8 + 12

SECOND EDITION

PERSONNEL MANAGEMENT FOR EFFECTIVE SCHOOLS

John T. Seyfarth
Virginia Commonwealth University

Allyn and Bacon
Boston • London • Toronto • Sydney • Tokyo • Singapore

To Susie and Chuck

Library of Congress Cataloging-in-Publication Data

Seyfarth, John T.
    Personnel management for effective schools / John T. Seyfarth. --
2nd ed.
        p.   cm.
    Includes bibliographical references and index.
    ISBN 0-205-16613-X
    1. School personnel management--United States.   2. School management
and organization--United States.   I. Title.
LB2831.5.S46   1996
371.2´01´0973--dc20   95-9231
                                                            CIP

Printed in the United States of America

10   9   8   7   6   5   4   3   2   1   99   98   97   96   95

Credits: Pages 4 and 6–9: Brown, Daniel J. *Decentralization: The Administrator's Guidebook to School District Change,* pp. 15, 20, 23, 24. Copyright © 1991 by Corwin Press,
Inc. Reprinted by permission of Corwin Press, Inc. Pages 7–9, 154, and 196: From
Prasch, John (1990). *How to Organize for School-Based Management.* Alexandria, VA: Association for Supervision and Curriculum Development. Copyright by ASCD. Used
with permission.

CONTENTS

PREFACE TO THE SECOND EDITION

The school reform movement that began in the early 1980s is alive and well, although the focus of the reformers' energies has shifted during the decade and a half that the movement has been underway. Early efforts sought to effect changes in curriculum and teaching practices, but as time has passed, attention has shifted to restructuring school governance. Site-based management has gained widespread acceptance as an alternative to the centralized bureaucratic structures that have been common in large school systems for 50 years or more.

Site-based management shifts decision making to schools, making it possible for those who work directly with students to have more influence on the decisions that affect students' academic progress. When site-based management is adopted in a district, the influence of personnel specialists diminishes, and that of teachers and administrators at the school level grows.

There is reason for optimism that this change in the structure of school governance will have a favorable effect on school operations, including personnel practice, but the optimism must be tempered with caution. The teachers, administrators, and parents who serve on school leadership councils usually come from a variety of backgrounds. Some of them have had training in personnel management, but many have not. Those with limited experience in personnel management can make decisions that hinder rather than advance the goal of instructional effectiveness.

The teachers and administrators who will serve on leadership councils in site-managed schools can help further the aims of the reform movement by increasing their knowledge of sound personnel practices and becoming aware of the potential impact of personnel actions on instruction. This second edition is written for the purpose of helping prepare these teachers and administrators for the challenges of self-governance, in the hope that they will be prepared to select well-trained and committed teachers and support staffs and to work to create conditions in school that facilitate their work, in order that our schools can truly become centers of inquiry and learning.

The second edition retains all of the popular features from the first edition and adds some new ones. A chapter on technology in personnel management has been added, new case studies are included, and the chapter on collective bargaining has been expanded to include descriptions of alternative negotiating models. In addition, the number of suggested activities has been increased and an Instructor's Manual is offered for the first time.

1

PERSONNEL MANAGEMENT AND EFFECTIVE SCHOOLS

This book is about managing people in schools. Its objective is to make prospective and practicing school administrators aware of the wide range of activities covered by the term *personnel management* and to present the best of current practice in personnel work. Effective personnel management practices are prerequisite to bringing about improved student learning, and all decisions relating to selection, placement, evaluation, development, promotion, and termination of employees should be made with that outcome in mind.

This book will be of interest to all school administrators whose responsibilities include any aspect of personnel management. All of the activities of personnel department staff members involve personnel management, and many of the duties of principals and assistant principals also fall under that heading. When a principal interviews an applicant for a secretarial position, plans a staff development program for faculty, or evaluates a counselor's performance, he or she is engaging in personnel management. The importance of the principal's role in personnel management is increasing as school districts move toward wider implementation of site-based management and decentralization of responsibility for some personnel decisions to the school level.

Most personnel decisions have either a direct or indirect impact on the quality of instruction. When a decision is made to employ a teacher, counselor, or aide, when a new personnel evaluation procedure is implemented, or when a compensation plan is adopted, there are likely to be implications for the quality of instruction. The potential impact of personnel decisions on instruction should be taken into account at the time these decisions are made. Our knowledge of teaching and learning is not yet extensive enough that we can always predict with a high degree of confidence what effects such decisions will have. However, as a result of advances in research on teaching, we are able to make these decisions now with much more confidence than was possible even a few years ago.

The book rests on three assumptions. The first of these is that capable teachers are essential to achieving quality education and that such teachers will always be in short supply. The supply of teachers fluctuates, depending on a number of factors, including salaries and demographic characteristics of the college student population, but the number of "good" teachers in the teacher pool will always fall short of the demand.

The second assumption holds that effective management of human resources requires thoughtful application of learned knowledge and skills. Some people are fond of saying, "I know a good teacher (or secretary, counselor, or social worker) when I see one," implying an intuitive ability to judge teaching success that is contradicted by research on the predictive validity of teacher selection criteria. Studies show that the ability to predict success in teaching requires a good deal of knowledge and perhaps some luck. As the supply of teachers grows, the task of selection grows progressively more challenging. Relying on strictly intuitive judgments when the number of applicants is large will almost certainly result in mediocre selection decisions, at best.

The third assumption is that proficiency in identifying and selecting quality teachers is not sufficient to solve the problems of teacher recruitment and retention if working conditions in schools are such that able teachers are induced to leave. Identifying and employing persons with the ability to become effective teachers is only the beginning. Principals and supervisors must create conditions in schools that facilitate teachers' work and help them to achieve success.

Plan of the Chapter

Important changes are taking place in our attitudes about the management of organizations. This shift has occurred in response to the growing realization among business and political leaders that U.S. firms face intense competition from global corporations. However, this rethinking of management practices is not limited to commercial enterprises. Governments and public organizations, including schools, are also adopting new methods and philosophies of administration in order to extend scarce resources and respond to criticisms of low quality and inefficient services.

This chapter provides the conceptual framework for the book. The chapter reviews the school reform efforts of the past decade and shows how an emphasis on decentralized decision making and new attention to quality are changing the way schools are run. The following topics are dealt with in this chapter: (1) personnel management and instruction, (2) educational reform,

(3) school decentralization, (4) school-based management, and (5) organizational effectiveness.

Personnel Management and Instruction

The model of school learning around which this book is organized is depicted in Figure 1.1. The model assumes that student learning is directly related to teachers' classroom behavior. That behavior is influenced by three factors: (1) teachers' knowledge of effective teaching techniques, the subject they teach, and appropriate ways of motivating students; (2) teachers' motivation to perform effectively on the job; and (3) availability of support services to enhance teachers' and students' efforts.

Personnel management functions determine the quality of instruction. Three personnel functions (selection, induction, and staff development) influence both teacher knowledge and motivation. Three functions (work environment, compensation policies, and accessibility of a mechanism for redressing employee grievances) attend to teacher motivation. Evaluation directly affects teacher behavior by making teachers aware of the school's expectations.

The personnel functions also help determine the quality of support services, and these services in turn influence teachers' and students' efforts. Support services include guidance and counseling, library, teacher aides, home/school visitors, instructional supervision, and so on.

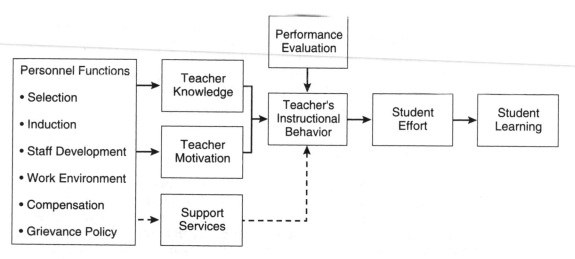

FIGURE 1.1   Relationship of Personnel Functions to Student Learning

Educational Reform

The educational reform movement that began in the early 1980s prompted efforts to change the operation and output of the schools. Most states responded to the warning by the National Commission on Excellence in Education (1983) that poor-quality schooling was a threat to the nation. Changes initiated in the states encouraged districts to adopt new instructional goals, promotion policies, teacher evaluation procedures, and graduation requirements, and to introduce a planning process and carry out a review of the curriculum (Cuban, 1984).

Some educators charged that these changes prevented school personnel from shaping the curriculum to students' needs (Snauwaert, 1993). In response to the argument that more comprehensive reforms were needed, state policymakers sought ways to redesign the education system. Two concepts were at the heart of the reform strategies they adopted—decentralization and participation.

Views of Organizations

Two views dominate thinking about management of organizations (Lawler, 1992). In the traditional view, management is centralized, top down, hierarchical, and bureaucratic. Lawler (1992) called this the *control-oriented approach*; it is also known as the *rational model*.

Rational Model
The rational model involves the following assumptions (Patterson, Purkey, & Parker, 1986):

1. Organizations have clear-cut goals that are understood and accepted by members, and activities of the organization are planned and coordinated for the purpose of achieving those objectives.
2. Information is available to decision makers to help them make informed decisions necessary to achieve the organization's goals.
3. Administrators have sufficient control to ensure compliance with long-range plans of the organization.
4. The external environment of the organization is stable and predictable and has little influence on decisions made within the organization.

In the second approach, which Lawler (1992) labeled the *commitment* or *involvement-oriented approach,* and which is also referred to as the *natural systems model,* managerial decision-making power is delegated to the level of the organization at which the work is done. Individuals at all levels are encouraged to offer input into decisions, and flexibility is encouraged in responding to changing needs of customers (Brown, 1991). Rather than being trained to respond in a standard way to a given problem, employees are expected to rely on their knowledge of the organization's mission and philosophy as guides to behavior and to decide for themselves how to respond when problems arise. Supervision is minimized, and all employees are expected to become thinkers and decision makers (Lawler, 1992).

Natural Systems Model

Assumptions underlying the natural systems model of organizations are (Patterson, Purkey, & Parker, 1986):

1. Organizations have multiple, competing sets of goals that are sometimes ambiguous.
2. Having access to information, support, and resources is the basis for power to make things happen. This power is distributed throughout the organization, not just at the upper levels of the managerial hierarchy.
3. No one group or individual has sufficient information or power to compel a high degree of coordination in the pursuit of goals; decisions are the outcome of bargaining and compromise.
4. The external environment undergoes constant change, is somewhat unpredictable, and seeks to influence decisions made within the organization.

Differences between the two views of organizations have to do with the way work is organized and managed. The control-oriented approach attempts to simplify and standardize tasks and to assign responsibility for certain functions to specialized units. Decisions about how work will be performed are made by individuals in high-level positions, and managers at all levels of the organization use supervision and incentives to motivate workers. Employees are able to perform well because they know what is expected of them and because they are supervised closely to ensure that the work is performed as intended (Lawler, 1992).

Both of these models contain elements of truth. Some organizations fit the natural systems model and others are closer to the rational type. The rational model of organizations envisions a world in which administrators' jobs are relatively straightforward and few conflicts are encountered in the process of establishing goals and carrying out the activities required to achieve them. However, the natural systems model paints a picture of the world that is closer to the reality that most administrators experience in their daily work. In the natural systems world, plans are made, but interference from the external environment and unforeseen problems within the organization sometimes block the implementation of those plans.

School reforms that began to appear during the second half of the 1980s shifted away from the control-oriented view of organizations toward the involvement-oriented approach. In many cases, these reforms provided for decentralized school governance and broader participation in decision making.

School Decentralization

There are two types of decentralization—horizontal and vertical. A school district is horizontally decentralized when authority is distributed among personnel in the district office. Assistant superintendents, supervisors, coordinators, and other specialists assume increased responsibility for specific decisions. Vertical decentralization occurs when authority is delegated downward in an organization. School-based management is an example (Brown, 1991).

Decentralization of Schools

The assumption behind vertical decentralization is that staff members in the schools understand students' problems and needs and are in a better position to make correct decisions about the use of resources than district staff members. Decentralization frees educators at the school site to take initiative to create effective responses to the educational needs of students (Martin, 1993). Administrators become facilitators, and other staff members' roles are expanded to include policy making and governance (Milstein, 1993).

Decentralization is not easily accomplished, and it entails costs as well as benefits. It requires district-level staff members to change the way they view their roles and it requires them to adopt a service orientation. Such a change is likely to be resisted, since many who are affected by decentralization struggled to attain their present positions and are unwilling to surrender their authority and influence easily (Wissler & Ortiz, 1988).

Organizations tend to become recentralized over time, and the success of decentralization depends on maintaining mechanisms that counter the drift toward recentralization (Wissler & Ortiz, 1988). Other problems that are encountered when authority is delegated downward include teachers who prefer not to participate in school governance decisions, principals who are unwilling to share their power and become facilitators and mediators, and absence of a pool of skilled people able to establish and maintain a cooperative work environment (Milstein, 1993).

Advocates of downward decentralization argue that administrators should delegate decisions about instructional methods and procedures to teachers since "no one knows better how to do a job than the person who does it." However, that statement is only true when workers are well informed about the relative advantages and disadvantages of alternative ways of performing a job. For that reason, redesigning jobs to permit jobholders to make decisions about work methods should be accompanied by staff development programs to prepare individuals to exercise that responsibility wisely (Lawler & Mohrman, 1991).

For all of the potential problems, there is general agreement that vertical decentralization can help reduce the bureaucratic control that many feel intensifies the problems of the schools. That has led to the introduction of school-based management, an arrangement that entails delegating authority over certain decisions to teachers and administrators in the schools.

School-Based Management

Almost one-fourth of school districts responding to a nationwide survey in 1989 reported they had adopted school- or site-based management (SBM), and an additional one-fourth were considering doing so (Prasch, 1990). A more recent National Education Association (1991) survey showed that about 30 percent of local association presidents who responded reported that the districts in which they worked had some form of SBM.

SBM constitutes a significant departure from the bureaucratized, centralized system of school governance that emerged during the Progressive Era in the United States (Snauwaert, 1993). For the first seven decades of the twentieth century, schools and school districts were consolidated into fewer and fewer units. The number of school districts dropped from 128,000 in 1932 to 15,000 in 1990, and the number of public elementary schools fell from 233,000 in 1932 to 44,000 in 1991 (*Historical Statistics*, 1975; McDowell, 1993).

Consolidation of Schools

The move toward fewer and larger districts and schools was undertaken primarily for reasons of efficiency, and although the residents of many communities were unhappy to see their schools closed, they agreed to the restructuring because of promised benefits for students. Many students had to travel great distances to school after consolidation took place, but the schools they attended were larger and better equipped, the teachers were better trained, and programs were more comprehensive than those in the schools they left.

However, consolidation had disadvantages as well as advantages. It increased the influence of educational bureaucracies, encouraged lack of responsiveness, and hampered accountability. SBM has been proposed as a remedy for the dysfunctional features of centralized school bureaucracies. It is promoted as a way of increasing flexibility, accountability, and productivity in schools (Brown, 1991). One superintendent described SBM as goal driven, needs responsive, results oriented, and teamwork/group operationalized (Prasch, 1990).

Under SBM, decisions that have traditionally been made by district office administrators are delegated to school councils or committees. Part of the appeal of SBM is the belief that it restores the essential mission of schools—instruction of students—to the center of educators' attention and it conveys a philosophy that all other activities of the district exist to support that mission (Prasch, 1990).

Features of SBM

Among the defining features of SBM plans are site-based budgeting to allow alternative uses of resources; governance committees composed of teachers, parents, and community members; increased autonomy in choice of staffing configurations and selection of personnel; power to modify the school's curriculum to serve specific needs of students; a process for obtaining waivers of local or state regulations; and an expectation for an annual report on progress and school improvement (Cawelti, 1989). Not all plans incorporate all of these features, but a school must have some of them in order to be considered an SBM school.

Districts differ in the types of services they choose to decentralize. Some districts delegate decisions about some parts of the budget but not about personnel or curriculum; some decentralize certain aspects of the curriculum; and others decentralize other decision areas. Other services are usually handled centrally. Purchasing is normally centralized, but teachers are encouraged to participate in decisions about the types of instructional materials and equipment to be purchased. Some experts recommend centralizing payroll, legal services, transportation, and food services (Prasch, 1990).

Site-based management frequently involves decentralization of the services provided by instructional coordinators and subject specialists. These individuals may be called on to provide help with staff development and training or to assist teachers with instructional or management problems. In some cases, schools that use these services pay a fee for them (Brown, 1991).

Advantages of SBM

A number of advantages and disadvantages of SBM have been identified. The claimed advantages include better programs for students; full use of human resources; higher-quality decisions; increased staff professionalism, satisfaction, loyalty, and commitment; development of staff leadership skills; clear organizational goals; improved communication; support for staff creativity and innovation; greater public confidence; enhanced fiscal accountability; and higher student achievement (David, 1989; Prasch, 1990).

Benefits from site-based decision making cited by respondents to the National Education Association (1991) survey were increased involvement of employees in decisions and improved coordination of programs and activities within schools. One local president cited as a benefit the fact that all participants come to meetings as equals. Others indicated that trust among teachers, parents, and administrators had risen, lines of communication had opened, and morale had improved. "Because more people have access to the decision-making apparatus, there is more room for new initiatives and addressing problems," according to one association president (National Education Association, 1991, p. 17).

An advantage of SBM that is mentioned more often than any other is increased flexibility in use of resources. One principal said, "We are now able to supply equipment like computers and the extra overhead projectors which the faculty felt they would never receive in the past." Another stated, "We placed $1000 in our professional development fund. . . . We could never do that before" (Brown, 1991, p. 24).

Disadvantages of SBM

Disadvantages of SBM mentioned most frequently include increased workloads for teachers and administrators; less efficiency; diluted benefits of specialization; uneven school performance; greater need for staff development; possible confusion about new roles and responsibilities; and coordination difficulties (Prasch, 1990).

A common complaint about SBM is that the planning process is highly time consuming, particularly during the first year of implementation (Brown, 1991). As a result, some teachers choose not to participate. They believe that the amount of time devoted to the tasks associated with site-based decision-making projects lessens their instructional effectiveness (National Education Association, 1991; Chapman, 1990).

The problems encountered in implementing SBM most often have to do with distribution of power. Some respondents to the National Education Association (1991) survey reported that superintendents and administrators attempted to give the trappings of power without its substance. Teachers who opposed SBM argued that under SBM they had little recourse against arbitrary and ineffectual principals (Bimber, 1993).

School-based management suffers when the participating parties cannot agree on its purpose. This disagreement often involves a question of whether SBM is primarily intended to draw more people into the decision-making process or to make schools more autonomous from central-office bureaucracies. If these questions are not resolved, and if, as is often the case, district administrators refuse to relinquish real power, SBM is likely to fail (Bimber, 1993).

Principals in schools with SBM assume new relationships with staff members. With professional staff, principals discontinue the role of overseer and operate on the assumption that teachers know their jobs. Only when a teacher proves to be indifferent or incompetent does a principal intervene to provide direct supervision. In many SBM schools, principals also assume a new role with noncertified personnel, such as custodians and food service workers, who become part of the decision-making process in the school (Prasch, 1990).

It is important to keep in mind that decentralization, participative decision making, school-based management, and bureaucracy are ideal types—that is, terms that represent socially constructed phenomena rather than objective realities. Schools with certain characteristics are said to have school-based management. However, these schools may differ from one another along a continuum ranging from complete autonomy in many areas at one extreme to limited autonomy in a few areas at the opposite extreme.

Schools are not political democracies. The ultimate power to make decisions about education is assigned in the United States to state legislatures and school boards, not teachers, parents, or administrators (Haller & Strike, 1986). Even in SBM schools, no action by a school council or teacher committee is final as long as the possibility exists that it might be overridden.

Personnel Management under SBM

In districts with school-based management, personnel decision making is altered in significant ways. Personnel staff members become facilitators, collecting and sharing information and coordinating activities of applicants and school staff members who interview them and decide whom to hire. District personnel staff members may be asked for information about legal requirements or for advice about what factors should receive most weight in selecting teachers, but they play a less active part in the final decision than is the case with more traditional forms of governance.

Organizational Effectiveness

Many organizational characteristics and outcomes have been used as indicators of effectiveness, including productivity, efficiency, profit, accidents, employee absenteeism, turnover, job satisfaction, and evaluations by external entities (Campbell, 1977). Ratings of the effectiveness of schools are usually based on efficiency, equality, or quality (Glasman, 1986).

Taxpayers' organizations and political leaders demand efficiency in use of resources; civil rights groups and parents argue for equality; and parents and employers who hire the schools' graduates seek quality. Most of the time the schools are able to maintain a balance in pursuit of these outcomes, but occasionally public opinion swings so strongly in favor of one of the three that the others are in danger of being neglected.

Efficiency as a Goal

Efficiency was the dominant theme in school administration during the early years of this century, when the new profession of educational administration was charged with the task of preparing the schools to accommodate a flood of students from immigrant families. Pressed by rapidly rising enrollments and limited resources, administrators turned to the corporate world to find ways to accomplish the task they had been assigned. From industry they borrowed the spirit, if not the methods, of scientific management. Efficiency continued to be emphasized in schools until the emergence of the human relations movement helped to achieve balance in the schools during the 1930s.

Equality as a Goal

The emphasis on equality came into prominence with the U.S. Supreme Court's decision ruling that segregated schools violated the constitutional rights of minorities. (*Brown* v. *Board of Education,* 1954, 1955). Interest in equality of educational opportunity broadened during the 1970s to include not only racial minorities and females but also students with mental and physical handicaps. The Education for All Handicapped Children Act mandated far-reaching changes in programs serving people with disabilities; it also required expansion of services and added safeguards to protect procedural rights of students.

Quality as a Goal

Quality of school programs is an issue that has received periodic attention from citizens and legislators, often in connection with national crises. The National Commission on Excellence in Education (1983) aroused the nation's concern when it declared that the United States was threatened by a rising tide of mediocrity as a result of the deteriorating quality of education. The Commission's report was one of many such studies that appeared about that time and that sounded similar themes.

Ironically, it was the publication of a study entitled *Equality of Educational Opportunity* (Coleman, 1966) that launched the debate on school effectiveness. The focus of the study was equality, as the title declared, but it had a good deal to say about educational quality as well. The study concluded that schools contributed relatively little to students' academic achievement and that most of students' cognitive growth could be accounted for by family background factors. These findings were disputed by critics who claimed that the research design and statistical treatment of the data magnified the impact of family factors on student achievement and diminished the schools' contributions to learning.

Effective Schools Research

We know that not all teachers are equally adept at producing learning and that some schools are more effective than others at increasing academic achievement. We know, too, that the differences are not attributable solely to family background characteristics of students, although those factors do affect school learning. In other words, schools do make a difference in what and how much students learn.

Considerable effort has been expended in recent years to increase our understanding of the factors that make certain schools and certain teachers more effective than others. Some of this research was underway before the Coleman report was published, but that event gave impetus to a group of studies known collectively as *effective schools research*. Those studies compared schools that were more effective in producing gains on standardized achievement tests with those that were less effective. Numerous factors were identified that seemed to account for the differences in school outcomes. Lezotte (1979) summarized the effective schools research by identifying six characteristics of effective schools:

1. Professional staff have a clear sense of the school's mission and direction.
2. Teachers believe that all students can master the basic skills; they also feel that they are capable of providing the necessary instruction to accomplish that objective.
3. Someone in the school, usually the principal, interprets the school's mission to students and staff and serves to facilitate communication between parents and teachers.
4. Students' progress is continually monitored.
5. Time is made available for students to learn.
6. Support of parents is solicited.

Research on Effective Teaching

Other studies have attempted to identify elements of the interaction between and among teachers and students that account for differences in the amount of learning occurring in classrooms. One group of studies focused on the relationship between teacher behavior in the classroom and student learning. The name applied to studies of this type is *process-product research* (Rosenshine, 1979). Process variables refer to behaviors exhibited by teachers and students, and product variables are those having to do with learning outcomes, usually achievement test scores.

Direct Instruction

The results of process-product research were catalogued by Kash and Borich (1982), although some of the items on their list (e.g., length of school day or school year) did not originate from studies of teachers. Two concepts that emerged from this research helped to explain differences in teacher effectiveness. One of these ideas was direct instruction, which involves what is sometimes called a *traditional teacher role*. Rosenshine (1979) described direct instruction this way:

> Direct instruction refers to academically focused, teacher-directed classrooms using sequenced and structured materials. It refers to teacher activities where goals are clear to students, time allocated for instruction is sufficient and continuous, coverage of content is extensive, the performance of students is monitored, questions are at a low cognitive level so that stu-

dents can produce many correct responses, and feedback to students is immediate and academically oriented. In direct instruction the teacher controls instructional goals, chooses materials appropriate for the student's ability, and paces the instructional episode. Interaction is characterized as structured, but not authoritarian. Learning takes place in a convivial academic atmosphere. The goal is to move the students through a sequenced set of materials or tasks. Such materials are common across classrooms and have a relatively strong congruence with the tasks on achievement tests. Thus, we are limiting the term "direct instruction" to didactic ends, that is, to instruction toward rational, specific, analytic goals. (p. 38)

This research revealed positive correlations between the use of direct instructional methods and student achievement score gains.

Academic Learning Time

The second concept originating with the process-product research was the notion of *academic learning time*, known more commonly as *time on task*. Academic learning time is best illustrated by considering a diagram consisting of three concentric circles (Berliner, 1984). The large outer circle represents allocated time for a particular subject or topic. The middle circle represents engaged time, or the time that students actually attend to what the teacher is saying or carry out content-relevant tasks under the teacher's direction. The small inner circle represents time spent on tasks at an appropriate level of difficulty—that is, those that permit a high success rate. This smallest circle represents academic learning time; it is the time during which students are actively engaged in performing tasks assigned by the teacher at which they are able to succeed a high percentage of the time.

Researchers discovered that more learning occurred in classrooms in which teachers maximized academic learning time. The concept is particularly useful because of the implications for practice that can be generated from it. For example, loss of learning may occur from reductions in allocated time resulting from a teacher's decision to spend more time on one subject than another or from students being assigned work that is too easy or too difficult. The easy work fails to hold their interest, thus lowering their engaged time, whereas work that is too difficult results in a low success rate. For an administrator or supervisor assisting teachers to improve instruction, the concept helps to identify alternative ways of correcting problems of low student achievement.

Process Variables

Research on effective schools suggests that teachers and administrators in these schools hold views about their work and their relationships to others that are different from those found in less successful schools. One of these features is that teachers in effective schools share a norm of collegiality. Such faculties are described by the members as "close" and able to work together.

Working together involves discussing, planning, designing, conducting, analyzing, evaluating, and experimenting with the business of teaching (Little, 1981). There are many ways by which such collaborative efforts can be brought about, and in order for a school to be truly effective, such collaboration must occur.

A second characteristic found in effective schools is acceptance by teachers of a norm of continuous improvement. Teachers in these schools are committed to the view that they can continue to learn about teaching, and they consider colleagues as potential resource persons who can help them to grow personally and professionally (Little, 1981).

Limitations of the Research

The research on effective schools is not without limitations. Many of the studies have been conducted in urban elementary schools, and it is not clear whether similar results would be obtained in other types of schools. The studies involve identifying correlations between school characteristics and learning outcomes, a method that does not permit cause-effect conclusions.

Another limitation of the research is the narrow definition of *effectiveness* used. In most of the studies, schools identified as effective are selected on the basis of higher-than-expected achievement test scores. This is a relative definition that can lead to a situation in which a school that is considered effective may have test scores that are equal to those of a school that is not rated effective. The definition also permits instability in effectiveness, since a school may be rated effective one year and ineffective the following year (Bossert, 1988).

A third weakness of the studies is that important school outcomes are ignored. Researchers concentrate on one outcome (student achievement) while overlooking other types of goals schools seek to accomplish (Bossert, 1988). From a research standpoint, the strategy is wise, but it has the effect of limiting the usefulness of the findings. In spite of these deficiencies, however, the research on effective schooling has enlarged our knowledge of what constitutes effective schools and how to achieve improved quality in our schools.

Principal's Role in Effectiveness

The importance of the principal's role in achieving effective instruction is a subject of some debate. It has been argued by some that teachers' decisions about what they teach are "impervious" to the principal's influence (Ross, 1982). Others maintain that "the nature and quality of leadership provided by administrators and supervisors is directly and positively related to . . . perceived effectiveness of instruction" (Lipham, 1982, p. 33).

The research suggests that some principals spend relatively little time on instructional leadership tasks, whereas others devote much of their attention to those responsibilities (Boyd & Crowson, 1981). Some of the ways in which principals influence the quality of instruction are participating in, defining, and reinforcing social norms; raising the professional aspiration levels of teachers; and providing for extensive teacher input into important curriculum decisions (Ross, 1982).

Leadership behaviors displayed by principals of effective schools are of four types (Bowers & Seashore, cited in Lipham, 1982):

1. Work facilitation, which involves scheduling, planning, and coordinating
2. Support, which involves actions that enhance teachers' and students' feelings of personal worth and importance
3. Interaction facilitation, which includes behavior that encourages teachers to develop close, mutually satisfying working relationships
4. Goal emphasis, which involves behaviors that arouse teachers' enthusiasm for attaining instructional goals and achieving excellence in performance

In effective schools, the principal exerts leadership by supporting and encouraging the staff and by serving as an advocate of change. The principal accomplishes this by being accessible and responsive to teachers, by encouraging teachers to try new ideas, and by arranging released time, financial support, and in-service training to assist teachers who are willing to try new ideas (Colorado Department of Education, 1982).

Administrators of effective schools set high but realistic standards for performance and they inform teachers, students, and parents about those standards. They hold high expectations of achievement for all students and emphasize the importance of academic achievement for all (Colorado Department of Education, 1982).

Some principals facilitate work and interaction by creating a "freedom to fail" atmosphere that encourages teachers to experiment without fear of being penalized when ideas flop. Effective administrators emphasize goals by establishing clear instructional priorities and facilitate work by creating organizational structures to carry out the tasks needed to accomplish them (Ross, 1982).

A popular image of successful principals depicts them as risk takers who are willing to ignore district policies in order to secure support for their staffs (Sarason, 1971; Watson, 1979). However, collective bargaining has exacted a toll among risk-taking administrators, who now are likely to encounter strong resistance both from teachers and from district administrators to actions that might be interpreted as violations of a collective bargaining agreement or board policy (Mitchell, Kerchner, Erck, & Pryor, 1981).

People who are employed in an organization usually interpret the words and actions of their immediate superiors as representing organizational policies and commitments. Since employees usually have limited information about the organization, they tend to accept superiors' views of it as authoritative. In the case of schools, a principal who espouses certain instructional outcomes is accepted by teachers as representing the official position of the district on those matters.

Thus, the principal is a central figure in bringing about improvements in instruction. In the absence of administrative direction, teachers tend to make curriculum choices based on their own interests and what they believe students will find interesting and relatively easy to learn. To change that behavior requires that instructional goals be identified and that support be provided for their attainment.

Research on the effect of school climate on academic achievement of students has shown that effective schools are more likely to have principals who stress the importance of academic achievement, help to coordinate instructional programs, and provide instructional materials for teachers' use. Other findings have shown that principals of successful schools establish high standards both for themselves and their schools and that they use their time to engage in activities that help to improve instruction. One study showed that principals of effective schools were more likely to hold an achievement orientation as opposed to a human relations orientation. Another study concluded that principals provided attitudinal and motivational leadership that created a sense of purpose among teachers and students, leading to increased achievement (Boyd & Crowson, 1981).

Summary

Personnel management practices have a direct impact on how much students learn by influencing teacher knowledge and motivation. Practices that increase knowledge and motivation lead to more student learning, and activities that decrease them result in less student learning. Personnel management occurs within an organizational context. Two models guide our thinking about organizations. The rational model holds that organizations have clear-cut, generally accepted goals and that organizational activities are carried out for the purpose of achieving those objectives. The model also assumes that administrators have sufficient information and control to ensure compliance with long-range plans and that the external environment has little influence on decisions made within the organization.

In contrast, the natural systems model assumes that organizations have multiple, sometimes ambiguous, goals and that power is distributed throughout the organization. This theory suggests that many parties become involved in making decisions, including some from outside the organization, and that bargaining and compromise are necessary in order to reach agreement.

Many states have decentralized school governance in recent years as a way of allowing greater decision-making autonomy to staff members in the schools. This move reverses a long-term trend toward fewer and larger school districts. In schools with site-based management, decisions on the budget and staff are made by committees composed of teachers, parents, and community members. In many districts these committees also have authority to modify the curriculum and can request waivers of certain local or state regulations.

References

Berliner, D. (1984). The half-full glass: A review of research on teaching. In P. Hosford (Ed.), *Using what we know about teaching* (pp. 51–77). Alexandria, VA: Association for Supervision and Curriculum Development.

Bimber, B. (1993). *School decentralization: Lessons from the study of bureaucracy*. Santa Monica, CA: Rand. (ERIC Document No. ED 357441).

Bossert, S. (1988). School effects. In N. Boyan (Ed.), *Handbook of research on educational administration* (pp. 341–352). New York: Longman.

Boyd, W., & Crowson, R. (1981). The changing conception and practice of public school administration. *Review of Research in Education, 9*, 311–373.

Brown, D. (1991). *Decentralization: The administrator's guidebook to school district change*. Newbury Park, CA: Sage.

Brown v. Board of Education of Topeka, 347 U.S. 483 (1954).

Brown v. Board of Education of Topeka, 349 U.S. 294 (1955).

Campbell, J. (1977). On the nature of organizational effectiveness. In P. Goodman & J. Pennings (Eds.), *New perspectives on organizational effectiveness* (pp. 13–55). San Francisco: Jossey Bass.

Cawelti, G. (1989, May). Key elements of site-based management. *Educational Leadership, 46*, 46.

Chapman, J. (1990). School-based decision-making and management: Implications for school personnel. In J. Chapman (Ed.), *School-based decision-making and management* (pp. 221–244). London: Falmer.

Coleman, J. (1966). *Equality of educational opportunity* (Vol. 1). Washington, DC: U.S. Government Printing Office.

Colorado Department of Education. (1982). *Indicators of quality schools*. Denver: Author. (ERIC Document Reproduction Service No. ED 239406).

Cuban, L. (1984). Transforming the frog into a prince: Effective schools research, policy, and practice at the district level. *Harvard Educational Review, 54*, 129–151.

David, J. (1989, May). Synthesis of research on school-based management. *Educational Leadership, 46*, 45–47, 50–53.

Glasman, N. (1986). *Evaluation-based leadership: School administration in contemporary perspective*. Albany: State University of New York Press.

Haller, E., & Strike, K. (1986). *An introduction to educational administration*. New York: Longman.

Historical statistics of the United States. Colonial times to 1970. (1975). Washington, DC: U.S. Department of Commerce, Bureau of the Census.

Kash, M., & Borich, G. (1982). Teachers. In H. Walberg (Ed.), *Improving educational standards for productivity* (pp. 49–72). Berkeley, CA: McCutchan.

Lawler, E. (1992). *The ultimate advantage: Creating the high-involvement organization*. San Francisco: Jossey-Bass.

Lawler, E., & Mohrman, S. (1991). High-involvement management. In R. Steers & L. Porter (Eds.), *Motivation and work behavior* (pp. 468–477, 5th ed.). New York: McGraw-Hill.

Lezotte, L. (1979). *A policy prospectus for im-*

proving urban education. (ERIC Document Reproduction Service No. ED 186495).

Lipham, J. (1982). Administrators and supervisors. In H. Walberg (Ed.), *Improving educational standards and productivity* (pp. 13–40). Berkeley, CA: McCutchan.

Little, J. (1981). *The power of organizational setting: School norms and staff development.* Paper presented at the annual meeting of the American Educational Research Association, Los Angeles. (ERIC Document Reproduction Service No. ED 221918).

Martin, L. (1993). *Total quality management in human service organizations.* Newbury Park, CA: Sage.

McDowell, L. (1993). *Public elementary and secondary schools and agencies in the United States and outlying areas: School year 1991–92.* Washington, DC: U.S. Department of Education, National Center for Education Statistics.

Milstein, M. (1993). *Restructuring schools: Doing it right.* Newbury Park, CA: Corwin.

Mitchell, D., Kerchner, C., Erck, W., & Pryor, G. (1981). The impact of collective bargaining on school management and policy. *Elementary School Journal, 89,* 147–188.

National Commission on Excellence in Education. (1983). *A nation at risk: The imperative for educational reform.* Washington, DC: U.S. Government Printing Office.

National Education Association. (1991). *Site-based decisionmaking: The 1990 NEA census of local associations.* Washington, DC: Author.

Patterson, J., Purkey, S., & Parker, J. (1986). *Productive school systems for a nonrational world.* Alexandria, VA: Association for Supervision and Curriculum Development.

Prasch, J. (1990). *How to organize for school-based management.* Alexandria, VA: Association for Supervision and Curriculum Development.

Rosenshine, B. (1979). Content, time, and direct instruction. In P. Peterson & H. Walberg (Eds.), *Research on teaching: Concepts, findings, and implications* (pp. 28–56). Berkeley, CA: McCutchan.

Ross, J. (1982). The influence of the principal. In K. Leithwood (Ed.), *Studies in curriculum decision making* (pp. 54–67). Toronto: Ontario Institute for Studies in Education.

Sarason, S. (1971). *The culture of the school and the problem of change.* Boston: Allyn and Bacon.

Snauwaert, D. (1993). *Democracy, education, and governance.* Albany: State University of New York Press.

Watson, B. (1979). The principal against the system. In D. Erickson & T. Reller (Eds.), *The principal in metropolitan schools* (pp. 40–54). Berkeley, CA: McCutchan.

Wissler, D., & Ortiz, F. (1988). *The superintendent's leadership in school reform.* New York: Falmer.

2

PLANNING FOR STAFFING NEEDS

Planning represents an effort to anticipate and shape the future. The process of planning involves identifying a desired future state, assessing conditions and trends that may influence the organization's ability to achieve that state, and developing strategies to reach the goal. Few organizations are successful for very long without planning.

This chapter addresses several issues related to planning in schools. Evidence suggests that schools will continue to be at a competitive disadvantage vis-à-vis other employers in seeking to attract and retain well-qualified personnel (Pounder, 1987). For that reason, it is important to anticipate staff needs and to plan carefully to recruit, select, and retain employees with the qualifications to help the district achieve its goals.

Plan of the Chapter

This chapter deals with the following topics: (1) strategic planning and (2) determining staff needs.

Strategic Planning

Strategic planning is a process through which stakeholders in an organization work together to assess the internal and external environments, identify an organizational mission and goals, and develop strategies for achieving the goals. Seldom do all members of an organization agree about the group's values and priorities, and one purpose of strategic planning is to help create a consensus around critical values (Sybouts, 1992).

A strategy known as *visioning* is used to help members develop consensus on values and goals. Employees organized into teams address five basic questions about the organization's future (Fear & Chiron, 1990):

- Where are we today?
- Where do we want to go?
- How are we going to get there?
- Who is responsible for what?
- How much will it cost and what are the benefits?

Strategic planning originated in industry but has been widely adopted by schools and other public service organizations (Conley, 1993). The process begins with the preparation of a mission statement, which is a declaration of a district's commitment to certain academic, social, and career outcomes for students and teachers and ways of achieving those outcomes (Sybouts, 1992). Each school's mission statement must be compatible with the district's mission. Once a mission statement has been agreed upon, goals and strategies are developed to specify how the school or district proposes to achieve the vision described in the mission statement. Exhibit 2.1 shows an example of a school's mission statement.

Planning is an attitude as well as an activity, and all members of the organization must be participants in order for planning to succeed (Hussey, 1985). In school districts, a task force made up of representatives from all levels of the workforce take the lead in planning. In schools with site-based management, the school council or parent-teacher committee has that responsibility.

Interactive Planning

Much long-range planning relies on a rational approach to preparing for the future. Planners collect data on a variety of indicators that show how well the organization is succeeding in achieving its goals and then develop strategies for improving performance where needed. This approach makes

---

Staff and students of Combs High School work together to create a learning atmosphere that encourages students to become responsible citizens and stimulates critical thinking and creativity. The faculty, in partnership with parents and the community, seek to promote excellence in all facets of school life and to offer a variety of instructional opportunities to enable students to master basic skills and expand their knowledge in all areas.

Recognizing that high expectations and regular evaluations of effort help to raise the quality of performance, teachers provide frequent evaluative feedback to students. School personnel periodically inform parents and the general public about the school's programs and performance and solicit their suggestions for improvement.

EXHIBIT 2.1 Model School Mission Statement for Combs High School

assumptions that are similar to the rational model of organizations that was discussed in Chapter 1.

An approach that makes some of the same assumptions about organizations as the natural systems model from Chapter 1 is the interactive model. In this model, the positivistic assumptions of rational planning are replaced by the belief that reality must be understood from the perspective of the individual. Interactive planning places less stress on rational approaches and gives more attention to social and political activities, taking into account differences in individuals' values and views of reality (Adams, 1988). When school councils engage in planning, it is usually of the interactive variety.

Interactive planning accepts conflict as a normal and expected part of human activity and proposes to minimize it by discussing and clarifying views of stakeholders until a consensus is reached. Advocates of the interactive approach to planning strongly believe that conflict must be explored and not ignored, as it often is when a rational approach to planning is followed (Hamilton, 1991).

No mission statement alone is sufficient to ensure that a school will achieve its goals. In order to realize the school's or district's mission, participants must first develop strategies for achieving the outcomes envisioned in the mission statement (Kaufman, 1992). The mission statement for Combs High School states that students and faculty members will work together to encourage intellectual curiosity and stimulate critical thinking. Some strategies that teachers could use to accomplish that result are:

- To provide at least one opportunity for every student to make a contribution during class discussions
- To plan at least one instructional activity each week that requires students to analyze their thinking processes
- To plan an assignment that requires students to read and comment on material (other than the textbook) that presents an alternative point of view about an issue of current interest in the field of study

Critical Issues Analysis

Strategic planning operates on two assumptions—that the future evolves from the present and that it will be different from the present (Hatten & Hatten, 1988). Planners use a process called *environmental assessment* to identify trends that are evident in the external environment that have implications for the organization's ability to accomplish its mission. One technique used to produce an environmental assessment is critical issues analysis.

Critical issues analysis begins with planners identifying potential critical issues and submitting each one to a test. The test involves three questions (Wilkinson, 1986):

1. Will the issue affect the performance of the organization?

2. Will it require allocation of organizational resources?
3. Can the organization reasonably expect to control or exert significant influence on the impact the issue has on the organization's performance?

If the answer to all three questions is *yes*, then the issue is a critical one.
Consider these examples of issues that might be considered by the faculty of a school engaged in developing a strategic plan:

1. The school's dropout rate has begun to rise in the past few years after a
period of stable or declining figures.
2. The school's faculty has half a dozen key members, including two department heads, who will retire within three years and who must be replaced.
3. The district is considering redrawing school boundary lines; the proposed
plan would shift 250 students to other schools and bring in a group of
about 120 new students, for a net loss of 130 (out of 1,200)
4. New textbooks in American history and mathematics will be reviewed
this year for adoption in the coming school year; review committees will
be appointed within one month.
5. Some teachers want the school to adopt a student conduct code that
would mandate specific penalties for violations of certain rules. The current code allows some discretion in enforcing rules, and some teachers
think that discipline is uneven.

Wilkinson's (1986) test questions will be applied to these five problems
to decide which ones qualify as critical issues.

Testing Issues

Question 1:   Which issues will affect the performance of the school? Loss
of key faculty members could affect the school's performance; changing
school boundary lines might also affect performance by changing the distribution of student achievement in the school. Adoption of a new student conduct code might help improve the school's performance by reducing disruptive behavior in classes. The increasing dropout rate and adoption of new
textbooks should have only a slight impact on the school's performance.

Question 2:   Which issues will require allocation of resources? All five issues potentially could involve allocation of resources. The proposed change
in boundary lines could result in the loss of teaching positions, and reviewing applications and interviewing teachers to replace those who retire will require some staff time. If teachers from the school are appointed to a district
textbook selection committee, if a decision is made to take action to lower
the dropout rate, or if the decision is made to develop a new student conduct
code, those actions will also require allocation of staff time.

Question 3:   On which issues can the school expect to have an impact? On two of the topics—hiring replacements for retiring faculty and implementing a student conduct code—the school can expect to have a major impact. On two issues—drawing new boundary lines and selecting new textbooks—the school has input, but the final decision will be made by others. On one issue— lowering the dropout rate— the school's influence is problematical, depending on the underlying causes.

Using Wilkinson's (1986) test, two issues (loss of key faculty members and a new student conduct code) qualify as critical items because all three questions are answered in the affirmative. For one issue (proposed changes in boundary lines), two questions were answered affirmatively. These results suggest that the potential loss of faculty members from retirement and the implementation of a new student conduct code should enter into the school's planning.

Futures Wheel

To help assess the probable impact of critical issues, planners prepare a futures wheel for each critical issue. An advantage of the futures wheel is that it helps planners trace the impact of an event two, three, or even four stages beyond the immediate results.

Figure 2.1 shows an example of a futures wheel illustrating how loss of key faculty members will affect the school program. One immediate outcome is that replacements must be selected and new mentors must be trained to take the place of those who have left. Some actions result in a series of reactions. For example, suppose a teacher who is retiring has been sponsor of the school's yearbook. In order to secure a replacement, the council decides to increase the salary supplement. That leads to requests for increased supplements from sponsors of other activities and may eventually result in reallocation of resources.

Ranking Issues

When the futures wheels have been completed, participating planners discuss the range of opportunities and threats posed by each issue under examination and rank them on three dimensions: probability, impact, and imminence. Probability and impact are rated on 10-point scales. For *probability,* a rating of 1 indicates that the rater believes the event is highly improbable, whereas a rating of 10 reflects a judgment that it is highly probable. For *impact,* 1 indicates negligible impact, whereas 10 indicates a judgment of major structural change. For *imminence,* a 3-point scale is used, with judges rating how soon a development is predicted to occur. Rating choices are near term (up to one year), medium term (next three years), and long term (next five years) (Wilkinson, 1986).

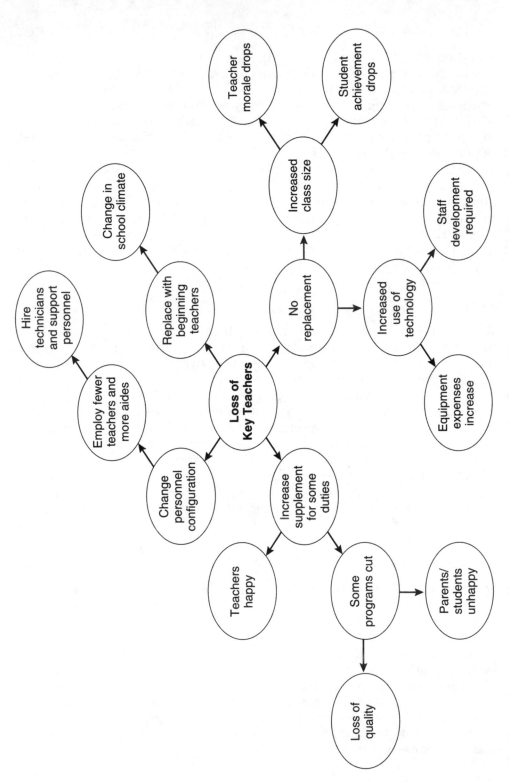

FIGURE 2.1 Futures Wheel Illustrating Effects of Teacher Shortage in Mathematics and Science

Source: Based on "Strategic Planning in the Voluntary Sector" by G. W. Wilkinson, in J. R. Gardner, R. Rachlin, & H. W. A. Sweeny (Eds.), *Handbook of Strategic Planning,* 1986, John Wiley & Sons, Inc.

Issue Brief

When the ratings have been compiled, the planners identify six to nine issues that are perceived as being most likely to occur, having the greatest impact on the organization, and being most imminent. For each of the issues selected for detailed examination and analysis, an issue brief is prepared, containing the following information (Wilkinson, 1986):

1. Title and definition of the issue
2. Identification of threats and opportunities related to the issue
3. Identification of driving influences—environmental forces that give the issue momentum and force
4. Potential outcomes of alternative scenarios
5. Impact on the organization of each of the scenarios
6. Planning challenges—a set of "need to" statements setting out the overall actions required of the organization to maximize opportunities or minimize threats

An example of an issue brief for the problem of impending retirement of faculty members appears in Exhibit 2.2.

Internal Organizational Assessment

An internal assessment describes the internal environment of an organization. An internal assessment for a school includes major strengths and weaknesses, the nature of the student body, school climate, financial restraints or resources, staff resources or limitations, facilities, equipment, internal politics, and school policies (Sybouts, 1992).

A variety of information about students appears in an internal assessment, including the number of students by gender, age, and socioeconomic levels. The assessment also notes trends related to grade-point average (GPA), honors, test scores, behavior, attendance, dropout statistics, rate of college attendance, and participation in school programs (Mauriel, 1989; Sybouts, 1992).

An internal assessment also contains information about the number of teachers, their level, and the quality of their training, experience, and competence; working relationships among teachers; type, quality, history, and reputation of the school's or district's programs; and the number and types of buildings, equipment, playgrounds, and stadiums (Mauriel, 1989).

The internal assessment also includes information about programs offered by the school or district, including test scores, enrollments in elective courses, course evaluation data from student and parent surveys, and awards received by students participating in debates, tournaments, and contests. Another measure of program quality is the percentage of graduates

I. Title
Impending retirement of key faculty members

II. Challenges and opportunities
Challenge: Contributions of the departing teachers—including curriculum development activities, mentoring of new teachers, and sponsorship of student
clubs and organizations—will be lost. Challenge is to find a way to replace the
contributions without adding an undue burden to other teachers' workloads.

Opportunity: Openings provide an opportunity to reconfigure the school's organizational pattern and replace expensive teachers with less expensive ones;
also an opportunity to hire teacher aides in place of teachers. If boundary lines
are redrawn, as appears likely, retirements offer an opportunity to achieve reductions in teaching staff without transfers or layoffs.

III. Driving forces
Age is the driving force for retirement.

IV. Prospects
Worst case: The only available satisfactory applicants have extensive experience and will draw higher salaries, squeezing the salary budget. Less experienced applicants will be unable or unwilling to take on all of the assignments
held by the retiring teachers, resulting in losses to instructional and extracurricular programs.

Current path: School will attract well-qualified applicants who will be able to
maintain the school's program offerings at reasonable cost.

Best case: Restructuring the school's organizational pattern and using a different mix of professional and paraprofessional personnel results in monetary
savings and improved programs.

EXHIBIT 2.2   Sample Issue Brief

Source: Based on "Strategic Planning in the Voluntary Sector" by G. W. Wilkinson, in J. R.
Gardner, R. Rachlin, & H. Sweeny (Eds.), *Handbook of Strategic Planning*, 1986, John Wiley &
Sons, Inc.

who are admitted to selective colleges and college attendance and completion rates (Mauriel, 1989).

It is advisable to select a few goals and to focus efforts on achieving those
rather than try to accomplish a large number of objectives (American Association of School Administrators, 1983). When a goal is agreed upon, it
should be tested for consistency with the mission statement, and one or
more strategies for achieving the goal should be identified (Sybouts, 1992).
Two examples of human resource goals for a school are shown here with accompanying strategies.

Goal No. 1:   Develop and implement a plan for teacher evaluation that enables teachers to grow professionally and increase their effectiveness and
maintain high job satisfaction.

Strategy: Appoint a committee to review criteria for evaluating teaching effectiveness now used by other schools and to present recommendations to the school council for proposed criteria to be used in this school.

Strategy: Appoint a committee to identify sources of information for evaluating teaching effectiveness using the criteria previously approved and to develop and test procedures for collecting the information. The committee's findings will be presented to the school council for approval.

Goal No. 2:   Implement a policy to permit teachers to develop individual professional development plans.

Strategy: Solicit opinions from teachers regarding the feasibility of individual professional development plans and their suggestions for operation of the program.

Strategy: Select volunteers to contact schools that have such plans in operation in order to obtain information about them and identify problems encountered in implementing them.

Strategy: Appoint a committee of teachers to review information obtained from teachers and from other schools and to make general recommendations for a policy.

Using results from the internal and external assessments, planners prepare a strategic plan for the district that contains both short-term (1 to 3 years) and long-term (4 to 10 years) goals. Key outcomes that should be addressed in the plan are (Lewis, 1983):

1. Instructional programs and services
2. Student learning and growth
3. Human resources
4. Financial resources
5. Physical resources
6. Community involvement and relations
7. Organizational management
8. Performance evaluation and training

Determining Staff Needs

The most common use of planning in schools is to prepare enrollment projections that enable the district to hire teachers and other personnel to staff the schools or, if enrollment is dropping, to make plans to reduce the size of school staffs. However, predicting future enrollments is tricky, since changing economic and social conditions can affect school enrollments.

Long-term predictions on school enrollments in the United States made in the early 1960s proved to be far from accurate because those who made them used assumptions that turned out to be faulty. Planners assumed that the birthrate would continue unchanged for the foreseeable future. They failed to anticipate the advancements in birth control that made family planning easier and more practical. As a result, the birthrate dropped and so did school enrollments. Enrollment projections are only as accurate as the assumptions upon which they are based.

Cohort Survival Method

The method that is used most often to predict future enrollments is called the *cohort survival method*. The word *cohort* originally referred to a division of soldiers in the Roman army. It has since come to mean any group of people who begin a venture together. People who were born in the same year or who were initiated into a college fraternity at the same time are examples of cohorts. For purposes of predicting school enrollments, we consider a cohort to be any group of students who start school together. A cohort may lose members when individuals move away or drop out of school, or gain members when students transfer into a school.

The cohort survival method is based on the assumption that the future will be like the past. For the short term, that is usually a safe assumption. Drastic changes in population do not normally occur within the space of a year or two, nor do people's habits change quickly. However, in school districts near military bases or in communities with industries that are sensitive to economic fluctuations, relatively large variations in enrollment can occur with no advance warning.

The cohort survival method is most accurate in districts in which school enrollments are relatively stable or in which enrollment trends are consistent. The method is less accurate in predicting enrollments for districts with fluctuating enrollments (Alspaugh, 1981). The accuracy of any prediction diminishes as the distance from the predicted event increases. Predicting enrollments one year in advance is more accurate than predicting enrollments 5 or 10 years ahead. There are two reasons for loss of accuracy over time. Unforeseen events can affect school enrollments, and errors in predicting near-term enrollments compound over time, creating ever-larger distortions.

Persons who calculate enrollment projections for school districts try to limit error to less than 1 percent of actual enrollments. A 1 percent error rate means that for a projection of 1,000 students, the actual enrollment will fall between 990 and 1,010, and that for a projection of 10,000 students, the actual enrollment will fall between 9,900 and 10,100. For small errors, districts are usually able to accommodate the difference by increasing (or decreasing) class sizes slightly or hiring an additional teacher or two. However, larger errors have more significant repercussions.

If enrollments exceed the projection by just 100 students, a district may have to employ several additional teachers and locate space for that many more classes. If projections call for more students than actually enroll, the district may be responsible for paying salaries for some teachers who are not needed.

Most districts that use cohort survival analysis prepare separate projections for each school and then combine them to obtain a district total. Since most districts now maintain automated enrollment data, it is fairly simple to carry out the necessary calculations at the district office. The results are usually reviewed by principals, who are sometimes aware of impending events such as a plant closing or construction of a new subdivision that will affect their schools' enrollments. With this information, adjustments are made and the final predictions prepared. Projecting an accurate district total is somewhat easier than predicting correct enrollments for individual schools since district enrollments are generally more stable.

Projecting First-Grade Enrollment

In those states where kindergarten is voluntary, accurate projections require the use of a census. However, if children are required to attend kindergarten, the methods discussed here can be used to obtain reliable enrollment projections. In preparing enrollment projections for kindergarten, data on the number of births 5 years earlier are used. In the example shown in Table 2.1, projections over a 5-year period in a district with increasing enrollments are averaged to obtain the mean enrollment ratio. In actual practice, enrollment figures for 10 years or even more are used in the calculations. Using more years produces more reliable estimates (Schellenberg & Stephens, 1987).

Retention Ratios

To project enrollments for grades 2 through 12, a retention ratio is calculated by dividing each year's enrollment at a given grade level by the previous year's enrollment at the next lower grade level. This procedure is repeated for each of five years prior to the current year. A mean retention ratio is obtained, and the mean is multiplied by the current year's enrollment in the next lower grade level to obtain the enrollment projection for the upcoming year. This procedure is illustrated in Table 2.2, using hypothetical data to project enrollments in grade 7 for a district with decreasing enrollments. When projected enrollments are obtained for all grades, they are added to the kindergarten projections to obtain the projected districtwide total enrollment.

When enrollment trends are evident, allowance should be made by adjusting the projection either up or down. If the enrollment ratio has increased each year for the previous five years, there is a good chance that it will continue to increase (although perhaps at a declining rate), and using the average for the previous five years will underestimate the enrollment. On the other hand, if the trend shows a decline over a five-year period, the enrollment ratio is likely to overestimate enrollments. Depending on the direction and magnitude of the trend, an adjustment of the final enrollment figure may be needed.

TABLE 2.1   Developing Kindergarten Enrollment
Projections for a District with
Increasing Enrollments

1 Birth Year	2 Live Births	3 Starting Year	4 Enrollment	5 Enrollment Ratio
1986	2073	1991	2019	.9740
1987	2097	1992	2044	.9747
1988	2105	1993	2069	.9829
1989	2118	1994	2093	.9882
1990	2121	1995	2136	1.0071
1991	2206	1996		

Step 1:   Divide the enrollment (col. 4) by the number of live births five years earlier (col. 2) to obtain the enrollment ratio (col. 5). The enrollment ratio for 1992 is 2044/2097 = .9747. A ratio greater than 1.00 means that the number of kindergarten students exceeded the number of births five years earlier.

Step 2:   Add the enrollment ratios and divide by 5 (.9740 + .9747 + .9829 + .9882 + 1.0071 = 4.9269; 4.9269/5 = .9854). This is the mean enrollment ratio.

Step 3:   Multiply the number of live births five years earlier by the mean enrollment ratio to obtain the projected enrollment for the 1996 school year (.9854 ↔2206 = 2174).

Most administrators prefer to underestimate rather than to overestimate enrollments because the potential cost to the district is smaller in the case of underestimates. Enrollments that exceed projections slightly can often be accommodated by increasing class sizes, but once a teacher has been hired there is no way that the money for his or her salary and benefits can be recaptured (unless a contingency clause has been included in the contract).

A sizable one-time increase or decrease in the retention ratio affects the mean ratio and may bias enrollment estimates. For example, in Table 2.2 the ratio for 1994 (.9351) is lower than the other figures and is probably an aberration. When it is used to calculate the mean retention ratio, the obtained figure will be likely to underestimate actual enrollments. When this happens, an adjustment can be made to correct the estimate.

Determining Staff Allocations

School systems rely on enrollment projections to determine how staff resources will be allocated. Teachers, aides, counselors, librarians, and assistant

TABLE 2.2 Developing Seventh-Grade Enrollment Projections for a District with Decreasing Enrollments

1 Year	2 6th-Grade Enrollment	3 Year	4 7th-Grade Enrollment	5 Retention Ratio
1990	2964	1991	2847	.9605
1991	2496	1992	2391	.9579
1992	2473	1993	2378	.9616
1993	2280	1994	2132	.9351
1994	2144	1995	2117	.9874
1995	2057	1996		

Step 1: Divide the seventh-grade enrollment by the previous year's sixth-grade enrollment to obtain the retention ratio (col. 5) for a given year. The retention ratio for 1991 is 2847/2964=.9605.

Step 2: Find the sum of the five enrollment ratios and divide by 5 (.9605 + .9579 + .9616 + .9351 + .9874 = 4.8025; 4.8025/5 = .9605). This is the mean retention ratio.

Step 3: Multiply the number of students enrolled in grade 6 in 1995–96 by the mean retention ratio to obtain the projected number of seventh-grade students for 1996 (2057 ↔.9605 = 1976).

principals are assigned on the basis of the number of students expected to enroll in each school. If the enrollment projections indicate that a school will have an increase in enrollment, a decision must be made whether additional staff are needed and, if so, in which positions or grade levels. Schools that lose students may have to give up positions.

Information about resignations and retirements are taken into account, and a determination is made on the number of employees who must be employed, transferred, or laid off. If additional staff members are needed, action is taken to initiate interviews with qualified applicants.

In recent years, school districts have begun to look at other factors in addition to enrollment in deciding how to allocate personnel. One plan is to award points to a school based on the types of students with particular needs. Schools might receive 1 point per student, with additional points for each child on free lunch, each child who is disabled, or each child who is gifted. Some districts grant additional faculty resources for schools with high mobility.

Staffing arrangements in site-managed schools are generally determined by the principal and teachers of the school, who have the option of reconfiguring staff to better meet the needs of the students. The faculty in a school might decide, for example, to hire fewer teachers and more aides or to do without an assistant principal in order to gain an additional teacher or several aides. Such a system provides a way to allocate staff that is equitable, and it lets each building control the configuration of staff to meet its needs.

Summary

Planning is an effort to anticipate and prepare for the future by mobilizing an organization's resources to attain a desirable future state. In strategic planning, a school identifies its goals and resources and develops strategies for attaining them. Strategic planners carry out a critical issues analysis by identifying forces that are expected to affect the school's operation, require allocation of resources, or can be influenced by the school. Following analysis and discussion, selected issues are chosen for further study and a brief is prepared for each issue.

One of the important tasks in human resource planning is projecting staff needs. This involves projecting enrollments and determining the number of personnel needed to staff the schools. Procedures are set in motion to recruit and select additional staff or, if enrollments are dropping, to reduce staff size.

The cohort survival method is the most widely used technique for projecting enrollments. This method is most accurate when school enrollments are stable or trends are consistent; it is least accurate when enrollments fluctuate.

Suggested Activities

1. Review the rational and natural systems models of organizations presented in Chapter 1. Then describe what would be involved in the process of planning if one embraced the beliefs of the rational model and how it would differ from the process of planning for a person who accepted the natural systems model of organizations.
2. A scan of the external environment assesses such factors as demographics, cultural climate, family structure, and the influence of other institutions and agencies. Choose a school that you are familiar with and write a paragraph describing the changes you anticipate in the external environment of that school during the next five years.
3. In preparing an internal scan, strategic planners look at strengths and weaknesses of a school, the nature of the student body, financial restraints or resources, staff resources or limitations, facilities, and equipment. Write one paragraph about each of two of these factors for the school you chose in Question 2.

4. Prepare a futures wheel showing the effects of the adoption of a new student conduct code with specified penalties for violation of school rules.
5. Prepare an issues brief for the topic of adopting a new code of student conduct.

References

Adams, D. (1988). Extending the educational planning discourse: Conceptual and paradigmatic explorations. *Comparative Education Review, 32*, 400–415.

Alspaugh, J. (1981, Summer). Accuracy of school enrollment projections based upon previous enrollments. *Educational Research Quarterly, 6*, 61–67.

American Association of School Administrators. (1983). *Planning for tomorrow's schools*. Arlington, VA: Author.

Conley, D. (1993, April). *Strategic planning in practice: An analysis of purposes, goals, and procedures*. Paper presented at the annual meeting of the American Educational Research Association, Atlanta. (ERIC Document Reproduction Service No. ED 358530).

Fear, R., & Chiron, R. (1990). *The evaluation interview* (4th ed.). New York: McGraw-Hill.

Hamilton, D. (1991). An alternative to rational planning models. In R. Carlson & G. Awkerman (Eds.), *Educational planning: Concepts, strategies, and practices* (pp. 21–47). New York: Longman.

Hatten, K., & Hatten, M. (1988). *Effective strategic management: Analysis and action*. Englewood Cliffs, NJ: Prentice Hall.

Hussey, D. (1985). *Introducing corporate planning*. Oxford: Pergamon Press.

Kaufman, R. (1992). *Mapping educational success*. Newbury Park, CA: Corwin.

Lewis, J., Jr. (1983). *Long-range and short-range planning for educational administrators*. Boston: Allyn and Bacon.

Mauriel, J. (1989). *Strategic leadership for schools*. San Francisco: Jossey-Bass.

Pounder, D. (1987). The challenge for school leaders: Attracting and retaining good teachers. In W. Greenfield (Ed.), *Instructional leadership: Concepts, issues, and controversies* (pp. 287–301). Boston: Allyn and Bacon.

Schellenberg, S., & Stephens, C. (1987). *Enrollment projection: Variations on a theme*. Paper presented at the annual meeting of the American Educational Research Association, Washington, DC.

Sybouts, W. (1992). *Planning in school administration. A handbook*. New York: Greenwood.

Wilkinson, G. (1986). Strategic planning in the voluntary sector. In J. Gardner, R. Rachlin, & H. Sweeny (Eds.), *Handbook of strategic planning* (25.1–25.23). New York: Wiley.

3

PREPARING FOR PERSONNEL SELECTION

Selecting school personnel involves matching applicants' qualifications to selection criteria. To the extent that a good match is achieved, employees will be successful in their work. However, when an applicant is placed in a position that does not fit his or her qualifications, the individual will experience frustration and will not do high-quality work.

Plan of the Chapter

This chapter presents a model of the selection process and explains how selection criteria are developed and applied to identify qualified applicants for vacant positions. Chapter 4 examines how information about applicants is obtained and evaluated. The following topics will be discussed in this chapter: (1) a model of the selection process, (2) identifying selection criteria, (3) job-specific selection criteria for teaching, (4) nonjob-specific selection criteria for teachers; and (5) selection criteria for support positions.

A Model of the Selection Process

The selection process has four objectives: (1) to ensure that individuals selected to work for an organization possess the knowledge, skills, and abilities to perform their jobs effectively; (2) to help individuals make informed decisions about whether to accept an offer of employment; (3) to create a sense of commitment to the organization on the part of new employees; and (4) to commit the organization to provide the support necessary for newly hired employees to succeed. A sound selection process results in hiring employees who possess the knowledge, skills, and abilities needed in the job for which they are hired and who are committed to the organization (Lawler, 1992).

To achieve the first objective, the employer identifies criteria related to successful performance on a job. Job-specific criteria are the knowledge, skills, and abilities that are integral to success in a specific position. Nonjob-specific criteria are characteristics that contribute to success in many different jobs. Knowledge of and ability to apply the principles of physical conditioning are examples of job-specific criteria for an athletic coach, just as ability to use a chisel is a job-specific criterion for a carpenter.

Nonjob-specific criteria are attributes that contribute to successful performance in many jobs. Examples of nonjob-specific criteria are the ability to express ideas clearly, regular attendance on the job, avoidance of alcohol and drug abuse, a positive attitude toward the job, and willingness to work cooperatively with other employees.

By assessing indicators of the selection criteria, an employer rates applicants for the position and hires the person whose qualifications best match the selection criteria. An example of an indicator of knowledge of the principles of physical conditioning is successful completion of a course on that topic, and an indicator of skill in word processing is the ability to type a document using a specified word-processing program with acceptable speed and with few errors.

Figure 3.1 graphically depicts the selection process. Job models, state and federal laws, mission statements, and research are used to identify the functions performed in a position. Selection criteria are generated from the list of functions, and indicators of the criteria are chosen. (Job models are described in a later section.) Information from applicants is compared to the criteria, and when a fit is found, that person is hired. Those whose attributes do not match the criteria are rejected. Since not all of the criteria are equally essential in a position, it is usually necessary to prioritize the criteria and give preference to applicants who are rated highest on those that are considered most critical.

The Americans with Disabilities Act (ADA) has brought about changes in the selection process by introducing the concept of *essential functions*. These are tasks that are fundamental to a particular job and that an employee must be able to perform in order to be considered qualified for the position.

Selection decisions have traditionally hinged on considerations of worth—that is, an individual's ability to make a contribution that is valued by the employer. If several candidates for a position were equally qualified, the candidate who was able to meet other needs of the employer, in addition to those required in the job for which he or she was applying, was hired (Scriven, 1990).

For example, an applicant for a teaching position who had experience in coaching tennis or field hockey might be chosen over an equally qualified applicant who lacked coaching experience, even though coaching was not required in the position. Under ADA, an employer who rejects an applicant

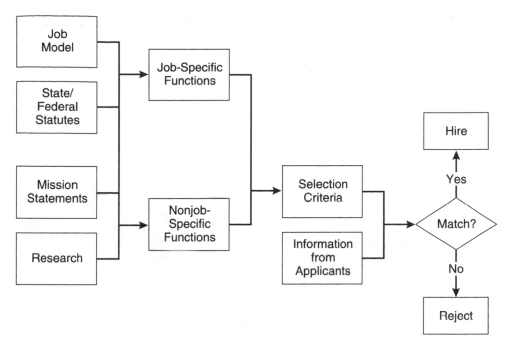

FIGURE 3.1   Model of the Selection Process

with a disability who is able to perform the essential functions of a position, with or without accommodation, and hires an applicant who is not disabled, on the basis that the person hired can perform certain peripheral functions, violates the law (Jacobs, 1993). Thus, the legislation forces employers to concentrate in selection of employees on job-specific criteria.

The identification of essential functions is achieved by analyzing information from the same sources that are used to identify selection criteria (job model, state and federal statutes, mission statement, and findings of related research). (See Figure 3.1.) The job model specifies the results that a jobholder is expected to accomplish and describes conditions under which the work takes place. State statutes spell out mandatory preparation and licensing requirements for personnel, and research identifies school characteristics and teacher attitudes and behaviors associated with increased student learning.

Determining whether a particular task is an essential function of a job involves consideration of three factors: the tasks that the position exists to perform, the number of employees available to perform a task, and whether a person hired for the position is chosen for his or her ability to perform the task (Fersh & Thomas, 1993). Consider a high school counselor whose primary duties include counseling students and providing information to help students choose a college or make vocational plans. On three or four occasions each year, the counselor visits nearby middle schools to counsel middle school students on the transition to high school. One applicant for the position is confined to a wheelchair and is unable, without help, to travel to other schools.

Can the district reject the applicant who is disabled in favor of someone who is physically able to travel? The answer probably depends on whether visiting middle schools is considered an essential function of the job. Since little of the counselor's time is devoted to that task and the counselor is not chosen primarily on the basis of his or her ability to do it, it is unlikely that these visits would be considered an essential function. Moreover, since it is possible to make an accommodation by assigning some other employee to visit the middle schools or by providing assistance for the counselor to make the trip, no rational basis exists for rejecting the disabled applicant.

Job-specific criteria are given more weight in the selection process under ADA than was true before that law was enacted. However, nonspecific criteria are still part of the picture, since some attributes are important to success in any undertaking. Employees who are faithful in attendance, who are cooperative with other workers and with supervisors, and who are able to do their jobs without close supervision are usually successful in whatever tasks they undertake. Employers need to exercise care, however, to avoid using nonjob-specific criteria that are peripheral to successful performance.

Identifying Selection Criteria

The primary source of information about the selection criteria for a position is a job description or job model. A *job description* identifies the position and describes the duties and responsibilities associated with it. The description usually gives some information about the school and the district in which the vacancy occurs. It includes a list of qualifications required in the position, and it may describe resources available to the incumbent.

Rochester (New York) schools use a generic job description for teaching positions (Haller, 1987). The description identifies the job goal as helping students "to learn subject matter and/or skills that will contribute to their development as mature, able, and responsible men and women" (p. 184).

Among the performance responsibilities for teachers identified in the Rochester job description are the following: planning programs that meet individual needs, interests, and abilities of students; creating an environment that is conducive to learning; guiding the learning process toward achievement of curriculum goals; establishing clear objectives and communicating those objectives to students; employing appropriate instructional methods and materials; evaluating students and providing progress reports as required; diagnosing learning abilities and disabilities of students on a regular basis; working cooperatively with staff, superiors, and community; assisting in implementing the school's rules of behavior; maintaining order in a fair and just manner; maintaining and improving professional competence; and attending meetings and serving on committees as appropriate.

The Rochester document is based on the assumption that all teaching jobs in a district are alike. In fact, teaching positions vary, depending on the subject and grade level taught and the school environment. Teaching a fifth-grade class in an elementary school with a multiethnic student population is a different experience, and requires different skills, than teaching English in a college preparatory high school. The results that are expected and the resources that are available to assist teachers in the two situations differ. Position descriptions that are specific to a particular school or job can help to target the selection process and increase the probability of making successful staffing decisions.

Writing a Job Model

An alternative to the traditional job description has been developed by Dailey (1982). The job model is an improvement over position descriptions because it focuses on results and makes it possible to focus the selection process on choosing an employee who can achieve those outcomes.

The job model presents a realistic picture of the job, including both its attractive and unattractive features. If a position is located in a school in an old building with out-of-date equipment and few supplies, the job model states those facts. If parents are cooperative and supportive of teachers, that too is reported. An effort is made to avoid presenting only the positive features of a position, since once a teacher is hired he or she soon becomes aware of the less attractive features of the situation and must be able to produce results in spite of them. Employees who are informed in advance of both the negative and positive features of a new position more often experience feelings of satisfaction than those who are told only the good news about the job (Wanous, 1980).

An example of a job model for the position of high school Spanish teacher is shown in Exhibit 3.1. The job model consists of three parts. The section entitled "Results Sought" describes the outcomes the Spanish teacher is expected to accomplish. This section is the heart of the job model because it helps to focus the search on the important task of identifying a candidate who can achieve those results. "Job Environment" describes characteristics of the school and community that are likely either to facilitate or hinder performance. Interviewers use the information in this section to investigate applicants' ability and willingness to overcome barriers and to use resources effectively to achieve specified results. Applicants use the information to weigh their feelings of adequacy to face the challenge presented by the position.

The "Priority Actions" section of the job model describes tasks that must be performed on the job. These may be actions that lead directly or indirectly to accomplishment of the results described under "Results Sought," or they

Results Sought

1. Students listening to a speaker describing familiar activities in Spanish are able to answer questions about the main ideas of the presentation in Spanish (level 1) and about details of the presentation in Spanish (level 2).

2. Students carry on a brief conversation with a Spanish-speaking person discussing daily events at home or school using limited vocabulary (level 1) or more extensive vocabulary (level 2).

3. Students write a brief (one-page) essay using regular verbs, present tense only (level 1) or both regular and irregular verbs, present and past tenses (level 2) on a familiar topic, when provided a stimulus in Spanish.

4. In English (level 1) or in Spanish (level 2) students present oral reports on elements of Hispanic culture, including religion, dress, history, and literature.

5. Students who complete one level are prepared to succeed at the next higher level.

6. Parents are familiar with their children's progress in Spanish and afford themselves of the opportunity for conferences with the teacher as needed.

Job Environment

The job is located in a high school in a rural/suburban area near a city of approximately 125,000 people. The school enrolls 1,200 students from low- and middle-income families; about one-fifth of the students are Black, Hispanic, or Asian. About 60 percent of the school's graduates attend college. Three foreign languages (French, German, and Spanish) are offered by the school. Level-1 classes typically have 25 to 30 students, and level-2 classes usually have between 20 and 25. Instructional materials that are integrated with the textbook, including audio- and videotapes and transparencies, are available for teachers' use.

Priority Actions

The successful Spanish teacher must speak and write Spanish fluently and must be able to motivate students from diverse backgrounds to apply themselves to the study of the language. The teacher must plan and present instruction that will enable students to attain facility in speaking and writing Spanish and must be able to diagnose students' deficiencies and provide appropriate instructional remedies. The teacher must be available to meet with students who request additional help and to confer with parents concerning their children's performance. The teacher must be able to work with teachers from other schools to develop the curriculum and select instructional materials.

EXHIBIT 3.1   Job Model: High School Spanish Teacher (Levels 1 and 2)

may be actions that help other persons in the school accomplish the results for which they are responsible. Examples of priority actions that might be required of a teacher are covering required curriculum content and assessing and reporting to parents on students' academic progress.

The first step in constructing a job model involves identifying the results sought. Schools are organizations with multiple and ambiguous goals. It is not easy in such organizations to reach consensus on results sought. The recommended procedure is to ask four or five persons who are familiar with the job to complete the following statement: "A person in this job is effective if he or she produces the result that . . ." (Dailey, 1982). Each contributor writes eight endings for the sentence and ranks these eight outcomes from most important (rank 1) to least important (rank 8).

To help in writing these statements, Dailey (1982) has offered this advice: "A 'result' should be a very *tangible* effect of work *useful to someone else* and contributing to the organization's reason for existing." Some educators focus on instructional strategies rather than results or outcomes of instruction. Statements such as "allow for individual differences" and "plan stimulating activities" describe actions, not results. Although these actions may lead to desirable outcomes, they are not tangible effects of work that are useful to others. Action statements belong under "Priority Actions."

The 6 to 10 statements that appear most often on contributors' lists are compiled under the "Results Sought" heading of the job model. Exhibit 3.2 shows examples of actions and corresponding results for several positions. Note that the results described in Column 2 of the exhibit are tangible effects that are useful to someone else. Textbooks are available for students' use, children play together in groups, assistant coaches work together, and so on. The actions described in Column 1 contribute to attaining those results, but they do not appear in the "Results Sought" section of the job model.

To prepare a description of the job environment, several individuals who are familiar with the position are asked to list forces that facilitate or hinder performance. The three most important facilitating forces are ranked +1 to +3, and the three most important hindering forces are ranked −1 to −3. These lists are then combined into a narrative statement under the heading "Job Environment." The description of the job environment should

Action	Result
Assistant principal manages textbook ordering, inventory, and storage	Textbooks are available in sufficient quantities when needed
Child care provider encourages children to take part in group activities	Children interact comfortably with peers in group activities
Football coach coordinates activities of assistant coaches	Assistant coaches understand their own and others' duties and work together effectively
English teacher covers material in the approved curriculum	Students demonstrate mastery of material in the approved curriculum

EXHIBIT 3.2   Examples of Actions and Results Sought

be a straightforward report of the factors that new employees will encounter in the position, including both positive and negative features.

Finally, a description of job demands is prepared by asking four or five persons who are familiar with the position to answer the questions that appear in Exhibit 3.3. When the results of this exercise are compiled, that information is written in narrative form and included in the section entitled "Priority Actions." The information generated by these three exercises is combined into a job model. Ideally, a separate job model is prepared for each vacancy, but that is not always practical. In those cases generic job models may be written for groups of positions (early childhood, special education/mentally retarded, high school physical education, and so on).

1. How important is it that the person in this position be able to perform the following activities?
   a. Make presentations to parent or community groups
   b. Prepare detailed lesson plans
   c. Meet with parents to discuss students' progress
   d. Lead a discussion about various aspects of the school's programs
   e. Lead a team of other professionals in planning and carrying out an assigned task
   f. Develop solutions to unique problems and obtain support to implement them
   g. Deal with children who are rowdy and disorderly
   h. Plan instruction for children who are mentally or physically handicapped
   i. Maintain accurate records of money, supplies, or student work
   j. Arrange public displays or performances of students' artistic work
   k. Develop and present instructional demonstrations
   l. Collect money or raise funds for special projects
   m. Monitor the school cafeteria, hallways, and parking lots
   n. Maintain a high degree of student involvement in academic tasks
   o. Conduct committee meetings to assess progress of students in special placements
   p. Arrange placements for students in community commercial businesses and government agencies
   q. Assist students to acquire job information

2. How important is it that the person who fills this job have motivation of the type described in each statement?
   a. Wants to produce a stable level of performance and be satisfied to work within routines
   b. Desires goodwill and affection from people and cares a great deal about having close relationships
   c. Wants to acquire and use influence and to exercise leadership
   d. Wants to set objectives in order to measure progress toward a better way of doing things
   e. Wants to acquire new or more intense experiences or to try new activities and ventures

EXHIBIT 3.3   Questions to Help in Writing Job Demands

Items listed under question 2 are from *Using the Track Record Approach: The Key to Successful Personnel Selection* by C. A. Dailey, 1982, AMACOM, New York.

Job-Specific Selection Criteria for Teachers

Teachers are hired to help students learn. They are expected to perform other duties as well, including maintaining records of students' attendance and academic accomplishments, serving on curriculum committees, and carrying out various managerial responsibilities. All of these are job-specific criteria, but none is more important than helping students to acquire knowledge, skill, and attitudes of respect for self and others.

Exhibit 3.4 lists six job-specific criteria that research has shown are related to effective teaching. The six factors are described in detail in the paragraphs that follow.

Ability to Organize and Manage a Class

Teachers who are good organizers and managers have fewer incidents of behavioral disruptions and hence less time lost to learning. These teachers announce rules to their students and explain the need for them, develop classroom routines that help make classroom activities run smoothly, deal with disruptive behavior promptly and firmly but fairly, and make efficient use of class time.

Ability to Motivate

Teachers who are good motivators are more effective at increasing student learning. Motivation includes such diverse activities as showing empathy for students' feelings, using persuasion to increase student effort, demonstrating enthusiasm for the subject matter, and using questioning to arouse student interest in the subject.

Ability to Communicate

Effective teachers are good communicators. They use illustrations and examples to help students understand, give clear explanations and specific di-

- Organize and manage a class effectively.
- Motivate students to learn.
- Communicate information effectively.
- Maintain student involvement in instructional activities.
- Believe in the educability of all children.
- Have extensive knowledge of subject.

EXHIBIT 3.4   Job-Specific Criteria for Teaching

Source: From "Do Teachers Make a Difference?" by A. Mood, in *Do Teachers Make a Difference?* (pp. 1–24). Washington, DC: U.S. Government Printing Office.

rections for completing assignments, and use language that students comprehend. These teachers frequently display a sense of humor that does not demean or ridicule students but helps to improve communication.

Ability to Maintain Student Involvement

This is the heart of good teaching. It involves planning activities that hold student interest, monitoring student work to diagnose students' performance, and adjusting the pace or difficulty level when needed.

Dedication to the Educability of All Children

Teachers with this attribute believe strongly that all children can learn, and they act on that belief by letting their students know they have confidence in their ability, praising students who learn new material, offering encouragement, assisting students to learn, and showing patience when students encounter difficulties with new material.

Knowledge of Subject

Knowledge of the subject area is necessary for effective teaching, but some research suggests that some administrators give preference to applicants who are average or below on measures of academic performance (Perry, 1981). Information about knowledge of subject is most likely to come from test scores, transcripts, and references. For the other criteria, the most useful sources of information are interviews with the applicant and references from persons who are familiar with the individual's teaching. Comments from previous principals and supervisors are frequently used sources of information about an individual's effectiveness in the classroom. Predicting future teaching success is more problematic in the case of beginning teachers, but that should not mean that beginners are ruled out in the selection process. It may be necessary that decision makers make an extra effort to obtain information that will help predict future performance about applicants who have not previously taught.

Applicants' own reports concerning previous teaching experiences are an important source of information in attempting to predict future teaching effectiveness, but self-reports are subject to distortion and must be viewed more critically than comments from references.

Nonjob-Specific Selection Criteria for Teachers

Important as it is, evidence of ability to teach effectively is not the only yardstick that is used in evaluating an applicant's qualifications. Other criteria also deserve attention. Some of these criteria originate in legal mandates established by the state or locality. For example, in all states teachers are required to hold a valid teaching certificate with endorsements in the subjects they teach, and are required to be free of infectious diseases.

Community Expectations

Community expectations are another source of criteria for selection of teachers. At one time, teachers were expected to exemplify community standards in their behavior, political activities, and moral beliefs (Sedlak & Schlossman, 1987). Those expectations have eased considerably in recent years, allowing teachers greater freedom in their personal lives, but in most communities the feeling prevails that teachers should be neat, well groomed, and have a good command of the English language. However, personnel administrators should be careful to distinguish between adherence to reasonable community expectations and deferral to social desirability factors.

Character and Adjustment Factors

Other criteria that are considered in making selection decisions are matters of character and adjustment that indicate an applicant will be likely to persist and succeed on the job. There are seven such factors: commitment, persistence, attitude toward authority, need for approval, temperament and adjustment, motivation to improve skills, and ability to function autonomously (Haberman, 1987).

Commitment
Commitment is revealed by evidence of pride and satisfaction in the work of teaching and by plans to remain in the field. A critical attitude is not incompatible with commitment if the intent of the criticism is to bring about improvement of the profession.

Persistence
Persistence is the action of continuing to pursue worthwhile objectives in the face of repeated discouragement and setbacks. It indicates maturity of character. Persistent teachers are not easily dissuaded from efforts to motivate students. They pursue their goals in spite of absence of support and lack of resources, and they are usually successful in attaining their goals.

Attitude toward Authority
Teachers' attitudes toward authority range from outright hostility to indifference to overdependence. These attitudes are formed in childhood through interaction with parents or guardians. A healthy attitude is one that permits the individual to accept legitimate authority without either feeling compelled to rebel or to submit passively. Mature teachers can disagree with a principal or supervisor without feeling either perverse satisfaction or dejec-

tion, and they are able to accept decisions with which they personally disagree without experiencing undue feelings of disappointment or anger. In hiring, it is advisable to give a preference to candidates with neither overly deferential nor hostile attitudes toward authority figures.

Need for Approval

Need for approval from students is fairly common among beginning teachers. However, most of them soon realize that they have an obligation to help children learn and that they cannot be effective teachers until they are able to place the welfare of the children they teach above their own emotional needs. Those who fail to acquire that insight find themselves unable to make reasonable academic and behavioral demands on their students, and are continually torn by the competing emotions of wanting to be liked while at the same time recognizing the need to assume a more adult role. High need for approval from students is a negative indicator for selection.

Temperament and Adjustment

Temperament and personal adjustment refer to an individual's typical mood patterns and satisfaction with life. A person may be an effective teacher even though he or she is subject to mood swings, and even a person who is not very satisfied with his or her life may nevertheless be effective in the classroom. However, given two candidates who, on the basis of all of the available evidence, promise to be equally effective teachers, a principal would be wise to select the candidate with the more stable temperament and better personal adjustment. These individuals are more likely to be flexible (that is, able to accommodate changes in routine without experiencing undue frustration or anxiety) and they are more likely to be able to work with other teachers and parents with a minimum of friction.

Motivation to Improve Skills

A teacher who is motivated to improve his or her skills is likely to be more effective in the classroom than one who must be persuaded to acquire new competencies. An applicant who inquires during an interview about opportunities for professional growth and development, including district-sponsored workshops and provision for travel to regional and national conferences, is revealing positive information about his or her motivation to improve. This type of interest should be noted by an interviewer and taken into account in the selection decision.

Ability to Function Autonomously

The ability to function autonomously is seldom cited as a desirable characteristic of a teacher candidate. In fact, it is more obvious by omission than by inclusion in the literature on teacher selection. In only one source reviewed for this chapter was professional autonomy mentioned (Wise, 1987).

East Williston Union Free District, located on Long Island near New York City, uses autonomy as one of the selection criteria for choosing teachers. Wise had this comment:

> *"Part of the mystique of the Wheatley School [East Williston's high school] is the autonomous teacher." "We look for the best." "If you get outstanding teachers, you get outstanding education for students." But "the best" does not mean the strongest academically. East Williston has turned away candidates with very strong academic backgrounds (Ph.D. level) in favor of people who have strong teaching experience. "We can help people to acquire content but we cannot help them to acquire concern." Behind those views is the belief in teaching as an autonomous profession wherein having found the best practitioners, the system allows professional teachers autonomy to practice. . . .*
>
> *Yet the search for independent performers is tempered. "We look for people who work harmoniously with other people in a situation where there is pressure to produce" is the official view. But too many strong personalities threaten the integrity of small groups. (pp. 102–103)*

Information from references who have observed a person's work firsthand can be especially useful in determining whether an applicant meets the criteria for a particular position. In addition to furnishing information about an applicant's character, references can provide insights into the individual's effectiveness in the classroom.

Selection Criteria for Support Positions

Some personal attributes are important in many jobs. Among them are emotional maturity, self-discipline, tough-mindedness, and ability to plan.

Emotional maturity is important for all persons who come in contact with children, including teacher aides, bus drivers, custodians, and clerical personnel. An emotionally mature person exhibits patience with children whose behavior can occasionally be trying and is able to maintain firm boundaries without feeling intimidated or reacting impulsively. An emotionally immature individual lacks the perspective to be able to look beyond his or her own needs in order to understand and respond to the needs and concerns of the child. Emotional maturity is especially vital for those who work with children who have problems of social adjustment or who are emotionally disturbed.

Self-discipline is important in jobs in which individuals work with minimal supervision and must schedule their work around frequent interruptions. Receptionists and secretaries, for example, need to possess self-discipline in order to persist in completing tasks in spite of interruptions from the telephone or from visitors. Custodians need self-discipline since they work without close supervision and must assume responsibility for monitoring heating and cooling equipment, changing lightbulbs, and, when the need arises, shoveling snow from school sidewalks, without being directed to do so.

Tough-mindedness refers to the ability to judge a situation objectively without excessive sentimentality and to persist in pursuing a course of action intended to correct a problem in the face of personal criticism. It is a trait that is especially important in those who are in personnel work or who deal with abusive individuals. Social workers who must initiate court action against families that keep their children out of school without good cause must be tough-minded and persistent in continuing to press these families to abide by the law.

Among the few jobs in which planning is not important are those that involve waiting on customers or manufacturing products on an assembly line. In those jobs, planning is usually done by someone else. In schools, planning is critical for success. Individuals in support positions must plan in order to have supplies on hand they need in their work, and they must plan the use of their time so they will be able to finish work on schedule.

Summary

Selection of personnel involves matching applicants to the selection criteria for a position. A basic objective of the selection process is to ensure that individuals who are hired possess the knowledge, skills, and abilities to perform effectively. The Americans with Disabilities Act holds employers responsible for evaluating applicants on the job-specific criteria for a position and their ability to perform the job, with or without accommodations, without regard to physical or mental disabilities. The job-specific and non-job-specific criteria that are essential for success on a job are the basis for selection decisions.

Selection criteria for a position are obtained from a job description or job model and other sources, including state and federal statutes. A job model lists results sought in a job along with descriptions of the job environment and priority actions. A result is a tangible effect of work that is useful to someone else that helps accomplish the unit's mission.

Among the criteria shown by research to be related to effective teaching are organizing and managing classes effectively, motivating students to learn, communicating information effectively, and maintaining student involvement in instructional activities. Among the selection criteria for support positions are emotional maturity, self-discipline, initiative, and tough-mindedness.

Suggested Activities

1. Work in teams to write a job model about a position held by one member of the group. Designate one individual to be a "resource person" and interview that person to obtain information.
2. Interview a person who holds a job different from yours and identify the essential functions of that position. Use the factors described in the chapter to identify the essential functions (position exists to perform the task, few employees can do the task, and employees are chosen for their ability to do the task).
3. Obtain a job description for a support position (counselor, school psychologist, visiting teacher, etc.). Use it to identify selection criteria and indicators for the position.
4. Read Case Study I (at the end of this book) and answer the questions that follow.

References

Dailey, C. A. (1982). *Using the track record approach: the key to successful personnel selection.* New York: AMACOM.

Fersh, D., & Thomas, P. (1993). *Complying with the Americans with Disabilities Act: A guidebook for management and people with disabilities.* Westport, CN: Quorum.

Haberman, M. (1987). *Recruiting and selecting teachers for urban schools.* New York: Columbia University, ERIC Clearinghouse on Urban Education.

Haller, E. (1987). Teacher selection in the city school district of Rochester. In A. Wise, L. Darling-Hammond, D. Berliner, E. Haller, P. Schlechty, B. Berry, A. Praskac, & G. Noblit (Eds.), *Effective teacher selection: From recruitment to retention—Case studies* (pp. 153–187). Santa Monica, CA: Rand.

Jacobs, R. (1993). *Legal compliance guide to personnel management.* Englewood Cliffs, NJ: Prentice Hall.

Lawler, E. (1992). *The ultimate advantage: Creating the high-involvement organization.* San Francisco: Jossey-Bass.

Mood, A. M. (1970). Do teachers make a difference? In *Do teachers make a difference?* (pp.

1–24). Washington, DC: U.S. Government Printing Office.

Perry, N. C. (1981). New teachers: Do the best get hired? *Phi Delta Kappan, 63,* 113–114.

Scriven, M. (1990). Teacher selection. In J. Millman & L. Darling-Hammond (Eds.), *The new handbook of teacher evaluation* (pp. 76–103). Newbury Park, CA: Sage.

Sedlak, M., & Schlossman, S. (1987). Who will teach? Historical perspectives of the changing appeal of teaching as a profession. *Review of Research in Education, 14,* 93–132.

Wanous, J. P. (1980). *Organizational entry: Recruitment, selection, and socialization of newcomers.* Reading, MA: Addison-Wesley.

Wise, A. (1987). Teacher selection in the East Williston Union Free School District. In A. Wise, L. Darling-Hammond, D. Berliner, E. Haller, P. Schlechty, B. Berry, A. Praskac, & G. Noblit (Eds.), *Effective teacher selection: From recruitment to retention—Case studies* (pp. 93–121). Santa Monica, CA: Rand.

4

OBTAINING INFORMATION
AND EVALUATING APPLICANTS

Selection decisions involve collecting information about the types and amount of knowledge, experience, and personal qualifications required in a position. Those details are then matched with information about the applicants, and the person whose qualifications most closely match the requirements for the position is hired. Chapter 3 dealt with writing a job model and using it to identify the essential functions and selection criteria for a position. This chapter explains how information about applicants is gathered and evaluated.

Plan of the Chapter

The selection process begins with the collection of information about applicants. This chapter focuses on sources of information about applicants for teaching positions. The chapter also deals with district transfer policies. The following sections appear in the chapter: (1) sources of information about applicants, (2) interviewing for selection, (3) types of interviews, and (4) transfer policies and student learning.

Sources of Information about Applicants

The district personnel office is responsible for gathering information about prospective employees, even in districts with school-based management. Initial screening of applicants is done by district-level staff members, and information gathered about qualified applicants is made available to decision makers in the schools.

There are five principal sources of information about applicants, and each is a potential contributor of data about applicants' qualifications. This information is used to determine whether the applicant meets the selection criteria for the position and is able to perform the essential functions of the job, with or without accommodation. The five information sources are the application form, transcripts, references, tests, and interviews.

Application Form

The application form should provide space for applicants to supply information about their educational background, including professional certification. It should also request information on the applicant's work history, including jobs held, dates of employment, and, for the most recent positions, the name of a person who is familiar with the individual's work and who is willing to provide a reference. The application form should provide enough information about an applicant that a selection committee can tell whether the individual is able to perform the essential functions of the position (Herman, 1994).

Questions that are not related to qualifications for performing a job should not appear on the application form since such information may be used for discriminatory purposes. Districts may ask about conviction of a crime if it pertains to a bona fide occupational qualification or business necessity, but inquiries about an applicant's arrest record should be avoided (*Education Law*, 1989). Questions dealing with race or ethnic background, religion, sex, or age should not be asked, although that information may be collected anonymously on preemployment inquiry forms. The legal ramifications of requesting this type of information are discussed in more detail in Chapter 12.

Other questions that are likely to be suspect are inquiries related to marital status or name of spouse, maiden name of female applicants, questions about the number and age of children or plans to have children, child care arrangements, organizational memberships, whether an applicant's spouse objects to the applicant's traveling, and whether an applicant is the principal wage earner in the family (*Education Law*, 1989). Employers are safe in asking whether an applicant has commitments that would interfere with regular attendance on the job and, if language fluency is a requirement on the job, whether the applicant is able to read, write, or speak other languages.

Employers may ask whether an applicant is over 21 years of age and whether he or she is a citizen of the United States. Noncitizens may be asked if they hold a valid work permit issued by the U.S. Immigration and Naturalization Service. Rather than ask applicants questions about their medical condition, employers are advised to describe the nature of the essential functions required on a job and ask applicants whether they will be able to perform those tasks and what accommodations, if any, they will need in order to perform them (Jacobs, 1993).

Transcripts

Some districts have attempted to simplify the application process by dropping the requirement that transcripts be submitted with the application. It is important that a transcript be obtained at some point in the selection process, however, in order to verify that the individual has indeed completed an approved course of study and received a college degree. Imposters have succeeded in posing as teachers, ministers, and physicians without holding a degree and, in a few cases, without ever having attended college. An official transcript bearing an embossed seal from the issuing institution is acceptable as valid evidence of an applicant's having attended that institution.

The transcript provides useful information about an applicant's academic achievements and course of study. Although a high grade-point average is no guarantee that an applicant will be successful in the classroom, other things being equal, individuals who do well academically in college generally achieve better results with children than those who are average or below.

References

Administrators often discount letters of references since many of them are one-sided, praising the applicant's strong qualities and avoiding mention of any faults. One authority describes written references as useful only for verifying employment history (Herman, 1994). However, in spite of legitimate questions about the validity of information from references, most districts require applicants to submit the names of three or four individuals who are acquainted with their work. In some districts, the application form for a professional position specifically requests the names of supervisors in all previous positions.

Some principals and personnel workers prefer to interview references by telephone, in the belief that they will be more honest in assessing an applicant orally than in writing. Telephone interviews also permit one to probe for additional information. However, some employers have adopted a policy of providing only factual information about previous employees, including dates of employment, positions held, and the reasons for leaving, if known. If a reference check reveals derogatory information or a significant discrepancy in information provided by the applicant, the applicant should be given the opportunity to explain (Drake, 1989).

These procedures are recommended for producing the best results from reference checks by telephone (Herman, 1994):

- Explain the purpose of the call and offer to call back at a later time in order to allow time for preparation, if needed.
- Explain that the reference check is the final step in preparing to make a job offer.

- Let the reference know that the interview will be confidential and that nothing he or she says will be revealed to the applicant.

Some districts provide a form on which references are asked to rate the applicant. Typically, such forms include a checklist of characteristics such as intelligence, persistence, initiative, oral and written language skills, and so on. There is usually a question about how long the reference has known the applicant and in what relationship, and there may be space for written comments. These forms have some advantages. They provide a standardized format that facilitates comparison of applicants' strengths and weaknesses, and, because they are convenient to complete, they are more likley to elicit a prompt response. One disadvantage of reference forms is that they have a low return rate.

Tests

In 1990, 44 of the 50 states required new teachers to pass one or more tests to be certified. Content knowledge was assessed in 25 states, and 26 examined basic skills. Tests of professional knowledge and in-class observations were also used (National Center for Education Statistics, 1993).

As a group, some minorities do not score as high on selection tests as other groups, raising a question about the fairness of using the tests for selection. The Supreme Court has held that the use of tests for selection is lawful if the test used is rationally related to a legitimate employment objective (*Washington* v. *Davis,* 1976). The Court has also affirmed the use of the National Teacher Examination for certification and salary purposes (*United States* v. *South Carolina,* 1978), but in *Griggs* v. *Duke Power Company* (1971), the Supreme Court disallowed the use of a general intelligence test for selection because the employer failed to show that the test results were related to job performance.

Teachers' organizations generally acquiesce in testing prospective teachers but oppose testing employed teachers. One professional group has identified a set of principles that it suggests be followed when test scores are used for selection decisions (Association of Teacher Educators, 1988). Among these principles are the following:

1. Tests should be validated for the purpose for which they are to be used. If a test is used for selection, it should have been validated for that purpose.
2. Tests should have a rational relationship to the job to be performed. That means that tests should be chosen to measure knowledge of subject or teaching techniques.
3. Cut-off scores on tests should be determined by an accepted empirical procedure rather than by arbitrary means.

4. Individuals should not be rank-ordered on the basis of test scores unless strong evidence exists that the test possesses criterion validity (that is, accurately predicts future performance).
5. Test scores should not be used to discriminate against a group or individual.

Interviewing for Selection

Interviews are used almost universally in employee selection, in all types of organizations. However, even though they are widely used, interviews are no more valid—and perhaps are less valid—than other ways of gathering information. Among the problems with interviews are the following:

1. Temporal placement of information influences interviewers' judgments. Positive information received early in the interview relates to more favorable judgments, and negative information results in less favorable judgments (Rowe, 1989).
2. Interviewers attach more weight to unfavorable information than to favorable information, but the reason is not clear. Some believe interviewers use negative information to narrow the list of applicants, thereby simplifying their jobs, but one author suggested that the attention to negative information indicates that interviewers are sensitive to the personal and organizational costs of hiring unqualified applicants (Rowe, 1989).
3. Interviewers may be subject to subconscious bias. Comparing an applicant with other persons who were interviewed earlier is called a *contrast effect* and is one of several biases that influences interviewers' judgments. Another is the *halo effect*, in which an interviewer's attitude about one characteristic influences ratings on all characteristics (Webster, 1982). A third source of bias is social merit considerations, discussed below.
4. Interviewers use only a limited number of dimensions in judging an applicant (Zedeck, Tziner, & Middlestadt, 1983).

Interviews are subject to the same legal scrutiny as written tests (Arvey, 1979). However, of the more than 8,000 employment practices cases reported between 1979 and 1987, fewer than 1 percent involved complaints about interviews. Nevertheless, interviewers should be aware that when courts do examine interviewing practices, questioning techniques are often a subject of scrutiny. Questions should be job relevant, and the same questions should be asked of all applicants (Campion & Arvey, 1989).

Using multiple interviewers can help avoid potential problems. A system for recording and storing information about the interview is recommended to avoid interviewers' being charged with bias or favoritism (Campion & Arvey, 1989).

The best results are obtained when individuals who conduct interviews are trained in their use and are familiar with the legal requirements governing employee selection. Topics that were described as inappropriate for use on application forms should also be avoided during interviews (Campion & Arvey, 1989).

Increasing Validity of Interviews

The validity of the interview as a selection device depends in large part on the interviewer's skills. Skills of interviewing can be learned, and training should be provided for those who screen applicants for teaching positions. One of the most important skills for interviewers to possess is the ability to put applicants at ease. This is done by greeting the applicant warmly and helping to break the ice by talking briefly about a topic of mutual interest (Hakel, 1982). Good interviewers avoid using words that are likely to create a defensive attitude on the part of an applicant. They also use body language to communicate their interest in what the applicant is saying and are sensitive to messages communicated by the applicant's body language (Moffatt, 1979).

Those who are adept at their work develop the skill of using implied or embedded questions. Implied questions involve paraphrasing or repeating what the applicant has said and then pausing. This is interpreted by the interviewee as a cue to elaborate. An example of an embedded question is this statement by an interviewer: "I am curious about the reasons for your statement that teaching second-graders is tougher than teaching high school students" (Magee, 1962).

Interviewers should be aware of the need to guard against bias in selection decisions. Interviewers can learn to avoid contrast and halo effects, but avoiding social merit bias is more tricky. A *social merit factor* is a trait or characteristic that inclines people to view another individual favorably. Social merit factors are the basis for one's initial attraction to other people in social situations. Individuals who are taller than average or who are strikingly attractive or who are graduates of prestigious universities are likely to be regarded by others more favorably than those who lack those advantages. Similarly, someone who has a poor complexion or a speech impediment is likely to be evaluated less favorably by other people than someone without those disadvantages. Social merit factors ordinarily have little to do with an individual's ability to perform effectively in a job, but interviewers may be influenced unconsciously to rate an applicant more or less favorably because of them.

Interviewers must be somewhat skeptical in order to be effective. Applicants who are eager to make a positive impression on an interviewer often omit negative information and embellish positive accomplishments. Interviewers learn to expect this and, by comparing information from several sources, are usually able to develop a reasonably accurate picture of an applicant's strengths and weaknesses.

In addition to comparing information provided by an applicant with that from other sources, there are three other methods skilled interviewers rely on to tell whether an applicant is truthful—internal consistency, the amount of unfavorable information provided, and clear evidence of exaggeration. *Internal consistency* refers to the absence of conflicting or contradictory answers. Since most people have encountered some unpleasant experiences on the job, a complete *absence of negative information* may mean that an applicant is withholding information. *Exaggeration* is the opposite of withholding information—it involves blowing up positive accomplishments to make them appear more significant than is warranted (Fear & Chiron, 1990).

Interview validity can be increased by use of the *behavior description interview technique* (Janz, 1989). In this approach, the interviewer asks questions about actual events an applicant has experienced in previous jobs or elsewhere. An individual's behavior in a previous situation is a more reliable predictor of how the person will act in similar situations in the future than responses to questions about hypothetical events. Focusing on an applicant's past behavior or track record is based on the principle that "a person can do again what he or she has done in the past" (Dailey & Madsen, 1980, p. 147).

The track-record approach somewhat mitigates the problem, which is inherent in what-would-you-do-if types of questions, of social desirability responses (Latham, Saari, Pursell, & Campion, 1980). A socially desirable response is one that an applicant believes will be more acceptable to the interviewer than a more honest response. Such responses may be given when an individual stands to gain something of value by creating a favorable impression on another person.

Asking an applicant to tell about a time when he or she took a particular kind of action or responded in a particular way to a problem situation reduces the possibility of the applicant's relying on socially desirable responses. For example, an interviewer might ask an applicant for a teaching position, "Tell me about a time when you helped a young child learn a new skill." Even persons who have no previous teaching experience may have taught a younger sibling to ride a bicycle or fly a kite. Descriptions of such incidents reveal a good deal about the kind of teacher a person will make.

If the applicant has taught, the possibilities for asking questions of this type are endless. The interviewer might ask, "Tell me how you taught your fifth-graders about the frontier in American history" or "How do you explain the concept of valence to your chemistry students?"

Sample Questions

Some sample questions that can be used to focus on past behavior in an interview are:

1. "Tell me about a time that you helped a child learn a new word in reading."
2. "I see that you have experience using the Lippincott reading program. I'd be interested in how you used these materials in the classroom."
3. "Middle school students often find math to be dull. Can you tell me what you have done to increase student interest in math?"
4. "What techniques have you used that work well in helping tenth-graders to improve their writing skills?"
5. "I'd like to hear about unusual materials you have used in your art classes."
6. "Discipline is always a challenge for teachers. What techniques do you rely on to keep order?"

For an applicant who has not held a full-time teaching position, questions that refer to student teaching or substitute teaching may be used. Substitute teachers often must rely on lesson plans prepared by the teacher whose place they are taking, so their responses to questions such as these may not be as reliable as indicators of future behavior as responses from teachers who have held full-time assignments.

Other questions that may be useful in assessing an applicant's potential teaching effectiveness are those that deal with working with colleagues, supervisors, administrators, and parents. An interviewer might ask, "What would you do if you wanted to introduce a new activity into a class you were teaching but had heard that the principal was opposed to the idea?" (Haberman, 1987).

A popular but not very useful question is to ask applicants to explain their philosophy of teaching. Interviewers ask it in the hope of finding out whether an individual's beliefs and attitudes about teaching are congruent with those held by others in the school, but applicants usually anticipate the question and give a rehearsed answer. Their answers may or may not reveal how they will actually behave on the job. Questions about past behavior yield insights into a person's action philosophy as opposed to a verbal philosophy and thus are more reliable indicators of future behavior.

Setting the Stage

The interviewer sets the stage for the interview by letting the applicant know what types of questions to expect and how the selection decision will be made. If the interviewer plans to take notes, that fact should be mentioned before formal questioning begins. Research has shown that note taking improves the interviewer's ability to recall information later (Webster, 1982). However, it may serve as a distraction. Interviewers should write down key words or phrases rather than entire sentences and prepare a written summary of the interview afterwards (Moffatt, 1979).

Mistakes to Avoid

Poor interviewing techniques interfere with the interviewer's ability to obtain information needed to rate an applicant's qualifications accurately. Some of the more common mistakes interviewers make are talking too much, jumping to conclusions, "telegraphing" the desired response to questions, allowing minor attributes to control a decision (Drake, 1982), and asking inappropriate questions.

Questions that can be answered *yes* or *no* or that have already been answered on the application blank should be avoided (Magee, 1962) unless there is reason to believe that an applicant has given misleading information on the application blank.

Types of Interviews

In a structured or standardized interview, all applicants for a job are asked the same set of prepared questions. The interviews are sometimes conducted by a team of interviewers who keep detailed notes on applicants' responses. There are several advantages to structured interviews. Notes from the interviews can be valuable in case legal action is initiated against the district for discrimination in hiring (Herman, 1994), and the structured format helps ensure that important topics are covered.

Screening Interview

For most professional positions, at least two interviews are held before a selection decision is made. The first is a screening interview, which is used to judge an applicant's personal and professional qualifications. If the applicant has the required qualifications, then he or she may be invited to take part in a selection interview.

The application is used as the basis for the screening interview. Only candidates who are clearly not qualified should be eliminated at this time. Candidates about whom there is a question should be given an opportunity to proceed to the selection interview, since some of them may be found to have strengths that compensate for certain weaknesses (Drake, 1989). Structured questions are usually used for screening interviews.

Selection Interview

The selection interview is used to help decide whether a qualified applicant is suited to fill a specific job vacancy. Selection interviews are longer, more intensive, and less structured than screening interviews. The questions asked by interviewers in the selection interview cover much the same material as the screening interview, but they are more specific and probing. In the selection interview, principals and teachers are interested in knowing whether an applicant possesses the professional skill and experience to perform the essential functions of a job and the personal qualifications needed for a good fit.

The selection interview is the time to examine in detail an applicant's views about various facets of the job for which he or she is being considered. To do this, interviewers use probes to encourage candidates to describe, expand, and elaborate on previous answers. Some examples of interview probes are (Moffatt, 1979):

- "I'd like to hear more about your thinking on that subject."
- "I'm not sure what you have in mind."
- "Why do you feel that way?"
- "Could you elaborate?"
- "Would you describe that in more detail?"
- "Tell me more."

Examples of interview questions that can be used to elicit information about the job-specific criteria for teaching identified in Exhibit 3.4 are shown in Exhibit 4.1.

Questioners in both types of interviews should be on the lookout for signals of possible problems that call for further investigation. Signs to be

---

Criterion: Is able to organize and manage a class effectively
Question: What classroom rules do you usually establish for students, and how do you introduce and explain the rules?

Criterion: Is able to motivate students to learn
Question: When you introduce a topic that is not a favorite with students, what do you do to build and hold their interest?

Criterion: Is able to communicate information effectively
Question: When you give an assignment that students are not familiar with, how do you make sure they understand what is expected?

Criterion: Is able to maintain student involvement in instructional activities
Question: How do you determine whether students understand new material, and what do you do if you find that they do not understand?

Criterion: Believes in the educability of all children
Question: What have you done in the past when you have had students who were not learning?

Criterion: Has extensive knowledge of subject
Question: What have you learned recently about the subject you teach that you did not know before, and how did you learn it?

EXHIBIT 4.1   Interview Questions for Selecting Effective Teachers

watched for are missing dates on work and education records, hints of drug use or abuse of alcohol, involvement in illegal activities of any kind, and reluctance to furnish names and addresses of previous work supervisors. Warning signals often turn out to be unfounded, but it is better to investigate and find nothing than not investigate and wind up with a problem employee (Hughes & Ubben, 1989).

Criminal Databanks

Some states now maintain criminal databanks with information about persons convicted of child abuse, kidnapping, and violent crimes. The district personnel office should routinely make use of any information that may be available to screen applicants for positions that involve contact with children in order to ensure that no one who poses a potential threat is hired.

Perceiver Interview

Some school districts use interview procedures developed by Selection Research Incorporated to select teachers and principals. The Teacher Perceiver Interview is used to select teaching personnel, and its counterpart, the Administrator Perceiver Interview, is used to screen administrative personnel (Berliner, 1987; Wendel & Breed, 1988).

Critical Incident Interview

An approach to a structured interview developed for business organizations can be adapted for use in teacher selection interviews (Latham, Saari, Pursell, & Campion, 1980). It is especially valuable with applicants who have not previously taught. This technique assumes that human behavior is goal oriented and that individuals choose behaviors with the intention of achieving certain results or outcomes. (This is also an assumption of goal theory, which is discussed in Chapter 6).

The technique involves identifying critical incidents that are likely to be encountered by an employee on the job. For a teacher, critical incidents might include a student who is disrespectful or disruptive, a situation in which a teacher is seeking to encourage critical thinking on the part of students through use of higher-order questions, or a child's difficulty in grasping new material. Each critical incident is described in a written narrative. The interviewer asks the applicant to read the narrative and indicate what action he or she would take if confronted with the situation described. The interviewer scores the applicant's response against benchmark answers prepared by a group of knowledgeable individuals who are familiar with the job. If the critical incidents highlight situations that are likely to be experienced in a specific position, applicants' responses can yield useful cues to probable behavior on the job.

When the incidents have been selected, teams consisting of four to six teachers and administrators independently prepare three benchmark answers to each problem. One of the prepared answers in each set is intended to identify the features of an answer that would receive a score of 5 (the highest score), one is a model of an answer worth 3 points, and the third is an example of an answer that would receive a score of 1 (the lowest). The interviewer refers to the benchmark responses as an aid to scoring applicants' answers, but applicants do not see the benchmark responses.

A response with a benchmark score of 5 represents the most complete response to the problem. It is an answer that would be given by an experienced teacher and takes into account all or most facets of the problem. A response rated 5 shows sensitivity, action aimed at resolving the problem, and a clear sense of professional responsibility. A response with a benchmark score of 1 represents a very limited response to the problem described in the narrative. It is an answer that might be given by a teacher with limited experience and knowledge of teaching or by a teacher who, despite having teaching experience, displays questionable judgment or lack of sensitivity. Such a response uses very little of the information provided in the narrative. The suggested plan of action is incomplete or addresses superficial aspects of the problem.

An example of a critical incident involving a child who fails to turn in his homework twice in one week is shown in Exhibit 4.2, along with three benchmark responses. Applicants' answers to a problem such as Will's will vary, of course. The benchmark responses in the example are used as guides to help interviewers score actual responses.

The three responses in the exhibit show a progression from little sensitivity for the child's feelings toward greater sensitivity and from failure to redirect students' attention to instruction toward prompt action to redirect their attention. An important component of the 5-point response that would probably not be found in less complete answers is the teacher's use of the incident to make Will aware of how other people respond to his behavior.

It is common practice for interviewers to pose hypothetical questions about incidents that teachers sometimes face and ask applicants what they would do in a similar situation. There are several important differences between that practice and the critical incident technique described here. First, a critical incident depicts a realistic but ambiguous problem with more than one possible response. It usually involves issues that teachers deal with on a daily basis.

Second, the critical incident approach yields insights into the applicant's thinking and judgment. The strongest applicants use the information from the critical incident to formulate a hypothesis and develop a plan of action based on testing the hypothesis. In the 5-point response to the problem in Exhibit 4.2, the respondent proposes to contact the parents for more information, a good idea since Will is not always truthful. A response such as that given in the 1-point benchmark shows that the applicant has made a decision without seeking additional information.

Will fails to turn in his language arts homework assignment for the second time this week. You want your fifth-graders to understand the importance of completing tasks on time, so you have told them that if they complete their homework on time they will receive a check for the day. Failing to do so results in a zero. When you ask Will why he doesn't have his homework, he replies, "Our house caught fire last night and my paper got burnt up."

Jason snorts. "It did not. Your house didn't burn down."

Will is indignant. "I didn't say it burnt down," he says. "I said it caught fire. It did, too. And my homework got burnt up."

Jason is shaking his head and mumbling, "He's lying, he's lying."

Others in the class are beginning to side with Will or Jason. Tonita, who lives near Will, says, "They did have a fire at Will's house last night. I saw the fire truck." Miguel disagrees. "It was a false alarm," he says. "There wasn't no fire."

You know that Will has an active imagination, but he seems to be telling the truth. What do you do?

Benchmark Response 1 (1 point): I would tell Will that he will receive a zero for not having his homework and that if he doesn't have his assignment completed by tomorrow he will have to stay after school.

Benchmark Response 2 (3 points): I would talk with Will in private to learn more about what happened. If there was no fire, I would give him a zero and make him stay after school for lying.

Benchmark Response 3 (5 points): I would first put the class back to work and, when I had a chance, talk with Will in private. I would call his mother or father to verify Will's account. If there was a fire, I would allow more time for Will to finish the homework. If Will made up the story, I would give him a zero and explain to him that creating stories for language arts is fine but that imagining events that didn't happen makes people think they cannot trust him to tell the truth.

EXHIBIT 4.2   Example of a Critical Incident

Transfer Policies and Student Learning

According to figures from the National Center for Education Statistics (1992), about 20 percent of teachers hired by the public schools in 1987–88 were first-time teachers. Slightly more than one-fourth were reentering teaching after an absence, and the remainder were transferring from other teaching positions.

Employees seek to transfer from one school to another for a number of reasons. Some want to transfer for convenience, whereas others seek to move to schools with better programs, facilities, or equipment. Still others hope to work with particular teachers or administrators or want to be assigned to a school with school-based management.

In many districts an effort is made to act on transfer requests before decisions are made to hire new teachers. This allows teachers who are already employed by the district to have the first choice of vacancies. Such a policy is helpful in sustaining teacher morale, but it can create problems when selection decisions are delayed while employed teachers are given the option to interview for vacancies.

Preference in Transfers

Some districts have policies that specify that teachers seeking transfers must be placed before new hires are made (Darling-Hammond, Wise, Berry, & Praskac, 1987). In other districts, the bargaining agreement gives transferring teachers the right to select the school in which they prefer to teach, subject only to the condition that teachers choose in order of seniority, with the most senior teacher having first choice (Haller, 1987).

Policies that give employed teachers the right of first refusal for available vacancies can delay decisions on selection and thereby prevent the district from issuing contracts to promising applicants. For that reason, some districts attempt to solve the problem of delay by issuing open contracts to qualified candidates. An open contract secures a commitment from the teacher but leaves the district the option of making a placement decision at a later time. A potential problem with this tactic is that the more highly sought after teachers may choose to sign with a district that offers an immediate placement decision.

Delays in offering teaching contracts can occur for a variety of reasons in addition to transfers. Whatever the reason, delays increase the likelihood that a district will lose out to other districts in the competition for teaching talent. A common reason for delays in making selection decisions is uncertainty regarding need, which is a factor when enrollment projections are unavailable or are suspected of being inaccurate, when finances are tight, or when late resignations are expected.

Caution in hiring teachers who may turn out not to be needed is important when the potential cost to the district can reach $50,000 per teacher, including salary and benefits. However, if experience has shown that the number of teachers needed consistently exceeds earlier projections, a district may offer a limited number of open contracts to promising applicants. This prevents the loss of teachers with strong qualifications to competing districts.

Equity in Transfer Practices

Placement and transfer decisions almost always raise questions of equity in the distribution of teacher talent. A district that relies solely on seniority in deciding transfer requests risks having all of its experienced teachers located in the most desirable schools, except for the individuals who principals reject. The end result of such a policy is maldistribution of teacher talent, with the most experienced teachers located in the more desirable schools and those with the least experience assigned to the less desirable schools. These are oftentimes schools with large proportions of children from poor and minority families. Staffing these schools exclusively with inexperienced teachers risks loss of learning.

Of course, experience is not necessarily synonymous with ability, and many inexperienced teachers are very capable, but the problem with open transfer policies is that the most able teachers do not remain long in schools that have little to offer in the way of rewards and prestige. In a profession in which there are limited opportunities for vertical mobility, teachers gravitate toward schools with better teaching conditions, a reputation for quality programs, or better facilities. This can create a problem for administrators who may be left with no alternative other than staffing less popular schools with beginning teachers.

Summary

Information about prospective employees is collected by the district office from five principal sources—application form, transcripts, references, tests, and interviews. The information is used to determine whether an applicant can perform job-specific functions.

Application forms and interviews are the most widely used methods for collecting information about applicants, but tests of knowledge of subject and methods of teaching are now in use in most states.

Interviews are more reliable when interviewers are taught methods of avoiding bias. A common but subtle form of bias is giving preference to certain individuals on the basis of social merit factors. The behavior description interview increases interview validity.

Critical incident interviews ask applicants to describe how they would handle realistic, work-related problems. The applicant receives a detailed description of the problem, and his or her answer is scored by comparing it to benchmark responses. This technique originated in industry and is especially valuable for assessing applicants' judgment.

Teacher transfers in schools are common, and they can affect the quality of instruction. A sound policy on teacher transfers maintains a balance of experienced and inexperienced teachers in all schools in the district.

Suggested Activities

1. Obtain application forms from three or four school districts and compare them. Can you identify a legitimate purpose for all of the questions that are asked? Is anything missing that should be included?
2. Work together with one or two other persons to write a critical incident for use in interviewing applicants for a teaching position. Identify the grade level and/or subject taught. When you finish writing the incident, write 1-point and 5-point benchmark responses.
3. Suppose you are the principal of a school and one of your teachers, whose spouse is being transferred to a position in another city, asks you to write a letter of reference. You have misgivings because the teacher is not effective. Discuss your ethical responsibilities in this situation and tell what you would do.

4. For the job you currently hold, list job-specific criteria that could be used to choose a replacement for you. Identify sources from which information about the criteria could be obtained and estimate the reliability of each source. Which sources are least reliable? Which are most reliable? Compare your response to another student's.

5. Look at Exhibit 3.4 in Chapter 3. Choose two job-specific criteria from the exhibit and write an interview question for each that could be used to help determine whether an applicant meets that criterion.

References

Arvey, R. (1979). Unfair discrimination in the employment interview. *Psychological Bulletin, 86,* 736–765.

Association of Teacher Educators. (1988). *Teacher assessment.* Reston, VA: Author.

Berliner, D. (1987). Teacher selection in the Mesa Unified School District. In A. Wise, L. Darling-Hammond, D. Berliner, E. Haller, P. Schlechty, B. Berry, A. Praskac, & G. Noblit (Eds.), *Effective teacher selection: From recruitment to retention—Case studies* (pp. 1–51). Santa Monica, CA: Rand.

Campion, J., & Arvey, R. (1989). Unfair discrimination in the employment interview. In R. Eder & G. Ferris (Eds.), *The employment interview: Theory, research, and practice* (pp. 61–73). Newbury Park, CA: Sage.

Dailey, C. (1982). *Using the track record approach: The key to successful personnel selection.* New York: AMACOM.

Dailey, C., & Madsen, A. (1980). *How to evaluate people in business.* New York: McGraw-Hill.

Darling-Hammond, L., Wise, A., Berry, B., & Praskac, A. (1987). Teacher selection in the Montgomery County Public Schools. In A. Wise, L. Darling-Hammond, D. Berliner, E. Haller, P. Schlechty, B. Berry, A. Praska, & G. Noblit (Eds.), *Effective teacher selection: From recruitment to retention—Case studies* (pp. 52–92). Santa Monica, CA: Rand.

Drake, J. (1982). *Interviewing for managers: A complete guide to employment interviewing.* New York: AMACOM.

Drake, J. (1989). *The effective interviewer: A guide for managers.* New York: AMACOM.

Education law: Vol. 2. (1989). New York: Matthew Bender.

Fear, R., & Chiron, R. (1990). *The evaluation interview* (4th ed.). New York: McGraw-Hill.

Griggs v. *Duke Power Company,* 401 U.S. 424 (1971).

Haberman, M. (1987). *Recruiting and selecting teachers for urban schools.* Reston, VA: Association of Teacher Educators.

Hakel, M. (1982). Employment interviewing. In K. Rowland & G. Ferris (Eds.), *Personnel management* (pp. 129–153). Boston: Allyn and Bacon.

Haller, E. (1987). Teacher selection in the city school district of Rochester. In A. Wise, L. Darling-Hammond, D. Berliner, E. Haller, P. Schlechty, B. Berry, A. Praska, & G. Noblit (Eds.), *Effective teacher selection: From recruitment to retention—Case studies* (pp. 153–187). Santa Monica, CA: Rand.

Herman, S. (1994). *Hiring right: A practical guide.* Thousand Oaks, CA: Sage.

Hughes, L., & Ubben, G. (1989). *The elementary principal's handbook: A guide to effective action* (3rd ed.). Boston: Allyn and Bacon.

Jacobs, R. (1993). *Legal compliance guide to personnel management.* Englewood Cliffs, NJ: Prentice Hall.

Janz, T. (1989). The patterned behavior description interview: The best prophet of the future is the past. In R. Eder & G. Ferris (Eds.), *The employment interview: Theory, research, and practice* (pp. 158–168). Newbury Park, CA: Sage.

Latham, G., Saari, L., Pursell, E., & Campion, M. (1980). The situational interview. *Journal of Applied Psychology, 65*, 422–427.

Magee, R. (1962). The employment interview: Techniques of questioning. *Personnel Journal, 41*, 241–245.

Moffatt, T. (1979). *Selection interviewing for managers.* New York: Harper & Row.

National Center for Education Statistics. (1992). *The condition of education, 1992.* Washington, DC: U.S. Department of Education.

National Center for Education Statistics. (1993). *Digest of educational statistics.* Washington, DC: U.S. Department of Education.

Rowe, P. (1989). Unfavorable information and interview decisions. In R. Eder & G. Ferris (Eds.), *The employment interview: Theory, research, and practice* (pp. 77–89). Newbury Park, CA: Sage.

United States v. *State of South Carolina,* 434 U.S. 1026 (1978).

Washington v. *Davis,* 426 U.S. 229 (1976).

Webster, E. (1982). *The employment interview: A social judgment process.* Schomberg, Ontario, Canada: S.I.P.

Wendel, F., & Breed, R. (1988, May). Improving the selection of principals: An analysis of the approaches. *NASSP Bulletin, 72*, 35–38.

Zedeck, S., Tziner, A., & Middlestadt, S. (1983). Interviewer validity and reliability: An individual analysis approach. *Personnel Psychology, 36*, 355–370.

5

SELECTING ADMINISTRATIVE
AND SUPPORT PERSONNEL

Finding qualified candidates to fill vacancies in schools is an ongoing challenge in most schools and districts. This chapter examines the procedures used to fill vacancies in administrative and support positions in schools and describes the duties performed by the individuals who hold those jobs. Finding the right people for these positions is critical in order for schools to run smoothly and offer effective instructional programs.

District office personnel, current principals, and those who contemplate becoming principals will be interested in the topic of selection of principals and assistant principals, for both personal and professional reasons, and in the material on selecting aides, counselors, and clerical personnel out of professional interest.

Plan of the Chapter

Teachers are indispensable in schools, but schools also depend on the people filling other roles in order to function smoothly and effectively. This chapter examines the processes involved in selecting administrative and support personnel for schools. It contains the following sections: (1) selection procedures, (2) selecting administrators, (3) managerial motivation, (4) progress toward equity, and (5) selecting other support personnel.

Selection Procedures

Selection procedures for administrative and support personnel parallel the procedures in teacher selection. The steps are:

1. Prepare a job model or job description.
2. Advertise the vacancy.
3. Conduct a preliminary screening of applicants and eliminate those who are not qualified.
4. Conduct first-round interviews with selected candidates.
5. Select finalists and conduct second-round interviews with them.
6. Announce the selection decisions and notify unsuccessful applicants.

Preparing a Job Model

The preparation of a job description or job model follows an analysis of the position to identify major tasks performed on the job or results expected. Information for the analysis may be collected either from interviews with those who currently hold the position or from questionnaires completed by them (Gatewood & Feild, 1987). The use of a job model or job description is important in defining the parameters of the search and selection process and helps avoid the problem of misperception of the position (Jentz, 1982).

The items in Exhibit 5.1 make up a generic list of duties that are commonly performed by elementary school principals, but the responsibilities associated with an actual position will vary from district to district and even from one school to another within a district. Duties of middle and high school principals are similar to those of elementary school administrators, except that secondary administrators usually deal with a larger number of people and activities. Secondary school administrators also spend more time planning and monitoring student activities than their elementary or middle school counterparts.

Preparing a list of duties such as those in Exhibit 5.1 is the first step in developing a job model for an elementary school principal. The list of duties is then converted to an inventory of results sought, and, finally, descriptions of the job environment and priority actions are added. A similar procedure would be used to develop job models for a middle or high school principal, assistant principal, counselor, media specialist, teacher aide, and school secretary.

Announcing the Vacancy

Most districts announce all administrative, supervisory, or counseling openings to current employees in order to give those who may be interested the opportunity to apply. Some negotiated agreements contain a clause requiring that teachers be notified of administrative and counseling vacancies. An issue of concern to individuals who are interested in moving up is whether vacancies are filled from within the district or from outside. Some school districts have ironclad policies of filling all vacancies from within, whereas others hire the most qualified candidate, regardless of location. Consistently hiring from within the district has the advantage of helping maintain high

1. Carries out policies of the board in such a way as to achieve and maintain the school's instructional effectiveness
2. Effectively utilizes resources of the district to enhance the school's instructional effectiveness
3. Plans and implements the instructional program of the school in cooperation with teachers, supervisors, and parents
4. Maintains complete and accurate records and monitors the instructional program of the school by reviewing indicators of instructional effectiveness
5. Works with district office staff and members of the school staff to recruit, interview, and select personnel for the school
6. Supervises teachers by means of classroom visits, conferences, and evaluations of performance
7. Provides or obtains assistance to help teachers overcome identified instructional problems
8. Recognizes individual teachers and students for significant accomplishments in teaching and learning
9. Obtains resources for and provides support and direction to enable school personnel to continue their professional development
10. In cooperation with teachers and parents, develops and implements a code of student conduct in order to create a school climate conducive to learning
11. Meets with parents to provide information and review and resolve concerns
12. Establishes and implements a process for prompt requisitioning of materials and equipment and informs personnel about the procedures
13. Oversees maintenance and cleaning of the building

EXHIBIT 5.1   Duties of Elementary Principal

teacher morale, but it runs the risk of developing inbred thinking. Hiring outsiders often brings fresh thinking into the system.

Advertising administrative openings outside of the immediate locality is common. Publications such as *Education Week* and metropolitan newspapers such as the *New York Times* regularly carry announcements of openings for school administrators. State and national professional associations for administrative and counseling personnel also maintain lists of openings in their respective fields.

Screening Applicants

Preliminary screening of applicants consists of checking the application form to be sure it is completely filled out and determining that the applicant has the necessary educational qualifications for the position and, when applicable, that he or she holds appropriate professional certification. Also at this time any tests that may be required are administered and scored.

Interviews and Reference Checks

A number of suggestions for conducting selection interviews with teachers were presented in Chapter 4. Most of the advice presented there applies equally to interviewing for administrative and support positions. The number of first-round interviews varies with the position and the number of applicants. For a principalship, it is not uncommon for 10 or more candidates to be invited to first-round interviews. For the position of teacher aide or secretary, there may be no more than 2 or 3 candidates. First-round interviews are intended to narrow the field to the most promising prospects, and if there are only a small number of applicants for a position, one round of interviews may be all that is needed. Discussion of selection criteria for each of the support positions will be presented later in this chapter. If needed, second-round interviews are conducted with the candidates whose qualifications appear to most nearly match the requirements of the position.

At this point, references are contacted and asked about the applicants' work record and performance in previous positions. That information is used to verify information furnished by the applicant and to help decision makers further narrow the field of candidates. The final step is to check appropriate criminal justice databanks in order to verify that applicants still under active consideration have not been convicted of a crime that would disqualify them from holding the position.

Announcing Decisions

Completion of second-round interviews is normally followed in short time by an announcement of the selection decision. The decision may be delayed if two equally strong prospects are vying for the position or if none of the finalists appears qualified. In the latter case, the decision may be made to reopen the search and interview additional applicants.

When a decision is made to hire an individual, that person normally receives word promptly, but the mail moves more slowly for those who were not chosen. Courtesy dictates that all active applicants (that is, those who participated in second-round interviews and have not withdrawn) are informed when the decision is made, but this practice is by no means universally observed.

Applicants from within the district who made the list of finalists should receive a personal communication, either in the form of a letter or a telephone call, informing them of the reasons they were not chosen and suggesting ways they might improve their chances of selection in the future. Those who are unlikely to receive serious consideration for future openings should be notified tactfully of that fact and encouraged to pursue other opportunities. Candidates not employed in the district should be informed when a decision has been made and encouraged to apply again in the future if their qualifications warrant that.

Selecting Administrators

Finding satisfactory replacements for administrative personnel who retire or resign and filling new administrative vacancies are high-priority activities in all school districts. With the growing use of school-based management and continued emphasis on improving school programs, the process of screening and selecting administrators is changing. Parents, teachers, and other employees of the school board are playing a more active role in the selection of administrators, on the assumption that those who help choose a leader will be responsive to that individual and work harder to ensure his or her success than those who have no voice in the selection.

Choosing a principal is an especially important decision because of the principal's potential influence on the quality of the instructional program in a school. In some districts with school-based management, principals are chosen by a local committee that includes teachers and parents, whereas in other districts, the committee makes a recommendation but does not make the final selection. Either method can result in high-quality choices if committee members are well informed with regard to the qualities that are desirable for principals.

Districts are making greater efforts now than in the past to develop a pool of persons who are qualified to hold administrative positions and to use valid methods of screening and selecting administrators. Some districts identify outstanding teachers and actively encourage them to enter administration rather than depend exclusively on self-selected applicants (Klauke, 1988).

Administrative internships are used in many districts to provide opportunities for teachers to gain firsthand experience with administrative duties and to learn more about district policies and procedures. The position of administrative aide, which involves half teaching and half administrative duties, is a popular type of internship. Positions such as administrative aide are assessment positions—jobs high in visibility that permit decision makers in the district to observe and evaluate an individual's potential for advancement (Gaertner, 1978/1979).

Districts are also beginning to use a variety of methods to collect information that will permit more valid inferences about applicants' potential leadership abilities. Simulations, written exercises, and situational questions are being used to assess candidates for the principalship and other administrative positions (Anderson, 1988).

School-based management places more responsibility for the quality of instructional programs on principals. It also requires that the process by which principals and assistant principals are selected receive more thought and attention than they have received in the past.

Selection of Principals

Most principals began their careers as teachers. Many of the skills that help one succeed in the classroom are useful in carrying out the responsibilities associated with the principalship. However, successful teachers do not always make successful principals—a fact that should be kept in mind in choosing administrators.

Principals are responsible for nine major functions related to the operation of the school. These duties may be delegated to other members of the administrative team or even occasionally to teachers, but the principal bears ultimate responsibility for their being carried out in a timely and effective manner. Principals and assistant principals should be selected on the basis of demonstrated evidence of successful previous performance or the potential for successful performance in these nine areas (Baltzell & Dentler, 1983):

1. Organization of the school setting
2. Resource and logistical management
3. Staff supervision
4. Staff evaluation
5. Staff development
6. Student discipline and safety
7. Instructional improvement
8. Curriculum innovation
9. Spokesperson or symbolic agent of both school and district

The nine functions are described in the paragraphs that follow, and suggestions are made for assessing applicants on each. In all cases, the strongest predictor of success is evidence of previous successful experience in a similar setting. Assessing applicants who have had no previous administrative experience and must be judged on the basis of their potential is one of the most difficult selection decisions administrators make. Many school districts now assign teachers who aspire to become administrators to part-time or temporary duties in which they have the opportunity to demonstrate their managerial abilities without having the responsibilities of a full-time position.

Organization of School Setting

This function involves establishing lines of authority and communication and clarifying responsibilities within a school. It is an indispensable part of effective management. Leadership experience outside of education, including volunteer work, can be useful for assessing an individual's prospects for success in this area. Those who evaluate applicants' qualifications should pay particular attention to experiences that involve coordinating or directing the activities of other adults. Some examples are serving as a volunteer coordinator for Boy Scout or Girl Scout programs, directing a United Way or other community agency fund drive, and organizing volunteer workers in community musicals, theater groups, rescue squads, and the like.

Experiences in education that are valid indicators of organizational ability include overseeing the reorganization of a department, in particular the merging of two or more specialties into a single organizational unit. The main considerations are the extent of an individual's contribution to the effort and its success.

Resource and Logistical Management

Principals are expected to manage fiscal accounts, supervise the distribution and use of equipment and supplies, and oversee the maintenance of the school building. These are managerial responsibilities that have implications for instructional effectiveness of the school. Teachers have similar responsibilities but on a much smaller scale. Few applicants will have had experience in this area unless they have held a managerial position inside or outside of education.

Staff Supervision

Supervision includes efforts to facilitate teachers' work. Other than department heads and those who have worked as administrative aides, most teachers have had little or no experience in supervising their colleagues. However, some have supervised teacher aides. In assessing supervision of aides, decision makers should consider the length, frequency, and quality of that supervision. These factors can be judged from teachers' self-reports if confirmed by other teachers or school administrators.

Summer school administrative assignments are another means by which teachers who aspire to become administrators demonstrate their supervisory ability. Ordinarily only a limited amount of supervision is carried out during summer school, but an administrator who supervises informally over a cup of coffee is demonstrating the potential for success in that area.

Staff Evaluation

In some districts, department heads are involved in teacher evaluation, and in a few cases, teachers even take part, but most teachers have had no experience with that responsibility. Some questions that can be asked of applicants for an administrative position that will help assess their readiness to evaluate teaching are:

1. What evidence would you look for in observing a fifth-grade teacher to show that students understand the material that is being presented?
2. How would you determine whether a teacher has diagnosed students' needs before presenting a lesson?
3. How would you judge whether a homework assignment given by a teacher whom you are observing is suitable for the students?
4. How could you tell during an observation how well a teacher is monitoring students' learning?
5. What would you look for as evidence that a teacher uses technology effectively in the classroom?

Staff Development

Staff development is examined in detail in Chapter 8. With school-based management, principals are assuming more responsibility for planning and presenting staff-development programs. However, this is an area in which even some persons with administrative experience are novices. In fact, some teachers have had more experience as trainers and peer coaches than the principals of their schools.

An applicant with little experience in planning or conducting staff development programs might be asked to describe some programs that he or she felt were particularly effective and to identify reasons for their effectiveness. Other evidence that can be deduced from an interview includes the applicant's self-identified developmental needs and aspects of program design about which the candidate is especially enthusiastic. An important factor in this area is the individual's knowledge of human and material resources that can be used in planning staff development programs. A strong candidate should be able to identify several nationally known staff development programs.

Student Discipline and Safety

The principal is ultimately responsible for student discipline and safety, but success in this area is dependent on his or her ability to develop among the teachers a shared sense of responsibility for the task. The most obvious indicator of future effectiveness in this area is the teacher's own record in the classroom. A teacher who successfully manages behavior of students in one classroom without being unduly repressive probably will be able to manage discipline on a schoolwide basis. However, there are important differences in the two settings. The teacher maintains a relationship with all students he or she teaches, whereas an administrator must administer discipline to students whom he or she knows only slightly.

Administrators have infrequent contact with most students but must still be able to use interpersonal influence to change students' behavior. The role of police officer is one that teachers dislike but one that administrators are often required to fill. Applicants with a strong aversion to that role will derive little satisfaction from serving as an assistant principal. Ideally, applicants for administrative positions should have experience in working with all types of children, including those from a variety of cultural backgrounds, children with physical, mental, or emotional disabilities, and children who are gifted and talented.

Instructional Improvement

Principals often are expected to take the lead in implementing instructional improvement in their schools. This involves achieving increased student learning within an existing or redesigned curriculum framework. Knowledge of instructional materials and various teaching methods and familiarity with the research on effective teaching (described in Chapter 1) are indicators of potential success in this area. Another criterion for assessing the ability to effect instructional improvement is knowledge of subject. A teacher who lacks comprehensive knowledge of a teaching field is unlikely to bring about instructional improvement.

Curriculum Innovation

What is being examined here is an applicant's inventiveness in developing new content or new ways of teaching. The principal's responsibility for curriculum innovation includes persuading teachers to develop new approaches to instruction and providing support for those who are willing to do so. Evidence from applicants' own classroom teaching experiences is useful in assessing future promise in this area. This may include experience in developing a new curriculum or in implementing a curriculum that has been developed at another level. Applicants with recent experience as a department head in a position that involved development or implementation of new curricula have acquired valuable preparation for the position of principal.

An interviewer would want to know the extent of the change initiated and the degree of leadership exerted by the applicant in bringing it about. Curricular innovation carried out in the applicant's own classroom without involvement of other teachers is not as strong evidence of competence in this area as are activities that demonstrate the candidate's ability to involve other teachers in adopting new methods or materials.

Spokesperson or Symbolic Agent

The spokesperson presents the organization's programs and point of view to the media and the public. Teachers rarely have the opportunity to serve as spokesperson for a school or district, but some perform a spokesperson role as part of the responsibilities involved in chairing district or association committees. An individual who serves as a delegate to professional conferences or who serves as union negotiator acquires valuable experience as a spokesperson. Poise and the ability to articulate a position are important for success in this area.

An individual's ability to function effectively as a spokesperson can be inferred from oral communication skills as well as from evidence of sensitivity to the views of others. Leaders are frequently required to summarize the views of groups with divergent opinions as a way of bringing about consensus on an issue. The ability to understand and verbalize a variety of positions on an issue, including those that differ from one's own, is a valuable asset to a school administrator. Evidence of this skill can be obtained from questions in which the candidate is asked to describe two divergent positions on an issue of current interest and to explain the strengths and weaknesses of each.

Selection of Assistant Principals

The selection of assistant principals has been characterized as "haphazard" and not guided by coherent policies and criteria (Hess, 1985). The assumption has been made that the principal is ultimately responsible for the administration of a school and that an assistant principal's lack of expertise can be compensated for by the principal's greater knowledge and skill, based on greater experience. The assistant principalship has long been thought of as an apprenticeship during which a novice acquires the skills of a master practitioner, the principal. Attention to selection procedures was not felt to be as important as placing a new assistant principal with an experienced and effective principal who could teach the newcomer the secrets of administrative success. Fortunately, this sentiment is waning.

Successful instructional programs require the "energy, talent, and commitment of a great many actors within each school building" (Spady, 1985, p. 118), including assistant principals. Most school districts now expect assistant principals to be contributing members of the administrative team immediately upon their appointment. Aspirants to administration learn the skills of the trade by means of district- or university-sponsored internships (Baltzell & Dentler, 1983), or they serve as administrative assistants part time while still teaching in order to learn the fundamentals of administering a school.

The assistant principal reports directly to the principal of a school and carries out duties assigned by him or her. These often have to do with maintaining the stability of the school as an organization, as opposed to attending to improving and strengthening the instructional program of the school (Reed & Himmler, 1985). One of the assistant principal's most important duties is to maintain order and discipline.

Among other tasks performed by assistant principals are developing an activity calendar and establishing a master schedule (Reed & Himmler, 1985). In some schools, they plan and coordinate orientation and assignment of new teachers, student teachers, and teacher aides, and participate in supervising and evaluating certificated staff. Assistant principals are also responsible for building maintenance, inventories of supplies and equipment, ordering and maintaining textbooks, and managing student attendance (Educational Research Service, 1984). In short, there is very little that principals do that is not also done by assistant principals.

Given the scope and importance of the evolving role of the assistant principal, the selection criteria for the position should be the same as those used in selecting principals. The differences in the selection criteria used for the two positions usually have to do with depth and length of experience, with the principal expected to have more varied experience, and with counterbalancing qualifications. That is, an effort is usually made to select an assistant principal whose subject field and administrative experiences complement rather than duplicate those of the principal.

Use of Tests for Selection of Administrators

Written Tests

About one-fourth of the states in the United States now require candidates for the position of principal to complete a written examination (Egginton,

Jeffries, & Kidd-Knights, 1988). One such examination is the specialty area test for educational administration and supervision developed by Educational Testing Service. Some states have developed their own tests, either independently or with the assistance of a testing firm, and a few large-city school districts have adopted testing procedures to help screen prospective administrators. Some of the tests now in use combine written exercises with in-basket exercises. On in-basket exercises, an examinee responds to telephone messages, memoranda, letters, and notes similar to those that principals might receive. In addition to imposing testing requirements, some state legislatures have introduced additional educational requirements for prospective school administrators, and others have mandated internship programs.

Assessment Centers

Many school districts increasingly rely on assessment centers to help in the selection of school principals, and some states now require aspirants for school administration to successfully complete an assessment center procedure. An assessment center is a series of exercises that simulate problems that might confront a school principal. Candidates record the decisions and actions they would take and are evaluated by a team of assessors who observe them in the process of carrying out a variety of simulated tasks (Gatewood & Feild, 1987).

The best known and most widely used assessment procedure was developed by the National Association of Secondary School Principals (NASSP). Participants in the NASSP centers are rated on 12 attributes (McCall, 1986). These attributes are described in Exhibit 5.2.

Although assessment procedures are considered tests in the technical sense, they avoid many of the objections that are raised to selection tests because they possess both construct and criterion validity. *Construct validity* refers to the accuracy with which an instrument measures psychological structures, functions, or traits (Landy, 1985). Assessment measures have construct validity because of the close match between the simulated tasks candidates are asked to perform and the actual work of school principals.

Criterion validity refers to the power of a test to predict performance on a particular job. Participants in assessment centers receive ratings in 12 areas in addition to an overall placement recommendation. A number of studies have shown that assessment center ratings are positively correlated with performance in a variety of jobs. A study of the relationship of performance of school administrators to assessment center ratings reported similar results (Schmitt, Noe, Meritt, & Fitzgerald, 1983). The dimensions most highly and consistently correlated with job performance of administrators were (1) leadership, (2) oral communication, (3) organizational ability, (4) decisiveness, (5) judgment, and (6) problem analysis. Ratings of school climate were not correlated with principals' performance on the assessment center tasks.

1. *Problem analysis*
   Ability to analyze information to identify the important elements of a problem
2. *Judgment*
   Skill in identifying and acting on educational priorities; making sound decisions with the information at hand
3. *Organizational ability*
   Skill in planning, scheduling, and controlling the activities of others; skill in using resources
4. *Decisiveness*
   Ability to recognize that a decision is required and making it
5. *Leadership*
   Skill in recognizing that a group requires direction and in involving others in solving problems
6. *Sensitivity*
   Skill in perceiving the needs and concerns of others and responding in a caring, supportive way
7. *Stress tolerance*
   Ability to perform under pressure without loss of effectiveness
8. *Oral communication*
   Ability to verbally express one's thoughts clearly and persuasively
9. *Written communication*
   Ability to write clearly and persuasively
10. *Range of interests*
    Knowledge of a broad range of subjects; involvement in activities that are unrelated to the job
11. *Personal motivation*
    Desire to perform well in situations that challenge one's abilities
12. *Educational values*
    Commitment to a coherent set of educational priorities

EXHIBIT 5.2   Skills Assessed in NASSP Assessment Centers

Source: "Twelve Skill Dimensions: Professional Benefits" by D. S. McCall, January 1986, *NASSP Bulletin, 70,* pp. 32–33.

Managerial Motivation

Although there is no single set of criteria that can ensure accurate selection of principals, applicants who have motivations that are similar to those of managers are somewhat more likely than persons without such motivations to succeed in managerial roles. Two well-researched psychological characteristics that identify managerial motivation are the need for power and the need for achievement (Stahl, 1983).

Need for power is not, as the name suggests, a desire to behave in dictatorial ways toward other people. It refers to the satisfaction that an individual receives from persuading others of the validity of his or her ideas. It might more accurately be called a "need for interpersonal influence" rather than need for power.

Need for achievement refers to the inclination to set challenging goals and strive to reach them. Individuals with this characteristic receive gratification from accomplishing demanding tasks or striving toward challenging goals. People with high need for achievement prefer goals that challenge their abilities but that they can, with hard work, expect to achieve.

In most research involving these two constructs, a projective instrument, the thematic apperception test, is used to assess an individual's placement on the achievement and power scales. Stahl (1983) developed a reliable paper-and-pencil test to measure these traits. He demonstrated that persons who hold positions as managers or who possess leadership qualities are more likely to score high on managerial motivation than nonmanagers and engineering students. Stahl operationally defined *managerial motivation* as consisting of a combination of high scores on both need for achievement and need for power. There is no difference in the incidence of managerial motivation based on gender or race. Women and minorities are equally as likely as men and whites to score high.

One trait that was found not to be related to managerial motivation was *need for affiliation*. This refers to an individual's desire to be liked and accepted by other people. One reason for the absence of an association between the two variables may be that managers occasionally need to take actions that are unpopular with those who work for them. Persons with high need for affiliation are often uncomfortable when faced with that prospect.

Progress toward Equity

The number of women and minorities serving as school administrators in the United States continues to be disproportionately small compared to their presence in the teaching force, but some progress has been made in achieving a better balance. The proportion of principalships held by women doubled during the decade of the 1980s. In 1979, about 15 percent of public schools had female principals (Adkison, 1985), but by 1990 that figure had risen to about 30 percent. Central city schools were most likely to be headed by women in 1990 (41 percent), and rural areas and small towns had the fewest female school administrators (34 percent of suburban schools and 22 percent of rural and small town schools) (National Center for Education Statistics, 1993b). Female administrators are much more common in elementary schools than in secondary schools. In 1990, 37 percent of public elementary schools were headed by women, compared to only 11 percent of secondary schools (National Center for Education Statistics, 1994).

The number of Black principals in public schools in the South dropped sharply in the late 1960s and early 1970s as a result of desegregation of schools in that region and the closing of many predominantly Black schools. Blacks were also underrepresented in administrative positions nationally during that period, and the disparity continues. In 1990–91, only about 7 percent of all public school principalships were held by Blacks. Black principals were most common in central city schools and in schools with large minority enrollments (National Center for Education Statistics, 1993b). Chapter 12 discusses ways by which school districts can avoid discrimination and ensure equal opportunity in selection for administrators and other personnel.

A number of reasons have been advanced to explain the discrepancies in the numbers of female and minority administrators, as compared to the number of teachers from those groups. Among the explanations are limited opportunities for socialization into administrative roles, limited visibility, and inaccessibility to informal networks (Yeakey, Johnston, & Adkison, 1986). It has also been suggested that women prefer jobs that allow them to devote time to home and family and that teaching is better suited than administration to the dual roles of careerist and homemaker (Shakeshaft, 1987).

Women's willingness to remain in the classroom rather than seek an administrative appointment has been attributed to lack of ambition, but that view has been challenged by those who suggest that men and women enter teaching for different reasons: Men choose to teach as a first step toward a career in administration, whereas for women, teaching is a goal in itself (Shakeshaft, 1987).

Reasons for Choosing Administration

Individuals choose to seek a career in school administration for a variety of reasons. Men and women cite different factors when they are asked to identify the attractions of an administrative career. Women cite financial factors more often than men, and women are more likely than men to give altruistic reasons for being attracted to administration. Women, much more often than men, cite the appeal of the work as a reason for their interest in administration. The opportunity to develop and use personal abilities is mentioned by both sexes about equally often (Adkison, 1985).

The Adkison study involved a relatively small number of administrators in one school district, and so the results should be interpreted with care, but the findings provide a clue that might help explain why more women do not apply for administrative positions. Almost 23 percent of the female respondents but only about 7 percent of male respondents cited altruistic reasons for wanting to be administrators. An example of an altruistic reason is to help children learn. Individuals with that motivation may feel they can accomplish their goal in the classroom as well as in the principal's office. For a woman who is already uncertain about her chances for promotion, such a rationalization would be easily accepted.

Need for Sponsorship

Women in positions of leadership more often than men cite the importance of encouragement from sponsors in attaining their positions. For these women, sponsorship of a relatively powerful superior appears to play a similar function in career advancement that informal networks provide for men. However, some experts suggest that sponsorship is no less critical for men than for women to advance in educational administration (Ortiz & Marshall, 1988). They argue that sponsorship limits competition and that "women have not enjoyed the benefits of the sponsorship process" (p. 126). They suggest that teaching and administration have evolved into separate, gender-specific occupations with different agendas and viewpoints.

Women who receive the support of a sponsor tend to be older than their male counterparts, since the accomplishments that bring about the recognition needed for sponsorship take time. They are also more oriented to instruction, having spent a good many years teaching and serving in quasi-administrative roles related to instruction. From the point of view of selecting promising administrative leaders for effective instruction, individuals who have demonstrated excellence in teaching and other instructional assignments over time represent a pool of talent that schools have yet to use to full advantage.

The lesson from research on equity in administrative selection procedures seems to be that the most promising candidates for positions as assistant principals or principals are not always selected. Some talented candidates choose not to apply, for reasons that are not entirely clear, whereas some who apply and are well qualified are not chosen.

Those who make selection decisions in schools have an opportunity to bring about instructional improvement by identifying and encouraging teachers with leadership potential to apply for positions as department head, assistant principal, principal, and supervisor. It is clear that some of these people will not apply unless they are encouraged to do so and receive support from those with influence over the final selection.

Many administrators value the ambition and initiative that an applicant displays by voluntarily applying for leadership roles in schools, but the importance of those traits may be overstated. Thorough knowledge of instruction and a time-tested commitment to teaching are assets that are likely to have more effect on instruction than self-identification for promotion.

Selecting Other Support Personnel

Counselors

The number of counselors in public elementary and secondary schools increased from about 14,600 in 1958 (*Digest of Education Statistics*, 1989) to 81,774 in 1991 (National Center for Education Statistics, 1993a). However, even though counselors are more common in schools now than in the past, there is not total agreement about their role. Teachers, students, parents, and principals all have opinions about an appropriate role for counselors, but they sometimes disagree.

A study of role expectations held for middle school counselors by the four groups found that parents and students held similar expectations and that teachers and principals held similar expectations. Parents and students viewed the counselor as primarily responsible for helping students with problems. Teachers and principals, on the other hand, thought of the guidance function as only part of what the counselor does; they attached equal importance to administrative tasks such as record keeping and scheduling (Remley & Albright, 1988).

Another study compared counselors' perceptions of their own role to principal's perceptions. The respondents in this case were counselors and principals in elementary, middle, and junior high schools in one midwestern state (Bonebrake & Borgers, 1984). The researchers found a high degree of agreement among the two groups in their ranking of 15 tasks performed by counselors.

Counselor Functions

Counselors perform 11 functions in schools (Chiles & Eiben, 1983):

1. Individual counseling
2. Group counseling
3. Group guidance
4. Educational planning and course selection
5. Career guidance and counseling
6. Appraisal
7. Consultation
8. Coordination, liaison, and referral
9. Program development, evaluation, and research
10. Public relations
11. Professional renewal

Individual counseling provides students with an opportunity to have professional assistance in a caring, nonevaluative environment to solve problems and make decisions. Group guidance is developmental and preventive in nature. In group counseling, the counselor facilitates interaction among members of a group of students who are attempting to solve common developmental problems. Counselors may train teachers to provide group guidance services.

Secondary school counselors assist students in making career plans and selecting courses appropriate for those plans, and provide guidance on how to meet high school graduation requirements. Career guidance and counseling is an organized group program that helps students prepare to select a career and enter the world of work.

Appraisal services include administering and interpreting standardized group achievement and aptitude tests. Consultation traditionally referred to collaborative work of two individuals focused on solving problems of a third person. Current definitions have been expanded to include giving advice to teachers on a number of topics, including classroom management and interpersonal communication.

Counselors often help to coordinate services provided by school and community agencies for a child. They serve as liaison from the school to community agencies and handle requests for information from student records from community individuals and groups. Counselors also perform a public relations service by informing parents and members of the community about guidance and counseling programs and services.

Factors that are considered in selecting counselors are the recency and quality of training and, in particular, exposure to a well-planned and comprehensive internship. Positive personal qualities are especially important for counselors because of the closeness of the relationship between the counselor and the students with whom he or she works.

Traits that have been identified as essential to success in counseling include accurate empathic understanding, communication of respect, warmth, sincerity, and specific expression (Herr, 1982). Depending on the nature of the assignment, other criteria will be added to those essentials. Additional qualifications include knowledge of occupational opportunity structures, knowledge of requirements for entry into various occupations, and the ability to relate effectively to parents and teachers.

Skills in which counselors are most likely to need additional training, as determined by a survey of experts, are counseling students from single-parent families, consultation skills with teachers, small-group counseling, and planning a comprehensive career development program. More than three-fourths of respondents identified those as critical training needs of school counselors (Comas, Cecil, & Cecil, 1987).

Given the emerging demographic profile of schools, the first task (counseling children from single-parent families) is one that counselors increasingly will be called on to perform. Other skills identified by the experts in which counselors are in need of training are ethical standards, drug abuse and alcohol counseling, and parent education (Comas, Cecil, & Cecil, 1987). All of these are areas about which interviewers may want to question counselor applicants during the selection process.

Librarians/Media Specialists

As the use of instructional technology becomes more common in schools, the role of the media specialist is increasing in importance. Librarians have traditionally been viewed by teachers and students as individuals who maintain silence in the library and see to it that books and magazines are in their proper places on the shelves. However, that view was never totally accurate, and it is becoming more out of date by the minute.

The title *media specialist* is intended to convey a sense of the emerging role of librarian. In addition to such traditional tasks as maintaining collections of a variety of sources of information, librarians now are expected to be familiar with current and constantly changing ways of storing and retrieving information.

This requires that they understand the operation of computers and be able not only to access information but also to train others to use the software by which accessibility is gained. To some extent at the present time and to a much greater degree in the future, librarians—or, more accurately, media specialists—will be expected to provide support for teachers who wish to develop instructional software and to help solve the problems that arise in the process of using individually developed or commercially produced programs.

Two attributes should be given primacy in the selection of media specialists. The first is an attitude that encourages students and teachers to use the media center and its materials extensively and often. Usage creates extra work for the staff, since books, magazines, records, filmstrips, fiche, recorders, and projectors that are taken from shelves and drawers must be returned to them. However, care should be taken to hire media specialists who will welcome usage of the media center as an indicator that the center is contributing to the vitality of the instructional program.

The second attribute to be looked for in a prospective media specialist is recent training. A person need not have just graduated in order to have up-to-date knowledge about instructional technology, but it is certain that anyone who completed their training more than three or four years previously and who has not had recent refresher training since graduating is out of date. This is one field in which training must be almost constant in order for a person to remain in touch.

Teacher Aides

The list of duties that aides perform to assist teachers is limited only by the teacher's imagination and the aide's abilities. Aides do everything from helping to fill out report cards, to planning and presenting plays, to tutoring students, to mixing paints (Nielsen, 1977). The job description for elementary school aides published by Kent (Washington) School District lists six functions of aides (Educational Research Service, 1984):

1. Assists teacher in management of student arrival and departure activities
2. Provides staff with clerical assistance such as typing, filing, duplicating, and organizing materials for distribution and recording information
3. Assists with personal needs of students
4. Supervises students at the elementary level during play periods and recess periods in and out of classrooms
5. Performs supportive tasks for a certified teacher that are primarily non-instructional in nature
6. Performs other duties as assigned

The list contains no mention of aides being involved in instruction, but in many classrooms, teacher aides extend instruction by the use of follow-up strategies to reinforce what students have been taught. Research indicates that aides can perform this role as effectively as teachers if they receive appropriate training (Love & Levine, 1992).

Aides are more common in elementary schools and special education classrooms than in other settings. In special education classes, aides assist teachers by attending to the physical and emotional needs of children who have disabilities.

The preferred candidate for the job of aide is someone who will be able to take directives from teachers but who does not need to wait to be told what to do. Experience with children is an advantage.

Secretaries

A school secretary's is the first voice heard by parents and others who call the school, the first person to whom new students talk, and the first individual contacted by visitors to the school (Drake & Roe, 1986). Secretaries are often known by more students than any other single individual, with the possible exception of the principal. Given the nature of this position and the extent of the secretary's contacts with the public, teachers, and students, careful selection for this position is critical.

It has been estimated that there are four million school secretaries in the United States and that 99 percent of them are females. Their duties can be classified into five categories (Rimer, 1984):

1. Public relations (greeting visitors, explaining school rules and policies to parents of new students, dealing with community organizations and special groups)
2. Student services (attending to nonlearning needs of students; performing as nurse, friend, disciplinarian; possessor of supplies and information)
3. Clerical (filing, typing, answering the telephone, record keeping, maintaining staff and student records, requesting or sending student information, writing letters, making announcements, operating office equipment, and maintaining office supplies)
4. Financial (collecting money, writing checks, making deposits, bookkeeping, filling out requisitions)
5. Office management (maintaining an attractive and businesslike environment; supervising clerical employees and student workers)

It should be clear from the foregoing that the secretary is first and foremost a public relations expert. In schools with more than one clerical employee, one serves primarily as gatekeeper, providing or denying access to the principal, receiving and transmitting telephone messages, and dealing with walk-in or call-in requests from students and teachers. The second employee then is assigned to handle clerical duties and office management chores and, when needed, to assist the head secretary with information requests.

A necessary qualification for the position of secretary is the ability to tolerate frequent interruptions without undue frustration. Regardless of the importance of the task being worked on, the secretary is expected to put it aside to handle a request from a student or teacher. Rarely is the secretary able to finish a task without being interrupted at least once. To work in such an atmosphere requires patience, flexibility, and a sense of humor. Some of the tasks that secretaries perform, most notably financial record keeping and check writing, require an atmosphere that permits concentration. In order to keep errors to a minimum, it is necessary to provide an opportunity for the secretary who performs those chores to retreat to a quiet, out-of-the-way room where there will be no interruptions. When selecting a secretary, it is important to recognize that not all individuals operate effectively in an atmosphere as busy as school offices often are. Care must be taken to select the person who can tolerate the noise and confusion without undue feelings of stress.

Because of their location in the center of the school's information flow, secretaries obtain considerable confidential information about teachers and students. Caplow (1976) noted that employees who have access to the manager of an organization and who possess information about other organization members acquire power that exceeds that allocated to them by the organization chart. He warned that such power can be a source of organizational problems and thus urged managers to keep the power of their assistants in check.

Summary

Successful schools depend on the quality of the personnel who run them. Besides teachers, schools require administrators, counselors, secretaries, teachers' aides, and other support staff. The selection process for these positions is similar to that used to select teachers, beginning with preparation of a job model or job description and announcement of the vacancy. Administrative vacancies receive priority attention in school districts because of the critical nature of the position. Principals perform nine functions, including organizing the school setting, supervising and evaluating teachers, supervising student discipline and safety, and encouraging instructional improvement. These functions should form the basis for assessing applicants for administrative positions.

Selection of assistant principals has been a neglected area, but with increasing attention to the importance of the principalship for school effectiveness, more care is being taken to select well-qualified assistants. People who possess managerial motivation (high need for achievement and power) generally succeed in positions of leadership. Minorities and women have made progress in increasing their representation in administrative ranks in school districts in recent years, but they are still underrepresented in comparison to their presence in the teaching force.

The number of counselors in schools has grown rapidly. Counselors provide a variety of services, including personal and group counseling and career guidance. Teacher aides perform a variety of duties to assist teachers. Secretaries help schools operate smoothly. Their ability to put upset parents and children at ease is important.

Suggested Activities

1. Interview an assistant principal and prepare a list of duties performed or results expected on the job. Compare duties performed by assistant principals to those performed by the principal.
2. Interview a school counselor and prepare a list of duties performed or results expected on the job. Compare lists from elementary, middle school, and high school counselors. In what ways are they alike? How do they differ?
3. Form three-member panels to debate the question: Should administrators be selected from within the district or recruited from outside the district? Cite evidence to support your position.
4. Write a letter of application for the position of school principal. Select two or three of the nine functions of principals described in this chapter and explain how your educational and work experiences have prepared you to perform those functions.

References

Adkison, J. (1985). The structure of opportunity and administrative opportunities. *Urban Education, 20,* 327–347.

Anderson, M. (1988). *Hiring capable principals: How school districts recruit, groom, and select the best candidates.* Eugene, OR: Oregon School Study Council.

Baltzell, D., & Dentler, R. (1983). *Selecting American school principals: A sourcebook for educators.* Washington, DC: National Institute of Education.

Bonebrake, C., & Borgers, S. (1984). Counselor role as perceived by counselors and principals. *Elementary School Guidance and Counseling, 18,* 194–199.

Caplow, T. (1976). *How to run any organization.* New York: Holt Rinehart.

Chiles, D., & Eiben, R. (1983). *Pupil personnel services recommended practices and procedures manual: School counseling.* Springfield, IL: Illinois State Board of Education.

Comas, R., Cecil, J., & Cecil, C. (1987). Using expert opinion to determine professional development needs of school counselors. *The School Counselor, 35,* 81–87.

Digest of education statistics. (1989). Washington, DC: U.S. Office of Education.

Drake, T., & Roe, W. (1986). *The principalship* (3rd ed.). New York: Macmillan.

Educational Research Service. (1984). *Job*

descriptions in public schools. Arlington, VA: Author.

Egginton, W., Jeffries, T., & Kidd-Knights, D. (1988, April). State-mandated tests for principals—A growing trend? *NASSP Bulletin, 72*, 62–65.

Gaertner, K. (1978/1979). The structure of careers in public school administration. *Administrator's Notebook, 27*(6), 1–4.

Gatewood, R., & Feild, H. (1987). *Human resource selection*. Chicago: Dryden.

Herr, E. (1982). Discussion. In H. Walberg (Ed.), *Improving educational standards and productivity* (pp. 99–109). Berkeley, CA: McCutchan.

Hess, F. (1985). The socialization of the assistant principal from the perspective of the local school district. *Education and Urban Society, 18*, 93–106.

Jentz, B. (1982). *Entry: The hiring, start-up, and supervision of administrators*. New York: McGraw-Hill.

Klauke, A. (1988). *Recruiting and selecting principals*. Eugene, OR: University of Oregon, ERIC Clearinghouse on Educational Management. (ERIC Document Reproduction Service No. ED 297481).

Landy, F. (1985). *Psychology of work behavior*. Homewood, IL: Dorsey.

Love, I., & Levine, D. (1992). *Performance ratings of teacher aides with and without training and follow-up in extending reading instruction*. Paper presented at the annual meeting of the American Educational Research Association, San Francisco. (ERIC Reproduction Service No. ED 349294).

McCall, D. (1986, January). Twelve skill dimensions: Professional benefits. *NASSP Bulletin, 70*, 32–33.

National Center for Education Statistics. (1993a). *Digest of education statistics*. Washington, DC: U.S. Department of Education.

National Center for Education Statistics. (1993b). *Schools and staffing in the United States: A statistical profile, 1990–91*. Washington, DC: U.S. Department of Education.

National Center for Education Statistics. (1994, January). Public and private school principals: Are there too few women? *Issue Brief*, pp. 1–2.

Nielsen, E. (1977). *Instructional aides*. Redwood City, CA: San Mateo County Office of Education. (ERIC Document Reproduction Service No. ED 238824).

Ortiz, F., & Marshall, C. (1988). Women in educational administration. In N. Boyan (Ed.), *Handbook of research on educational administration* (pp. 123–141). New York: Longman.

Reed, D., & Himmler, A. (1985). The work of the secondary assistant principal: A field study. *Education and Urban Society, 18*, 59–84.

Remley, T., Jr., & Albright, P. (1988). Expectations for middle school counselors: Views of students, teachers, principals, and parents. *The School Counselor, 35*, 290–296.

Rimer, A. (1984, Fall). Elementary school secretary: Informal decision maker. *Educational Horizons, 63*, 16–18.

Schmitt, N., Noe, R., Meritt, R., & Fitzgerald, M. (1983). *Validity of assessment center ratings for the prediction of performance ratings and school climate of school administrators*. (ERIC Document Reproduction Service No. ED 236777).

Shakeshaft, C. (1987). *Women in educational administration*. Newbury Park, CA: Sage.

Spady, W. (1985). The vice-principal as an agent of instructional reform. *Education and Urban Society, 18*, 107–120.

Stahl, M. (1983). Achievement, power and managerial motivation: Selecting managerial talent with the job choice exercise. *Personnel Psychology, 36*, 775–789.

Yeakey, C., Johnston, G., & Adkison, J. (1986). In pursuit of equity: A review of research on minorities and women in educational administration. *Educational Administration Quarterly, 22*, 110–149.

6

MOTIVATION OF PERSONNEL

Educational reforms that were implemented in the schools during the 1980s were based on stated or implied beliefs about human motivation. The effort to increase teachers' salaries reflected the belief that people value money and are more likely to enter or remain in an occupation if the financial rewards are attractive (Sedlak & Schlossman, 1987). Policies that gave teachers a larger voice in decisions about their work originated in the conviction that people prize autonomy and will be attracted to occupations that offer it (Lortie, 1969).

Those of us who work with other human beings make daily decisions that reflect our beliefs about human motivation. Our theories of motivation may be simple or elaborate, primitive or sophisticated. Some of us base our beliefs about human motivation on research, whereas others operate on the basis of personal experience, yet we all carry around in our heads a model of motivation that guides our actions. The purpose of this chapter is to provide personnel managers, including principals and personnel department staff members, with a better understanding of what motivated behavior is and how human motivation levels can be increased. Knowing more about motivation should help administrators become more effective personnel managers.

Plan of the Chapter

Motivation is a central feature of the effective teaching model presented earlier (Figure 1.1). The model shows that teacher motivation and knowledge are precursors to the teaching behaviors that lead to student learning. This chapter suggests ways of applying what we know about motivation to the problem of improving instructional effectiveness in schools. The chapter covers the following topics: (1) meaning of work motivation, (2) expectancy theory, (3) equity theory, (4) goal-setting theory, (5) job satisfaction in teaching, and (6) job satisfaction and teacher turnover.

Meaning of Work Motivation

The factors that influence people in choosing an occupation and in carrying out the tasks associated with a particular job have been studied by organizational psychologists for many years. Most of the research on motivation in the workplace has taken place in industrial settings. Nevertheless, much of what has been learned can be applied to those who work in schools.

Work motivation has been referred to as a set of forces "that originate both within as well as beyond an individual's being, to initiate work-related behavior, and to determine its form, direction, intensity, and duration" (Pinder, 1984, p. 8) and as having to do with "the conditions responsible for variations in the intensity, quality, and direction of ongoing behavior" (Landy, 1985, p. 317). By combining elements of these descriptions, we arrive at a definition that is suitable for our purposes.

Work motivation refers to conditions responsible for variations in the intensity, quality, direction, and duration of work-related behavior. Variations in the quality of work produced by employees may arise from either motivational or knowledge differences. If an employee is not achieving satisfactory results, it is necessary to ascertain whether the problem originates with lack of motivation, lack of knowledge, or both.

Psychologists have advanced several theories to explain how people become motivated to perform a job and what factors within the individual or in the work setting influence the level of motivation experienced. We will examine three theories that are of particular interest to school administrators because of their potential for improving our understanding of work motivation among teachers. The three theories are:

1. *Expectancy theory:* Advocates believe that people are motivated by the opportunity to earn incentives.
2. *Equity theory:* Advocates believe that people expect a balance between effort expanded and rewards received and lose motivation when that balance is missing.
3. *Goal-setting theory:* Advocates believe that people are motivated to achieve identified goals.

Each theory has its own implications for administrative action. An administrator who believes that employees are motivated by expectancy will attempt to identify and distribute incentives to increase teacher motivation. One who believes in equity theory will try to provide more generous rewards to employees who work hard and withhold some rewards from those who put forth less effort. Administrators who subscribe to goal-setting theory will attempt to identify long- and short-range goals that are personally meaningful to employees and help the employees to achieve those goals.

These theories are described in more detail in the following sections.

Expectancy Theory

Expectancy theory is based on the premise that workers perform tasks to gain incentives and that motivation is a function of the value of the incentive to the individual. Vroom incorporated three concepts into his model of expectancy motivation—valence, instrumentality, and expectancy—so the theory is sometimes referred to as VIE theory (cited in Pinder, 1984).

1. *Valence* refers to the positive or negative feelings attached to work outcomes. For example, money received for performing a job has positive valence for most workers, whereas working in a dirty environment has negative valence. For teachers, student success has positive valence. Some work outcomes that have negative valence for teachers are unnecessary paperwork and being required to monitor hallways, restrooms, and bus-loading areas.
2. *Instrumentality* refers to the perceived connection between a work outcome and some object or event that has positive valence for an employee. An employee must believe that something he or she does on the job will lead to a desirable result in order for motivation to occur. According to the theory, a teacher who has been asked by the principal to serve on a textbook committee will be more motivated to serve if he or she believes that by doing so, something pleasant will be forthcoming. The teacher must believe that the task (serving on the committee) is instrumentally related to an incentive he or she values. That might be the principal's approval, or it might be the opportunity to improve the instructional program.
3. *Expectancy* refers to the employee's perception of the probability of successfully achieving a work outcome. In the preceding example, the teacher who has been asked to serve on the textbook committee may decide not to do it if she believes that she lacks the requisite knowledge and skills. Her expectancy of satisfactorily performing the task is low.

Work outcomes include tasks performed on the job, but they may also include what we refer to as *opportunities*. For example, the chance to attend a workshop to improve one's skills is a work outcome, but most of us would not refer to it as a task. This distinction is important because with it we can use expectancy theory to help explain why teachers are sometimes not motivated to participate in staff development activities.

Expectancy theory is illustrated in Figure 6.1. The figure shows how a work situation leads to a condition of motivation or lack of motivation for an employee. The employee considers a work outcome, which might be an in-service program offering instruction on a new way to teach music. The teacher asks first, "Can I achieve the work outcome?" This might involve several other considerations, including "Do I have the time to take this in-service class?" "Is Tuesday afternoon a convenient time for me?" "Can I learn the material?" If the answer to any of these questions is *no*, the teacher will not be motivated for this particular work outcome. If the answer to all of the questions is *yes*, the teacher moves to the next decision block.

At this point, the teacher considers whether there is an incentive to perform the outcome. The music teacher in the example might decide that the workshop could result in her acquiring new instructional techniques that

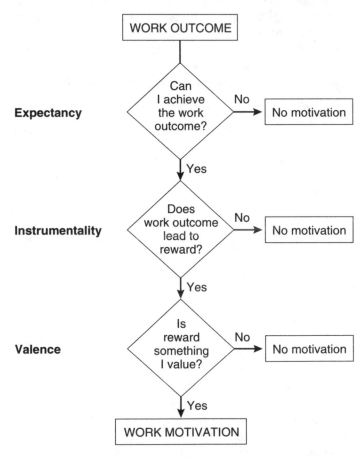

FIGURE 6.1 Flowchart Illustrating Expectancy Theory

would increase student interest in music. If student interest (and the resulting student learning) have positive valence for the teacher, then she will be motivated to attend the workshop.

Consider another situation: A district offers a salary increment to teachers who agree to teach in schools with concentrations of low-achieving students. A teacher considers first whether he or she can perform the task. If the job involves working with children with learning problems, the teacher may decide that he or she lacks the necessary skills. However, if the teacher feels able and qualified to do the job and the salary increment is attractive, he or she will accept the offer.

Some psychologists have commented recently that the use of rewards and incentives as motivators raises ethical questions. Some have also challenged their effectiveness in increasing motivation. Kohn (1993) stated, "Rewards, like punishments, can usually get people to do what we want for a while. In that sense, they 'work.' But my reading of the research, corroborated by real-world observation, is that rewards can never buy us anything more than short-term compliance" (p. 784).

Kohn (1993) has written specifically about motivating learners, but he believes that similar conclusions apply to other situations. He argues that when incentives are used to change behavior—whether to persuade people to quit smoking or to wear seatbelts—the use of incentives works as long as rewards are forthcoming, but when the rewards are withdrawn, individuals revert to earlier behaviors.

Those who have ethical objections to incentives suggest that their use amounts to an effort to control people's behavior, and they are opposed to that because they feel that it denies individuals the right of free choice. The debate about the use of incentives will continue, since both sides are convinced that they are correct and that the opposition is mistaken. In the meantime, the use of incentives in the workplace will probably go on Those who supervise personnel in schools should keep in mind that individuals differ. What is rewarding for one person may not be so for another. Finally, they should also remember that, as a general rule, educators attach less importance to extrinsic rewards than to intrinsic satisfactions from their work.

Rewards and Incentives

For an incentive to have an effect on performance, it is necessary that the employee anticipate receiving it and understand that certain performance standards must be met in order to qualify to receive the reward. Anticipation differentiates *rewards* from *incentives,* terms that are often and incorrectly used interchangeably (Mitchell, Ortiz, & Mitchell, 1983).

Incentives are of three types: material, solidary, and purposive (Clark & Wilson, 1961). *Material* incentives are tangible rewards such as money and prizes awarded to employees who attain specified levels of performance.

Solidary incentives come from association with members of a group. Peer acceptance and support are examples of solidary incentives. *Purposive* incentives are rewards that are related to the purpose for which an organization exists. Giving teachers a greater voice in decisions about their work is an example of a purposive incentive.

Examples of incentives under the three categories identified by Clark and Wilson (1961) are:

Material Incentives

1. Fewer extra-duty assignments
2. Financial assistance

Solidary Incentives

1. Recognition or praise for performance
2. Assistance and support from peers

Purposive Incentives

1. Assignments that utilize special knowledge and skills
2. Opportunities for professional growth and development

Guidelines for Expectancy Motivation

Using expectancy theory to motivate teachers is more likely to succeed if administrators follow these guidelines:

1. Select incentives that are valued by teachers. Schools made relatively little use of purposive and solidary rewards, even though teachers generally respond positively to them. Direct financial incentives to teachers seem to have promise for attracting teachers to specific assignments such as schools with large numbers of non-English-speaking students or schools located in neighborhoods with a high rate of crime. They can also be used to achieve specific goals, such as raising achievement test scores. However, financial incentives do not work as well in raising the overall level of quality of teaching performance (Johnson, 1986). These issues will be discussed in more detail in Chapter 10.
2. Be sure that teachers understand the instrumental connection between work outcomes and incentives. If the connection between the work outcome and the incentive is not clear, no motivation will occur. Some merit pay programs fail because teachers do not understand what they must do to earn the merit increase.
3. Select work outcomes that are attainable. Teachers must believe that a work outcome is attainable in order for expectancy to affect their work behavior. Choosing work outcomes that are beyond the reach of most teachers defeats the purpose of using rewards and incentives.

4. Make incentives available to all teachers but allow the individuals to decide whether to seek them. Do not use incentives to achieve work outcomes that are expected or required of all employees. For example, teachers should not be offered incentives for being on time to school.
5. Make sure that teachers who achieve designated work outcomes receive the associated reward.

Equity Theory

Equity theory can be illustrated by a story about a man who has just bought a new car at what he feels is a bargain price. The man searched for a dealer who would consider an offer and then negotiated with the salesperson to get the best deal possible. After considerable effort, he succeeded in buying the automobile with the equipment he wanted at a price substantially below the list price. A week later, he tells a friend about his good fortune and learns that the friend has that day bought an identical car from the same dealer at an even lower price.

The car buyer's evaluation of his own performance changed when he learned that someone else had been more successful than he. Adams (1965) suggested that employees evaluate the rewards they receive by comparing them to the rewards received by others. Thus, a teacher who receives a $1,000 salary increment will feel satisfied if other teachers received the same amount or less but dissatisfied if others received more.

To whom do employees compare themselves in making equity judgments? According to equity theory, an interpersonal standard is the basis for judgment. Individuals compare their effort/reward ratio to that of other employees in the same organization who hold similar jobs. For example, a school counselor might compare the amount of effort he or she expends on a job and the rewards received to those of another counselor in the same school or to those of a counselor in another school in the same system (Goodman, 1974).

Reducing Tension

Equity theory suggests that employees compare their own and others' effort/reward ratios and feel satisfied if the ratios are equal and dissatisfied if they are unequal. If Allan and Barry both work equally hard but Allan receives a promotion and Barry does not, both will experience feelings of psychological tension. They may try by various means to allay the tension, including cognitive distortion. For example, Barry may tell himself, "Maybe Allan works harder than I thought" or "Allan talks a good game, and the boss believes him."

A second way to relieve psychological tension is to change one's inputs. Barry may decide not to work so hard, or he may elect to change his priorities on the job in order to devote more effort to activities that are rewarded. He may also act to change the comparison. One way to do that is to tell himself, "Allan may be a better salesman, but I'm a better manager." Or he may say, "A promotion is not worth it if I have to neglect my family to get it." Finally, Barry may leave the job altogether.

Allan may experience some of the same tension that Barry feels, and if so he will probably react in some of the same ways. For example, he might distort reality by telling himself, "I always thought Barry was kind of lazy." Or he may decide to change his inputs by working less hard in order to avoid further alienation from Barry.

Equity theory helps one to understand teachers' opposition to merit pay and other forms of performance-based compensation. Since most of these programs rely on principals' ratings to determine which teachers will receive salary increases, teachers fear that principals may reward their favorites and ignore all others. Teachers seem to be less concerned about inequities in the single salary schedule than they are about possible inequities in performance-based compensation plans.

Equity theory assumes that employees have accurate information about the amount of effort their colleagues expend, but in education that assumption is often faulty. Since teachers seldom observe one another's work directly, they lack complete information about the work habits of others. Nevertheless, they form judgments about which of their colleagues work hard and which do not, basing those conclusions on inconclusive evidence, such as how late a teacher stays at school and whether he or she carries work home.

Even though an employee may be misinformed about how hard colleagues work, it is the beliefs one holds that provoke the responses predicted by equity theory. Thus, the perception of inequity has the same effect on employee behavior as actual inequity.

Guidelines for Equity Motivation

Using equity theory to motivate teachers is most likely to be successful when administrators follow these guidelines:

1. Differentiating rewards on the basis of performance will increase productivity but may also increase intragroup conflict. If harmonious relations and minimal conflict are important, distribute rewards equally among members.
2. Whenever possible, give all employees the chance to work toward rewards, but if rewards are offered to some groups and not others, make certain that the individuals understand and accept the reasons for the differentiation. Providing clerical assistance to employees who serve on a curriculum revision committee is acceptable, but providing such assis-

tance to coaches who already receive a salary increment is likely to be perceived as inequitable.

3. Achieve a balance between the effort required and the value of the reward. Rewards that are of little value should be more easily attained than those that are of greater value. In education, the cost of incentive programs is always a concern. Costs may be capped by limiting the number of incentive awards given, but a more equitable approach is to increase the amount of effort required to gain a reward, so that fewer people try for them.

4. In education, perceived inequities most often arise in connection with evaluating performance. If no objective and valid way of measuring performance exists, managers are vulnerable to charges of unfairly rewarding favorites. To avoid the charge, appoint a committee of teachers to set standards for deciding which individuals shall receive rewards.

Goal-Setting Theory

One reason that games are highly motivating is because they have clear and challenging goals. Whether playing bridge, video games, or touch football, participants understand the objective of the activity and enjoy the challenge of trying to attain it. A number of psychologists contend that clear-cut and challenging goals are as effective for motivating people in work settings as in recreational situations. Locke and Latham (1984) suggested that people gain a sense of accomplishment and efficacy from attaining goals, provided the goals are sufficiently challenging and success is not either impossible or meaningless.

Goal-setting theory has been shown to work in psychological laboratories as well as actual work environments when the goals are accepted by the people involved. Studies have shown that individuals who were assigned more challenging goals outperformed those who received moderately difficult or easy goals. Also, individuals who were given specific goals did better than those who were given vague admonitions such as "Do your best."

Goal setting is a form of self-leadership. Organizations use a variety of external control mechanisms for influencing employee behavior, including evaluation, rules and policies, and supervisory oversight. In recent years, however, organizations have begun to place more emphasis on internal controls. By working to achieve commitment by employees to the organizational mission and goals, these organizations hope that the need for external mechanisms of control will diminish.

Self-leadership refers to an inclination by an employee to engage in behaviors that contribute to the accomplishment of an organization's mission and that are performed in the absence of any external constraint (Manz, 1986). Employees engage in self-leadership because they are committed to the goals and purpose of the organization that employs them. In schools with school-based management, self-leadership assumes greater importance because these schools do not have access to the full range of external controls on employees that are available to districts with centralized administrative structures.

Locke and Latham (1984) stated that goals are motivating for employees even though they were not involved in setting them. Teachers may differ from other employees in that respect, however, since teachers believe that setting instructional goals is an important function of their jobs. Goals that are set by the administration are more likely to be accepted by teachers if the principal justifies the choice of goals and offers to provide support to members in attaining those outcomes.

Guidelines for Goal Setting in Schools

When goal setting is used as a motivational device for employees in schools, the following principles should be kept in mind:

1. There is some evidence that goal setting works better when employees are confident of their ability to achieve goals (Carroll & Tosi, 1973). Supervisors may need to provide interpersonal support for employees who lack confidence in their ability to achieve a goal. Individuals who are new to the job may be especially uneasy about identifying performance goals.
2. Performance goals should reflect the outcomes envisioned in the school's strategic plan and mission statement. Other documents that can be helpful in formulating goals are job models and incentive pay plans or career ladders.
3. A way should be found to measure progress toward individual or group performance goals and to share the findings. Detailed feedback helps in several ways. It reduces uncertainty concerning which behaviors are most appropriate in the pursuit of goals, and it provides information about the relative importance of various goals (Ashford & Cummings, 1983). Feedback is more likely to be perceived accurately if it follows the performance without delay, is positive, and is given relatively frequently (Ilgen, Fisher, & Taylor, 1979). The motivational value of feedback is influenced by the extent to which it conveys to the recipient a sense of competence.
4. Employees will be more committed to performance goals that are chosen consensually by members of work teams.

Using Goal Setting for Evaluation

Goal setting is commonly used in schools as part of the evaluation process. Teachers choose annual goals and are evaluated on their success in achieving them. In such programs, it is advisable for principals and teachers to discuss how goal attainment will be measured and to set a date for achieving the goals (Locke & Latham, 1984). The time limit is ordinarily one year, but interim reviews of teacher performance at periodic intervals during the year are recommended. Teacher evaluation schemes that involve teacher-selected outcomes are reviewed in more detail in Chapter 9.

Guidelines for Goal Setting in Evaluation

When goal setting is used as an adjunct to teacher evaluation, the following guidelines should be considered:

1. Individual teachers should select goals that help advance the school's established mission. The principal can help by reviewing individuals' goals for compatibility with the objectives of the school.
2. Since individuals vary in their abilities and stage of professional development, some variance in goal difficulty is to be expected. However, employees should be advised to maintain a reasonably comparable level of difficulty in the goals they select. If one individual chooses very challenging targets while another picks only easy ones, the effect will be to create feelings of inequity and demotivation.
3. When an organization asks employees to identify performance goals, it should commit itself to help the employees achieve the goals they choose. To avoid the frustration and discouragement that arise from seeking unrealistic results, employees should be advised to select attainable goals, and supervisors should work to obtain the resources employees need in order to achieve them (Katzell & Thompson, 1990).
4. Employees should be assisted to write goal statements that are clear and concise, describe measurable outcomes, and require a significant and continuing effort. Since most goal statements represent a year's work, a problem that is sometimes encountered is that the goals are too modest. A goal that can be accomplished within a month or two is not sufficiently challenging. Employees often think of goals as being an addition to their normal workload. In fact, the goal statement should incorporate the activities that are part of normal responsibilities.
5. Employees are understandably concerned about the possibility of being penalized if they select goals that are too difficult and they fail to achieve them. That fear can be reduced by giving individuals an opportunity to revise their goals if it turns out they are unable to accomplish as much as they had expected.

Job Satisfaction in Teaching

A persistent question in the minds of administrators and organizational psychologists has to do with the relationship between job satisfaction and performance. It is frequently assumed that by creating conditions that increase employees' levels of satisfaction, we will obtain increased productivity, but the evidence for a connection between the two is not strong.

The median correlation from studies that examined the relationship between satisfaction and performance was about 0.14 (Vroom, 1964). In practical terms, that means that when an employee's level of satisfaction increases, the job performance will improve slightly, or that when job performance improves, job satisfaction levels will rise a little. The direction of the cause-effect relationship is not clear. Some experts believe that satisfaction results from performance rather than the other way around (Lawler & Rhode, 1976).

Two explanations for the low correlation between satisfaction and productivity have been advanced. One is that in many jobs productivity is determined by the speed at which an assembly line moves or a machine operates. Employees' feelings do not influence the machines' speed (Fincham & Rhodes, 1988). A second explanation is that employees may feel satisfaction for reasons that are unrelated or negatively related to productivity. For example, a vendor in a sports stadium might prefer to watch sporting events rather than sell popcorn and peanuts. Watching teams play reduces sales but increases the employee's feelings of satisfaction with the job.

Satisfaction and Self-Concept

The relationship between performance and satisfaction is thought by some to be mediated by self-concept; that is, when the work requires the use of abilities an individual values, then performance and satisfaction will be associated. On the other hand, a worker who performs well at a task that requires the use of talents the individual does not value will experience little or no increase in satisfaction (Vroom, 1964). This explains why teachers derive relatively little satisfaction from performing routine tasks such as monitoring hallways, cleaning blackboards, and supervising cafeterias. For most of us, the skills required to carry out these tasks are not those that we think of as an integral part of our self-identity.

Sources of Dissatisfaction in Teaching

There are several sources of dissatisfaction in teaching of which principals and other personnel administrators should be aware. Some dissatisfaction is inherent in the work, but some is amenable to change.

One source of teacher dissatisfaction is simple boredom. Teaching becomes highly repetitive after a short time, and for some people repetition leads to boredom. During the first year in the classroom, teachers have the benefit of novelty. Everything is new and much must be learned. Beginning with the second year, the teacher begins to repeat activities and content, and after a few more years, the teacher has done everything at least once.

This repetitiveness, while in some ways a lifesaver for overworked teachers, is also the source of boredom. Some teachers seem to be able to avoid becoming bored, possibly because of the nature of the subjects they teach, but boredom is an occupational hazard for many. Administrators can help relieve boredom by providing stimulating staff-development programs, providing for conference travel and sabbatical leave, and arranging transfers to new situations for teachers who request them.

Another source of dissatisfaction that is prevalent in teaching is interruptions and distractions. Teachers complain frequently about intercom announcements that interrupt their classes, but they also feel distracted by visitors and paperwork (Plihal, 1981). Principals in many schools have taken steps to reduce the number of interruptions. Some allow announcements only once a day except for emergencies.

Another cause of frustration for teachers is lack of teaching resources. In many districts there is simply not enough money to permit teachers to purchase the maps and charts, filmstrips and viewers, paper and scissors that they need in order to teach in the way they prefer. One-half of the teachers interviewed in a study reported that the teaching materials in their schools were "poor" or "barely adequate" (McLaughlin, Pfeifer, Swanson-Owens, & Yee, 1986). Unfortunately, administrators often have little control over budgets, other than to request the money to purchase needed materials and supplies.

Teachers who are assigned to teach subjects that they are not qualified to teach or for which they lack interest are likely to cite that as a cause of frustration and dissatisfaction. Administrative decisions to assign teachers to teach courses for which they have inadequate preparation create incompetence (McLaughlin et al., 1986). Although it may not be possible to avoid misassignment of teachers in every case, it is possible to reduce the number of instances.

Teacher selection procedures should be reviewed if schools frequently find themselves short of teachers in certain fields. Problems are most likely to arise in fields with an undersupply of teachers, such as science and mathematics, and in fields that are affected by enrollment fluctuations. Changing selection procedures to give preference to teachers who are certified in more than one teaching field and helping teachers to acquire additional endorsements in fields with teacher shortages can help alleviate the problem.

Many teachers feel dissatisfied because of the pervasive sense of failure they experience in trying to work with children who have suffered deprivation either because of family failures or poverty. Teachers report that they are forced to take on parenting roles in order to respond to the needs of children from single-parent or dual-career families. Working with students who are learning disabled in mainstreamed settings and large classes are other sources of frustration for many teachers (McLaughlin et al., 1986). Unfortunately, administrators have relatively limited resources with which to attack the problems of poverty and neglect. The needs of children such as these far exceed the resources available to assist them. It may be of some help for administrators to stress to teachers the need to adopt realistic expectations.

Suggestions for administrative actions that will help address teacher dissatisfaction arising from the sources discussed are shown in Exhibit 6.1.

Sources of Satisfaction in Teaching

Satisfaction with one's work occurs when there is a close match between performance goals and the actual performance (Campbell & Pritchard, 1976).
Ironically, teachers might feel higher levels of job satisfaction if they were
able to lower the performance expectations they hold for themselves. To
some extent that appears to happen during the first few years in the classroom. Individuals who begin teaching with unusually high ideals soon learn
to temper their expectations in order to more closely match the realities they
must deal with on a daily basis (Blase, 1980).

For most teachers, satisfaction from their jobs arises from the opportunity to perform tasks that they believe are socially significant and that yield
intrinsic satisfactions. Of 10 sources of satisfaction from teaching identified
by teachers in one recent study, the 4 highest ranked were intrinsic rewards
(Plihal, 1981). The 10 items are listed in Exhibit 6.2.

The principal is an important actor in creating conditions that lead to
teacher satisfaction. One study reported that teachers are more satisfied with
their work when principals have "a firm sense of professional autonomy" and

Source of Dissatisfaction	Administrative Action
Boredom	Rotate teaching assignments
	Provide workshops and seminars on new content and methods
	Provide educational leave
Interruptions	Schedule announcements once a day
	Use volunteers to reduce teacher responsibility for fundraising
	Train teachers in classroom management
Misassignment	Provide support for training teachers assigned out of field
	Examine qualifications of all teachers and reassign accordingly
	Consider changes in curriculum
	Provide supervisory support for teachers out of field
Lack of Resources	Obtain support from other sources
	Reallocate instructional budget to most needed items
	Encourage sharing of supplies
Working with At-Risk Children	Frequent praise
	"Time Out" for teachers to help them reduce stress
	Expert supervisory assistance

EXHIBIT 6.1   Administrative Responses to Teacher Dissatisfaction

- Knowing that I have "reached" students and they have learned
- Enjoyment of experience and/or use of skills
- Development of personal skills (mental and physical)
- The activity itself: the pattern, the action, the world it provides
- Friendship and companionship
- Chance to use influence
- Respect from others
- Time (especially summers) for travel and holidays
- Security of income or position
- Salary

EXHIBIT 6.2   Sources of Satisfaction for Teachers

Source: J. Plihal, *Intrinsic Rewards of Teaching.* Paper presented at the annual meeting of the American Educational Research Association, 1981. ERIC Document Reproduction Service No. ED 200599.

"regard their staff members as competent, independent professionals" (Morris, 1981, p. 1). Schools with large proportions of satisfied teachers were compared with schools in which the proportion of satisfied teachers was smaller. It was found that principals of the schools with fewer satisfied teachers more often reported that "poor teaching or teachers" was a problem in the school, than was the case in schools with more satisfied teachers (Morris, 1981, p. 4).

Job Satisfaction and Teacher Turnover

Attrition is an important problem in teaching, as it is in many occupations. It has been estimated that about 15 percent of beginning teachers leave the field of teaching during the first two years and that between 40 and 50 percent dropout during the first seven years (Schlechty & Vance, 1983). The 15 percent attrition rate for new teachers in the first and second year of teaching compares to an estimated rate of 6 to 9 percent for experienced teachers.

Teachers as a group are more satisfied with their work than people in most other occupations (Rodman, 1986), but their satisfaction is affected by the conditions of their work. A study in Great Britain found that the more discipline problems beginning teachers encountered, the more likely they were to leave teaching (Veenman, 1984). Some teachers leave the profession because they are discouraged by what they perceive as a lack of success in the classroom, and others decide that they are not temperamentally or intellectually suited for the job. Not all teachers leave because of dissatisfaction, however. Some teachers leave involuntarily because of enrollment declines or changes in their family situation.

 Inadequate salary was the most frequently cited reason for leaving teaching by those who had taken jobs in other fields in one of the few studies of the topic. Some 60 percent of respondents named that factor. Most of the leavers had improved their financial situation as compared to a group of persons who were still teaching. About 38 percent of former teachers, compared to 13 percent of current teachers, earned $30,000 or more a year from their jobs, and only about 32 percent of former teachers, compared to about 42 percent of a sample of current teachers, earned less than $20,000 a year (Metropolitan Life Insurance Company, 1985).

Working conditions, including lack of input, nonteaching duties, and paperwork, were second in frequency of mention in the Metropolitan Life (1985) survey; they were named by 36 percent of the former teachers. Student-related reasons ranked third in frequency of mention, named by 30 percent of the respondents (Metropolitan Life Insurance Company, 1985).

Academically Able

There is evidence that academically able teachers are more likely to leave the profession as compared to those with less academic ability (Schlechty & Vance, 1981). The reason is not clear, but it is possible that teachers with higher levels of ability have more career options than less able individuals.

Organizational Correlates of Attrition

There has been very little research on organizational features of schools that are related to higher levels of teacher turnover. In one of the few studies that has been done, it was found that of the organizational characteristics studied, compensation factors were most strongly related to retention. Four of five items dealing with compensation were negatively correlated with teacher turnover. The items were higher beginning salaries for teachers, teachers paid for service on curriculum committees, teachers' hospital insurance premiums paid by the district, and summer employment for teachers available (Seyfarth & Bost, 1986).

Some evidence indicated that working conditions are positively correlated with teacher retention. In districts in which educational leaves for teachers were available and in which teachers helped select other teachers, teacher retention was higher, as compared to districts without those features. Interestingly, tuition payments for graduate study were associated with higher rather than lower teacher attrition (Seyfarth & Bost, 1986).

Demographic Correlates of Attrition

Several demographic factors correlate with employee retention. Among those that have been shown to be related to attrition are length of service, age, level of skill, and education level. Workers who are younger, who have been with an employer a shorter length of time, and who have fewer skills and less education are more likely than employees without those traits to leave their jobs (Price, 1977). School districts that employ relatively large numbers of young teachers can expect to have higher than average turnover rates. However, teachers with higher levels of education are more, rather than less, likely to leave their jobs. That may be the result of increased awareness of job opportunities among teachers who hold advanced degrees.

Teacher turnover may be an indicator of teachers' lack of satisfaction with their jobs or have to do with factors in their personal lives or the economy. Many of the teachers who leave classrooms do so because of family reasons, either to bear or care for children or to move with a spouse to another locality. There is not much that principals and personnel administrators can do to reduce attrition that is related to family factors. However, in order to be able fully to understand the causes and implications of teacher attrition, it is necessary to keep detailed information on teacher mobility and the reasons for it.

In some districts, teachers who resign from their jobs are interviewed or asked to complete a questionnaire explaining their reasons for leaving. Although the validity of this information is debatable, it is an important source of data about an area of human behavior in which our knowledge is very limited. Unexplained increases in turnover may reveal previously unsuspected morale problems. An investigation is called for if turnover rates increase suddenly, particularly when the increase occurs among groups of teachers with normally low attrition.

Turnover generally refers to employees who leave a company or district altogether, but information about teacher transfers can also give clues about teacher motivation. Teachers transfer from one school to another in order to find more pleasant working conditions or greater convenience.

At the district level, a transfer has no effect on the overall composition of the teaching force, but at the school level it does. If an experienced teacher in a school is replaced by a less experienced one, the net result may be a decline in instructional effectiveness within the school. Principals should therefore be concerned with discovering the true reasons for teachers' requests for transfer and their decisions to leave the profession.

Not all attrition is to be deplored. Both from an individual point of view and from the point of view of the district, some is necessary and desirable. Individuals who discover that they have made the wrong career choice should be encouraged to seek other outlets for their talents, and school districts should move quickly to terminate new teachers who, after provision for reasonable assistance, show little or no improvement.

The profession erects relatively few barriers to those who seek to become teachers. It is argued by some that ease of entry is desirable for reasons of equity (Sykes, 1983), but the training of individuals who are not intellectually or temperamentally suited for teaching imposes on both the individuals and the districts that employ them the cost of correcting earlier errors of choice and judgment.

Summary

Motivated and knowledgeable teachers are essential ingredients of effective schools. Motivation refers to conditions responsible for variations in the intensity, quality, direction, and duration of work-related behavior. Expectancy theory explains variations in motivation as attributable to responses to the opportunity to earn rewards. Equity theory holds that motivation is affected by perceptions of fairness, and goal-setting theory suggests that people are motivated to achieve identified goals. It is often assumed that satisfaction is positively correlated with performance on the job, but the evidence shows that the correlation is weak. Happy employees are not necessarily outstanding performers. For teachers, satisfaction is related to reaching children, whereas dissatisfaction arises from factors that impede effective teaching.

Suggested Activities

1. Consider the following situation: Marie Nader teaches fifth grade in an inner-city elementary school. Most of her students come from single-parent welfare families and receive little encouragement at home to work hard in school. Marie is regarded by her principal and fellow teachers as a hard-working and effective teacher, but she feels discouraged by her lack of progress in reaching her students. Marie has been in the school two years and is the youngest member of the faculty. Most of the other teachers have taught in the school for years and are complacent about its problems. As principal of the school, you receive a telephone call from a city businessperson offering a one-time gift of $5,000 to be spent any way you choose to help the school. What will you do with the money? Suppose the businessperson tells you that the money must be spent on or for teachers. What will you do in that case? What effect would you expect your proposed project to have on teachers' motivation? What theory of motivation are you using?

2. The principal of an elementary school announces that she is instituting a teacher-of-the-month award. The winning teacher will have his or her picture posted in the front hall and receive a plaque. He or she will also be treated to a free luncheon by the principal. Teachers will be judged on the basis of classroom neatness and student behavior. What theory of motivation is the principal using? What is the likely effect of the award on teacher behavior?

3. The district appropriates money to be used for instructional materials and supplies and directs principals to distribute the money to teachers in whatever way they choose. The principal of Gold Avenue Elementary School decides to divide the money equally among all teachers in the school. According to equity theory, what is likely to be the effect on

teacher motivation of this decision? Which teachers are likely to be most motivated and which least motivated by this plan?

4. In the same district, the principal of Beach Middle School asks teachers to submit a request for the purchase of supplies and material they were unable to purchase with the normal allotment. He appoints a committee of teachers to evaluate the proposals and make awards. What is the likely effect of this plan on teacher motivation at Beach Middle? What motivation theory is the principal using?

5. Evaluate these performance goals proposed by teachers. Use the criteria provided and decide whether the goal is acceptable as written or if it needs to be revised. Specify on which, if any, criteria the goal is deficient. *Criteria:* (a) Clarity (Is it clear what the teacher must do to achieve the goal?); (b) Relevant (Is the goal related to the teacher's assignment and to the school's mission?); (c) Realistic (Does the teacher possess the necessary authority and resources to accomplish the goal?); (d) Measurable (Is it possible to measure the teacher's progress toward achievement of the goal?); (e) Challenging (Is the goal sufficiently challenging?)
Goals:

1) I want to improve my attendance record this year and to reduce the number of times I am absent from school.

2) My goal this year is to diagnose my students' performance more often so that I can plan to better meet their needs.

3) I plan to do more extensive planning this year, including weekly and daily lesson plans in all subjects.

4) I plan to set a faster pace this year so that I will be able to cover more material by the end of the year.

References

Adams, J. S. (1965). Inequity in social exchange. In L. Berkowitz (Ed.), *Advances in experimental social psychology* (Vol. 2, pp. 267–299). New York: Academic Press.

Ashford, S. J., & Cummings, L. L. (1983). Feedback as an individual resource: Personal strategies of creating information. *Organizational Behavior and Human Performance, 32,* 370–398.

Blase, J. J., Jr. (1980). *On the meaning of being a teacher: A study of the teacher's perspective.* Unpublished doctoral dissertation, Syracuse University, Syracuse, NY.

Campbell, J. P., & Pritchard, R. D. (1976). Motivation theory in industrial and organizational psychology. In M. D. Dunnette (Ed.), *Handbook of industrial and organizational psychology* (pp. 63–130). Chicago: Rand McNally.

Carroll, S., & Tosi, H. (1973). *Management by objectives: Applications and research.* New York: Macmillan.

Clark, P. B., & Wilson, J. Q. (1961). Incentive systems: A theory of organizations. *Administrative Science Quarterly, 6,* 129–166.

Fincham, R., & Rhodes, P. (1988). *The individual, work and organization.* London: Weidenfeld and Nicholson.

Goodman, P. (1974). An examination of referents used in the evaluation of pay. *Organizational Behavior and Human Performance, 12,* 170–195.

Ilgen, D. R., Fisher, C. D., & Taylor, M. S. (1979). Consequences of individual feedback on behavior in organizations. *Journal of Applied Psychology, 64,* 349–371.

Johnson, S. (1986, Summer). Incentives for teachers: What motivates, what matters. *Educational Administration Quarterly, 22,* 54–79.

Katzell, R., & Thompson, D. (1990, February). Work motivation: Theory and practice. *American Psychologist, 45,* 144–153.

Kohn, A. (1993). Rewards versus learning: A response to Paul Chance. *Phi Delta Kappan, 74,* 783–787.

Landy, F. J. (1985). *Psychology of work behavior* (3rd ed.). Homewood, IL: Dorsey.

Lawler, E. E., & Rhode, J. G. (1976). *Information and control in organizations.* Pacific Palisades, CA: Goodyear.

Locke, E. A., & Latham, G. P. (1984). *Goal setting: A motivational technique that works!* Englewood Cliffs, NJ: Prentice Hall.

Lortie, D. C. (1969). The balance of control and autonomy in elementary school teaching. In A. Etzioni (Ed.), *The semi-professions and their organization* (pp. 1–53). New York: Free Press.

Manz, C. (1986). Self-leadership: Toward an expanded theory of self-influence processes in organizations. *Academy of Management Review, 11,* 585–600.

McLaughlin, M. W., Pfeifer, R. S., Swanson-Owens, D., & Yee, S. (1986). Why teachers won't teach. *Phi Delta Kappan, 67,* 420–426.

Metropolitan Life Insurance Company. (1985). *Former teachers in America.* New York: Author.

Mitchell, D. E., Ortiz, F. I., & Mitchell, T. K. (1983). *Work orientation and job performance: The cultural basis of teaching rewards and incentives.* Riverside, CA: University of California.

Morris, M. B. (1981). *The public school as workplace: The principal as a key element in teacher satisfaction* (Technical Report No. 32). Los Angeles: University of California, Graduate School of Education.

Pinder, C. C. (1984). *Work motivation: Theory, issues, and applications.* Dallas: Scott, Foresman.

Plihal, J. (1981). *Intrinsic rewards of teaching.* Paper presented at the annual meeting of the American Educational Research Association. (ERIC Document Reproduction Service No. ED 200599).

Price, J. L. (1977). *The study of turnover.* Ames: Iowa State University Press.

Rodman, B. (1986, May 7). Teachers' job satisfaction seen greater than that of other college graduates. *Education Week,* p. 4.

Schlechty, P. C., & Vance, V. (1981). Do academically able teachers leave education? The North Carolina case. *Phi Delta Kappan, 63,* 106–112.

Schlechty, P. C., & Vance, V. (1983). Recruitment, selection and retention: The shape of the teaching force. *The Elementary School Journal, 83,* 469–487.

Sedlak, M., & Schlossman, S. (1987). Who will teach? Historical perspectives on the changing appeal of teaching as a profession. *Review of Research in Education, 14,* 93–131.

Seyfarth, J. T., & Bost, W. A. (1986, Fall). Teacher turnover and quality of working life in schools: An empirical study. *Journal of Research and Development in Education, 20,* 1–6.

Sykes, G. (1983). Public policy and the problem of teacher quality: The need for screens and magnets. In L. S. Shulman & G. Sykes (Eds.), *Handbook of teaching and policy* (pp. 97–125). New York: Longman.

Veenman, S. (1984). Perceived problems of beginning teachers. *Review of Educational Research, 54,* 143–178.

Vroom, V. H. (1964). *Work and motivation.* New York: Wiley.

7

INDUCTION

People who are hired to fill a job they have not previously held have many questions about the work and the organization that will employ them. For those who are entering a field for the first time, the questions focus on job duties and expectations, income, opportunities for advancement, fellow workers, and one's superiors. Some of these questions are answered in the interview or in orientation sessions, but many are not. Unfortunately, most employers provide little information to help employees feel comfortable in their new work setting. What the new employee learns is usually learned from other employees, varies in accuracy, and reflects the attitudes of those employees toward the employing organization.

Plan of the Chapter

Organizations that provide planned induction programs for new employees increase the chances that those employees will obtain accurate information about the job and the organization and that they will be more satisfied and productive as a result. Identifying the purposes of induction programs for teachers and principals and suggesting ways of planning programs that will help meet their needs for information are the goals of this chapter. The chapter is written for principals and district staff members who work with new teachers. The following topics are examined: (1) expectations and teaching reality, (2) induction of new employees, (3) types of induction programs, (4) content of induction programs, (5) mentors and teacher induction, (6) induction and career development, (7) administrative leadership in induction, (8) recommendations for principals, and (9) induction for administrators.

Expectations and Teaching Reality

One of the reasons mentioned most frequently by educators for choosing a teaching career is a special interest in working with children or young people (Jantzen, 1981). Other reasons mentioned frequently are "a life-long opportunity to learn," "an opportunity for exercising individual initiative," and "the opportunity for service to mankind." In their choices of reasons for choosing a teaching career, students reveal their expectations for their lives as teachers. To the extent that these expectations are fulfilled by their experiences in the classroom, these teachers are likely to feel satisfied with their choice of career, but if their expectations are not met, they may feel disappointed and even cheated. Many of those who experience dissatisfaction probably ultimately leave the profession altogether.

First Year of Teaching

The first year in the classroom is an important time in the life of the new teacher. Few periods compare in impact and importance with the first year (Johnston & Ryan, 1983). It is a time of transition. Some teachers are on their own for the first time in their lives, and they face the difficult tasks of learning a new and challenging job, finding a place to live, locating transportation, and making friends. The demands are daunting, and it should not be surprising that many new teachers experience trepidation.

Many teachers discover during their first year in the classroom that the idealistic expectations they held for the job are dashed. They discover that instruction requires endless hours of preparation, usually at the end of an exhausting day of teaching, and that this preparation interferes with their social lives. They also find that students are not as eager to learn as they had expected them to be (Blase, 1980).

One of the main problems new teachers must learn to deal with is discipline. They find the role of classroom disciplinarian a difficult one to assimilate. One new teacher wrote:

> *My biggest worry now is keeping a straight face. I just cannot seem to keep from laughing at the kids. Partly, I'm sure, it's just me—but I'm sure other new teachers face the same problem. I cannot seem to get mad at them and I laugh many times when I shouldn't. I guess I lack a detachment which can only come with time. (Morris, 1968, p. 10)*

Within a few weeks, the same teacher was writing:

> *All of my problems with my third period class seem to be concentrated on one boy. The problems are not all his fault but he personifies them. I really believe that it is physically impossible for him to stay quiet and in his seat*

for a whole period. This one kid has really gotten to me!! To top it off, he is in my homeroom and I have to face him for a solid 90 minutes right in the middle of the day. (Morris, 1968, p. 11)

Many beginners are surprised to realize that the stern admonitory tones they have heard other teachers use and that they had thought they would never adopt become second nature to them after they have been teaching a few months. They also see their fantasies of being friends with their students fade in the cold light of classroom reality. This experience of dissonance between the expectations one brings to a new job and actual experiences at work are not limited to teaching. New entrants into most occupations report similar experiences. A term that has been applied to this experience is *reality shock*. Two types of factors have been cited as leading to reality shock (Veenman, 1984).

Personal causes have to do with the individual. They include personality characteristics that are not suited to teaching and attitudes that are uninformed and out of place. Situational factors that contribute to reality shock include inadequate professional preparation, teaching assignments for which the new teacher has no prior preparation, lack of materials and supplies, absence of clear instructional objectives, isolation, overcrowded classes, and a school climate that is not conducive to instruction (Huling-Austin, 1986; Veenman, 1984).

Induction of New Employees

Induction of new employees begins with the selection process. When an applicant is treated courteously and given regular feedback on the progress of his or her application, the organization is demonstrating that it cares about its employees and that an individual may expect to be treated with respect and fairness if hired. Conversely, an applicant who is treated rudely or who receives no information about his or her prospects for employment infers a different message about the organization's attitudes.

Once a selection decision is made, the employer may attempt to make the new employee's entry into the work setting easier. Also, to maintain productivity, the employer usually provides orientation and assistance. However, induction is not limited to first-time workers. In many organizations, all new employees, regardless of whether they have previously worked elsewhere, are included in the induction program.

Five purposes for induction programs for beginning teachers have been identified: (1) to improve teacher effectiveness, (2) to encourage promising new teachers to remain in teaching by offering support and assistance, (3) to promote the professional and personal well-being of new teachers, (4) to communicate district and school cultures to beginning teachers, and (5) to satisfy state mandates (Hirsh, 1990a).

An implicit objective of most induction programs is to help new employees feel more comfortable in the work setting. New employees may feel overwhelmed by the unfamiliar world they have entered. This is especially true for teachers, who are isolated from their peers for most of the time they are at work. This isolation can be particularly demoralizing for beginning teachers because they often have no acquaintances among their colleagues. Moreover, many beginning teachers find that although most of their colleagues are helpful, some are not (Applegate, Flora, & Lasley, 1980). Support that comes from working closely with colleagues is often missing from teaching (McPherson, 1979).

Changing conditions in education that have made teaching more difficult and stressful have underscored the need for well-designed induction programs. Among the conditions that make teachers' work more difficult today than in the past are the increasing numbers of at-risk children in the schools, a curriculum that is more extensive and varied and which is increasingly prescribed by state or local authorities, and the introduction of new technologies that teachers are expected to master (Mager, 1992).

Types of Induction Programs

The definition of *induction* used in this book is a series of planned activities developed for the purpose of acquainting new employees with an organization. It also includes equipping them with knowledge, skills, and attitudes that will enable them to function effectively and comfortably in the work setting. Three distinct types of induction programs are in use in public schools.

Orientation Programs

The simplest of these three types consist of orientation sessions to introduce new teachers to the school and the community. These programs provide information about the district, help new employees to become better acquainted with the community in which they will be working (Kester & Marockie, 1987), explain performance expectations and help new employees to learn what is expected of them on the job, provide some emotional support, promote employees' personal and professional well-being (Huling-Austin, 1986), and clarify the organizational hierarchy (Pataniczek & Isaacson, 1981). These programs tend to be of short duration, and the emphasis is on information dissemination.

About 80 percent of first-year teachers in one study reported they participated in orientation sessions of one kind or another (Pataniczek & Isaacson, 1981). Orientation sessions are not always well received by teachers. Although the teachers in the study reported that they valued the information they received, many felt that equally good results could have been achieved by providing the information in a faculty handbook. One administrator described traditional orientation programs as boring to old-timers and confusing to beginners (Hunt, 1968).

Performance Improvement Programs

The second type of induction program incorporates some of the features of the first type and also seeks to help new members internalize the norms of the group they seek to join (Schlechty, 1985). Some of these programs have multiple objectives, whereas others have limited scope and narrowly focused goals. Two of the most important of the objectives identified for this type of induction program in schools are helping beginning teachers to improve their instructional effectiveness and reducing attrition of new teachers (Huling-Austin, 1987).

Among the topics that are likely to be especially useful for beginning teachers seeking to improve their instructional effectiveness are workshops at which discipline and classroom management procedures are explained; conversations with subject-area specialists who provide an orientation to the district curriculum and help locate resources and share lesson plans and tests; explanations of performance assessment procedures; and assistance in preparing a professional development plan (Hirsh, 1990b). This type of program often continues over a semester or a full year. In addition to receiving information about the school and the district, participants usually receive individualized assistance with their teaching from an administrator, supervisor, or, increasingly, another teacher.

The simplest type of assistance consists of responses to requests for help. More complex kinds of assistance include classroom observations combined with feedback. These observations may be provided by other teachers but are separate from the normal evaluation procedures. Mentoring programs are included in this category. They are characterized by intensive involvement of an experienced teacher with a beginner and may deal with many facets of the new teacher's experiences (Anderson & Shannon, 1988).

Induction for Certification

The third type of induction program operates under state mandate and requires beginning teachers to demonstrate mastery of specified teaching competencies. This type of program is primarily evaluative in nature, but in some of these programs, evaluation is combined with limited assistance.

In some states, beginning teachers are required to demonstrate that they possess certain teaching competencies in order to receive a permanent teaching certificate. In most of these programs, an assessment or assistance team is designated to work with one or more beginning teachers. Usually, the team includes among its members one principal and one experienced classroom teacher. Some programs provide training for the team members, although the training is often brief and may be limited to use of a particular classroom observation instrument. Team members observe the beginning teacher and may give feedback on the teacher's performance along with recommendations on corrective actions (Defino & Hoffman, 1984).

Improving Effectiveness

The mental and behavioral skills that teachers require in order to be successful include the ability to group discrete events into meaningful units, to discriminate among classroom events that have short- or long-range significance, to monitor and control the duration of events, and to interpret events and take action with a minimum of delay (Rubin, 1982). Experienced teachers are more likely to be competent in these behaviors than individuals who are in the classroom for the first time. An induction program can help new teachers acquire these skills by providing opportunities to interact with and observe teachers who have the skills.

Reducing Attrition

Attrition is an important problem in many occupations, including teaching. Data from one study cited by Grissmer and Kirby (1987) showed that about 20 percent of new teachers left after one year in the classroom. The researchers estimated that only about 30 percent of the men and 50 percent of women would be teaching five years after entering the profession. Some people who leave teaching do so because they decide that they are not temperamentally or intellectually suited for the job, whereas others depart because they are discouraged by what they perceive as a lack of success in the classroom. (See Chapter 6 for a discussion of attrition as a motivational problem.)

Not all teachers who decide to leave the profession are unsuited for the job. Some depart because they become discouraged or frustrated with the demands of the job and the conditions under which they work. Some of these individuals could have been successful and effective teachers if the conditions in the schools in which they worked had been less difficult or if support and assistance had been provided.

Academically able teachers are more likely to leave the profession as compared to those with less academic ability (Schlechty & Vance, 1981). The loss of able employees is always a source of concern to employers. The question is whether more of these capable teachers would be retained in teaching if they were provided with the support and assistance needed in order for them to feel successful in their work.

Little information is available on which to base predictions about the efforts of well-planned induction programs on teachers' career decisions. However, there is reason for optimism that such programs will help to retain good teachers, at least during the first few critical years in the classroom. Assistance provided during that time to these teachers, even if it reached only a relatively small number, could make a considerable difference in terms of the quality of the teaching staffs in schools.

Content of Induction Programs

The content of induction programs in schools is often based on locally produced or published reports of surveys of needs identified by beginning teachers. The most comprehensive review of published studies was Veenman's (1984) report. He summarized findings from 83 studies published in North America, Europe, and Australia. The 10 most frequently perceived problems from these 83 studies are listed here in order of frequency of mention.

1. *Classroom discipline*
2. *Motivating students*
3. *Dealing with individual differences*
4. *Assessing students' work (tie)*
4. *Relations with parents (tie)*
5. *Organization of classwork (tie)*
5. *Insufficient materials and supplies (tie)*
6. *Dealing with problems of individual students*
7. *Heavy teaching load resulting in insufficient preparation time*
8. *Relations with colleagues (Veenman, 1984, pp. 154–155)*

Competent mentor teachers can assist beginning teachers with most of the problems on Veenman's list, but some of the problems require administrative action. For example, a mentor teacher might help a beginning teacher to deal more effectively with classroom discipline and student motivation, but the mentor teacher would likely be unable to help solve problems related to lack of materials and supplies or heavy teaching load, since those factors usually result from policy decisions.

There is some evidence that the kinds of assistance beginning teachers actually seek are different from the needs they identify on questionnaires. One study found that requests for assistance with classroom discipline constituted only 5.2 percent of beginning teachers' requests for assistance from mentor teachers, although it headed the list of problems cited by beginning teachers in the studies reviewed by Veenman (1984) (Odell, Loughlin, & Ferraro, 1986–87). That was the lowest frequency of seven assistance categories.

Beginning teachers most frequently requested assistance with instruction (35 percent), followed by system requests (20.6 percent) and resource requests (14.5 percent). System requests had to do with "information related to procedures and guidelines of the school district" (p. 53), and resource requests were related to "collecting, disseminating, or locating resources for use by the new teacher" (p. 53) (Odell et al., 1986–87).

These results suggest that teachers respond to questionnaires from a different frame of reference than has been assumed. Their responses may indicate which problems teachers believe are most critical to their success as a teacher, not necessarily those for which they are most likely to seek help. The findings also show that when a new teacher does not ask for assistance with a particular problem, it does not necessarily indicate that he or she feels comfortable with that situation. There is a good deal of evidence that teachers refrain from asking for help if they believe such requests will be interpreted as evidence of lack of teaching competence. New teachers may not ask for help with classroom discipline yet nevertheless welcome and profit from any assistance that is made available.

Supplementing Preservice Training

Induction and staff development programs must sometimes provide training that was not incorporated into the new teacher's preservice preparation. As more schools adopt school-based management, it will be necessary for teachers to receive training in the leadership skills required by the added responsibility that structure requires. Many preservice programs presently offer little or no preparation in assuming leadership roles (Stallings, 1984).

Principals' leadership styles vary from laissez faire to directive, and teachers must learn to accommodate themselves to a variety of styles as administrators come and go or as teachers themselves transfer from school to school. Very few preservice programs address differences in principals' leadership styles, nor do they prepare new teachers to adapt to these different approaches. Induction is an appropriate time to help beginning teachers identify and respond in an appropriate way to the leadership behaviors of principals and supervisors with whom they work. In some schools, a small group of influential teachers exert leadership, and beginning teachers must be able to recognize such coteries and be able to work effectively through them (Stallings, 1984).

Other groups that new teachers must learn to take into account in their work include parents and professional organizations. Parents are more interested and involved in school affairs in some districts than in others, but in no school is it wise to ignore parents. Professional organizations are much more powerful in certain districts than in others, but they too are a force of which new teachers should be aware (Stallings, 1984).

Mentors and Teacher Induction

Induction programs in schools serve several different purposes, as noted earlier. The design of the program depends on the purpose for which the program was established. One of the most popular components of induction programs is the mentor teacher. This position goes by a variety of names, including *buddy teacher, support teacher, cooperating teacher,* and *teacher advisor.* Several studies have shown that mentor teachers have been instrumental in helping beginning professionals to acquire increased teaching competence (Gray & Gray, 1985; Zahorik, 1987).

One of the reasons for the success of mentors is that teachers are accustomed to seeking help from colleagues. Most teachers prefer to talk to another teacher when they have a question rather than seek assistance from a supervisor or administrator (Pataniczek & Isaacson, 1981).

In part, the preference for conferring with other teachers is related to convenience. It is usually easier to locate another teacher than to find a supervisor or administrator, but new teachers are often afraid that asking for help from the principal may raise questions in the administrator's mind about their competence. To avoid that possibility, some teachers avoid asking for help, or they go to a teacher whom they think they can trust.

Mentor teachers perform a variety of functions, including planning and presenting orientation and staff development sessions, assisting new teachers to locate and organize curriculum materials, and providing consultation and classroom assistance (Wagner, 1985). They also provide political information and advice, publicize their proteges' accomplishments, protect their proteges, and offer advice and assistance to those considering career moves (Anderson & Shannon, 1988).

In a recent study examining teachers' beliefs about mentoring (Ganser, 1993), two factors were named most often by mentors who were asked to cite the most useful contributions mentors make to beginning teachers. These were providing support and encouragement and informing new teachers about school and district policies, procedures, and paperwork.

Among the obstacles to effective mentoring cited most frequently were the lack of time for meeting and observations, personality conflicts between teacher and mentor, lack of administrative support, unclear roles or lack of training for the role, and mismatches between beginning teachers and mentor teachers due to differences in assignment or philosophy of teaching (Ganser, 1993).

Mentoring programs work better when the teachers who are chosen as mentors are experienced, competent, and willing to serve. It is desirable that they teach the same discipline as the teacher they mentor, have a planning period at the same time, be located near the classroom of the new teacher, have similar beliefs about teaching and learning, and be willing to serve as mentor. Finally, the two teachers should have compatible personalities and temperament (Huling-Austin, 1987).

Training Mentor Teachers

Training for mentor teachers is an important part of a successful induction program. The complexity of the skills required to function effectively in a support role should not be underestimated. It is sometimes assumed that teachers who perform well with children will be equally effective with adults (Wagner, 1985). Unfortunately, that is not always true.

Even when training is provided, "school systems cannot expect that experienced teachers will be able to provide effective assistance to beginners in a systematic way" (Thies-Sprinthall, 1986, p. 13). It seems safe to say that training that is brief and superficial is not likely to have much impact on the ability of mentor teachers to affect the behavior of beginning teachers. The training they receive should be designed to convey the knowledge and skill they will need in working with beginning teachers. Two of the important skills are knowledge of a variety of teaching models and the ability to explain and demonstrate the conditions under which each is appropriate (Thies-Sprinthall, 1986).

Induction and Career Development

Commercial and industrial organizations in particular emphasize the career development aspect of induction. In some firms, mentors are assigned to new employees and serve as sponsors to help the new worker establish informal networks inside and outside the company. Mentors also serve as teachers, and they are particularly helpful in assisting beginners to understand the organization's culture, including both written and unwritten rules and norms. They provide feedback on both performance and interpersonal relations and allow learners to test their assumptions about the organization. Mentors occasionally play devil's advocate by challenging an employee's perceptions or behavior. Finally, mentors play the role of coach by sharing their own career histories and struggles as a way of providing emotional support to beginning employees who experience difficulties in getting their ideas accepted (Farren, Gray, & Kaye, 1984).

Career Development in Schools

Some public school induction programs incorporate career development features. For example, the state of California has enacted legislation under which local school boards may elect to initiate a mentor program with state financial support. The legislation requires that mentors be credentialed and experienced classroom teachers who have demonstrated exemplary teaching ability as indicated by effective communication skills, subject-matter knowledge, and mastery of a range of teaching strategies, and are recommended by a teacher-dominated selection committee (Wagner, 1985). Mentors are appointed for terms of up to three years, during which time they teach a reduced classload and receive a stipend in addition to their regular salary. For most teachers in programs such as these the opportunity to gain critical experience and acquire new skills outweighs the importance of added fiscal benefits.

In California, the school district receives $2,100 for each mentor teacher to offset the cost of training and released time. Idaho initiated a plan in 1989 that grants school districts $1,000 for each first-year employee. It can be used for supplemental pay and released time or to contract with a higher education institution to provide assistance to beginning teachers and administrators (Cornett & Gaines, 1992).

Administrative Leadership in Induction

The role of the principal in induction varies depending on the type of program. In orientation programs, principals often play a major part both in planning and presenting information sessions for teachers. The principal's work may be supplemented by district supervisors and other teachers.

In performance effectiveness programs, the principal is usually involved in selecting and training mentor teachers and in monitoring the operation of the program. This involves conferring with mentors and beginning teachers periodically to identify and resolve problems. In certification programs, the principal's involvement is usually limited to evaluating beginning teachers and providing feedback on their performance. Assistance is usually provided by trained assessors.

The three types of programs vary in their potential to influence the behavior of beginning teachers. Orientation programs have low potential for impact, whereas the performance effectiveness and certification programs have relatively high potential. The impact of a mentor teacher on the behavior of a beginning teacher depends on the mentor's skills and the prevailing norms in the school. The principal can play an influential role in performance effectiveness programs by careful selection of mentors, by providing instruction and guidance to help them carry out their duties, and by encouraging a climate of high instructional standards among all teachers.

One of the problematic aspects of programs that use mentors is helping experienced teachers to overcome a reluctance to comment on their colleagues's work. One author (Zahorik, 1987) made the following observation:

> *Teachers must come not to fear exposing their classroom practices. They must see that knowledge of their classroom behavior by others as well as by themselves is essential to improvement. . . . Changing teachers' views of teaching is obviously a difficult and lengthy process, but it seems to be an unavoidable first step to developing collegiality, improving instruction, and making teaching satisfying work. (p. 395)*

Principals can help by encouraging all teachers to be more open in their teaching and by reassuring those who are observed by colleagues that they will not be evaluated on the basis of collegial observations.

Induction programs are subject to fail when unreasonably high expectations are held for them. They cannot be expected to overcome problems related to resource scarcity or policy limitations. Induction does not remove the need for ongoing staff development activities aimed at raising or maintaining the quality of the instructional program, and it does not take the place of performance evaluation.

Principals should be aware of the danger that induction may make poor teachers feel good about doing a poor job (Huling-Austin, 1986). Other potential problems arise when teachers without supervisory training or experience attempt to assist beginning teachers in improving their instructional practices or when narrowly defined instructional models are prescribed for all teachers, leading to standardized practice (Thies-Sprinthall, 1986).

Induction is not a substitute for instructional leadership. Clearly defined performance expectations are essential for effective instruction, and induction programs cannot take the place of that ingredient. Principals are sometimes surprised to hear that performance expectations are not clear, since they are clear to them. What is needed is continuous reinforcement of behavioral expectations as employees learn new roles (Kurtz, 1983).

Recommendations for Principals

Even in districts without formal induction programs, principals can anticipate and remove some of the obstacles to effective teaching that are frequently encountered by teachers who are in their first year of teaching. If followed, the following practices will help beginning teachers to attain success during their first year in a school (Kurtz, 1983):

1. Plan special in-service sessions for beginning teachers throughout the school year with timely topics addressing the concerns of that group. Information is timely if it is presented when teachers need it. If presented before the need arises, the information is likely to be disregarded; if it is presented afterwards, it is worthless.

Beginning teachers want help in evaluating student work and assigning grades, but a presentation on that topic will be more successful if presented about halfway through the first grading period than if it is scheduled for the opening of school or the week grades are due.

2. Pair beginning teachers with experienced teachers, matching individuals for subject taught, physical proximity, and teaching philosophy. In some districts, the bargaining agreement places limits on the types of activities that teachers may be asked to participate in and the amount of time they may commit to such activities. Within the contract's limitations, attempt to involve teachers who are warm and supportive and who have demonstrated they are effective at producing student learning. Spell out what is expected of the support teacher, but avoid asking that individual to perform as a mentor unless training is provided.

3. If the school has a mentor program, plan to meet periodically with mentor teachers to review their experiences working with beginning teachers and, when necessary, to identify general problems that need attention.

4. Avoid allowing beginning teachers to end up with only the courses and students more senior teachers do not want. If the bargaining agreement permits it, limit new teachers' preparations to the fewest number possible and assign students who are known to be disruptive to more experienced teachers. Be aware, however, that this action may be controversial, since some experienced teachers will resent being imposed upon and will accuse beginners of not carrying their load.

5. Exercise care and judgment in making extra duty assignments in order to avoid jeopardizing the teaching effectiveness of beginning teachers. The first year in the classroom is a demanding experience, and most beginning teachers require large amounts of preparation time. Burdening new teachers with extra duty assignments will make it much more difficult for them to be effective in bringing about student learning.

6. If an induction program is offered, schedule sessions for beginning teachers separately from the sessions for experienced teachers but give beginners the opportunity to attend both. Administrators who are responsible for the programs should choose content that is relevant to teachers' needs. Refer to the research by Veenman (1984) and Odell, Loughlin, and Ferraro (1986–87), presented earlier in this chapter, for ideas on relevant content.

Induction for Administrators

Most administrators learn the skills they need on the job in informal ways, either by trial and error or by observing an experienced administrator. Some are fortunate enough to begin their careers working with an experienced educator who is able to articulate issues that need to be considered as decisions are made, and who is willing to assist the beginner by talking through each new type of problem as it arises.

Principals who work with an assistant principal who has had no previous administrative experience should plan to spend time with the new assistant outlining duties and discussing the teachers' expectations of administrators. A useful guide on how to conduct such an induction activity is provided by Jentz (1982).

Interviews

Among the steps Jentz (1982) has recommended are helping the new assistant principal to learn more about the school's culture and procedures by scheduling him or her to conduct interviews with individuals with whom the assistant principal will be working in the coming months. For example, if the assistant is expected to help prepare the school's budget, interviews would be scheduled with the school bookkeeper and with the district business officer. The assistant principal would also want to talk to several department heads about budgeting, purchasing procedures, and handling of payments and fees.

These interviews serve several purposes. First, they allow the assistant to make initial contacts with individuals with whom he or she will be working in the future. Second, they serve to acquaint the assistant principal with existing rules and procedures as they are interpreted by the individuals involved and alert him or her to problems that may exist in the implementation of the rules. Since policies are sometimes ignored in practice, it is a good idea as well for the new administrator to read the district's policies on fiscal accounting in order to learn "what the book says."

Third, the interviews convey to those upon whom the administrator must rely for assistance when developing the budget that the assistant principal is interested in their opinions. This will facilitate future working relationships. Similar interviews can be conducted in connection with other duties for which the administrator will have responsibility.

Preparing Work Plans

Beginning assistant principals can also be helped by preparation of detailed work plans for the year. Jentz (1982) recommended preparing a chart that shows each of the major policy areas for which the assistant principal is responsible (e.g., budget, teacher absence, student enrollment, student discipline, and so on) arrayed along one dimension and a calendar on the second. Deadlines for completion of specific tasks related to each of the policy areas are noted.

In a separate document, Jentz (1982) recommended listing a detailed sequence of steps that must be accomplished in carrying out the duties assigned to the assistant. For example, one step in preparing a budget is to notify department heads of the date for submission of a tentative budget request along with guidelines for preparing it.

The principal very likely will not have the time to prepare this chart for the assistant, but the assistant should be asked to keep a record of the steps involved in carrying out major duties and to prepare a copy for the principal. This record can later be typed and kept for future referral.

Summary

Induction involves planned activities developed for the purpose of acquainting new employees with an organization and equipping them with knowledge, skills, and attitudes to enable them to function effectively and comfortably in the work setting. Three types of induction programs are common in public schools: orientation, performance effectiveness, and certification. The first year of teaching is a transitional year for many teachers, and for some the experiences in the classroom create reality shock.

Mentor teachers can help reduce the impact of reality shock by giving new teachers a sounding board and a source of advice and suggestions. Mentors who are selected with care and trained to perform the functions of the role can be of value in helping new teachers to deal with the problems they encounter. The most frequently mentioned problem areas identified by new teachers include student discipline, motivating students, and providing individual assistance.

Administrators should be aware of potential problems in implementing teacher induction programs and should be aware that induction does not reduce the need for instructional leadership and does not replace performance evaluation responsibilities of principals. In schools with no formal induction program, principals can make life easier for first-year teachers by appointing a support teacher to assist the new teachers and by relieving new teachers of extra duty assignments and unnecessarily heavy teaching duties.

Induction for administrators should provide the individual with the opportunity to learn about the responsibilities of the position by talking to people with whom he or she will work. Specific guidelines on major tasks are helpful to those who are new to an administrative job.

Suggested Activities

1. Prepare a short five-minute talk to welcome new teachers to your school and to give them a brief history of the school and the community.
2. Working with a classmate, one of you interview a person who has recently completed the first year of teaching, and the other interview a person who recently served as a mentor for a beginning teacher. Ask each individual what he or she perceives as the advantages and disadvantages of mentoring for themselves and for the person with whom they worked. Compare the answers and report your findings to the class.
3. From the *Dictionary of Occupational Titles* select an occupation about which you have little knowledge. Suppose you have been selected for a job in that occupation. Write five questions you would like to have answered in an induction program. How many of your questions might also be asked by a beginning teacher? (The *Dictionary of Occupational Titles* is published by the U.S. Department of Labor and is available in most libraries.)
4. Prepare a plan for a semester-long induction program for new teachers. Specify instructional objectives for each session and identify a possible presenter.
5. Read Case Study II (at the end of this book) and answer the questions that follow.

References

Anderson, E. M., & Shannon, A. L. (1988, January/February). Toward a conceptualization of mentoring. *Journal of Teacher Education, 39,* 38–42.

Applegate, J. H., Flora, V. R., & Lasley, T. J. (1980, October). New teachers seek support. *Educational Leadership, 38,* 74–76.

Blase, J. J., Jr. (1980). *On the meaning of being a teacher: A study of the teachers' perspective.* Unpublished doctoral dissertation, Syracuse University, Syracuse, NY.

Cornett, L., & Gaines, G. (1992). *Focusing on student outcomes: Roles for incentive programs.* Atlanta: Southern Regional Education Board. (ERIC Reproduction Service No. ED 358058).

Defino, M. E., & Hoffman, J. V. (1984). *A status report and content analysis of state mandated teacher induction programs.* Austin: University of Texas, Research and Development Center for Teacher Education. (ERIC Document Reproduction Service No. ED 251438).

Farren, C., Gray, J. D., & Kaye, B. (1984, November/December). Mentoring: A boon to career development. *Personnel, 61,* 20–24.

Ganser, T. (1993). *How mentors describe and categorize their ideas about mentor roles, benefits of mentoring, and obstacles to mentoring.* Paper presented at the annual meeting of the Association of Teacher Educators, Los Angeles. (ERIC Document Reproduction Service No. ED 354237).

Gray, W. A., & Gray, M. M. (1985, November). Synthesis of research on mentoring beginning teachers. *Educational Leadership, 43,* 37–43.

Grissmer, D., & Kirby, S. (1987). *Teacher attrition: The uphill climb to staff the nation's schools.* Santa Monica, CA: Rand.

Hirsh, S. (1990a, Fall). New teacher induction: An interview with Leslie Huling-Austin. *Journal of Staff Development, 11,* 2–4.

Hirsh, S. (1990b, Fall). Designing induction programs with the beginning teacher in mind. *Journal of Staff Development, 11,* 24–26.

Huling-Austin, L. (1986, January–February). What can and cannot reasonably be expected from teacher induction programs. *Journal of Teacher Education, 37,* 2–5.

Huling-Austin, L. (1987). Teacher induction. In D. M. Brooks (Ed.), *Teacher induction: A new beginning* (pp. 3–23). Reston, VA: Association of Teacher Educators.

Hunt, D. W. (1968, October). Teacher induction: An opportunity and a responsibility. *NASSP Bulletin, 52,* 130–135.

Jantzen, J. M. (1981, March–April). Why college students choose to teach: A longitudinal study. *Journal of Teacher Education, 33,* 45–48.

Jentz, B. (1982). *Entry: The hiring, start-up, and supervision of administrators.* New York: McGraw-Hill.

Johnston, M. J., & Ryan, K. (1983). Research on the beginning teacher: Implications for teacher education. In K. R. Howey & W. E. Gardner (Eds.), *The education of teachers: A look ahead* (pp. 136–162). New York: Longman.

Kester, R., & Marockie, M. (1987). Local induction programs. In D. M. Brooks (Ed.), *Teacher induction: A new beginning* (pp. 25–31). Reston, VA: Association of Teacher Educators.

Kurtz, W. H. (1983, January). How the principal can help beginning teachers. *NASSP Bulletin, 67,* 42–45.

Mager, G. (1992). The place of induction in becoming a teacher. In G. DeBolt (Ed.), *Teacher induction and mentoring: School-based collaborative programs* (pp. 3–33). Albany: State University of New York Press.

McPherson, G. H. (1979). What principals should know about teachers. In D. A. Erickson & T. L. Reller (Eds.), *The principal in metropolitan schools* (pp. 233–255). Berkeley: McCutchan.

Morris, J. (1968, October). Diary of a beginning teacher. *NASSP Bulletin, 52,* 6–22.

Odell, S. J., Loughlin, C. E., & Ferraro, D. P. (1986–87, Winter). Functional approach to identification of new teacher needs in an induction context. *Action in Teacher Education, 8,* 51–57.

Pataniczek, D., & Isaacson, N. S. (1981, May–June). The relationship of socialization and the concerns of beginning secondary teachers. *Journal of Teacher Education, 32,* 14–17.

Rubin, L. (1982). Instructional strategies. In H. J. Walberg (Ed.), *Improving educational standards and productivity: The research basis for policy* (pp. 161–176). Berkeley: McCutchan.

Schlechty, P. C. (1985, January/February). A framework for evaluating induction into teaching. *Journal of Teacher Education, 36,* 37–41.

Schlechty, P. C., & Vance, V. (1981). Do academically able teachers leave education? The North Carolina case. *Phi Delta Kappan, 63,* 106–112.

Stallings, J. A. (1984). Implications from the research on teaching for teacher preparation. In R. L. Egbert & M. M. Kluender (Eds.), *Using research to improve teacher education* (pp. 128–145). Washington, DC: ERIC Clearinghouse on Teacher Education.

Thies-Sprinthall, L. (1986, November/December). A collaborative approach for mentor training: A working model. *Journal of Teacher Education, 37,* 13–20.

Veenman, S. (1984). Perceived problems of beginning teachers. *Review of Educational Research, 54,* 143–178.

Wagner, L. A. (1985, November). Ambiguities and possibilities in California's mentor teacher program. *Educational Leadership, 43,* 23–29.

Zahorik, J. A. (1987). Teachers' collegial interaction: An exploratory study. *Elementary School Journal, 87,* 385–396.

8

STAFF DEVELOPMENT

All personnel functions have a direct or an indirect impact on school effectiveness, but none has a greater potential effect than staff development and training. Staff development provides opportunities for teachers and other professional and support personnel to acquire new skills and attitudes that can lead to the changes in behavior that result in increased student achievement.

However, despite its promise, staff development often fails to achieve the results that planners hope for and expect (Popham, 1984). This chapter examines some of the reasons that staff development is less successful than it might be and reviews how staff development is changing in response to shifting expectations and the emergence of new organizational forms in schools.

Plan of the Chapter

This chapter addresses these topics: (1) functions of staff development, (2) characteristics of effective staff development, (3) planning for staff development, and (4) staff development for administrators and support personnel.

Functions of Staff Development

Staff development has been defined as any activity or process intended to improve skills, attitudes, understandings, or performance in present or future roles (Fullan, 1990). The definition emphasizes one aspect of staff development—to effect change—but ignores another purpose, which is to secure compliance with district policies and procedures (Evertson, 1986). Schlechty and Crowell (1983) called the latter the maintenance function of staff development. They explained that this function refers to activities intended to "keep things from getting worse" (p. 55) by reminding people "of what it is assumed they already knew but have forgotten" (p. 56).

Incorporating this idea into the preceding definition results in a more accurate description of staff development. In this book, *staff development* is defined as any activity or process intended to maintain or improve skills, attitudes, understandings, or performance of professional and support personnel in present or future roles. (One author [Duke, 1990] makes a distinction between *staff development* and *professional development*. Staff development is described as designed for groups and focused on school and district goals, whereas professional development is meant to produce increased personal understanding and awareness for individuals.)

Types of Change

Change may occur in more than one way. Change in the way work is performed is referred to as *technological change* (Schlechty & Crowell, 1983). Examples of technological change include revisions in the curriculum content and the introduction of new ways of delivering instruction, such as using television or computers. Changes in the design of programs as well as changes in the ways students are managed and motivated also fall under the rubric of technological change.

Changes in the way people relate to one another are referred to as *structural changes* (Schlechty & Crowell, 1983). Structural change may involve a reassignment of duties or a change in the way power and authority are allocated in schools. Addition of new positions, such as teacher aide, or changes in responsibilities and rewards, such as those that occur when a career ladder is introduced, are examples of structural changes (Schlechty & Crowell, 1983). Site-based management is another example of a structural change. Some structural changes are aimed at empowering teachers, but some authorities are skeptical of the value of these changes for improving student learning (Geisert, 1988).

Thus, staff development may be used to support technological or structural change or to serve a maintenance function. A change of one type may lead to change of the other kind. Introduction of certain technological changes in schools leads to alterations in power and authority relationships. When a school purchases computers for students' use, it is introducing a technological change, but the new technology may also trigger structural changes, as teachers begin to develop cooperative working arrangements in order to facilitate access to the machines.

Accommodating Teachers' Needs

People have different needs as they attempt to implement the two types of change, and it is necessary to design staff development programs that accommodate these needs. When they implement new teaching methods or content, teachers want specific and practical suggestions on how the new technology will work, to see demonstrations of it, and to be allowed to try it out in a threat-free environment and receive feedback. They prefer to adapt new techniques to their situations rather than implement them whole. Finally, teachers want to be convinced that the strategy they are being asked to adopt is superior to that they have been using.

In the case of structural change, employees need to have a clear conception of how the change will affect them. Changes that are perceived as altering relations among people have the potential to reduce security and are likely to be resisted unless teachers are convinced of the need for the change. The preferred presenter of a technological change is someone with expertise in the new technology, whereas the preferred presenter of structural change is someone who is trusted by those who will be affected. Expertise is less important in this case than a reputation for honesty and fairness. Thus, for a staff development session involving structural change, a presenter might be an administrator in whom teachers have confidence and who can help allay feelings of threat aroused by the proposed alterations in roles, responsibilities, and relationships.

Characteristics of Effective Staff Development

What is an effective staff development program? Effectiveness may be measured by any of four outcomes—teacher reactions, teacher knowledge, teacher behavior change, and increased student learning (Wade, 1984/1985). Teacher reactions are evaluative ratings and comments provided by teachers following training. Teacher knowledge is measured by pre- and posttests preceding and following training that show how much participants have learned from the sessions. Teacher behavior change occurs when teachers use strategies acquired from staff development in their classrooms. Student learning gains are increased scores on achievement tests or other measures of growth that occur following the introduction into classrooms of teaching techniques learned during staff development.

Teacher reaction is the least valid indicator of program effectiveness but the easiest to measure, whereas student learning is the ultimate test of success but the most difficult to verify. Staff development is most effective in producing gains in teacher learning and least effective in producing increases in student learning (Wade, 1984/1985).

It is to be expected that staff development will have less impact on student learning than on the other three outcomes. Student learning outcomes occur only if two of the other three outcomes are also achieved. Teachers must learn the techniques presented in staff development sessions and must actually employ them in their classrooms before the staff development can be considered a success. If teachers fail to learn the new procedures or do not use them correctly, the program may not result in increased student learning. Using the four outcomes identified earlier as criteria of effectiveness, several characteristics have been identified as typical of effective programs.

Length of Training

Some studies have reported that the length of training sessions has no statistically significant relationship to the four outcomes (teacher learning, teacher reaction, behavior change, and student learning) (Wade, 1984/1985). However, it is reasonable to believe that more time will be needed to teach material that is high in complexity (Sparks, 1983). The finding of no difference may indicate that length of staff development sessions is dictated by the school calendar rather than by the complexity of the content to be taught.

A scheduling plan that has been shown to produce good results is a series of brief (three-hour) workshops spaced at intervals of two or three weeks over a period of several months (Mohlman, Kierstad, & Gundlach, 1982). Presenting small amounts of new material at each of several sessions rather than crowding all of it into one or two meetings helps teachers gradually integrate the new practices into their existing routines. Teachers also find it easier to cope with concerns aroused by change when the innovations are presented at a more leisurely pace (Sparks, 1983).

Size of the training group seems to make little or no difference in the outcome of training, but the composition of the group does make a difference. More learning occurs when elementary and secondary teachers receive training together than when they are separated (Wade, 1984/1985). However, this may have to do with the content of joint sessions and not only with the composition of the group.

Feedback and Support

Research is clear on the need for feedback and support for teachers who are implementing new classroom practices. The principal is an important source of this support. Both teacher learning and behavior changes are more likely to occur when the principal is supportive of the change (Sparks, 1983).

Support from other teachers is also important. Peer coaching is a technique designed to be used by teachers and administrators to help other teachers learn new teaching behaviors (Joyce & Showers, 1988). Teachers receive training in a new technique, including information about the skills and strategies and the rationale for their use. They practice the new technique in their classrooms while a coach observes. Afterwards, the observer-coach critiques the teacher's performance, demonstrates the technique, and makes suggestions for improvement. The teacher and coach then discuss appropriate ways to use the new strategy. Using coaching triads rather than pairs increases the amount of feedback each participant receives and reduces the "mutual admiration society" aspect that sometimes occurs when two teachers coach one another (Duttweiler, 1989).

Coaching offers several advantages that are not found in more traditional staff development arrangements. Because teachers who are coached are likely to spend more time practicing new strategies and are more likely to receive immediate feedback on their performance, behavioral change can be expected to occur. Joyce and Showers (1988) claimed that coached teachers use newly learned techniques more appropriately than teachers who do not have the benefit of coaching. They also suggested that coached teachers retain their knowledge of new techniques longer and have a clearer understanding of the purpose and uses of the strategies.

Showers (1985) reported that coached teachers show much higher levels of behavior change than teachers who receive the same training without coaching, but other researchers have not found the same results (Sparks, 1983). The effectiveness of coaching probably depends on the coach's skill, the complexity of the behavior being learned, and the teacher's receptiveness to change.

Peer observation alone appears to be about as effective as peer coaching in producing behavior change among teachers when it is carried out in an atmosphere of trust. There are several reasons for this. Classroom observers pick up ideas that they use in their own teaching, and they often become more aware of their own teaching behavior as a result of watching others teach. Observing also helps to free teachers from the psychological isolation that pervades many schools (Sparks, 1983).

Congruence and Ease of Adoption

Teachers are more likely to adopt strategies for use in their classrooms when they fully understand them and when the strategies are congruent with their teaching philosophies. Difficulty of implementing new techniques is another consideration that influences teachers' decisions. If the time and effort required to learn or use them are excessive, teachers are unlikely to adopt them (Doyle & Ponder, 1977).

Most teachers would like to find methods and materials that produce better results than those they are using, and they are inclined to try innovations that promise to do that (Guskey, 1986). For staff developers, the implications of those facts are clear. They should select strategies that have been shown to be effective in increasing student learning and should plan workshops to include clear explanations and demonstrations showing how the techniques work.

The research reviewed in this section provides direction for administrators who are responsible for planning and coordinating staff development programs. The characteristics associated with more effective programs are those that should be incorporated into staff development programs for teachers. Empirical research has yielded some clues that help explain why staff development programs fail to achieve the results we envision for them, but we are still learning.

Why Staff Development Is Ineffective

Four facts about staff development programs help explain why they sometimes fail to achieve improved instructional results. One is the lack of coordination of staff development activities with other programs aimed at improving instruction (Howey & Vaughn, 1983). Coordination can be improved by training department heads and supervisors in providing follow-up for teachers who have received training in new teaching techniques. This can be done by allocating resources to purchase professional books and tapes that provide additional information about the new strategies, by encouraging curriculum committees to incorporate elements of the new techniques into curriculum guides, and by providing support for conference travel for teachers and supervisors who wish to learn more about the technology.

A second fact that helps account for the failure of staff development to bring about change is the absence of continuity in training (Howey & Vaughn, 1983). Continuity provides the reinforcement that ensures that teachers will continue to use new teaching strategies. The key to continuity is follow-up activities, which provide teachers with feedback that shows them how well they are doing in implementing newly learned techniques and that addresses their concerns related to implementation of the new strategies (Killion & Kaylor, 1991).

Third, staff development programs are often designed with the intention of changing the behavior of individuals but making no provision for collaborative learning. It has been predicted that in the future the focus of staff development will shift from individual teachers to groups of teachers who have common interests and who are willing to serve as resources to one another for the purpose of enhancing professional growth (Smylie & Conyers, 1991).

Fourth, staff development fails because of weaknesses in training designs (Showers, Joyce, & Bennett, 1987). It seems clear that if teachers are to use in their classrooms what they learn in staff development sessions, the sessions must be carefully planned. There are two important elements in planning for transfer of training. One is providing teachers with information about the theoretical base on which new practices are founded. Knowledge of theory improves the probability that a teacher will successfully transfer the learned skill to his or her classroom. The second requirement for successful transfer is that what is learned must be related to what the trainee does on the job. Unrelated skills are neither transferred nor retained (Hinson, Caldwell, & Landrum, 1989).

Planning for Staff Development

Due to the increasing costs of staff development, district superintendents are anxious to see evidence that the programs are producing the desired results. Productive programs are brought into being by careful planning, including consideration of three factors—assignment of responsibility, design of the program, and evaluation of the results.

Responsibility

Staff development activities involve a great many persons. Moore and Hyde (1981) found that the teacher/developer ratio ranged from 63 teachers for each full-time equivalent staff development position in the district with the most intensive program to 92 teachers per full-time equivalent development position in the district with the least intensive program.

A decision that must be made is whether to operate staff development as a centralized or decentralized activity. Some districts offer a unified program for all teachers, whereas others leave decisions on the content, format, and timing of developmental activities to the staff of each school.

School-Based Programs

In districts with site-based management, much of the responsibility for staff development programs is delegated to the school; mandatory districtwide in-service programs cease to exist. The primary function of district staff members shifts from initiation and organization of training sessions to facilitation and support of activities initiated at the school level (Duttweiler, 1989; Smylie & Conyers, 1991). This change is accompanied by a shift in resources, with schools assuming responsibility for administering staff development budgets (Shanker, 1990).

Principals and teachers share the leadership for planning and presenting staff development activities for professional staff members at the school. The principal focuses attention on staff development by informing staff members of opportunities for professional growth, by distributing professional and curriculum materials to them, by seeking staff members' opinions about current issues related to their work, by increasing staff members' awareness of new developments, and by encouraging teachers to try new practices (McEvoy, 1987).

The idea of assigning responsibility for staff development to faculty members in each school is based on the belief that "the individual school is the most viable unit for effecting educational improvement" (Goodlad, 1983, p. 36). Goodlad admits that this position cannot be defended on the basis of research or common practice but rather as "a reasonable working hypothesis" (p. 39).

Several claims for the superiority of decentralized staff development are made by proponents. One is that school-based programs, by directly involving teachers in decisions about program content and format, lead to higher levels of interest and commitment. Advocates also claim that site-based programs increase collaboration among and between teachers and principals (Howey & Vaughn, 1983), that site-based programs are more flexible, and that program offerings are more relevant and practical than offerings in programs that are centrally directed.

Decentralized programs also have potential disadvantages. One of the main drawbacks is the heavy demand they make on the time of the principal and teachers who are involved in planning and presenting training workshops. Most principals feel they already have too little time for instructional leadership responsibilities, and adding more duties further complicates that problem. School-based programs are also somewhat less efficient than centralized operations since some duplication across schools is unavoidable.

Staff developer is a new role for most teachers, and although most who attempt it have credibility with their colleagues and are successful, problems are occasionally encountered. Moving from teacher to staff development leader in the same school can be difficult, and some teachers prefer not to attempt it. Further, in schools with strong individualistic cultures, the lack of cohesiveness can threaten the success of school-based staff development programs (Joyce, 1990).

The arrangement recommended in this book is to encourage school faculties to plan their own staff development activities when they have identified specific objectives that apply to the school and that are most appropriately addressed at the school level. A centralized option should also be available for schools that are not prepared to undertake their own effort.

Time for Staff Development

Teacher time for staff development falls into four categories (Moore & Hyde, 1981). *Salaried work time* includes all hours during which teachers are on duty. *Released time* includes periods during which substitutes are hired to release teachers from teaching duties. *Stipend time* is time outside of regular work hours during which teachers participate in staff development and are paid a salary supplement. *Personal time* is time that is teachers' own. Negotiated contracts often limit the use of teachers' personal and stipend time. It is important to check the contract before scheduling activities during those times.

Use of teachers' personal time for developmental purposes is the least costly option for the district, but it is also the least feasible. Some teachers are willing to use their own time to work toward a master's degree, but few willingly participate in staff development activities on their own time. A better approach is to schedule occasional activities during work time before and after school. However, teachers prefer to reserve this time for planning, conferring with parents, personal errands, and housekeeping. The other two options (stipend time and released time) are feasible options and are about equally costly.

Design of the Program

A number of models of staff development programs have been proposed in the literature. A typical example is this model, adapted from Siedow, Memory, and Bristow (1985). It consists of these steps: (1) establish priorities, (2) determine in-service objectives, (3) plan content, and (4) choose methods of presentation.

Establish Priorities

Priorities are of four types: (1) districtwide—the district identifies a list of priorities for all schools; (2) individual—a variety of classes and activities are offered from which individuals choose those in which they are most interested; (3) school—staff members collectively identify issues and concerns they wish to address; and (4) school community—school personnel, students, and parents work together to set priorities (Moore & Hyde, 1981).

School and district priorities can be identified by reviewing planning documents and mission statements. Sections dealing with instructional programs and services, student learning and growth, human resources, and performance evaluation and training should be examined (Lewis, 1983).

To assess individual priorities, employees may be asked to identify their own growth needs, or supervisors, principals, and department heads list areas in which teachers ask for assistance. Exhibit 8.1 shows a survey instrument for collecting information from teachers to supplement data from other sources, including test results, evaluation reports, audits, and accreditation studies (Kramer & Betz, 1987).

For districts with school-based programs, the Georgia State Department of Education (1990) has recommended forming a staff development committee in each school to conduct a needs assessment to identify areas requiring attention.

Determine In-Service Objectives

When priorities have been established, the next step is to select objectives. Typically, these are described in terms of changes in teacher or student knowledge, attitudes, and behavior. Objectives should be selected for the purpose of improving the quality of instruction (Joyce & Showers, 1988), for bringing about cognitive development or professional and career development of teachers (North Dakota State Department of Public Instruction, 1986), or for effecting changes in the structural arrangements in schools.

Objectives may be stated either as individual or group outcomes. An example of an individual objective is: "All participants will demonstrate familiarity with five techniques for teaching thinking skills to students in the

Directions: The information you provide will be used in planning for staff development activities in the district. Please answer all questions thoughtfully and truthfully.

1. How many years (total) teaching experience do you have?
2. What grade level(s) do you teach?
3. What subject(s) do you teach?
4. What is the highest degree that you hold?
5. When did you last take a college course in your subject specialty?
6. With which of the following groups would you prefer to attend a staff development workshop?
    ❏ Teachers from your own school
    ❏ Teachers from other schools in this district
    ❏ Teachers from other districts
    ❏ Mixed groups, including teachers and administrators from this district
    ❏ Mixed groups, including teachers and administrators from other districts
7. What is your preference of day and time for staff development sessions?
8. From the following list, select the three workshops you would be most interested in attending.
    ❏ Time on task
    ❏ Classroom organization and management
    ❏ Classroom climate
    ❏ Learning styles
    ❏ Teacher-made tests
    ❏ Higher-order thinking
    ❏ Using technology in the classroom
    ❏ Effects of teacher expectations on student achievement
    ❏ Curriculum revision
    ❏ Lesson design
    ❏ Teaching students with special needs
    ❏ Preparing an individualized educational plan
    ❏ Teaching gifted children
    ❏ Site-based management
    ❏ Assessing student performance
    ❏ Working with parents and the community
9. Can you suggest presenters for any of the topics on the list? (If so, list the name of the topic and the presenter.)
10. Would you be willing to serve as a workshop leader presenting a topic in which you have received previous training? (If yes, give your name and school and the topic you can present.)

EXHIBIT 8.1   Assessment of Staff Development Needs of Teachers

grade level or subject they teach and will commit themselves to try all five techniques in their classes within one month." A group objective could be stated in the following way: "Participants will collectively identify methods of increasing time on task that have worked in their own classes and will agree to try at least two new methods in their classes and discuss the results with colleagues within one month."

Plan Content

Once the objectives of the program are selected, the decision about content is simplified. Both objectives and content should take into account the realities of the school as an organization and a social system and should recognize the teacher as a person and professional. Staff development programs are often presented with little or no thought given to school norms and teacher role relationships that affect the implementation of new technologies (North Dakota State Department of Public Instruction, 1986).

Some examples of topics related to improving instruction are the social climate of the school, revision of particular curriculum areas, teaching strategies, use of technology, student learning styles, and teaching students with special needs (Joyce & Showers, 1988). The research on effective schools suggests other possible topics, including time on task, behavior management, organization and grouping, lesson design, instructional sequencing, and teacher expectations (Mohlman et al., 1982). Brookover and associates (1982) described 11 staff development modules on a variety of topics, including effective learning climate, grouping, classroom management, cooperative learning, and use of assessment data.

When planning staff development programs that involve technological change, it is important to bear in mind that teachers are not likely to be persuaded about the value of a new technique until they have seen for themselves that it works. If a technique works without being unduly costly of teachers' time and effort, they will be more likely to embrace it than if it is unproven. Staff developers should therefore concentrate on selecting strategies that have been shown to work and should offer assistance and support for teachers who are trying the new procedures.

Teachers are more likely to try new ideas when the presentation focuses on concrete practices rather than theoretical issues. Attention to specific rather than global teaching skills is also helpful. Presenters who have credibility with teachers and those who address teachers' personal concerns related to adopting the change are more likely to be successful in achieving teacher support for change (Guskey, 1986).

Planners should take maximum advantage of the resources available to them. An important source of assistance for staff development is local colleges and universities. At one time colleges and universities were the primary providers of professional development for school personnel, but today, with most school districts having developed their own programs, few teachers rely exclusively on colleges and universities for developmental opportunities (Little, 1990). Nevertheless, coursework should not be overlooked as one component of an effective staff development program.

Some of the most effective programs are those in which a school district and a university reach an agreement under which the university offers coursework tailored to meet an identified need of the district. One example was the Houston Teaching Academy, which offered a program to prepare teachers to work in inner-city schools (Arends, 1990).

In Maryland, the University of Maryland and Montgomery County Schools cooperated to form the Minority Teacher Education Project. The district hired minority individuals with bachelor's degrees as teacher aides and gave them released time to participate in a two-year program at the university that led to their receiving a teaching credential (Arends, 1990).

College work is especially valuable for teachers who are assigned to teach out of their field or who entered teaching through an alternative certification route. In 1991, 39 states provided for alternative certification of teachers in at least some specialty areas. As a rule, teachers with alternative certification have a strong background in a content area but are not as well grounded in pedagogy. Many of them need coursework in instructional methodology and human learning. Teachers who came through a traditional teacher preparation program some years ago or who have been reassigned to a new teaching field often need additional training in a content area (National Center for Education Statistics, 1993).

The numbers of individuals who are teaching out of their field are not large. Even in special education, a field of chronic shortages, 88 percent of all teachers were fully certified in 1987–88 (National Center for Education Statistics, 1993). Nevertheless, the lack of expertise among these teachers can be a significant area of need to be addressed by staff development.

Other resources available to staff developers are state departments of education, which usually have on their staffs specialists in the major subject fields who can be called on for information about instructional materials and in-service ideas. In some localities, curriculum centers are also available to help schools meet developmental needs of teachers. In whatever form staff development is offered, planners need to offer instruction in both content and process (Mell & Mell, 1990).

Choose Methods of Presentation

Staff development workshops are likely to be most successful when they incorporate four components: (1) presentation of theory, (2) demonstration of a teaching strategy, (3) initial practice, and (4) prompt feedback (Showers et al., 1987). The more complex the behavior being taught, the greater is the need for a training design that incorporates all four elements. The addition to the first two elements of the opportunity to practice and receive performance feedback dramatically increases the likelihood that teachers will retain and use what they learn (Showers et al., 1987). Practice and feedback appear to be especially important when the behavior being learned is unfamiliar to the learner (Sparks, 1983).

Sessions that are planned for beginning teachers should use a structured, directive approach. Teachers with more experience prefer to learn ways to add variety to their teaching and favor a collaborative approach (Burden & Wallace, 1983).

To prepare teachers to use specific instructional techniques, the following format is recommended (Stallings, 1985):

1. *Baseline/pretest:* Teachers are observed for target teaching behaviors. Profiles are prepared showing how frequently each behavior is used. From the profiles, teachers consult with supervisors and set goals.
2. *Information:* Information is provided to participating teachers linking research and practice. Teachers are checked for understanding.
3. *Guided practice:* Teachers adapt the new techniques one at a time to their own context and style. After trying the new methods, they assess them and are provided feedback from peer observers. Leaders obtain a commitment from participants to try the new method in their own classes and provide support and encouragement for the change.
4. *Posttest:* Teachers are observed again and a new profile is prepared. Teachers set new goals and assess the training program for effectiveness.

Evaluation

Evaluation of staff development programs is often carried out as an afterthought with little or no advance planning. Time spent in planning the evaluation will yield rewards in increased confidence in the findings. A comprehensive evaluation plan involves assessing the four outcomes of staff development identified earlier (Wade, 1984/1985). Exhibit 8.2 shows sources of data for a comprehensive evaluation of a staff development program.

Provide Follow-Up Assistance and Reinforcement

The initial presentation of a new program or technique is only the first step in implementing change. Providing regular feedback to teachers who are charged with implementing the model and providing sustained support and followup after the initial training are critical elements of an effective staff development program (Guskey, 1986). Feedback can be provided by other teachers who have had sufficient training in the technique to be able to guide their peers in its use.

Staff Development for Administrators and Support Personnel

Professional development for administrators does not receive much attention in most school districts. Principals who wish to grow professionally can usually find the necessary financial support, and their schedules are flexible enough to permit them to be away from their buildings for training purposes. However, many districts do not require or even encourage principals to engage in professional development activities (Hallinger & Greenblatt, 1989).

The principal's job is a demanding one; in most schools, principals have very little time that is not already committed. Moreover, most principals feel a sense of responsibility to be available in case a problem should arise in their

Outcome	Items
Teacher Reactions	Convenience of time and day of session
	Convenience of the location
	Comfort of the room
	Ability of presenters to make concepts clear and to maintain interest
	Presenters' knowledge of subject
	Appropriateness of the content for teachers' own schools or classrooms
	Probability of using strategies presented in the workshop
	Estimated need for feedback and followup
Teacher Knowledge	Teachers' estimates of their knowledge of subject before and after attending session
	Pre- and posttest to measure knowledge gain
	Desire to learn more about the subject
Behavior Change	Teachers' estimate of frequency of use of new strategy one month after attending session
	Data from classroom observers showing frequency of use
	Teachers' estimates of difficulty of use (time involved, student understanding and receptivity)
	Teachers' estimates of likelihood they will continue to use strategy
Student Learning	Results of experimental research on student gains in classes with teachers using new techniques, compared to students in classes with teachers using old techniques
	Students' estimates of amount they learn when teachers use new versus old techniques
	Data from classroom observers on student interest and participation in classes using new versus old techniques

EXHIBIT 8.2   Information to Be Collected in a Comprehensive Evaluation of Staff Development Programs

schools. For these reasons, many principals spend little or no time on their own professional development, even though they encourage their teachers to do so.

Principals who take advantage of professional development opportunities for themselves report that they do so because it helps them to grow and learn or helps them avoid burnout. One principal commented, "It's very important to me to continue to learn. It's self-satisfying, it makes me feel good about myself." Another stated, "[I] need energy from outside, otherwise I'd be burned out or bored out" (Hallinger & Greenblatt, 1989, p. 71).

Periodic surveys of principals' and supervisors' needs can help those responsible for staff development to provide sessions that will help principals and supervisors to feel better prepared to deal with the dual responsibilities of school management and instructional leadership. Perennial issues of concern to both groups include evaluation of teaching performance, supervision of teachers, and conducting postobservation conferences. Other topics appear periodically as issues of interest. In one survey of principals, the following topics received frequent mention (Olivero, 1982):

1. *School climate:* Principals were interested in learning how to analyze school morale and in being able to understand the relationship between climate and school policies. Principals expressed a need to be able to take action to develop more positive climates in their schools.
2. *Team building:* Principals asked to learn more about use of interpersonal skills to achieve improved collegial relations among teachers in their schools.
3. *Internal communications:* Principals hoped to improve two-way communication among staff members and with students, community members, and other district personnel.

The results of administrators' performance in assessment centers can also be used as a source of data on staff development needs of this group. A study of assessment center results for 94 practicing and aspiring principals found that the administrators were rated highest in group leadership and oral communication and lowest in problem analysis and creativity. The results indicated that improvement was needed in instructional leadership skills for practicing principals and in organizational ability for aspiring principals (Elsaesser, 1990). Staff development opportunities in instructional leadership, group leadership, and organizational ability were readily available to the aspiring and practicing principals who participated in that study, but training opportunities in resourcefulness, decisiveness, creativity, and judgment were limited (Elsaesser, 1990).

Individualized Development Plans

Because individual needs and interests vary, the ideal approach to professional development is to allow each individual to design a program uniquely suited to his or her needs and interests. The Nebraska Council of School Administrators has developed such a plan, called the Nebraska Professional Proficiency Plan (Joekel, 1994), which permits administrators to plan their own professional development agenda.

Under the plan, an administrator works with a mentor to develop an individualized plan that includes, among other things, a list of career goals, descriptions of personal strengths and areas of needed improvement, and identification of one immediate goal. With the assistance of the mentor, the administrator brainstorms and lists activities that will help him or her to achieve the immediate goal and develops a means to monitor accomplishment of tasks leading to the goal (Joekel, 1994).

The administrator compiles a performance portfolio to document his or her progress toward attainment of the goal. After reviewing the portfolio, the mentor approves or recommends refinements or additional evidence. Upon completion of the individual development plan, the administrator and mentor submit a report to the state Council of School Administrators, which, upon approving the report, issues a certificate of accomplishment (Joekel, 1994).

Career Counseling for Administrators

Most businesses provide extensive in-service training for their managers because they believe that it is a good investment for the individual as well as for the firm, but education lags in this regard (Daresh, 1987). Many corporations provide career counseling services to managers, but few school districts do so. The decision to leave the classroom in order to take an administrative position is a major change in career direction. Most people who consider such a career change would like to have the opportunity to discuss the topic with a sympathetic listener; unfortunately, they can't. Career counseling could help individuals consider all aspects of a decision more carefully and result in better quality decisions.

Some districts now arrange for prospective administrators to take part-time administrative assignments as a way of assessing their administrative potential. For the individual, such an arrangement is a growth experience; through it he or she learns what the job is like and acquires experience that can be used at a later time. The district receives the individual's services and acquires information about his or her ability.

Some new ideas are being tried in administrator in-service. One of these is a program that focuses on analyzing real-life problems. Participating administrators write short reports that describe an actual administrative problem and tell how the problem was handled. These reports become the focus of discussions that permit other administrators to relate how they have handled similar situations in the past and to suggest alternatives that might be tried. State departments of education have recognized the need for improvements in administrative staff development offerings, and some now sponsor administrative academies that offer training for superintendents and other administrators (Daresh, 1987).

Some districts now recognize that many growth experiences are available to administrators other than those represented by traditional staff development. An example of one such approach is provided by Elam, Cramer, and Brodinsky (1986). It is a growth chart on which an administrator makes a record over the course of a year of a variety of activities in which he or she has participated that have led to professional growth. Some of the categories include reading, writing, research, conventions, conferences, meetings, speeches, association or community activities, travel, college courses, visits to other schools or businesses, and participation in cultural activities.

Suggestions for improving in-service training for administrators are similar to those for teachers. Planners are advised to personalize staff development activities by focusing program content on areas of identified need and providing opportunities for participants to build on their experiences as

administrators. Demonstration, modeling of new skills, and providing opportunities for practice both in the training session and on the job are other
recommendations. Performance feedback is important while a new skill is
being learned (Pitner, 1987).

Like staff development for teachers, administrative training should provide for both personal and professional growth and should be related to identified district instructional goals. Training should be cumulative, with sessions designed to build on previous offerings (Pitner, 1987).

Training for Staff Support Personnel

Some school districts operate comprehensive training programs that provide
in-service opportunities and college courses for clerical and paraprofessional
personnel. Such a program is offered to personnel in Los Angeles schools,
where teachers' aides are able to participate in a program leading to an associate or baccalaureate degree from a local community college. Employees
who complete a bachelor's degree in an approved teacher preparation program are hired by the district as teachers (DeVries & Colbert, 1990). The Los
Angeles school district also offers in-service training for clerical and crafts
employees. These classes focus on skills development, including clerical
skills, student discipline for bus drivers, computer operation, and food service operation (DeVries & Colbert, 1990).

Summary

Staff development has a significant potential for influencing instructional effectiveness. Staff development refers to any activity or process intended to
maintain or improve skills, attitudes, understandings, or performance of professional and support personnel in present or future roles. Research on effectiveness of staff development programs has yielded findings related to
length and scheduling of training sessions, size and composition of the
group, and ease of adoption. In districts with school-based management, responsibility for staff development is being delegated to schools. Planning for
staff development in a school begins with creation of a planning committee
and the completion of a needs assessment. A comprehensive staff development program should include developmental opportunities for administrators and training for support staff.

Suggested Activities

1. School-based management is an example of a *structural change*. One of
   the characteristics of structural change is that organizational roles are
   modified. Describe the changes that take place in the roles of teachers

and administrators when a school adopts site-based management, and describe a staff development program to help prepare individuals for the new roles.

2. *Technological change* refers to new ways of organizing thinking or doing work. Some technological change leads to structural change. Give three examples in your experience of technological change that has led to changes in the way people relate to one another in the organization.

3. Interview the training director of a company or agency other than a school. Some examples of agencies you might contact are a health department, social service agency, bank, electric or gas utility, or hospital. Find out who is served by the training program, the type and frequency of offerings, and the background and qualifications of the training staff. Compare the program in the agency you study to the staff development operation in a school district.

4. Imagine you are the principal of a school and write a memorandum to the director of professional development in your district, arguing in favor of initiating a plan to introduce teacher coaches into all schools. Support your arguments with evidence from published research or statements of knowledgeable experts and suggest ways of implementing the teacher-coach program.

5. Plan a three-hour in-service session for principals on a topic of your choice. Prepare an outline of the activities to be included and the handouts, tapes, films, or transparencies that will be used.

References

Arends, R. (1990). Connecting the university to the school. In B. Joyce (Ed.), *Changing school culture through staff development* (pp. 117–143). Alexandria, VA: Association for Supervision and Curriculum Development.

Brookover, W., Beamer, L., Efthim, H., Hathaway, D., Lezotte, L., Miller, S., Passalcqua, J., & Tornatzky, L. (1982). *Creating effective schools: An in-service program for enhancing school learning climate and achievement.* Holmes Beach, FL: Learning Publications.

Burden, P. R., & Wallace, D. (1983, October). *Tailoring staff development to meet teacher needs.* Paper presented at the Association of Teacher Educators meeting, Wichita, KS. (ERIC Document Reproduction Service No. ED 237506).

Daresh, J. C. (1987). Administrator in-service: A route to continuous learning and growing. In W. Greenfield (Ed.), *Instructional leadership: Concepts, issues, and controversies* (pp. 328–340). Boston: Allyn and Bacon.

DeVries, R., & Colbert, J. (1990). The Los Angeles experience: Individually oriented staff development. In B. Joyce (Ed.), *Changing school culture through staff development* (pp. 203–217). Alexandria, VA: Association for Supervision and Curriculum Development.

Doyle, W., & Ponder, G. (1977). The practicality ethic and teacher decision-making. *Interchange, 8,* 1–12.

Duke, D. (1990, May). Setting goals for professional development. *Educational Leadership, 48,* 71–75.

Duttweiler, P. (1989, Spring). Components of

an effective professional development program. *Journal of Staff Development, 10,* 2–6.

Elam, S., Cramer, J., & Brodinsky, B. (1986). *Staff development: Problems and solutions.* Arlington, VA: American Association of School Administrators.

Elsaesser, L. (1990, April). *Using assessment center results to determine subsequent staff development activities for principals.* Paper presented at the annual meeting of the American Educational Research Association, Boston. (ERIC Document Reproduction No. ED 318763).

Evertson, C. (1986). Do teachers make a difference? Issues for the eighties. *Education and Urban Society, 18,* 195–210.

Fullan, M. (1990). Staff development, innovation, and institutional development. In B. Joyce (Ed.), *Changing school culture through staff development* (pp. 3–25). Alexandria, VA: Association for Supervision and Curriculum Development.

Geisert, G. (1988, November). Participatory management: Panacea or hoax? *Educational Leadership, 46,* 56–59.

Georgia State Department of Education. (1990). *School-focused staff development guide.* Atlanta: Author.

Goodlad, J. (1983). The school as workplace. In G. Griffin (Ed.), *Staff development* (pp. 36–61). Chicago: University of Chicago Press.

Guskey, T. (1986, May). Staff development and the process of teacher change. *Educational Researcher, 15,* 5–12.

Hallinger, P., & Greenblatt, R. (1989, Fall). Principals' pursuit of professional growth: The influence of beliefs, experiences, and district context. *Journal of Staff Development, 10,* 68–74.

Hinson, S., Caldwell, M., & Landrum, M. (1989, Spring). Characteristics of effective staff development programs. *Journal of Staff Development, 10,* 48–52.

Howey, K., & Vaughn, J. (1983). Current patterns of staff development. In G. Griffin (Ed.), *Staff development* (pp. 92–117). Chicago: University of Chicago Press.

Joekel, R. (1994, January). Nebraska Professional Proficiency Plan. *Design for Leadership: Bulletin of the National Policy Board for Educational Administration, 5,* 5–7.

Joyce, B. (1990). The self-educating teacher: Empowering teachers through research. In B. Joyce (Ed.), *Changing school culture through staff development* (pp. 26–40). Alexandria, VA: Association for Supervision and Curriculum Development.

Joyce, B., & Showers, B. (1988). *Student achievement through staff development.* New York: Longman.

Killion, J., & Kaylor, B. (1991, Winter). Follow-up: The key to training for transfer. *Journal of Staff Development, 12,* 64–67.

Kramer, P., & Betz, L. (1987). *Effective inservice education in Texas public schools.* (ERIC Document Reproduction Service No. ED 290205).

Lewis, J. Jr. (1983). *Long-range and short-range planning for educational administrators.* Boston: Allyn and Bacon.

Little, J. (1990). Conditions of professional development in secondary schools. In M. McLaughlin, J. Talbert, & N. Bascia (Eds.), *The contexts of teaching in secondary schools: Teachers' realities* (pp. 187–223). New York: Teachers College Press.

McEvoy, B. (1987, February). Everyday acts: How principals influence development of their staff. *Educational Leadership, 44,* 73–77.

Mell, B., & Mell, C. (1990). An experience in Anchorage: Trials, errors, and successes. In B. Joyce (Ed.), *Changing school culture through staff development* (pp. 229–242). Alexandria, VA: Association for Supervision and Curriculum Development.

Mohlman, G., Kierstad, J., & Gundlach, M. (1982, October). A research-based inservice model for secondary teachers. *Educational Leadership, 40,* 16–19.

Moore, D., & Hyde, A. (1981). *Making sense of staff development: An analysis of staff development programs and their costs in three urban school districts.* (ERIC Document Reproduction Service No. ED 211629).

National Center for Education Statistics.

(1993). *America's teachers: Profile of a profession.* Washington, DC: U.S. Department of Education.

North Dakota State Department of Public Instruction. (1986). *Professional development model: A wholistic approach.* Bismarck, ND: Author. (ERIC Document Reproduction Service No. ED 286868).

Olivero, J. (1982, February). Principals and their inservice needs. *Educational Leadership, 39*, 340–344.

Pitner, N. (1987). Principles of quality staff development: Lessons for administrator training. In J. Murphy & P. Hallinger (Eds.), *Approaches to administrative training in education* (pp. 28–44). Albany: State University of New York Press.

Popham, W. (1984). Assessing the impact of staff development on educational improvement. In Connecticut State Department of Education, *Professional development planning guide: A primer for local school districts* (pp. 95–99). Hartford, CT: Author.

Schlechty, P., & Crowell, D. (1983). *Understanding and managing staff development in an urban school system.* Washington, DC: National Institute of Education. (ERIC Document Reproduction Service No. ED 251519).

Shanker, A. (1990). Staff development and the restructured school. In B. Joyce (Ed.), *Changing school culture through staff development* (pp. 91–103). Alexandria, VA: Association for Supervision and Curriculum Development.

Showers, B. (1985, April). Teachers coaching teachers. *Educational Leadership, 42*, 43–48.

Showers, B., Joyce, B., & Bennett, B. (1987, November). Synthesis of research on staff development: A framework for future study and a state-of-the-art analysis. *Educational Leadership, 45*, 77–87.

Siedow, M., Memory, D., & Bristow, P. (1985). *Inservice education for content area teachers.* Newark, DE: International Reading Association.

Smylie, M., & Conyers, J. (1991, Winter). Changing conceptions of teaching influence the future of staff development. *Journal of Staff Development, 12*, 12–16.

Sparks, B. (1983, November). Synthesis of research on staff development for effective teaching. *Educational Leadership, 41*, 65–72.

Stallings, J. (1985). *How effective is an analytic approach to staff development on teacher and student behavior?* Nashville: Vanderbilt University, Peabody College. (ERIC Document Reproduction Service No. ED 267019).

Wade, R. (1984/1985, December-January). What makes a difference in inservice teacher education? A meta-analysis of research. *Educational Leadership, 42*, 48–54.

9

EVALUATING EMPLOYEE PERFORMANCE

Evaluation of performance is a fact of life in most work settings, and even though it may be carried out in a routine and perfunctory manner, few individuals approach the experience with indifference. All employees potentially stand to gain or lose from evaluation, but in schools, it is not only teachers and other personnel who have something at stake. Parents and students can also benefit from evaluation, since evaluation procedures properly carried out lead to improved instruction.

In many schools, teacher evaluation has little effect on teacher performance. It is carried out to fulfill the requirements of state statutes, board policy, or union contracts. In such cases, evaluation

> *does little for teachers except contribute to their weariness and reinforce their skepticism of bureaucratic routine . . . [and] does little for administrators except add to their workload. It does not provide a mechanism for a school system to communicate its expectations concerning teaching. (Darling-Hammond, 1986, pp. 531–532)*

Two of the most common problems in teacher evaluation are the relative infrequency of classroom observations and the unrealistically high ratings teachers receive. A majority of teachers report they are observed by an evaluator no more than twice a year, and a substantial number (about one in six) say they have never been observed. Elementary school teachers and younger teachers, including those with less experience, are observed slightly more often than teachers in middle and high schools and those who have been teaching longer (Educational Research Service, 1985).

All employees tend to rate themselves high on performance and are disappointed when they receive lower ratings from superiors than they feel they deserve. On the whole, however, teachers are rated high. One study showed that about 41 percent of teachers surveyed viewed themselves as belonging in the top 10 percent of all performers (a striking finding in itself); however, an even larger proportion (48 percent) reported that their superiors rated them among the top 10 percent. Put another way, the evaluators rate teachers even higher than they rate themselves.

There is nothing inherently wrong with high ratings, and it is human nature to prefer to avoid giving others low ratings. The problem is that personnel who receive higher ratings than they deserve may be lulled into believing that they have no need for further improvement.

Plan of the Chapter

This chapter deals with the following topics: (1) purposes of performance evaluation, (2) criteria for evaluating school personnel, (3) models of teacher evaluation, (4) characteristics of successful evaluation programs, (5) state-mandated evaluation systems, (6) legal considerations in personnel evaluation, and (7) evaluation of administrative and support personnel.

Purposes of Performance Evaluation

The Joint Committee on Standards for Educational Evaluation (1988) has identified the following purposes for evaluation of educational personnel: "Evaluation of educators should promote sound education principles, fulfillment of institutional missions, and effective performance of job responsibilities, so that the educational needs of students, community, and society are met" (p. 21).

This chapter examines two types of evaluation for educational personnel. *Summative evaluation* refers to assessment carried out for accountability purposes. This type of evaluation is usually conducted annually or semi-annually, and the results are used to make decisions about individuals, such as whether to grant tenure, to seek termination or transfer, to place an individual on a career ladder, or to make a salary adjustment (Educational Research Service, 1978). *Formative evaluation* serves a developmental function. Its purpose is to help an individual employee improve his or her effectiveness on the job by providing feedback and coaching (Educational Research Service, 1978).

The formative and summative sides of performance evaluation are sometimes in conflict. Formative evaluation relies on the creation and maintenance of a bond of trust between the employee and the evaluator. Summative evaluation, because of the high stakes involved and the emphasis on judging, risks undermining the trust that is essential to helping employees learn new job-related behaviors (Wise, Darling-Hammond, McLaughlin, & Bernstein, 1984). Some authorities believe that formative and summative evaluation cannot be reconciled in the same evaluation system and suggest that the two functions should be separated (Knapp, 1982).

Although formative and summative evaluation are the most common reasons for conducting performance evaluations, other purposes are served as well. Evaluation is sometimes used to validate selection criteria, to provide a basis for career planning, and to select individuals to receive merit pay awards or promotions to positions of greater responsibility (Educational Research Service, 1978).

Selecting Summative Instruments

Care must be exercised in selecting or constructing instruments to be used for summative evaluation. When they are used for decisions about individuals, instruments should have high reliability and criterion or predictive validity. *Criterion validity* refers to the degree of relationship between scores on an instrument and employees' subsequent performance on the job.

Reliability refers to whether different evaluators agree in their ratings of the same teacher and whether an individual evaluator is consistent in his or her ratings. Training of evaluators is necessary in order to ensure reliability. Instruments used for summative purposes should also be tested to ensure that they do not discriminate on the basis of teacher gender or race, or produce different results when applied to teaching situations involving variations in subject matter, class size, or type of student (Smith, Peterson, & Micceri, 1987).

Criteria for Evaluating School Personnel

Workers are evaluated on the basis of possessing certain personal characteristics, demonstrating behaviors associated with successful performance, or producing specified results. The characteristics, behaviors, and results used to judge performance are called *criteria*. To identify criteria for use in evaluating an individual in a position, the job model for that position (see Chapter 3) is a logical place to start. The "Priority Actions" and "Results Sought" sections of the job model are useful sources of criteria for performance evaluation. The "Results Sought" section lists outcomes the employee is expected to achieve, and the performance evaluation should be based on the degree to which the employee has successfully attained those results.

Teachers are asked to perform a number of tasks, but none is more important than instruction. For both formative and summative evaluation, attention to instruction is prominent. Accordingly, the main emphasis in this chapter is on evaluating performance of instructional tasks. The model of student learning depicted in Chapter 1 (Figure 1.1) showed that student learning results from teacher behaviors, which in turn are influenced by teacher knowledge and motivation. If the bottom line is student outcomes, why not measure those results directly rather than relying on indirect indicators of teaching effectiveness?

In some occupations, results are readily available and are easily measured. In sales, for example, the best indicator of employee performance is the number of units sold or the dollar value of sales completed during a given period of time. To the sales manager, a salesperson's personal characteristics are less important than the revenue the employee generates. In manufacturing operations, the quantity of a product produced is a measure of employee performance, and in clerical work the number of letters typed or the number of customer questions answered are measures of employee productivity.

However, the "product" of teaching is the content of children's minds. This output is not tangible, nor is it easily attributed to the efforts of a single teacher, since the learner's responses in a given situation are influenced by all previous experiences. Learning outcomes are not easily measured, and cause-effect relationships between teacher behavior and learning are far from clear. Learning gains achieved by a child during the course of a year result in part from the efforts of the current teacher and in part from the child's previous teachers and from experiences outside of school.

Selecting Criteria

The criteria selected for use in evaluating teachers should be supported by research and experience showing they are related to desirable learning outcomes. The evaluator has the task of determining whether a teacher uses validated teaching behaviors and must also judge whether the behaviors are used in appropriate situations. Teaching behaviors cannot be prescribed as a physician would prescribe a drug for an infection; the teacher must understand when a particular behavior is called for and must be able to call it forth at that moment. This decision must take into consideration the teacher's instructional objectives, the types of students in the class, and the situation in the classroom at a given moment (Knapp, 1982).

The evaluator must consider two questions in assessing teaching performance: Is the teacher able to perform the behavior in question? and Does the teacher use the behavior when it is appropriate to do so and not use it when its use is inappropriate? The first question is a matter of knowledge; the second is a matter of judgment.

Five criteria commonly used to evaluate instruction are knowledge of subject, preparation and planning, implementing and managing instruction, student evaluation, and classroom environment. Exhibit 9.1 provides sample items for each of these criteria that are appropriate for summative evaluation purposes.

Knowledge of Subject:
1. Teacher demonstrates understanding of the subject being taught.
2. Teacher helps learners to understand the significance of the topics or activities studied.

Preparation and Planning:
1. Teacher prepares instructional plans on both a daily and long-term basis.
2. Teacher makes advance arrangements for materials, equipment, and supplies needed for instruction.
3. Teacher develops teaching procedures to match lesson objectives.
4. Teacher prepares plans for use by substitute teachers in case it is necessary to be absent.
5. Teacher works cooperatively with colleagues in the school and district to develop curriculum and select instructional materials.

Implementing and Managing Instruction:
1. Teacher makes the goals of instruction clear to all students.
2. Teacher monitors students' performance and adjusts the pace and difficulty level of instruction as needed.
3. Teacher reviews material previously learned before introducing new concepts.
4. Teacher maintains student interest and attention by using a variety of instructional modes.
5. Teacher frequently checks students' understanding of new material and reteaches when indicated.
6. Teacher makes use of students' ideas to introduce new concepts and reinforce previously learned material.
7. Teacher allocates instructional time to activities that produce the highest rates of student learning.
8. Teacher asks content-related questions that most students are able to answer correctly.

Student Evaluation:
1. Teacher regularly assigns, collects, and evaluates students' homework.
2. Teacher uses both teacher-made and standardized tests to check student progress.
3. Teacher provides feedback on student performance.
4. Teacher uses results of student evaluations to modify the pace or scope of instruction.
5. Teacher provides detailed directions for completing assignments and evaluates students' work on the basis of specified criteria.

Classroom Environment:
1. Teacher is fair and impartial in dealings with all students, including those of different races and nationalities.
2. Teacher behaves toward all students in a friendly and accepting manner.
3. Teacher displays high expectations for the amount and quality of work to be performed by students and expresses confidence in their ability.
4. Teacher maintains a businesslike learning climate without being humorless or repressive.
5. Teacher provides a safe, orderly, and attractive environment.
6. Teacher uses nonpunitive and preventive techniques for minimizing disruption and maintaining learner involvement.

**EXHIBIT 9.1   Sample Items for Summative Evaluation of Teachers'
Instructional Effectiveness**

Some of the items in Exhibit 9.1 are behaviors that teachers are always expected to display. Being fair and impartial in dealings with students, making profitable use of class time, and providing a safe classroom environment are behaviors that are always appropriate. Other items from the instrument represent behaviors that teachers should use most of the time but may elect not to use in certain situations. An evaluator must decide whether the decision to use or not to use one of these behaviors was a sound one.

Effective Teaching Research

Some of the items in Exhibit 9.1 are based on effective teaching research, which identifies teacher behaviors associated with student learning. A summary of that research was presented in Chapter 1. For example, setting instructional goals and communicating them to students, monitoring students' progress, and providing feedback are all derived from this research. Teacher expectations for the amount and quality of work produced by students has also been found to be related to increased learning (Brookover et al., 1982). Obtaining information to rate a teacher on these items usually involves classroom observation. Information on other criteria may be obtained from other sources, including conversations with the teacher and others and student test scores (Ryan & Hickcox, 1980).

Surprisingly, teachers often are not sure what standards are used to assess their performance. Almost one-half of teachers in one study reported they did not know what criteria were used to evaluate them, yet the principals in the schools in which these teachers taught indicated that their teachers knew the criteria (Natriello & Dornbusch, 1980/1981). The authors wrote:

> *Informing teachers of the criteria used to evaluate them is of prime importance if procedures for teacher evaluation are to have any impact on modifying and improving teacher performance. If teachers are unaware of the criteria and standards used to judge their performance, they are in no position to direct their energies along lines desired by the school organization. (p. 2)*

Site-based management (SBM) introduces a new element into evaluation of teachers. SBM is based on the assumption that greater autonomy for teachers will translate into increased learning for students. However, that will happen only if teachers are willing to use their new freedom to experiment with new ways of doing their jobs and are willing to abandon techniques that do not work and retain those that do. Teachers who prefer to be told what to do and who will not accept responsibility for the success or failure of their efforts do not fare well in SBM schools. In these schools principals must include among the criteria for evaluating teachers the extent to which teachers assume leadership for improving instruction (Prasch, 1990).

Flags and Alerts

One way to make teachers aware of criteria of effective teaching (and also of practices that should be avoided) has been developed by a school district in Colorado (Maglaras & Lynch, 1988). Desirable practices are labeled "green flags," and those that are to be avoided are called "red alerts." Examples of green flags in mathematics classes include heterogeneous grouping, high student interest and teacher enthusiasm, applying mathematics to real-life situations, use of manipulatives, and availability of enrichment activities for all students.

Red alerts are practices that "if seen consistently, call for explanation; they should usually be avoided" (Maglaras & Lynch, 1988, p. 59). Some examples of red alerts from mathematics are giving no homework or excessive amounts of homework, chalkboard work for no purpose, teacher grading papers while students do homework, no diagnostic testing, students not understanding the purpose of homework assignments, and no use of calculators.

Models of Teacher Evaluation

There are several models of teacher evaluation in use in schools. The assumptions about teaching, and about evaluation of teaching in particular, vary from one model to another. Three models that are in widespread use in schools will be examined in this chapter. They are the remediation, goal-setting, and portfolio models. Exhibit 9.2 presents a brief summary of the major points about each model, including the purpose, objectives, assumptions, and typical methods of operation.

Remediation Model

In districts that use the remediation model, teachers who receive unsatisfactory summative evaluation readings are required to participate in formal remediation sessions to correct identified weaknesses (Pfeifer, 1986). Assistance is provided to the teacher either by the principal or assistant principal or by other teachers or supervisors from the district office. The assistance usually consists of two parts—didactic instruction and classroom practice. The teacher tries new techniques with students while an observer provides performance-related feedback.

Under the remediation model, teachers who fail to meet performance standards may be required to demonstrate improved proficiency in specified areas or face termination. Assistance is provided to help teachers expand their skills, and if no improvement is noted after a reasonable time, action is taken. In some programs a committee of observers, including peers, evaluates the teacher's performance and makes a recommendation

	Remediation Model
Purpose:	Correct identified weaknesses
Objective:	Bring all teachers to a minimum level of performance
Assumption:	It is possible to specify effective teaching behaviors and teach them
Method:	Assess, provide feedback, reassess
Works best with:	Teachers with correctable teaching problems
Evaluator skills:	Ability to provide clear, specific directions
Possible problems:	Heavy demands on evaluator's time; offers no challenge to more competent teachers; deemphasizes variety in teaching

	Goal-Setting Model
Purpose:	Involve teachers and administrators in choosing individualized evaluation criteria
Objective:	Increase teacher autonomy and commitment
Assumption:	Teachers are professionals and able to assess their own developmental needs
Method:	Teacher prepares annual goals statement; principal reviews, approves, or amends it and evaluates teachers' attainment
Works best with:	Experienced, motivated teachers
Evaluator skills:	Ability to help teachers write relevant performance objectives and guide teachers into productive channels; ability to evaluate on individualized criteria
Possible problems:	Weak or overly ambitious goals; lack of consensus on what constitutes attainment of objective

	Portfolio Model
Purpose:	Base teacher evaluation on documented evidence of effective performance
Objective:	Encourage teachers to cooperate in formulating high standards of practice
Assumption:	Teachers will be able to assemble a collection of evidence that will present an accurate picture of teaching skills
Method:	Teachers maintain a file of handouts, tests, reports, student evaluations, documentation of teaching practices, and other information and submit it to the evaluator
Works best with:	Experienced teachers in a variety of areas; especially well suited to teachers of art, music, and vocational subjects
Evaluator skills:	Ability to synthesize a profusion of details into a meaningful assessment of an individual's performance
Possible problems:	Teachers: Time required to prepare portfolio; temptation to impress with flashy packaging Administrators: Amount of time required to review portfolios; need to equate evidence from many different sources

EXHIBIT 9.2   Comparison of Three Evaluation Models

for continued employment or termination. In other districts the evaluation process is carried out in the usual way, with the principal observing and rating the teacher's performance and recommending appropriate action.

An assumption upon which the remediation model is based is that individuals can become effective teachers by mastering a limited number of teaching behaviors identified in the research literature as related to student learning. The object of such a program is to bring all teachers to a minimal level of competence using specific instructional criteria such as those shown in Exhibit 9.1

The remediation model works best with teachers who have correctable problems, who are motivated, and who have the ability to profit from instruction. Classroom management is an example of a problem for which teachers can usually be helped by the remediation approach. The model is most successful when specific corrective techniques can be prescribed and when support is provided to help teachers expand their skills.

The model requires evaluators to spend a good deal of time observing teachers and providing feedback. A few spaced observations over the course of a school year are not sufficient for solving most problems. For severe problems, observations should be scheduled two or more times per week, but for mild deficiencies, biweekly or monthly visit should suffice. Because of these time demands, the remediation model is usually not practical for use with more than a small number of teachers.

A variation of the remediation model that has received relatively little attention to date is to use staff development to remediate identified deficiencies. This approach helps overcome some of the problems with the model of individual remediation described earlier by reducing somewhat the demands on principals' and supervisors' time (Knapp, 1982).

Goal-Setting Model

Goal-setting models of teacher evaluation involve teachers in selecting the criteria for evaluation. In this approach, each teacher selects developmental goals and identifies strategies for achieving them. These strategies might include observing other teachers, coursework, workshop attendance, or readings (Darling-Hammond, 1986). This approach is used most often for formative evaluation purposes. Goal statements are prepared individually but usually reflect a current schoolwide or systemwide emphasis. A typical goal-setting plan requires a participating teacher to meet with the evaluator near the beginning of the school year to establish the year's goals. The principal may approve the proposed workplan as submitted or amend it by adding additional goals or by revising those submitted by the teacher.

Once a goal statement has been agreed to by both parties, it becomes part of the teacher's personnel file and constitutes a contract between the teacher and the district. In most such plans the principal meets with the teacher once or twice during the year to check on progress. If necessary, the goals may be amended or revised at these meetings.

The goal-setting model presumes that teachers are able to identify their own developmental needs. It is not well suited for teachers who are having difficulty with classroom management or instructional organization, and in some schools that use goal-setting plans, teachers with identified deficiencies do not participate (Tesch, Nyland, & Kernutt, 1987).

The plan is most effective when teachers' efforts are coordinated. When all teachers in a school work together toward improving questioning techniques, for example, the impact on students is far greater than when each teacher works independently of colleagues.

Several problems may be encountered in implementing a goal-setting evaluation plan. One potential problem is disparities in the difficulty of the goals chosen by teachers. Some teachers select goals that require little or no effort, whereas others identify objectives so ambitious that they exceed the time and other resources available to accomplish them. Both cases require the evaluator to exercise critical judgment in reviewing proposed workplans.

A second problem may arise at the end of the year when teachers are evaluated on the attainment of their approved goals. Unless the evaluator and teacher have agreed beforehand what will constitute evidence of achievement of goals, disagreements may occur. Evaluating goal attainment is further complicated by questions of equity when a teacher who has set ambitious goals fails to attain them, while another teacher proposes and easily achieves a modest list of accomplishments. Should the evaluator rate the more ambitious teacher lower for failing to reach all of the proposed goals, or should the difficulty of the outcomes be taken into account in evaluating the teachers?

The major strength of the goal-setting approach is that it gives teachers autonomy in identifying and working toward attainment of professional objectives. Autonomy is a key to building commitment (Hawley, 1982). Goal-setting plans involve considerably more teacher input than the remedial plan (described earlier) and allow for flexibility in the determination of the criteria upon which teachers are evaluated. Their success is dependent on whether teachers approach the program seriously. It is most likely to be successful when used with teachers who are experienced and willing to assume responsibility for their professional development.

Portfolio Model

Portfolios are used to document changes in students' academic performance over time, and the idea has been borrowed for use as a device in evaluating teachers. Teachers prepare a portfolio by assembling a variety of information pertaining to their teaching and presenting it to an evaluator. The evaluator—usually the principal—reviews the information, forms a picture of the teacher's style and effectiveness, and prepares an evaluative report on the teacher.

Portfolio evaluation appeals to teachers because it gives them more control of the evaluation process, but many teachers find that collecting the information they need to assemble a file is onerous. The process is somewhat less burdensome if specific guidelines are available showing what to include and what to omit. In most portfolio plans, teachers receive a checklist or outline of the materials they are expected to include in the portfolio. Items on the list include the following (Bird, 1990):

- Lesson plans
- Sample tests
- Sample handouts
- Samples of completed student work
- Grade distributions
- Student evaluations
- Parent comments
- Teaching license or certificate
- Professional development activities
- Documentation of teaching practices, including video tapes of class sessions

Teachers may also be asked to prepare a resumé with information about educational background, professional experience, and professional leadership activities. Leadership activities include serving as an officer for a professional association or taking part in regional or statewide service activities such as serving on accreditation teams. District leadership activities that are included on the resumé include chairing committees for staff development or textbook selection. Activities for the school, such as serving as a mentor to another teacher or serving as grade-level chair or department head, are also featured in the resumé.

Portfolios will be used as one part of the process of assessment leading to national certification of teachers being developed by the National Board for Professional Teaching Standards. The Board has proposed to develop standards for certifying teachers in 34 fields, including limited English proficient, special education, and exceptional needs children. Pilot tests were recently undertaken for early adolescence language arts, the first area of certification to be tested (National Center for Education Statistics, 1993).

The portfolio to be prepared by teachers seeking national certification would document teachers' planning, evaluation, and classroom discussion skills. A written test covering knowledge of the teaching field and a series of assessment exercises would also be required (National Center for Education Statistics, 1993).

Characteristics of Successful Evaluation Programs

McLaughlin (1990) pointed out that improving evaluation requires increasing the district's capacity by equipping principals and other supervisory staff members with the skills and strategies needed to carry out effective evaluation processes. Few principals are able to maintain evaluation systems that result in improved teaching outcomes without encouragement and backing from the district. Districts need to ensure that evaluation processes are integrated in a seamless web with staff development and curriculum development, so that knowledge gained from one process informs the others. District leadership, including commitment of resources, is one of several factors identified as characteristic of successful evaluation programs (Wise et al., 1984).

A second important feature of such programs is training for evaluators. The skills required of evaluators include methods of observation, data collection and analysis, conferencing, report writing, goal setting, and teacher remediation techniques (Conley, 1987). One university, in cooperation with the state administrators' association, recently initiated an experiment to test procedures for training and certifying administrators in teacher appraisal techniques (McIntire, Hughes, & Burry, 1987).

Peer Evaluation

Other attributes of successful teacher evaluation plans are that all participants understand how the system works and are aware of the rationale for the criteria upon which they are evaluated. Understanding and awareness are most easily attained by active teacher participation in the design and implementation of evaluation procedures. Although teachers' unions have traditionally opposed peer evaluation, some have agreed to participate in pilot tests of programs that place teachers in an active role in the evaluation process (Buttram & Wilson, 1987). Most successful evaluation plans distinguish between teachers who have demonstrated competence or mastery and those who are inexperienced or who have identified deficiencies (Conley, 1987).

Evaluating Evaluation Systems

The purpose of performance evaluation is to improve a school's ability to accomplish its mission (Stronge & Helm, 1991). If the system in use fails to do that, it should be changed or replaced. When educators consider ways of improving performance evaluation, they often assume that problems with the system can be resolved by developing a better observation instrument or rating form. In fact, what is usually needed is agreement among those who have a stake in performance evaluation regarding its purpose and uses.

Two types of performance evaluation were described earlier in the chapter. Formative evaluation helps to improve an individual's performance on the job, and summative evaluation is used for decision-making purposes. The process of evaluating a performance evaluation system should begin by determining which of the two types is needed. If both are required, then a decision must be made about whether to attempt to combine both into one plan.

If the evaluation plan is intended primarily to assist in making personnel decisions, the evaluation of it should consider how well it performs that function. Are the recommendations clear-cut and free of ambiguity, and do they result in actions that are sound and defensible? If not, the plan may need an overhaul, or those who administer it may need to be better trained in its use.

A good summative evaluation system specifies minimally acceptable performance, and employees are aware that if their performance does not measure up, they may be in jeopardy of a demotion, a cut in pay, or termination. If the reason for an individual's failure to attain a minimally acceptable level of performance is lack of skill, then consideration should be given to providing training and assistance to help correct the deficiency (Guzzo & Gannett, 1988).

If, on the other hand, the evaluation plan was meant to help improve individual performance, an evaluation of the system should consider first whether it is being used for that purpose. Evaluation plans are sometimes subverted for uses other than the intended ones, and it is not uncommon for data from a formative evaluation system to be used for summative purposes. When that happens, employees lose confidence in the evaluation program and either ignore it or resist participating in it.

If it is determined that the information collected from performance evaluations is being used as intended, the next question is whether individuals are able to perform better as a result. If evaluators can point to specific instances of increased individual effectiveness that can be traced directly to evaluation feedback, it is fair to conclude that the evaluation plan is working. But if no specific evidence is available—even though participants may feel positive about the plan—there is a question about its value. In that case, consideration must be given to ways of changing the operation of the evaluation system in order to bring it into line with the stated purpose.

Characteristics of the evaluator and the quality of information provided to teachers influence the extent to which workers benefit from performance evaluation. An evaluator's credibility, relationship to the employee, and ability to model suggestions have all been found to be positively correlated with the appropriate use of evaluation information. Characteristics of the information received by teachers from evaluation sources, including the quality of suggestions and the persuasiveness of the evaluator's rationale for improvement, are also related to the value of the evaluation process for teachers (Duke & Stiggins, 1990).

Both types of evaluation plans are more likely to be successful if they are accepted and supported by those who are evaluated. Teachers look for three features that they regard as indicators that an evaluation plan is likely to be beneficial. First, teachers consider whether it encourages self-improvement. Second, they judge whether evaluators demonstrate, both in their personal attitudes and in the mechanics of evaluating an individual's performance, appreciation for the complexity of teaching. Finally, they consider whether the procedures employed are fair and likely to provide protection of their rights (Darling-Hammond, Wise, & Pease, 1983).

Administrators should not overlook the motivating potential of performance feedback. Knowledge of results is an important motivator (Lawler, 1973), and feedback sets the stage for new learning by pinpointing areas in which improvement is needed. Performance evaluation is one of the few ways by which teachers receive information about the results of their efforts. They gauge their success in the classroom by how their teaching is rated.

The design of evaluation instruments should take their potential motivating effects into account. Teachers pay heed to the criteria on which they are evaluated and adjust their performance accordingly (Hoenack & Monk, 1990).

State-Mandated Evaluation Systems

Some states have recently instituted mandatory programs for evaluating teachers. Although the plans differ from state to state, they have some common characteristics. In Tennessee, evaluation is tied to a statewide career ladder program (Furtwengler, 1985). Teachers who are candidates for advancement to Career Levels II and III are observed and evaluated by three evaluators using a uniform evaluation system developed by the state. For lower-level positions, district administrators and supervisors evaluate teachers in compliance with state guidelines that specify six criteria for judging teaching effectiveness. The criteria are planning, teaching strategies, evaluation, classroom management, professional leadership, and communication.

The Texas Education Agency developed the Texas Teacher Appraisal System to serve several purposes. Data from teacher observations are used for decisions about contract renewal or placement on a career ladder. The information also serves as an indicator of the need for staff development programs related to particular teaching skills (Barnes, 1987).

The instrument developed by the state education agency in Kentucky for use with that state's teacher career ladder is similar to one used in Texas. The Kentucky instrument consists of six functional areas (planning, management of student conduct, instructional organization and lesson development, presentation of subject matter, verbal and nonverbal communication, and evaluation of students). Unlike the Texas instrument, which consists of items describing behaviors associated with greater student learning or higher student satisfaction, the Kentucky instrument contains both positive and negative indicators.

Because of the states' greater resources, teacher evaluation instruments developed at that level are frequently of higher quality than those that originate at the district level. Evaluation instruments developed in the state of Florida, for example, use research-based items focusing on instructional processes. During the development process, items were tested to establish reliability and job-relatedness and to permit future studies of predictive validity (Florida Coalition for the Development of a Performance Measurement System, 1983).

A study by the Southern Regional Education Board (SREB) (1991) of state-sponsored teacher evaluation systems identified several strengths and weaknesses of these programs. Among the strengths identified by the SREB were the use of research on effective teaching; requiring beginning teachers to demonstrate satisfactory classroom performance prior to initial licensure; introducing a set of common terms and concepts with which to discuss teaching performance; and linking evaluation of teaching with professional development.

The SREB (1991) report also identified some weaknesses of state-sponsored teacher evaluation programs. Among these were the absence of attention to teachers' knowledge of the subject they teach; an overreliance on classroom observation and little use of other means of documenting teaching effectiveness; the failure to assess the relationship between teachers' practices and student outcomes; and the lack of attention to developing ways of identifying the most competent teachers.

Legal Considerations in Personnel Evaluation

Because of tenure, teacher evaluation decisions more often provoke legal challenges than evaluations of other personnel. To protect teachers' rights to procedural fairness, most states impose specific requirements for conducting performance evaluations. Some states require that teachers be notified in advance of the criteria upon which they will be evaluated, and, in case deficiencies are found, that teachers be informed of the nature of the problems. Other requirements establish a minimum number of classroom observations as part of the evaluation process or specify a deadline for completing the process (Webb, 1983). Districts are allowed latitude in establishing performance criteria (McCarthy & Cambron-McCabe, 1987).

Negotiated contracts also contain provisions regulating teacher evaluation. Board negotiators generally prefer to limit such provisions to general descriptions of evaluation procedures and to avoid committing principals to make a specific number of observations, meet specified deadlines for completion of the evaluation process, or notify teachers of performance deficiencies (Deneen, 1980).

However, specifying evaluative criteria either in the contract or in a policy statement has advantages for both the board and for teachers. Publicizing the standards on which teachers will be judged allows teachers to prepare to meet them and allows administrators to assess them. It also avoids reliance on unreliable, invalid, and legally indefensible criteria (Gross, 1988).

Training for evaluators should include information about applicable provisions of state law, state or district policy, and the master contract that affect evaluation. Failure to comply with these requirements can nullify a district's attempt to terminate or place a teacher on probation. Issues related to termination of teachers are examined in more detail in Chapter 15.

Performance Criteria

Legal challenges to evaluation decisions most often take the form of questions about the performance criteria used. Basing unsatisfactory ratings on criteria for which direct links to student learning do not exist are likely to invite legal challenge. Two examples of questionable criteria that are still in use in some districts are appearance or grooming and personal lifestyle. Unless the district is able to show that a teacher's appearance or behavior outside of school has a direct relationship to teaching effectiveness or poses a threat to students, it is unlikely to be successful in a court test (Deneen, 1980).

In reviewing district actions, courts have taken into account, in addition to the factors already enumerated, whether teachers are given an opportunity to correct their weaknesses and whether they are provided with assistance and sufficient time for implementing improvements. Courts may also consider the question of whether the reasons given teachers for unsatisfactory ratings are stated clearly enough to provide direction for correcting deficiencies (Webb, 1983).

The use of student achievement gains to assess teacher performance raises legal questions that are not at issue when other criteria are employed. The use of student test results in teacher evaluation is relatively uncommon, judging by the small number of dismissal cases in which such evidence has been used to document unsatisfactory teacher performance. One authority recommends that student achievement data be used only as supporting evidence for dismissal, not as the sole or primary reason for the action (Groves, 1984, cited in Carter, 1985).

Evaluation of Administrative and Support Personnel

Exhibit 9.3 shows seven criteria that are used to evaluate school administrators. These are generic criteria that can be applied with appropriate adaptations to all administrators, from assistant principal to superintendent. Some of the criteria in the exhibit are taken from the Texas statute that prescribes evaluation of school administrators in that state. For each position to be evaluated, a specific list of duties or results expected would be prepared, and the administrator's performance would be rated against that list.

The scope of duties for which administrators are responsible varies. Principals and superintendents are responsible for all areas, but the director of personnel is primarily responsible only for personnel administration.

Administrators are evaluated by their immediate superiors, and the superintendent is evaluated by the board. Principals in small districts are

1. *Instructional management:* Improves instruction by: (a) monitoring student achievement and attendance and using the data to improve programs, (b) assisting teachers to design effective instructional strategies and select appropriate instructional materials, (c) providing mechanisms for articulation of the curriculum, and (d) supporting programs designed for students with special needs

2. *School/organizational improvement:* Brings about improvement in school programs by: (a) collaborating to develop and achieve consensus for an organizational mission statement, (b) organizing to permit and encourage teamwork among staff members pursuing common goals, (c) encouraging an attitude of continuous improvement in curriculum, instruction, and operations on the part of all staff members, (d) arranging for and promoting opportunities for professional development designed to meet identified needs of staff, and (e) providing current information about innovative programs and technologies to staff members

3. *School/organizational climate:* Fosters a positive climate by: (a) assessing and planning for improvement of the environment, (b) reinforcing excellence, (c) promoting an atmosphere of caring and respect for others, and (d) encouraging broad participation in decisions about school programs and operations

4. *Personnel management:* Manages personnel effectively by: (a) recognizing exemplary performance, (b) encouraging personal and professional growth, (c) administering personnel policies and regulations consistently and fairly and recommending changes when needed, (d) securing necessary personnel resources to meet objectives, and (e) periodically evaluating job performance of assigned personnel

5. *Management of facilities and fiscal operations:* Responsibly manages facilities and fiscal operations by: (a) compiling budgets and cost estimates that enable the organization to accomplish its mission, (b) ensuring that facilities are maintained and upgraded as needed, and (c) overseeing school operations, including attendance, accounting, payroll, and transportation

6. *Student management:* Promotes positive student conduct by: (a) developing and communicating guidelines for student conduct that help students feel safe and valued, (b) ensuring that rules are enforced consistently and without favor, (c) appropriately disciplining students for misconduct, and (d) effecting collaboration among teachers and parents in managing student conduct

7. *School/community relations:* Ensures community support by: (a) clarifying the mission of the school(s) to members of the community, (b) taking an active part in deliberations of school councils and advisory committees, (c) seeking support for school programs from the community, (d) participating in activities that foster rapport between schools and the community

EXHIBIT 9.3   Performance Criteria for Administrators

usually evaluated by the superintendent. In larger districts, they may be evaluated by an assistant or associate superintendent.

Some administrator evaluation plans provide for input from subordinates or others who work with the individual. For example, teachers may be asked to evaluate the principal's instructional leadership or community relations skills. In some systems, administrators design their own evaluation form to collect information from subordinates, and they are encouraged to construct items that will be of use to them in planning professional development activities.

There are sound reasons why subordinates' opinions should not be the sole basis for judging administrative performance, but there are equally convincing arguments in support of giving subordinates a voice. Administrators must on occasion make decisions that leave some subordinates unhappy, and they need to be buffered from the resentment that follows such actions. Nevertheless, information from subordinates can provide a perspective on administrative performance that is not available from other sources.

Since most district office personnel provide support services for the schools, it makes sense to ask teachers and principals to evaluate their performance. Teachers are a valuable source of information about curriculum supervisors and instructional specialists, since they are the recipients of the services provided by those personnel. Principals are in a position to evaluate at least some aspects of the operations of departments of transportation and maintenance.

Summary

Evaluations of educators should promote sound education principles, fulfillment of institutional missions, and effective performance of job responsibilities, so that the educational needs of students, community, and society are met (Joint Committee on Standards for Educational Evaluation, 1988). Performance evaluation may be either formative or summative in nature. Formative evaluations are intended to help individuals perform more effectively; summative evaluations support decisions on promotion, transfer, and termination.

Three models of teacher evaluation used in schools are the remediation model, goal-setting model, and portfolio model. Each serves specific purposes. Successful evaluation programs are characterized by strong district support, including training for teacher evaluators. Legal challenges to evaluation decisions are less likely when teachers are informed about the procedures and the evaluation policy is carefully followed by those responsible for implementing it.

Suggested Activities

1. Three characteristics of evaluation plans that are valued by teachers are (a) protection against arbitrary or biased evaluations, (b) recognition of the complexity of teaching, and (c) provision for professional growth. Describe how you would develop a design for a teacher evaluation plan incorporating these features.

2. Below are goal statements written by four teachers in a school. Imagine that you are the principal of the school and that you use the goal-setting model of evaluation. Prepare a brief response for the author of each goal statement indicating whether the statement is acceptable as written and, if so, how you propose to measure goal attainment. If the statement needs to be amended, suggest how it might be improved.

Teacher A: "I plan to try to have a perfect attendance record this year."

Teacher B: "I will contact the parents of all my students during the first grading period to let them know how their child is doing in school and to offer suggestions on how they can help their child to do better work at school."

Teacher C: "I will attend a professional conference this year (either the teachers' association meeting in April or a conference on teaching talented and gifted students sponsored by the State Department of Education in November)."

Teacher D: "I will take part in a staff development workshop on teaching thinking skills for science in October. I will try out three of the techniques in my class and will share what I learn with other teachers in my department."

3. One of the problems with portfolio evaluations is deciding how to use the information submitted by a teacher in a portfolio. Select three or four items from the list of items to be included in a teacher evaluation portfolio and be prepared to discuss what you might learn from each piece about a teacher's instructional effectiveness if you were the teacher's evaluator. *Example:* Suppose a teacher includes examples of classroom tests in a portfolio. What could you learn about his or her teaching from examining these tests?

4. A frequently heard complaint about summative evaluation plans is that they seldom lead to dismissal of incompetent teachers. Do you agree? If so, explain why you believe it is true. Do you believe the problem is lack of training for those who administer teacher evaluations, opposition from teacher unions contesting the dismissal of members, or courts that are inclined to support teachers' rights over administrators' efforts to improve school performance?

References

Barnes, S. (1987). *The development of the Texas Teacher Appraisal System*. Paper presented at the annual meeting of the American Educational Research Association, Washington, DC. (ERIC Document Reproduction Service No. ED 294323).

Bird, T. (1990). The schoolteacher's portfolio: An essay on possibilities. In J. Millman & L. Darling-Hammond (Eds.), *The new handbook of teacher evaluation* (pp. 241–256). Newbury Park, CA: Sage.

Brookover, W., Beamer, L., Efthim, H., Hathaway, D., Lezotte, L., Miller, S., Passalacqua, J., & Tornatzky, L. (1982). *Creating effective schools.* Holmes Beach, FL: Learning Publications.

Buttram, J. L., & Wilson, B. L. (1987, April). Promising trends in teacher evaluation. *Educational Leadership, 44,* 4–6.

Carter, B. (1985). *High expectations: A policy paper on setting standards for student achievement.* Stanford, CA: Stanford University School of Education, Education Policy Institute.

Conley, D. T. (1987, April). Critical attributes of effective evaluation systems. *Educational Leadership, 44,* 60–64.

Darling-Hammond, L. (1986). A proposal for evaluation in the teaching profession. *Elementary School Journal, 86,* 532–551.

Darling-Hammond, L., Wise, A., & Pease, S. (1983). Teacher evaluation in the organization context: A review of the literature. *Review of Educational Research, 53,* 285–328.

Deneen, J. (1980). Legal dimensions of teacher evaluation. In D. Peterson & A. Ward (Eds.), *Due process in teacher evaluation* (pp. 15–43). Washington, DC: University Press.

Duke, D., & Stiggins, R. (1990). Beyond minimum competence: Evaluation for professional development. In J. Millman & L. Darling-Hammond (Eds.), *The new handbook of teacher evaluation* (pp. 116–132). Newbury Park, CA: Sage.

Educational Research Service. (1978). *Evaluating teacher performance.* Arlington, VA: Author.

Educational Research Service. (1985, September). *Educator opinion poll.* Arlington, VA: Author.

Florida Coalition for the Development of a Performance Measurement System. (1983). *A study of measurement and training components specified in the Management Training Act.* Tallahassee, FL: Author.

Furtwengler, C. (1985). *Evaluation procedures in the Tennessee Career Ladder Plan.* Paper presented at the annual meeting of the American Educational Research Association, Chicago. (ERIC Document Reproduction Service No. ED 259012).

Gross, J. (1988). *Teachers on trial: Values, standards, and equity in judging conduct and competence.* Ithaca, NY: Cornell University, New York State School of Industrial and Labor Relations.

Guzzo, R., & Gannett, B. (1988). The nature of facilitators and inhibitors of effective task performance. In F. Schoorman & B. Schneider (Eds.), *Facilitating work effectiveness* (pp. 21–41). Lexington, MA: Lexington.

Hawley, R. (1982). *Assessing teacher performance.* Amherst, MA: Education Research Associates.

Hoenack, S., & Monk, D. (1990). Economic aspects of teacher evaluation. In J. Millman & L. Darling-Hammond (Eds.), *The new handbook of teacher evaluation* (pp. 390–402). Newbury Park, CA: Sage.

Joint Committee on Standards for Educational Evaluation. (1988). *The personnel evaluation standards: How to assess systems for evaluating educators.* Newbury Park, CA: Sage.

Knapp, M. (1982, March). *Toward the study of teacher evaluation as an organizational process: A review of current research and practice.* Paper presented at the annual meeting of the American Educational Research Association, New York.

Lawler, E. (1973). *Motivation in work organizations.* Monterey, CA: Brooks/Cole.

Maglaras, T., & Lynch, D. (1988, October). Monitoring the curriculum: From plan to action. *Educational Leadership, 46,* 58–60.

McCarthy, M., & Cambron-McCabe, N. (1987). *Public school law: Teachers' and students' rights.* Boston: Allyn and Bacon.

McIntire, R., Hughes, L., & Burry, J. (1987, April). The training and certifying of teacher appraisers. *Educational Leadership, 44,* 62.

McLaughlin, M. (1990). Embracing contraries: Implementing and sustaining teacher evaluation. In J. Millman & L. Darling-Hammond (Eds.), *The new handbook of teacher evaluation* (pp. 403–415). Newbury Park, CA: Sage.

National Center for Education Statistics. (1993). *America's teachers: Profile of a pro-*

fession. Washington, DC: U.S. Department of Education.

Natriello, G., & Dornbusch, S. (1980/1981). Pitfalls in the evaluation of teachers by principals. *Administrator's Notebook, 29*, 1–4.

Pfeifer, R. (1986). *Integrating teacher evaluation and staff development: An organizational approach*. Stanford, CA: Stanford University, Institute for Research on Educational Finance and Governance. (ERIC Document Reproduction Service No. ED 270506).

Prasch, J. (1990). *How to organize for school-based management*. Alexandria, VA: Association for Supervision and Curriculum Development.

Ryan, D., & Hickcox, E. (1980). *Redefining teacher evaluation*. Toronto: Ontario Institute for Studies in Education.

Smith, B., Peterson, D., & Micceri, T. (1987, April). Evaluation and professional improvement aspects of the Florida perfor-mance-measurement system. *Educational Leadership, 44*, 16–19.

Southern Regional Education Board. (1991). *Teacher evaluation programs in SREB states*. Atlanta: Author.

Stronge, J., & Helm, V. (1991). *Evaluating professional support personnel in education*. Newbury Park, CA: Sage.

Tesch, S., Nyland, L., & Kernutt, D. (1987, April). Teacher evaluation—Shared power working. *Educational Leadership, 44*, 26–30.

Webb, L. (1983). Teacher evaluation. In S. Thomas, N. Cambron-McCabe, and M. McCarthy (Eds.), *Educators and the law* (pp. 69–80). Elmont, NY: Institute for School Law and Finance.

Wise, A., Darling-Hammond, L., McLaughlin, M., & Bernstein, H. (1984). *Teacher evaluation: A study of effective practices*. Santa Monica, CA: Rand.

10

COMPENSATION AND REWARDS

Education is a labor-intensive enterprise. A larger share of school funds is spent to pay personnel than for any other purpose. Estimates of the proportion of school budgets allocated for personnel costs range from 60 to 90 percent (Chambers, 1978; Johns, Morphet, & Alexander, 1983; Jacobson, 1987; *How Is Minnesota. . .* , 1993). Personnel funds are expended in accordance with a compensation plan that, if well designed, can help the schools to achieve their strategic goals.

Compensation plans have three broad objectives—to attract, retain, and motivate qualified and competent employees (Cascio & Awad, 1981). It is desirable that a compensation plan be acceptable to taxpayers, who seek assurance that cost-effective compensation procedures are being followed, and to employees, who are concerned that compensation practices are orderly, fair, and consistent.

Plan of the Chapter

Fair and adequate compensation are important issues in personnel management. Districts that offer competitive salaries and benefits are able to attract and hold well-qualified teachers, and equitable compensation plans help them to maintain employee morale and motivation. This chapter deals with the following topics: (1) sound compensation plans, (2) single salary schedule, (3) attracting and holding employees, (4) adequacy of teacher pay, (5) balance in teachers' salaries, (6) equity in teacher pay, (7) alternative pay plans, (8) keeping costs under control, (9) administrators' salaries, and (10) constructing a salary schedule.

Sound Compensation Plans

Sound compensation plans have six features. They are externally competitive, are internally equitable, are internally balanced, offer incentive, limit cost, and provide adequately for employees' needs (Cascio & Awad, 1981). These six features help to achieve three organizational imperatives described by Katz (1973)—attracting and retaining members, obtaining commitment, and motivating members to perform role-related behaviors and respond with innovative behavior when appropriate.

Competitiveness improves a district's ability to attract and retain workers; adequacy and balance are important for increasing employee commitment and retention; and equity and incentive help a district to motivate members to perform role-related tasks and to respond with innovative behavior. The sixth factor, cost, impinges on a district's ability to sustain a compensation program.

Single Salary Schedule

It has been estimated that 99 percent of all teachers in the United States teach in districts that use single salary schedules (Murnane & Cohen, 1986). A single salary schedule uses only two factors in determining the salaries of all employees in each job classification: experience and level of education. Historically, the single salary plan is fairly young. The first use of the idea occurred in 1920, when Lincoln (Nebraska), Denver, and Sioux City (Iowa) put single salary schedules into effect. The idea spread rapidly; by 1927, 165 cities had adopted the plan (Morris, 1972).

Teachers' organizations pushed for the adoption of the single salary plan as a way of achieving a more professionalized teaching force. Supporters argued that the plan would encourage professional growth, contribute to a feeling of unity and satisfaction among teachers, equalize pay for men and women, increase tenure, attract better-quality teachers to elementary schools, and encourage teachers to teach at that level rather than aspire to teach in high school.

Critics suggested that the single salary plan was contrary to the law of supply and demand and that it was a "subterfuge" invented by administrators who wished to be freed of the burdensome task of rating teachers on merit. Those who were against the idea argued that elementary teachers did not need extensive educational preparation and that educational attainment in itself was not a criterion of teaching ability. Their bottom-line argument was that the cost of the single salary proposal was excessive (Morris, 1972).

Districts that use the single salary schedule sometimes provide a fixed dollar increment at each step. The increment represents a proportionally larger adjustment for teachers near the bottom of the scale as compared to those near the top. To provide step increments that are proportionally equal, many districts use indexed schedules in which the dollar amounts vary but the rate of increase is fixed.

Since attrition is highest in the first few years after an individual is hired (Mark & Anderson, 1978), it would seem to make sense to provide proportionally larger raises to teachers near the low end of the scale and smaller increases to those at the top in order to hold teachers who might otherwise leave. However, the evidence for the effectiveness of such an approach is not strong. Jacobson (1987) found that in the two regions of New York state that he studied, proportionally larger increases in the middle of the scale were more strongly related to retention of teachers than were adjustments at either top or bottom.

Critics claim that the single salary schedule lacks motivational power. None of the three motivational theories described in Chapter 6 would predict that the single salary schedule would be an effective motivator. Since the single salary schedule provides equal compensation for teachers with similar levels of experience and education without regard to effort, equity theory would regard it as demotivating for highly productive teachers.

Expectancy theory suggests that incentives must be contingent on performance in order to have a motivating effect on employees, but most single salary plans grant salary increases automatically as employees gain additional experience. Raises are not contingent on performance. Thus, expectancy theory would predict a dampening effect on motivation from a single salary pay plan.

Only goal-setting theory would regard the single salary schedule as neutral in its effect on motivation. In goal-setting theory, compensation is important to motivation only if it serves to make goals clearer. Since there is no strong relationship between performance goals and single salary plans, the theory would predict no motivational effect on employees.

Defenders of the single salary schedule acknowledge that it has weaknesses, but argue that there is no alternative approach that does not have even more problems. Later in this chapter, three proposals for changing the way teachers are compensated will be examined. These alternatives are merit pay, incentive pay, and career ladders.

It is unlikely that the single salary schedule will disappear. Its widespread use and strong appeal to teachers and many administrators militate against its being replaced. However, we can expect to see new models of teacher compensation being adopted by school districts.

Attracting and Holding Employees

A district's compensation is externally competitive when the district is able to attract a sufficient number of qualified applicants to fill all of its vacancies. Typically, districts in the same regional labor market offer salaries that are reasonably close. One district may offer salaries that are lower than the prevailing level in the region and yet be able to attract the employees it needs if it has offsetting advantages that help compensate for the lower salaries.

Offered salary is probably the single most important factor that applicants consider in making a decision about a job. There is some evidence that salary plays a more important role in decisions of beginning teachers than it does for experienced teachers (Jacobson, 1989). A possible explanation is that new teachers lack the information to make knowledgeable judgments about such factors as fringe benefits and working conditions.

In most districts with single salary schedules, regular increases are provided for the first 12 or 15 years a teacher is employed. After that, longevity increases are scheduled every fifth year or so. Practically speaking, however, teachers in the United States reach the peak of their earning power within 15 years following their entry into the field. This is in contrast to other professions, in which salaries continue to rise throughout most of one's career.

A salary schedule may be made more competitive by increasing salaries across the board or by providing targeted increases. If the district is losing experienced teachers, it may decide to provide targeted increases at the upper end of the salary schedule. On the other hand, if it is having problems attracting beginning teachers, the decision may be made to raise salaries at the bottom end of the schedule.

Another approach is to add more steps to the schedule. Experience increments might be scheduled for 20 rather than 15 years. Experience increments average about 4 percent per year (Bacharach, Lipsky, & Shedd, 1984), so adding 5 additional steps onto a 15-step scale, each providing a 4 percent increase, results in a top-of-the-scale compounded figure that is 21.7 percent higher than the 15-step maximum. However, as long as teachers' salaries lag behind those in other occupations, administrators will be under pressure to maintain or decrease the number of steps in the schedule rather than to increase them.

Many workers discovered that inflation consumed their salary increases during the 1970s. By the end of the decade, many were no better off, and some were worse off in terms of buying power, than they had been when the decade began. The losses in real income were more severe for teachers than for members of other occupations (Bacharach et al., 1984). Some of the ground lost by teachers during the 1970s was regained in the 1980s. The National Education Association reported that teachers' salaries rose more in purchasing power between 1984 and 1986 than at any time since the 1950s ("NEA Reports Sharp Rise," 1986).

Between 1988 and 1990, the average salary in the United States for a teacher with a bachelor's degree and no teaching experience increased from $18,035 to $19,931 (National Center for Education Statistics, 1993b), just enough to keep up with inflation. However, between 1989 and 1992, the average salary of all instructional staff members actually decreased in about one-half of the states (Augenblick, Van de Water, & Fulton, 1993). The salary increases won by teachers during the 1980s moved teaching into a slightly more competitive position with respect to other occupations, but salaries for teachers continued to lag behind those of most occupations that require a bachelor's degree.

In 1990–91, college graduates with degrees in teaching were paid on average $10,000 less those individuals who majored in computer science and $6,100 less than persons with degrees in mathematics or physical science. However, teachers fared better in comparison with graduates holding degrees in biology, communications, and public affairs. Biology majors averaged annual salaries that were about $1,400 more than teachers, but individuals with degrees in communications or public affairs both earned slightly less, on average, than teachers (National Center for Education Statistics, 1993b).

One option available to teachers to increase their income is to obtain an advanced degree. Districts offer salary increments of about 5 percent of the base salary to teachers who earn a master's degree.

Reasons for Low Salaries

To what can the disparity between teachers' salaries and the salaries of workers in other occupations with comparable educational requirements be attributed? In part, the decline in teachers' salaries during the 1970s was the market's response to an oversupply of teachers. However, even during periods of short supply, teachers make relatively lower salaries than members of most other comparable occupations.

Teachers, of course, work fewer days per year than full-time employees in most other fields. They are on the job between 182 and 190 days per year (Educational Research Service, 1985), compared to about 225 days per year for most other workers—a difference of about 17 percent. But teachers salaries' appear to be lower than expected, even when this difference is taken into account.

One factor that appears to contribute to low salaries in teaching is the composition of the teaching force. Bird (1985) used Census Bureau data to compare salaries of teachers to those of persons with similar levels of education employed outside of teaching. Mean income from wages for the nonteaching group was $19,707 in 1983, compared to $14,145 for teachers. The nonteaching group had somewhat less education (16.3 years compared to 17.7 years) but included more males (60.2 percent versus 20.0 percent) and more Whites (88.6 percent versus 79.0 percent).

On an annualized basis, teachers did about as well as a nonteaching group of workers with characteristics similar to those found in teaching, but they did less well than nonteachers with different demographic characteristics. Bird's conclusion was that sex discrimination accounted for the lower salaries in teaching and concluded that "the challenge facing education policymakers today is to seek a new teacher pay comparability strategy to fit a market in which the results of a history of sex discrimination may be disappearing" (Bird, 1985).

Adequacy of Teacher Pay

Adequacy refers to whether employees receive sufficient pay and benefits to permit them to maintain a decent standard of living. Workers whose salaries are too low to permit them to afford a middle-class lifestyle often take second jobs in order to supplement their earnings. This practice, called *moonlighting*, is more common among teachers than members of other occupations. About one-fourth of teachers in public schools earned income from a second, nonteaching job during the 1990–91 school year, and one-third had earnings from extra duty assignments for the school system, including coaching athletic teams or sponsoring student clubs. Teachers earned an average of $4,400 from nonteaching jobs and $1,900 from school-related extra duty assignments in that year (National Center for Education Statistics, 1993a).

There has been relatively little research on the extent of moonlighting among teachers or of its effects on the individual's attitudes toward the primary job. In one of the few studies of this phenomenon, researchers found that about 13 percent of the 329 Texas teachers they surveyed held second jobs after school or on weekends and holidays. They worked nearly 13 hours a week and earned slightly more than $3,500 a year at the second job. About 31 percent of the respondents also worked during the summer breaks, with average earnings of about $1,900. Teachers who moonlighted year-round thus increased their income by about $5,400 on average (Henderson & Henderson, 1986).

The most common type of outside employment among teachers in the Texas study was sales, reported by 35 percent of respondents. Next in frequency of mention were school-related work (24 percent) and music (15 percent).

Cross-National Comparisons

How do U.S. teachers do economically in comparison with their counterparts in other parts of the world? One recent study compared the economic situations of teachers in the United States and Japan (Barro & Lee, 1986). The findings showed that beginning teachers in Japan make 20 to 25 percent less than the average beginning teachers in U.S. schools, but that the lower starting salaries are balanced by long-term gains.

A Japanese teacher with the equivalent of a bachelor's degree who remains in teaching will eventually earn three times the beginning salary, compared to two times or less in most school districts in the United States. The reason for this substantial difference in the long-term rewards of teaching in the two systems has to do with the "topping out" of teachers' salaries. After about 15 years, U.S. teachers no longer qualify for annual increments, but Japanese teachers continue to receive increases each year until retirement.

Balance in Teachers' Salaries

Although salaries are the most visible part of personnel costs and the item that employees most often consider in deciding whether to accept a job offer, they are only part of the total compensation package. Fringe benefits are an important part of the compensation picture. Benefits include immediate and deferred payments employees are entitled to receive by virtue of working in a particular organization. The best known benefits are various kinds of leave, medical and hospital insurance, and retirement contributions.

Three types of benefits are common in school districts:

1. *Collateral benefits:* These are direct and indirect forms of compensation that are received without expenditure of additional effort. Examples are sick leave, medical insurance, and retirement contributions. More than 95 percent of public schools in the United States offered medical insurance to teachers in 1990, retirement benefits were available to teachers in 99 percent of the schools, and dental insurance was offered by 67 percent of the schools (National Center for Education Statistics, 1993a).

2. *Nonsalary payments:* These are supplementary payments made to individuals who perform duties above and beyond their regular assignments. Coaching and sponsoring various activity groups are the most common examples of nonsalary payments. Data from the National Center for Education Statistics (1993a) showed that public school teachers who performed extra-duty assignments earned $1,940, on average, during the 1990–91 school year.

3. *Noneconomic benefits:* This category includes any features of a job that make it more attractive, whether or not the employer thinks of them as benefits. Intrinsic rewards are included here. Examples of noneconomic benefits are small class size, duty-free lunch, a planning period, and motivated students.

The cost of fringe benefits averages between 20 and 30 percent of teachers' salaries. A survey of Illinois schools showed that the average cost of fringe benefits in that state was almost 28 percent of the average teaching salary for the year 1983–84 (Booth, Carlson, & Johnson, 1985).

The cost of health insurance has increased rapidly in recent years. In the state of Minnesota, health insurance benefits for professional staff members rose 58 percent between 1986 and 1991, almost four times the rate of increase in total spending for personnel salaries and benefits during the same period of time (*How Is Minnesota. . .* , 1993).

Equity in Teacher Pay

The Equal Pay act of 1963 requires employers to refrain from discriminating against female employees by paying them less than males are paid for performing the same or similar jobs. Few cases involving teachers have been decided by the courts under the Equal Pay Act, since teachers' salaries are commonly assumed to be gender neutral. However, a study of teachers' salaries found that female teachers in public high schools school earned $1,134 less, on average, than their male counterparts. The discrepancy in salaries of female and male teachers was even greater in private high schools.

The disparity persisted even when differences in educational attainment, experience, and teaching field were taken into account. The researchers concluded that the differences were the result of male teachers receiving more credit for previous teaching experience than females (Bradley, 1989).

In the few cases involving charges of unequal pay for female teachers under the Equal Pay Act, courts have held that schools may not pay female coaches less than male coaches for assignments that involve similar levels of effort. In one case, a plan to provide a salary supplement for male heads of household was struck down (McCarthy, 1983).

Since the passage of the Equal Pay Act, some progress has been made in closing the gap between men's and women's incomes, but discrepancies remain. Women who work in occupations that are dominated by women, including teaching, nursing, and secretarial work, generally earn less than men. However, a female employee has no redress under the Equal Pay Act unless her employer pays a male more to do a similar job.

Comparable Worth

In an attempt to address discrepancies that are based on occupational groupings, some women have sued, charging discrimination under Title VII of the Civil Rights Act. In one of these cases, nursing supervisors in Denver claimed they were discriminated against because they were grouped for pay purposes with other jobs held predominantly by women rather than being placed in a class of jobs that included more males. The nursing supervisors claimed that they performed work that was equal in importance to that performed by men and should be paid equally. The concept involved in this case is comparable worth. To date, courts have avoided requiring a comparable worth standard (Landy, 1985).

Aside from adequacy, employees value equity more highly than any other feature of compensation. Opposition of teachers to merit pay is based on a fear of potential inequity. There is no widely accepted objective measure of equity, since people's perceptions vary depending on their definitions of their own and others' contributions and rewards. Moreover, objective judgments of equity are difficult when individuals have access to incomplete information about an organization's compensation policy and practices.

Alternative Pay Plans

Employers use a variety of compensation plans designed to increase employee motivation and commitment or to strengthen the relationship of pay to performance. Business corporations use compensation to help them achieve certain strategic objectives. Pay-for-performance plans, group and individual incentive plans, profit sharing, and various types of bonuses are widely used by private employers.

The field of education has been more cautious than the private sector about adopting alternative pay arrangements. The forms of alternative compensation used most widely in schools are merit pay, incentive pay, and career ladders. These plans are described in detail here.

Taxpayers are in favor of providing differentiated pay for teachers. In their report entitled *Time for Results,* the National Governor's Association recommended developing compensation plans that would recognize differences in function, competence, and performance of teachers (Alexander, 1986). However, taxpayers and politicians often are not aware of the difficulties involved in implementing alternative pay plans.

There is confusion regarding terminology in discussions of alternative pay plans. Terms such as *pay-for-performance, incentive pay, merit pay,* and *career ladder* are used interchangeably and without precision in the media. The terms to be used in this chapter will be defined by reference to features that differentiate them from other types of compensation plans. You should be aware that the descriptions given here are pure types and that in practice a particular plan may incorporate features of two or even three of these types.

Merit Pay

Merit pay is a form of compensation in which workers who perform similar duties are paid on the basis of the quality of performance (Thornton, 1986). Compensation increases may be awarded to individuals or to groups and may be added to an individual's salary or given as a one-time bonus (Milkovich & Milkovich, 1992). Merit pay awards in education are based on performance ratings by a principal or supervisor using either input or output factors or both (American Association of School Administrators, 1983a).

Input factors are teacher characteristics such as cooperation and enthusiasm, or performance factors such as using specified teaching techniques. Output evaluations base merit increases on the results of instruction, usually a measure of student cognitive gains, such as scores on a standardized achievement test. Teachers may be rated individually or collectively for eligibility for merit pay.

Merit pay was widely used in the United States in the 1920s and 1930s but its use faded when districts converted to single salary schedules. A 1978 survey showed that about 4 percent of districts had merit pay plans in effect for teachers and that another 4.7 percent were considering instituting such plans (Thornton, 1986).

Proponents of merit pay believe that it motivates teachers to improve their performance. They argue that merit pay is in widespread use in industry and that it is successful there. This claim is sometimes disputed. Bishop (1986) estimated that only about 1.2 percent of industrial employees worked under piece-rate plans and that 1.9 percent worked on commission. Merit pay generates considerable opposition from teachers' unions, although the president of the American Federation of Teachers has specified conditions under which his union would be willing to support merit pay (McGuire & Thompson, 1984).

Objections to merit pay for teachers focus on the subjective nature of teacher evaluation and the divisive nature of the competitive motives merit pay is believed to arouse. Since there are few truly objective measures of teaching performance, merit pay plans usually rely on principals' judgments regarding which teachers deserve merit raises. This requires trust on the part of teachers in the principal's ability to correctly interpret the meaning of the criteria and accurately assess the degree to which each teacher meets them (Lawler, 1981). Some teachers lack confidence that principals can be trusted to administer merit pay plans equitably, even though most administrators themselves believe they are capable of doing so.

Another objection to merit pay is voiced by those who fear that the competition for salary increases will demoralize employees and destroy cooperation. This threat is felt to be especially great in pay plans with a predetermined limit on the number of workers who qualify (Ballou & Podgursky, 1993).

However, a recent nationwide study of attitudes of teachers toward merit pay found that, contrary to popular opinion, a majority of teachers (55.2 percent) approved of merit pay, which was defined as a "pay bonus for exceptional performance in a given year" (Ballou & Podgursky, 1993, p. 53).

Incentive pay and career ladders were favored by even larger percentages. Additional pay for additional duties was approved by almost 90 percent of respondents, additional pay for teaching in a "high priority" (inner-city) school was endorsed by more than three-fourths of the respondents, and career ladders received approval of more than 70 percent. Additional pay for teaching in a shortage field, such as mathematics or science, was approved by almost 54 percent of the respondents (Ballou & Podgursky, 1993).

A number of school districts in the United States have tried merit pay and abandoned it after a short time. One of the few plans to survive more than a few years is located in a St. Louis County (Missouri) school district, where it has been in operation since 1953. An important feature of the plan, and one that probably contributes to its longevity, is the attention given by administrators to teacher evaluation procedures. Principals' evaluation reports are carefully reviewed by district officials, who suggest ways that principals can improve their assessment procedures (Natriello & Cohn, 1983).

There is a need for research that examines the effects of merit pay on employee attitudes and performance. Compensation experts point out that the amount and timing of a merit increase have an effect on its motivational value, but little is known about how to structure merit pay plans in order to produce gains in worker output (Milkovich & Milkovich, 1992) or employee acceptance of the philosophy of merit pay.

Expectancy theory and goal-setting theory (Chapter 6) propose two possible explanations for merit pay's potential effectiveness as a motivator. Goal-setting theory suggests that merit pay and incentive pay plans motivate employees by making goals and expectations clear. Expectancy theory implies that employees are motivated to obtain the incentive (in this case, increased salary).

Incentive Pay

Incentive pay is a salary supplement or bonus paid to teachers who fulfill specified conditions established by the district to help it attain certain goals or solve particular problems (American Association of School Administrators, 1983a). Examples include payments to teachers who are willing to teach in schools with high concentrations of educationally disadvantaged children or who teach hard-to-fill positions teaching subjects such as mathematics or science. Incentive pay is also given by some districts to teachers who attain certain educational or professional growth objectives. The amount of these awards varies. For teaching in a difficult school, a teacher may receive a bonus of $1,500 to $2,000 per year, and for achieving professional growth objectives, the payment is often equivalent to the cost of tuition for a graduate college course.

Houston Independent School District successfully used an incentive plan to recruit teachers with scarce subject specialties. The Houston plan paid salary supplements ranging from $600 to $1,000 per year for teachers of mathematics, science, bilingual, and special education.

Career Ladders

The best known example of a career ladder is that adopted statewide in Tennessee in 1984. That plan provides five levels of teaching competence: Probationary, Apprentice, and Career Levels I, II, and III. Teachers on the top three rungs of the ladder earn from $1,000 to $7,000 per year in salary supplements (Thornton, 1986). Advancement in the Tennessee plan is based on performance and experience. Teachers move from the probationary to the apprentice stage in one year and remain at that level for three years. A minimum of five years of experience at career levels I and II is required before a teacher can advance to the next higher step. All promotions on the ladder require demonstration of satisfactory performance and a review of performance conducted by assessment teams that consist of teachers, principals, and supervisors (Thornton, 1986).

Most career ladder plans, including the one in Tennessee, assign additional responsibilities to teachers as they advance up the ladder. These duties may include supervising other teachers or planning and leading curriculum or staff development activities.

Advantages and Disadvantages

All compensation plans have both advantages and disadvantages. Single salary schedules have the advantage of being easily administered and acceptable to most teachers. These plans also have one major weakness: They fail to attract and hold enough high-quality teachers.

Merit pay plans have three potential advantages. By rewarding employees who have above-average productivity, they help to attract quality employees, provide an incentive for greater effort by current employees, and reduce the level of attrition among more productive employees (Bishop, 1986).

However, any plan that bases compensation on performance evaluation is likely to encounter problems. It is expensive to obtain data on worker productivity, and the information that is obtained is often low in reliability. Even in industry, supervisory ratings are often used to assess productivity, and research shows that those ratings are not very reliable. An added complication of the use of merit pay for teachers is the evidence that teacher performance is not consistent over time. Teachers who achieve above-average learning gains with their students one year may be average or even below average the next.

Aside from the technical difficulties involved in implementing merit pay, there are questions about the soundness of the psychological assumptions upon which it is based. Some researchers (Deci, 1972) have found that activities that are intrinsically motivating—that is, those that are performed only for the pleasure of performing them—lose some of their intrinsic motivation if a reward is offered for performing them. Moreover, the research has shown that individuals who are given tangible rewards for engaging in activities that are intrinsically motivating engage in the activities less often after they are rewarded. Some educators interpret these findings to mean that teachers who derive pleasure from teaching may experience less satisfaction from it when merit pay is implemented, and hence may lose interest in teaching well.

One other potential problem with merit pay was cited by Bishop (1986). He noted that monetary rewards and promotions increase an employee's visibility and make the person more attractive to other employers, thus raising the possibility of increased turnover among more productive workers. He proposed using less visible incentives, including praise, desirable job assignments, increased autonomy, participation in selecting coworkers, and opportunities for travel, in place of financial rewards.

Nonsalary rewards may have greater motivational potential for teachers than salary bonuses, according to a study of teachers' preferences of performance rewards (Kasten, 1984). That study involved 26 teachers, 15 of whom reported no interest in merit pay. "Strong interest" in tuition grants was reported by 20 of the teachers, and 21 were strongly interested in the opportunity to have time off to attend conferences. The opportunity to work with student teachers was also of strong interest to 20 of the teachers, and 21 reported a strong interest in receiving money to be spent on classroom enrichment.

One of the problems with merit pay is that many more employees believe they should receive awards than qualify for them. A recent study of teachers' ratings of themselves and their colleagues (Hoogeveen & Gutkin, 1986) found that teachers rated themselves higher than they rated their peers and that their self-ratings were higher even than the average ratings given all teachers by the principal.

A question investigated by Hoogeveen and Gutkin (1986) had to do with whether teachers agree on the identity of superior performers. In all three of the small elementary schools involved in the study, one teacher was nominated by more than one-half of his or her colleagues as deserving merit pay. This finding suggests that there is a reasonably high degree of consensus in some faculties. Whether similar results would be obtained in larger elementary schools or in high schools, however, is not known.

Career ladders are meant to provide opportunities for teachers to move through a series of positions of expanding responsibility, greater task variety, and increasingly attractive monetary rewards. They are designed for the purpose of attracting and retaining able teachers. However, career ladders, like merit pay, are more expensive to operate than single salary schedules and, if not adequately funded, can result in greater competition and less cooperation among teachers. Moreover, if advancement on a career ladder is based on the results of performance evaluation, teachers are likely to experience the same concerns that they report for merit pay (Timar, 1992).

Incentive pay has the advantage of being effective in attracting better-quality applicants for positions that are normally difficult to fill. Incentive pay has no effect on teacher performance, except indirectly, and it is more costly than the single salary schedule (although potentially less expensive than merit pay or career ladders).

Keeping Costs under Control

A critical criterion by which a compensation plan is judged is cost. If the cost is excessive, proposed increases will have little support from either taxpayers or board members. Whether the cost of a proposed pay plan is reasonable or excessive depends on one's point of view. What is reasonable to the members of a union may be considered excessive by the board. The objective must be to maximize the five criteria described earlier in this chapter while at the same time maintaining acceptable cost limits.

The American Association of School Administrators (1983b) reported that beginning salaries for teachers would have to be increased an average of 35 percent in order to attain the goal of making teachers' salaries competitive with those paid in other professions with similar educational requirements. The increases required to reach such a goal would have ranged from a low of 14.2 percent to a high of 58.5 percent in the 28 districts surveyed.

The cost of merit pay and other similar programs depends on the size of the awards and the number of teachers who qualify for them. The problem is illustrated by the experience of Fairfax County (Virginia) school officials. During a one-year pilot test of a proposed merit pay program, school officials discovered that the number of teachers who qualified for a 10 percent salary increase on the basis of performance evaluations exceeded the predicted number by 3.4 percent. The additional cost to the district, had the plan been in effect, would have exceeded one-half million dollars ("Fairfax Officials," 1987).

The Educational Research Service (1983) reported that districts with operational merit pay plans gave awards to teachers ranging from $28 to $6,000. The average of the lowest amount received by a teacher in the surveyed districts was $804, and the average of the highest amounts was $1,738. An average of 26 percent of teachers received awards. The definition of merit pay used in that survey differs from the one presented in this chapter, and the costs would have varied somewhat if the definition used here had been applied.

A rough estimate of the cost of merit pay can be obtained by multiplying the anticipated average award by the number of teachers expected to qualify. Using the midpoint of the high-low award range reported by Educational Research Service as the average award size and 26 percent as the number of recipients, a district could anticipate investing about $24,300 per year for each 100 teachers employed ($934 × .26 × 100). Giving larger awards or giving awards to more teachers would increase the cost, and smaller or fewer awards would lower it.

Administrators' Salaries

Salaries for administrators represent about 8.5 percent of the average district budget, according to one study (Chambers, 1978). Table 10.1 shows the minimum (starting) salaries for nine administrative positions in 1993–94 for districts with the largest (25,000+) and smallest (300–2,499) enrollments.

The data in Table 10.1 show that for five of the six district office positions in the table, administrators in large districts earned higher salaries than those who worked in the smallest districts. However, principals and subject

TABLE 10.1   1993–94 Minimum Salaries of Selected
Administrators in Large and Small School
Districts and Ratios

	Large Districts	Small Districts	Ratio
Superintendent	$107,954	73,738	1.46
Asst. Superintendent	62,051	53,282	1.16
Director of Instruction	53,716	44,779	1.20
Director of Finance	53,877	36,412	1.48
Director of Personnel	52,509	41,799	1.26
Instructional Supervisor	40,539	44,003	.92
Elementary Principal	45,691	47,737	.96
Middle School Principal	40,580	44,336	.92
High School Principal	42,421	47,161	.90

Source: Salaries Paid Professional Personnel in Public Schools, 1993–94. Arlington,
VA: Educational Research Service, 1994.
   Note: Large districts are those with enrollments of 25,000 or more students; small districts enroll between 300 and 2,499 students.

matter supervisors in small school districts had higher starting salaries than their counterparts in the large districts. Superintendents and directors of finance in large districts earned almost 1.5 times the salaries of their counterparts in small districts, whereas principals in large districts earned 4 to 10 percent less than principals in small districts.

Merit pay for administrators is more common than for teachers. A 1978 study found that 15.3 percent of school districts offered merit pay for administrators, compared to only 4 percent with merit pay plans for teachers (Kienapfel, 1984). At least one state has adopted a statewide career ladder plan for administrators and supervisors (North Carolina Department of Public Instruction, 1984). The North Carolina plan consists of four steps, beginning with Provisional status and advancing through Career Statuses I, II, and III.

An individual must spend a minimum of two years at each step before being eligible to advance to the next higher level. Advancement is based on satisfactory performance and demonstrated professional growth, including completion of continuing education credits appropriate for the position and related to the needs of the individual (Kienapfel, 1984). Advancement from one Career Status level to the next results in a salary increase of 10 percent in addition to the normal 5 percent step increment.

Some districts have abolished salary schedules for principals and offer only minimum and maximum salaries. Salaries are determined individually, based on several factors such as the size of the school served and the quality of the individual's performance.

Constructing a Salary Schedule

Salary schedules are usually developed by firms that specialize in employee compensation. The task is one that requires a considerable amount of expertise and a great deal of data. The first decision to be made in developing a salary schedule is the number of grades or levels to be included. Henderson (1985) defined pay grades as convenient groupings of a wide variety of jobs that are similar in difficulty and level of responsibility but with little else in common. The number of grades to be incorporated into a schedule varies depending on the number of employee specialties and the extent to which the district administration wishes to be able to make small distinctions in compensation.

Each grade is subdivided into 10 to 15 steps to provide for differences in experience and level of educational attainment. The different between the lowest step in adjacent grades in school district salary schedules typically ranges from 2.5 to 4 percent, and there is obviously considerable overlap across grades.

The procedure used to establish salaries for dissimilar jobs is *job evaluation* (Landy, 1985). A job evaluation involves these steps:

1. Select the jobs to be evaluated and choose the evaluation factors. The factors should be skills or abilities that are required to varying degrees in all of the positions and for which salary differences can be justified. An example of a factor that is frequently used is education; people who hold jobs requiring higher levels of education receive higher salaries than those whose jobs require less education, other things being equal.
2. Collect information about the positions from a variety of sources, including interviews, job descriptions, and observations.
3. Using information collected in step 2, rate the jobs being evaluated by assigning points for each criterion. Sum the points to obtain a total for each position. This activity is normally carried out independently by members of a committee who compare their ratings after they are completed and discuss differences until a consensus is reached.
4. Rank the positions by point totals agreed upon in step 3. Select a few key positions and assign salaries to those by investigating salaries for similar positions in nearby districts.
5. Assign salaries to the remainder of the positions by comparing the point totals for those positions to the point totals for the key positions.

Job evaluation should result in a salary schedule that is internally consistent and externally competitive. It is necessary to repeat the procedure about every 10 years because jobs change over time and their relative importance to the district shifts. As duties evolve and new specialties emerge, some positions must be moved up or down on the scale to preserve internal competitiveness.

Summary

A well-designed compensation plan should help a district to accomplish the objectives of attracting and holding employees and helping employees to engage in reliable task-related behavior and, when appropriate, to be spontaneous and innovative in carrying out a job. Six features of a sound compensation plan are competitiveness, adequacy, balance, equity, incentive, and reasonable cost. A competitive salary structure enables an organization to attract employees; adequacy and balance help to hold them; and equity and incentive assist in motivating employees to higher productivity. Reasonable cost permits the organization to continue to offer an attractive compensation package to its employees.

Most school districts in the United States use single salary schedules, in which teachers are paid on the basis of education and experience. Three other approaches to teacher compensation are being tested in some districts. Merit pay rewards teachers who are judged above average in effectiveness; career ladders establish steps in which teachers may advance in both income and prestige; and incentive pay involves salary supplements for teachers who possess scarce skills or fulfill specific contractual requirements such as accepting a difficult teaching assignment. All of these plans have advantages and disadvantages that should be considered before a decision is made to implement one or more of them.

Job evaluation is a procedure by which a school district equates jobs with different content for purposes of compensation. It is used to eliminate inequities in salaries and to ensure that all salaries are commensurate with level of responsibility.

Suggested Activities

1. In trying to construct a salary schedule that is externally competitive, a school district must sometimes sacrifice internal equity. Discuss the relative importance of these two features. Under what conditions is it advisable to increase external competitiveness at the cost of internal equity? What problems may arise as a result?

2. The argument is sometimes made that dollars spent increasing beginning salaries have a bigger payoff for a school district than those spent on raises for experienced teachers. Discuss the merits of that argument and cite reasons why you believe it is or is not true. How do you explain research showing that increases in the middle of the salary schedule have more impact on retention than those at the lower or upper ends?

3. Adding additional steps to existing salary schedules has been proposed as a way to make teaching more competitive with other occupations. However, that idea has little support among teachers. Why do you think teachers do not favor adding steps?

4. A study cited in this chapter showed that some school personnel hold two jobs during the academic year. What are the factors that contribute to teachers and other employees working at two jobs? What is the likely effect of a second job on teachers' effectiveness? What policy should districts adopt with regard to second jobs?

5. One way by which classroom teachers can increase their income is to obtain an advanced degree. However, the salary increase teachers receive from holding a master's degree is relatively small. Estimate the cost to a teacher of obtaining a master's degree and, using the present salary schedule in your district, determine how long it would take a teacher to make back that cost. Is the decision to obtain an advanced degree a rational decision from an economic point of view? What noneconomic factors influence teachers to decide to pursue an advanced degree?

References

Alexander, L. (1986). Time for results: An overview. *Phi Delta Kappan, 68,* 202–204.

American Association of School Administrators. (1983a). *Some points to consider when you discuss merit pay.* Arlington, VA: Author.

American Association of School Administrators. (1983b). *The cost of reform: Fiscal implications of "A nation at risk."* Arlington, VA: Author.

Augenblick, J., Van de Water, G., & Fulton, M. (1993). *How much are schools spending? A 50-state examination of expenditure patterns over the last decade.* Denver: Education Commission of the States.

Bacharach, S., Lipsky, D., & Shedd, J. (1984). *Paying for better teaching: Merit pay and its alternatives.* Ithaca, NY: Organizational Analysis and Practice.

Ballou, D., & Podgursky, M. (1993, October). Teachers' attitudes toward merit pay: Examining conventional wisdom. *Industrial and Labor Relations Review, 47,* 50–61.

Barro, S., & Lee, J. W. (1986). *A comparison of teachers' salaries in Japan and the U.S.* (ERIC Document Reproduction Service No. ED 273630).

Bird, R. E. (1985). *An analysis of the comparability of public school teacher salaries to earning opportunities in other occupations.* Research

Triangle Park, NC: Southeastern Regional Council for Educational Improvement. (ERIC Document Reproduction Service No. ED 256070).

Bishop, J. (1986). *The recognition and reward of employee performance.* Paper presented at a conference on the New Economics of Personnel, Tempe, AZ. (ERIC Document Reproduction Service No. ED 268376).

Booth, R., Carlson, M., & Johnson, S. (1985). *Collective bargaining in Illinois schools, 1984–85.* Springfield, IL: Illinois Association of School Boards.

Bradley, A. (1989, December 13). New study finds a gender gap in teachers' salaries. *Education Week,* pp. 1, 12.

Cascio, W., & Awad, E. (1981). *Human resources management: An information systems approach.* Reston, VA: Reston Publishing.

Chambers, J. (1978). *An analysis of educational costs across local school districts in the State of Missouri, 1975–76.* Denver: Education Commission of the States.

Deci, E. (1972). The effects of contingent and noncontingent rewards on intrinsic motivation. *Organizational Behavior and Human Performance, 8,* 217–220.

Educational Research Service. (1983). *Merit pay plans for teachers: Status and descriptions.* Arlington, VA: Author.

Educational Research Service. (1985). *Scheduled salaries for professional personnel in public schools, 1984–85.* Arlington, VA: Author.

Fairfax officials still unsure of the cost of teacher merit pay. (1987, May 13). *The Washington Post*, p. B1, B9.

Henderson, R. (1985). *Compensation management* (4th ed.). Reston, VA: Reston Publishing.

Henderson, D., & Henderson, K. (1986). *Moonlighting, salary, and morale: The Texas teachers' story.* (ERIC Document Reproduction Service No. ED 269374).

Hoogeveen, K., & Gutkin, T. (1986). Collegial ratings among school personnel: An empirical examination of the merit pay concept. *American Educational Research Journal, 23,* 375–381.

How is Minnesota spending its tax dollars? (1993). St. Paul, MN: Office of the State Auditor.

Jacobson, S. (1987). *The distribution of salary increments and its effect on teacher retention.* Paper presented at the annual meeting of the American Educational Research Association, Washington, DC.

Jacobson, S. (1989). Change in entry-level salaries and its effect on teacher recruitment. *Journal of Education Finance, 14,* 449–465.

Johns, R., Morphet, E., & Alexander, K. (1983). *The economics and financing of education* (4th ed.). Englewood Cliffs, NJ: Prentice-Hall.

Kasten, K. (1984, Summer). The efficacy of institutionally dispensed rewards in elementary school teaching. *Journal of Research and Development in Education, 17,* 1–13.

Katz, D. (1973). The motivational basis of organizational behavior. In M. Milstein & J. Belasco (Eds.), *Educational administration and the behavioral sciences: A systems perspective* (pp. 319–346). Boston: Allyn and Bacon.

Kienapfel, B. (1984). *Merit pay for school administrators: A procedural guide.* Arlington, VA: Educational Research Service.

Landy, F. (1985). *Psychology of work behavior.* Homewood, IL: Dorsey.

Lawler, E. (1981). *Pay and organization development.* Reading, MA: Addison-Wesley.

Mark, J., & Anderson, B. (1978). Teacher survival rates: A current look. *American Educational Research Journal, 15,* 379–383.

McCarthy, M. (1983). Discrimination in employment. In J. Beckham & P Zirkel (Eds.), *Legal issues in public school employment* (pp. 22–54). Bloomington, IN: Phi Delta Kappa.

McGuire, C., & Thompson, J. (1984). *The costs of performance pay systems.* Denver: Education Commission of the States.

Milkovich, G., & Milkovich, C. (1992, November/December). Strengthening the pay-per-formance relationship: The research. *Compensation and Benefits Review, 24,* 53–62.

Morris, L. (1972). *The single salary schedule: An analysis and evaluation.* New York: AMS Press. (Original work published 1930).

Murnane, R., & Cohen, D. (1986). Merit pay and the evaluation problem: Why most merit pay plans fail and a few survive. *Harvard Educational Review, 56,* 1–17.

National Center for Education Statistics. (1993a). *Schools and staffing in the United States: A statistical profile, 1990–91.* Washington, DC: U.S. Department of Education.

National Center for Education Statistics. (1993b, March). Teacher salaries—Are they competitive? *Issue Brief,* pp. 1–2.

Natriello, G., & Cohn, M. (1983). *Beyond sanctions: The evolution of a merit pay system.* Paper presented at the annual meeting of the American Educational Research Association, Montreal.

NEA reports sharp rise in teacher pay. (1986, April 24). *The Washington Post,* p A7.

North Carolina Department of Public Instruction. (1984). *North Carolina career development plan for administrators, supervisors and other certified personnel.* Raleigh: Author.

Thornton, R. (1986). Teacher merit pay: An analysis of the issues. In R. Thornton & J. Aronson (Eds.), *Forging new relationships among business, labor and government* (pp. 179–199). Greenwich, CT: JAI Press.

Timar, T. (1992). Incentive pay for teachers and school reform. In L. Frase (Ed.), *Teacher compensation and motivation* (pp. 27–60). Lancaster, PA: Technomic.

11

CREATING PRODUCTIVE WORK ENVIRONMENTS

"In fundamental ways, the U.S. educational system is structured to guarantee the failure of teachers" (McLaughlin, Pfeifer, Swanson-Owens, & Yee, 1986). That indictment was not written by a disgruntled teacher. It was authored by four educational researchers in one of the nation's leading universities, who reached that conclusion after interviewing 85 teachers about the conditions of their work. Despite evidence that the charge is not true in many schools, it is difficult to deny that in too many cases it accurately describes reality.

Why do many people find psychological success in their work so elusive? To what extent are structural conditions in schools responsible for the sense of frustration and defeat that teachers and members of support staffs experience? What can administrators do to make schools more conducive to success? These are questions that are addressed in this chapter.

Plan of the Chapter

Chapter 6 described three theories of employee motivation and their effect on human performance. However, working conditions in many schools are such that even motivated employees are unable to achieve maximum productivity. This chapter examines how environments in schools inhibit employee productivity and it suggests ways of creating more productive work environments. The chapter considers four topics: (1) psychological success and work environments; (2) qualities of productive work environments; (3) teacher stress and burnout, and (4) employee assistance programs in schools.

Psychological Success
and Work Environments

All human beings strive to experience psychological success. One way by which they are able to do that is by performing competently in some personally valued task (Hall & Schneider, 1973). Teachers as well as students gain self-esteem when they believe they are performing capably a task that they value, and they experience satisfaction from the feeling that they are using their abilities appropriately and effectively (McLaughlin et al., 1986).

The environments in which people work may either increase or decrease the likelihood that they will experience psychological success. When conditions in the work environment prevent them from meeting their expectations, disappointment and frustration follow. Self-esteem suffers and the individual withdraws emotionally and perhaps physically by leaving the organization (Hall & Schneider, 1973). If the employee is not able to change jobs, continued frustration produces stress that may eventually lead to job burnout.

Unfortunately, the work environment in some schools does little to help employees experience psychological success. Surveys have shown that teachers believe that working conditions in schools limit their effectiveness and contribute to feelings of frustration (Corcoran, 1990).

Among the conditions about which teachers have expressed most concern in these surveys are low salaries and limited opportunities for advancement; heavy workloads; limited contacts with colleagues; shortages of materials and supplies for teaching; limited input into school decisions; lack of support from administrators; unfair or unhelpful evaluation practices; unavailability of stimulating professional development opportunities; rundown or outdated facilities; and lack of respect from administrators, students, and parents (Corcoran, 1990). Similar concerns are expressed by other school employees, including counselors, aides, nurses, and secretaries. Many of the conditions that limit employee productivity in schools are so common that they are taken for granted as characteristic of these occupations.

Some conditions found in schools prevent employees from doing their best work, whereas others simply make it more difficult to do a good job. Many teachers manage to be effective in spite of large classes by taking work home on evenings and weekends, and they overcome the lack of materials and supplies by buying them from their own funds. Other employees cannot solve their problems as easily, however. A counselor who is assigned to an office in which her conversations with students can be overheard by others is unable to conduct confidential counseling sessions with students, and a teacher who cannot be confident of receiving support from the principal must avoid teaching topics that offend sensitive parents.

Fortunately, the prospects for creating and sustaining productive work environments in schools have improved as our knowledge of the factors that contribute to employees' feelings of psychological success have increased.

Based on recent research, we can identify elements of the work setting that employees rank as most important, and it should come as no surprise that some of these are factors about which teachers expressed concern. The elements identified by employees as most important were having a good relationship with one's supervisor; being treated as an important person; receiving adequate and fair compensation; working in a safe, healthy, and stress-free environment; having a job that is socially relevant; and having opportunities for growth and development (Bruce & Blackburn, 1992). Other job factors to which employees attach importance are good relationships with co-workers, having a job with variety, being involved and informed, and being able to maintain a balance between work and family responsibilities (Bruce & Blackburn, 1992).

School administrators, in general, and personnel administrators, in particular, need to find ways to create more productive working environments in schools. Although it may be true that administrators have little or no control over some conditions that cause psychological stress for employees, they are able to influence others.

Qualities of Productive Work Environments

Productive work environments are those that enable employees to perform their jobs effectively and to experience psychological success while doing it. These environments generally have five characteristics:

1. Supportive administrative leadership
2. Opportunity to work collaboratively with others
3. Respect for people as individuals
4. Opportunity to use one's knowledge and skill and to receive feedback on one's performance
5. Necessary resources to do the job

When one of these conditions is missing, teachers are less likely to be able to carry out their work successfully and hence are not as likely to experience psychological success.

Supportive Leadership

Leaders achieve results by influencing members of the group to work toward attaining group goals. Four types of leadership behavior may be involved (House, 1971):

1. *Directive leadership:* The leader spells out expectations to subordinates.
2. *Supportive leadership:* The leader treats subordinates as equals and shows concern for their well-being.

3. *Participative leadership:* The leader involves subordinates in advising about or actually making decisions concerning their work.
4. *Achievement-oriented leadership:* The leader identifies challenging work-related goals and communicates to subordinates confidence in their ability to achieve them.

Supportive, participative, and achievement-oriented leadership are the critical elements of a productive work environment. Directive leadership is also necessary on occasion. Leaders must be able to determine which type of leadership is needed in a given situation and to exhibit the behaviors associated with that type. They may differ in the types of leadership they prefer. Some principals rely primarily on participative leadership to achieve results, by delegating instructional duties to department heads and teachers. Others identify a small group of innovative teachers and use achievement-oriented leadership to encourage them to try new ideas and share with other teachers those that work (Little & Bird, 1987).

A large body of research suggests that when workers are given the opportunity to make decisions about how to organize and carry out their work, their satisfaction and commitment increase. In most cases, their performance also improves, but occasionally changes are limited to reductions in sick days, turnover, and other indirect indicators of performance (Louis & Smith, 1990).

Participative leadership is particularly important in schools, but the evidence indicates that few teachers believe they have much influence over decisions about their work. Data collected nationally in 1990–91 showed that fewer than 40 percent of teachers in public schools reported they had a great deal of influence over decisions about discipline policy, in-service training, ability grouping, and curriculum development. However, the level of self-reported influence varied somewhat across district types (National Center for Education Statistics, 1993b).

The number of teachers who reported having a lot of influence changed slightly between 1987 and 1990, increasing by a small amount in two areas, decreasing slightly in another, and remaining unchanged in the fourth (National Center for Education Statistics, 1993a). This finding was surprising since during this time school-based management was widely adopted in American schools (Cawelti, 1994).

Although a participative style of leadership has several important benefits, there are limitations to be considered. Participative decisions take more time than directive decisions, and if employees are called on to make decisions for which they lack the necessary interest, knowledge, or experience, the quality of their decisions is likely to be poor (Landy, 1985).

Increasing Trust

Supportive leadership helps build trust between administrators and employees. Leaders gain employees' trust by exhibiting consistent and predictable behavior and by demonstrating a commitment to helping individuals do a better job. Trust is important; without it, administrators' efforts to influence employees' behavior are likely to fail. Workers who trust their boss are more willing to accept his or her influence since they believe the supervisor will not suggest a course of action that will harm them.

Principals use a variety of strategies to demonstrate support for teachers, including involving them in important decisions; doing things with them; being positive, cheerful, and encouraging; being available and accessible; and being honest, direct, and sincere. They also exercise supportive leadership by collecting and disseminating information to staff members, assisting teachers with their tasks, facilitating communication within the school and between the school and community, and establishing procedures to handle routine matters (Leithwood & Montgomery, 1986).

Principals who wish to become more effective in supportive leadership should make a point of talking with teachers often about their personal and instructional interests and concerns. Teachers would like opportunities to discuss a variety of issues, including their own career plans and training needs, their concept of education, and the content of their courses. However, most teachers have relatively few chances to talk with administrators even about issues of immediate concern, including adjustments in work assignments, their own performance, their need for materials and supplies, instructional problems, and teacher-parent relationships. On only two topics do teachers report having fairly frequent conversations with principals. Those are student achievement and behavior (Bacharach, Bauer, & Shedd, 1986).

Administrators exhibit achievement-oriented leadership by alerting employees to new practices and encouraging them to experiment. They help obtain the resources employees need in order to try out new ideas, and they provide advice on implementation of innovative practices. Principals who make opportunities for teachers and other professional employees to attend conferences are also exhibiting achievement-oriented leadership.

Some principals hesitate to initiate discussions about teaching for fear of being perceived as intruding (Corbett, 1982). They consider teachers to be autonomous professionals who know their work and need no direction from an administrative superior. However, most teachers do not share that view of their role. They think of principals as colleagues with expertise in dealing with a variety of teaching problems, and welcome the chance to talk with them.

Teachers' morale is higher in schools in which principals provide support by offering constructive suggestions, displaying interest in improving the quality of the educational program, encouraging superior performance standards in the classroom, maintaining egalitarian relationships, offering social and managerial support, and standing behind teachers in conflicts with students and parents (Gross & Herriott, 1965).

Even though the press of managerial duties limits the time available for principals to perform as instructional leaders (Deal, 1987) and even though involving teachers in a participative style of leadership makes sense, the principal must retain the title of leader both symbolically and in fact. No other individual carries the authority to speak for the school as a whole in resolving differences of opinion regarding allocation of resources and in making decisions regarding goals. The role of instructional leader is one that the principal can and should carry. A participative mode of decision making, when appropriate, enhances the principal's instructional leadership rather than detracts from it.

Collaborative Work Arrangements

In schools with site-based management (SBM), the responsibility for student success moves from the central office to the schools. One of the first jobs that must be undertaken by SBM schools is team building. This involves helping employees to envision new roles that permit and encourage collaboration between and among staff members, students, parents, and the community (Payzant, 1992). Even noncertified, staff such as custodians and food service workers, assume new roles in SBM schools and assume more responsibility for accomplishing the school's mission (Prasch, 1990). SBM does not guarantee that communication will be better or that teachers, counselors, and other employees will cooperate more closely, but it does provide an opportunity to create conditions under which these things are possible.

Under school-based management, decisions about curriculum that were formerly made at the district level are made by the faculty and staff of the school. Each school must decide how to allocate the resources it receives. Schools have the freedom to hire more aides and fewer teachers if they choose to do so, or they may divert some of the money from teachers' salaries into technology.

Teachers often describe the schools in which they work in terms of how close teachers are to one another and how willing they are to work together. Working together encompasses many activities—discussing, planning, designing, analyzing, evaluating, and experimenting (Little, 1981).

Most teachers look for opportunities to share with colleagues what they are doing in their classrooms, but many prefer to speak with those whom they know well and for whom they feel an affinity. Few are willing to speak out in faculty meetings unless group norms supporting such sharing exist. Principals should proceed slowly, encouraging sharing by minimizing threats but avoiding pressuring anyone to speak.

Accepting a collaborative mode of operation in schools requires first adopting an attitude that improvement is necessary and desirable. If teachers have not fully accepted that value, the principal should make its adoption the first priority. After that, administrators can suggest activities that will permit teachers to work collaboratively for more effective instruction. Some examples of ways teachers collaborate appear in Exhibit 11.1.

Design and prepare instructional material
Design curriculum units
Research material and ideas for curriculum
Write curriculum
Prepare lesson plans
Review and discuss existing lesson plans
Persuade others to try a new idea or approach
Make collective agreements to test an idea
Invite other teachers to observe one's classes
Observe other teachers
Analyze practices and effects
Teach others in formal inservice
Teach others informally
Talk publicly about what one is learning or wants to learn
Design inservice sessions
Evaluate the performance of the principal

**EXHIBIT 11.1   Examples of Collegial
                 Cooperation in Teaching**

*Source: The Power of Organizational Setting: School Norms and Staff
Development* by J.W. Little, April 1981. Paper presented at the annual meeting of the American Educational Research Association,
Los Angeles, CA. ERIC Document Reproduction Service No. ED
221918.

Respect for Individuals

Teachers and other school employees desire respect from others, including
their colleagues on the job, administrators, parents, students, and the community at large. Lack of respect has led many teachers to believe that their
work is unimportant and unappreciated (Louis & Smith, 1990).

Lack of respect for others is demonstrated in a number of ways, both obvious and subtle. Behavior that indirectly shows disrespect erodes an individual's self-confidence and sense of efficacy, whereas more overt manifestations can lead to an individual's experiencing a threat to his or her
psychological security. The potential power of lack of respect on individuals
is evident in the results of a recent survey of employees' work-related fears.

Employees who admitted they avoided discussing a work-related issue because of fear of repercussions were asked to identify the fear that prevented
their being more open. The most common response of these employees was
fear of loss of credibility or reputation. Some 27 percent of respondents cited
that concern, more than expressed a fear of lack of career advancement (16
percent), loss of employment (11 percent), or transfer or demotion (4 percent) (Ryan & Oestreich, 1991).

Employees who experienced fear related to their work reported that their
concerns had created negative feelings about the organization or about
themselves or had a negative impact on the quality or quantity of their work.

Some reported that, as a result of the fear, they were taking more care to avoid actions that might expose them to repercussions or were engaging more often in politically oriented behavior by cultivating "connections" with powerful individuals in the organization. Others reported that they were contemplating a transfer to a job outside the organization or had engaged in petty revenge or sabotage (Ryan & Oestreich, 1991). The researchers also found that employees who reported being fearful less often put forth extra effort to complete a task, more often attempted to hide mistakes, and less often engaged in creative thinking or risk-taking behavior on the job (Ryan & Oestreich, 1991).

Supervisory behaviors are a source of anxiety for many employees. Behaviors that are especially likely to arouse fear, whether the supervisor intends it or not, are silence, glaring, abruptness, insults and put-downs, blaming, yelling and shouting, and an aggressive, controlling manner. Poorly managed personnel systems, particularly with respect to implementing reductions in force, also increase employee anxiety (Ryan & Oestreich, 1991).

Suggestions for administrators that will help lessen the level of fear in an organization include recognizing its presence and harmful effects and avoiding behaviors that are known to increase it. Administrators who wish to lower the level of anxiety are also advised to reduce ambiguous behavior, to talk about sensitive issues that are likely to arouse fear and that employees may be embarrassed to bring up on their own, and to welcome criticism (Ryan & Oestreich, 1991).

Using Knowledge and Skill

Few experiences are more important for employees' feelings of well-being than holding a job that allows them fully to use their knowledge and skill. Most young workers are less satisfied in their jobs than more experienced individuals, and the reason is that entry-level jobs tend to be less demanding and offer fewer opportunities for these workers to use the knowledge and skill they have acquired from their training.

Employees who are required to stretch in order to meet challenging aspects of their jobs are generally happier in their work and more productive than those for whom the job is a familiar routine. Of course, mastery is partly a function of one's experience, and the longer an individual is in a job, the less likely it is that he or she continues to be challenged by it. For that reason, the opportunity to move into new positions or take on demanding new duties that force the employee to acquire new skills and knowledge are important for maintaining employee interest and involvement.

For many school employees, school-based management provides such challenges. Teachers, counselors, and other employees who are unaccustomed to participating in decisions outside of their own immediate area of responsibility must learn new skills in order to participate fully in the operation of the school once SBM is introduced. Among these skills are developing and implementing a school improvement plan; learning to work effectively as a member of a team; and gathering, analyzing, and reporting data. Training in these skills can produce benefits in the form of a more efficient and effective transition to SBM (Holcomb, 1993).

Facilities and Resources

In many schools, the building itself is a hindrance to effective teaching (Olson, 1988). Buildings that are not kept clean or in which maintenance work is neglected, either because of lack of funds or employee indifference, are less pleasant places to work than those in which facilities are clean and well maintained.

Although amount of space is a more common problem, the quality of space is also a concern of teachers (Bacharach et al., 1986). *Quality* refers to availability of electrical outlets, running water, telephone, adequate lighting, and privacy. It also encompasses furnishings, including desks, and electronic equipment such as computers.

Good teaching is hindered by the shortage of textbooks, equipment, and supplies. It is not uncommon for teachers to have too few microscopes, maps, and computers for their classes, and in some schools even textbooks must be shared. Adequate facilities and resources do not by themselves guarantee teacher satisfaction or effectiveness, but they help (McLaughlin & Yee, 1988).

Class size influences teachers' feelings of efficacy. Large classes are more difficult to manage and cause more work for the teacher. Teachers much prefer smaller classes to larger classes and generally approve of spending additional resources on reducing class sizes, even though that may mean smaller salary increases.

When school districts receive additional funds, less than half of the new money is spent on instructional resources, including reductions in class size and teacher salaries. About 40 cents of each new dollar goes to reduce class size, and 9 cents is spent for salary increases (Picus, 1993).

Teacher Stress and Burnout

Like most human service occupations, teaching is stressful work. All teachers experience some stress, and although its effects can be reduced, it cannot be eliminated entirely from teachers' work. Indeed, one probably would not want to do so even if it were possible, for a job with no stress whatever would be exceedingly dull.

Some teachers are better prepared, both by temperament and training, to deal with stress, but excessive and prolonged stress saps any teacher's energy and sharply reduces productivity. Administrators should be especially sensitive to conditions that create stress. Among the conditions that lead to high levels of teacher stress are excessive pressure to produce student learning gains and teaching students who are disruptive and disrespectful.

Types of Stress

There are at least four sources of stress in schools (Albrecht, 1979). *Time stress* occurs when the time allotted for completing a task is insufficient or when inflexible deadlines are established for completion of work assignments.

Situational stress arises when the situation in which a person is placed creates a psychological threat that exceeds the individual's ability to cope (Albrecht, 1979). An example of situational stress that is unfortunately common in schools occurs when teachers must deal with students whose emotional, psychological, and physical needs exceed the families' and the school's resources for assistance. Teachers feel overwhelmed by the problems of these children, and they experience guilt and anger because of their powerlessness to correct the conditions contributing to the children's difficulties (Grant, 1983).

Encounter stress is experienced when a person is forced to deal with other individuals whose behavior is unpleasant or unpredictable (Albrecht, 1979). An example of a situation that induces encounter stress for teachers is having to deal with parents who are angry and abusive.

Anticipatory stress occurs when an individual experiences anxiety about an upcoming event (Albrecht, 1979). Teachers may experience anticipatory stress prior to issuing report cards or before a classroom observation visit by the principal.

Symptoms of Stress

The experience of stress is manifested in feelings of fear, anxiety, depression, and anger. The individual subjected to prolonged stress experiences fatigue, reluctance to go to work, withdrawal, hypersensitivity to criticism, and hostility and aggression toward others (Cedoline, 1982).

Stress also produces physiological effects, such as changes in skin conductance, heart rate, and blood pressure. Individuals are unlikely to be aware of physiological changes except when the level of stress experienced is quite high. However, the physiological manifestations of stress exact a cumulative toll on mental and physical health.

Stress can also affect cognitive functioning. Some stress is desirable for optimal performance, but exposure to unrelenting stress results in a marked decrease in performance (Lazarus, 1968).

Over time, the frustration, anger, disappointment, and guilt that teachers experience have a cumulative effect on their feelings about themselves and about their work that results in a condition known as *burnout.* Burnout has been defined as a form of alienation characterized by the feeling that one's work is meaningless and that one is powerless to bring about change that would make the work more meaningful. The experience of meaninglessness and powerlessness is intensified by the feeling that one is alone and isolated (Dworkin, 1987).

Teachers who are experiencing job burnout often exhibit cynicism and negativism (Freudenberger, 1977). They are likely to be inflexible and rigid and to demonstrate reduced concern for students and fellow workers (Maslach & Pines, 1977).

Factors in Burnout

Factors that contribute to teacher burnout are role ambiguity (having a job in which duties are not clearly spelled out); responsibility/authority imbalance (having insufficient authority to carry out the responsibilities one has been assigned); a workload that is either too heavy or too light; inability to obtain information needed to carry out one's responsibilities; and job insecurity (Milstein, Golaszewski, & Duquette, 1984).

Relationships with superiors are related to stress experienced by some teachers. Teachers who receive no performance feedback from principals and who feel that they are unable to influence administrators' decisions about their work are more likely to experience stress (Litt & Turk, 1985).

Administrators can help reduce the stress teachers experience by following some commonsense precautions:

1. Reduce time pressures by alerting teachers early to upcoming deadlines and by providing directions and assistance to help teachers complete paperwork requirements.
2. Assist teachers in obtaining help for students with emotional and psychological problems; if district resources are not available, appeal to community service agencies and service clubs for help.
3. Provide training to help teachers deal with disruptive students and, when necessary, provide support for teachers who are experiencing problems with student behavior.
4. Remove the dread of performance evaluation by pointing out that everyone can improve in some area; give teachers the opportunity to evaluate the school administration.
5. Provide feedback to teachers on their classroom performance, including specific suggestions that will help them be more effective teachers.
6. Offer to participate in parent conferences when teachers request it; provide training in planning and carrying out parent conferences.
7. Make time for informal conversations with teachers and give them a chance to talk about whatever they wish to talk about, bearing in mind that the most conscientious teachers are most subject to burnout.

8. Plan faculty outings that provide a break from the routine and allow teachers to have a good time with colleagues.
9. Help discouraged teachers maintain perspective by reminding them of past successes. Invite former students who have done well back to the school to talk about their successes and how their teachers helped them succeed.

Employee Assistance Programs in Schools

Employees' productivity may be affected by problems that originate on the job or elsewhere. In the past, supervisors could suggest that an employee with problems seek help, but if the worker chose not to do so, there was little the supervisor could do about it. Individuals with medical problems were usually willing to seek help because in most cases the employer provided insurance to cover the cost of medical care. But when the problem was not a medical one, many employees did not know where to go to find help, or if they did, they avoided going. Many of these cases involved individuals with problems of alcohol abuse, for which treatment was expensive and not readily available.

A number of companies instituted counseling programs to assist individuals whose work was affected by alcohol or drug abuse and other mental health or personal problems. Gradually, these programs came to be known as *employee assistance programs*. They are now widespread in industry and are becoming more commonplace in school districts.

An employee assistance program consists of policies and procedures for identifying and assisting employees whose personal or emotional problems hinder their job performance. Counselors in an employee assistance program also provide a valuable service by advising principals and other administrators about how to work more effectively with employees who have various kinds of mental health or personal problems (Hacker, 1986). Most administrators are not trained to work with problem employees, and they can perform their jobs more effectively if they have access to professional advice on dealing with such workers.

Wellness Programs

Because of escalating costs of all types of health care, many industrial concerns and some schools districts are now offering wellness programs, which emphasize good health practices for all employees. The idea of a wellness program is to help employees prevent illness by using sound judgment in decisions on nutrition, weight control, exercise, and use of drugs, tobacco, and alcohol.

Summary

All human beings want to experience psychological success. One of the most common ways by which they seek to do that is by performing competently in some personally valued task. Schools are structured in such a way that teachers frequently experience failure in their efforts to help children grow and develop.

Productive working environments are characterized by supportive administrative leadership; opportunities to work collaboratively with others and receive respect from others, including administrators, colleagues, and parents; opportunities to use one's knowledge and skill and to receive feedback on one's performance; and the resources one needs to do the job.

Four types of leadership used by administrators to achieve desired results are directive, supportive, participative, and achievement-oriented leadership. All four types are appropriate in particular situations. Directive and achievement-oriented leadership behaviors provide clear guidelines for teachers to follow and make goals more salient. Supportive leadership increases trust between teachers and administrators and helps to foster norms of collegiality, which in turn facilitate the introduction of participative leadership. Participative leadership increases commitment to group decisions.

Teachers often experience stress because of the conditions under which they work. Conditions that are particularly conducive to stress are pressure to produce learning gains and disruptive and disrespectful students. Prolonged stress leads to physical and emotional symptoms characterized by a loss of interest in work and in the welfare of others. Administrators should be sensitive to the need to provide supportive leadership to alleviate teacher stress.

Employee assistance programs help individuals whose job performance is affected by personal or mental health problems. Wellness programs are designed to help all employees avoid illness by using sound health practices.

Suggested Activities

1. An item that almost always shows up on lists of desirable characteristics of work environments in schools is *supportive administrative leadership*. Explain what is meant by that phrase and give one or two specific examples of it from your own experience. Tell what you think are the necessary ingredients of supportive leadership and why school employees attach so much importance to it. Are school personnel different from people in other occupations in this respect?

2. Suppose you are preparing for an interview for the position of assistant principal in a school. Write a list of questions you might ask the principal or other personnel in the school that would yield useful information

about the environment of the school. Explain what you would expect to learn from the questions you wrote.

3. A number of people have observed that some stress is desirable and that the total absence of stress makes life boring. Nevertheless, individuals vary in their tolerance for stress. Is some stress acceptable to you? Think of one or two situations in which you have experienced "pleasant" stress and an equal number in which you have experienced "unpleasant" stress. What is the difference between the two? Do you deal with "pleasant" stress differently from the way you handle "unpleasant" stress? If so, why? Do you agree that teaching is a "stressful" occupation? Why or why not?

4. Individuals value opportunities to work collaboratively with one another, but in schools such opportunities are few in number. Tell what action you might take as a school administrator to create an environment in a school that would increase the number of opportunities for personnel to work together.

References

Albrecht, K. (1979). *Stress and the manager.* Englewood Cliffs, NJ: Prentice Hall.

Bacharach, S. B., Bauer, S. C., & Shedd, J. B. (1986). The work environment and school reform. *Teachers College Record, 88,* 241–256.

Bruce, W., & Blackburn, J. (1992). *Balancing job satisfaction and performance: A guide for human resource professionals.* Westport, CT: Quorum.

Cawelti, G. (1994). *High school restructuring: A national study.* Arlington, VA: Educational Research Service.

Cedoline, A. J. (1982). *Job burnout in public education.* New York: Teachers College Press.

Corbett, H. D. (1982). Principals' contributions to maintaining change. *Phi Delta Kappan, 64,* 190–192.

Corcoran, T. (1990). Schoolwork: Perspectives on workplace reform in public schools. In M. McLaughlin, J. Talbert, & N. Bascia (Eds.), *The contexts of teaching in secondary schools: Teachers' realities* (pp. 142–166). New York: Teachers College Press.

Deal, T. E. (1987). Effective school principals: Counselors, engineers, pawnbrokers, poets . . . or instructional leaders? In W. Greenfield (Ed.), *Instructional leadership: Concepts, issues, and controversies* (pp. 230–245). Boston: Allyn and Bacon.

Dworkin, A. G. (1987). *Teacher burnout in the public schools: Structural causes and consequences for children.* Albany: State University of New York Press.

Freudenberger, H. (1977). Burn out: Occupational hazard of the child care worker. *Child Care Quarterly, 6,* 90–99.

Grant, G. (1983). The teacher's predicament. *Teachers College Record, 84,* 593–609.

Gross, N., & Herriott, R. (1965). *Staff leadership in public schools: A sociological inquiry.* New York: Wiley.

Hacker, C. (1986). *EAP: Employee assistance programs in the public schools.* Washington, DC: National Education Association. (ERIC Document Reproduction Service No. ED 281267).

Hall, D. T., & Schneider, B. (1973). *Organizational climates and careers: The work lives of priests.* New York: Seminar Press.

Holcomb, E. (1993). *School-based instructional leadership: A staff development program for school effectiveness and improvement.* Madison, WI: National Center for Effective Schools.

House, R. L. (1971). A path-goal theory of

leader-effectiveness. *Administrative Science Quarterly, 16,* 321–338.

Landy, F. J. (1985). *Psychology of work behavior.* Homewood, IL: Dorsey.

Lazarus, R. S. (1968). Stress. In D. L. Sills (Ed.), *International encyclopedia of the social sciences* (Vol. 15, pp. 337–348). New York: Macmillan.

Leithwood, K. A., & Montgomery, D. J. (1986). *Improving principal effectiveness: The principal profile.* Toronto: Ontario Institute for Studies in Education.

Litt, M. D., & Turk, D. C. (1985). Sources of stress and dissatisfaction in experienced high school teachers. *Journal of Educational Research, 78,* 178–185.

Little, J. W. (1981, April). *The power of organizational setting: School norms and staff development.* Paper presented at the annual meeting of the American Educational Research Association, Los Angeles. (ERIC Document Reproduction Service No. ED 221918).

Little, J. W., & Bird, T. (1987). Instructional leadership "close to the classroom" in secondary schools. In W. Greenfield (Ed.), *Instructional leadership: Concepts, issues, and controversies* (pp. 118–138). Boston: Allyn and Bacon.

Louis, K., & Smith, B. (1990). Teacher working conditions. In P. Reyes (Ed.), *Teachers and their workplace: Commitment, performance, and productivity* (pp. 23–47). Newbury Park, CA: Sage.

Maslach, C., & Pines, A. (1977). The burn-out syndrome in the day care setting. *Child Care Quarterly, 6,* 100–113.

McLaughlin, M. W., Pfeifer, R. S., Swanson-Owens, D., & Yee, S. (1986). Why teachers won't teach. *Phi Delta Kappan, 67,* 420–426.

McLaughlin, M. W., & Yee, S. M. (1988). School as a place to have a career. In A. Lieberman (Ed.), *Building a professional culture in schools* (pp. 23–44). New York: Teachers College Press.

Milstein, M. M., Golaszewski, T. J., & Duquette, R. D. (1984). Organizationally based stress: what bothers teachers. *Journal of Educational Research, 77,* 293–297.

National Center for Education Statistics. (1993a). *America's teachers: Profile of a profession.* Washington, DC: U.S. Department of Education.

National Center for Education Statistics. (1993b). *Schools and staffing in the United States: A statistical profile.* Washington, DC: U.S. Department of Education.

Olson, L. (1988, September 28). Work conditions in some schools said "intolerable." *Education Week,* pp. 1, 21.

Payzant, T. (1992). Empowering teachers and enhancing student achievement through school restructuring. In L. Frase (Ed.), *Teacher compensation and motivation* (pp. 454–481). Lancaster, PA: Technomic.

Picus, L. (1993). *The allocation and use of educational resources.* Brunswick, NJ: Consortium for Policy Research in Education.

Prasch, J. (1990). *How to organize for school-based management.* Alexandria, VA: Association for Supervision and Curriculum Development.

Ryan, K., & Oestreich, D. (1991). *Driving fear out of the workplace.* San Francisco: Jossey-Bass.

12

LEGAL ISSUES IN PERSONNEL MANAGEMENT

The legal authority to employ, assign, transfer, suspend, and terminate teachers is assigned by the states to local school boards, and the boards are given wide latitude in the exercise of that power (Hudgins & Vacca, 1985). The large majority of personnel decisions are made by school boards on the recommendation of an administrator. For that reason, principals and district administrators who are involved in personnel management activities should be aware of legal ramifications of personnel decisions.

Although they delegate considerable power over personnel matters to school boards, the states maintain professional preparation requirements for teachers, counselors, and administrative personnel. The states also prescribe other qualifications for those positions, including age, moral character and citizenship (*Education Law*, 1989). In addition, an extensive body of federal and state legislation forbids discrimination in employment practices against members of protected classes, and all citizens of the United States receive certain protections under the Bill of Rights.

Most of the actions taken during the process of recruitment, selection, and placement of employees—including advertising, preparation of application forms, and conducting interviews—are potential areas of legal vulnerability. Also included under the aegis of the law are decisions to transfer, promote, discipline, or dismiss employees. The best protection against violating these laws is to be well informed about statute and case law relating to all facets of personnel management. This chapter will examine the legal issues involved in personnel management in schools.

Plan of the Chapter

This chapter covers the following topics: (1) hiring and assigning employees; (2) antidiscrimination legislation; (3) types of discrimination; (4) defending personnel practices; and (5) affirmative action and reverse discrimination.

Hiring and Assigning Employees

The states delegate to school boards authority to hire and assign or reassign and terminate employees. The states also establish rules governing the preparation and certification of professional personnel, including teachers, counselors, school social workers, school psychologists, and administrators. State laws and regulations specify the course of study that the various personnel must complete and stipulate licensing procedures, including tests of general or professional knowledge. School boards may establish higher standards than those specified by the state, but they may not lower the standards.

Most states require school personnel to be free of communicable diseases, and school boards sometimes establish other policies dealing with employee health. All such regulations are subject to review under federal statutes that protect employees that are disabled against discrimination. Some states prohibit school boards from establishing a residency requirement, but where it is permitted, courts have usually upheld residency rules as long as the boards were able to establish a rational basis for the policy (*Wardwell* v. *Board of Education of the City School District of Cincinnati*, 1976).

The use of competitive examinations as part of the selection procedure is legally defensible provided the board can show that the test is validly related to the requirements of the position. Chapter 4 reported on several cases in which courts have ruled on the use of tests for the selection of teachers.

Boards have the authority to assign teachers to any school in the district as long as the action is not in violation of the bargaining agreement or the teacher's contract. Reassignments that are perceived as involving a demotion are subject to legal challenge, but as a general rule, courts have upheld the board in these cases except when the position to which the teacher was transferred differed significantly in responsibility or pay from the previous one (McCarthy & Cambron-McCabe, 1987).

State statutory provisions are considered part of the contract between the teacher and the board, and district policies and procedures are implicitly incorporated into the contract. For that reason, care should be taken in preparation of employee handbooks, in order to ensure that they accurately reflect district policy (Strahan & Turner, 1987).

Antidiscrimination Legislation

Discrimination occurs when decisions about selection, placement, promotion, compensation, discipline, or dismissal of individuals are made on the basis of characteristics other than qualifications, ability, and performance (McCarthy, 1983). A number of state and federal statutes, regulations, and executive orders forbid discrimination in recruiting, selecting, placing, promoting, and dismissing employees. In this section, some of the more important federal statutes relating to discrimination will be reviewed.

Civil Rights Act of 1964

The most significant piece of legislation dealing with discrimination in employer/employee relations is the Civil Rights Act of 1964, as amended. Title VII of that act covers all employers with 15 or more employees, including state and local governments as well as schools and colleges. Religious institutions are exempt with respect to employment of persons of a specific religion.

The law prohibits discrimination with respect to compensation and terms, conditions, or privileges of employment on the basis of race, color, national origin, sex, or religion. The legislation also prohibits limiting, segregating, or classifying employees or applicants for employment in any way that deprives an individual of employment opportunities or otherwise adversely affects his or her status as an employee.

Title VII is administered by the Equal Employment Opportunity Commission (EEOC), which administers most federal legislation dealing with employment rights. The EEOC has no adjudicatory authority, but most claims of discrimination under Title VII must be reviewed by the EEOC before legal action is taken against an employer. If, following an investigation, the Commission concludes that the law has been violated, it attempts to persuade the employer to eliminate the illegal practice. If this approach does not work, the Commission will issue a finding confirming that a basis for legal action exists (van Geel, 1987).

The Pregnancy Discrimination Act of 1978 extended the protections of Title VII of the Civil Rights Act to pregnant employees. This law requires employers to treat pregnancy the same as other temporary medical conditions. Except where state law establishes conditions that make separate policies necessary, school divisions are advised to establish a single policy on medical leave, including maternity leave (Hubbartt, 1993).

Age Discrimination in Employment Act of 1967

The Age Discrimination in Employment Act (ADEA) of 1967, as amended in 1986, enjoins discrimination against individuals above the age of 40 in hiring, assignment, training, promotion, and the terms and conditions of employment (McCarthy & Cambron-McCabe, 1992). Under the ADEA, employers may offer incentives to induce employees to retire early as long as such plans are not used to circumvent the intent of the legislation.

The legislation makes it unlawful to give preference to a younger person over an older one if the older person is within the protected range. For example, a district that promotes a 45-year-old employee rather than a 60-year-old because of the latter's age when the two are equally qualified would be guilty of age discrimination, just as it would be for promoting a 25-year-old employee over an equally qualified 40-year-old. The act offers no protection against discrimination based on age for individuals who are outside the protected range. Thus, refusing to hire a 21-year-old applicant on the basis of age is not unlawful.

An employer charged with violating the Age Discrimination in Employment Act may disprove the charge by showing bona fide occupational qualification (BFOQ). For example, a director hiring an actor to play the part of a 25-year-old man in a play could lawfully select a younger person over an applicant within the protected age range solely on the basis of age. An employer who uses age as a qualification for employment must be able to show a reasonable relationship between the requirement and job performance. This is usually done by citing a connection between employee age and safe performance (van Geel, 1987).

Equal Pay Act of 1963

The equal Pay Act of 1963 forbids an employer from paying higher wages to employees of one sex than it pays to those of the opposite sex for jobs that require equal skill, effort, and responsibility and that are performed under similar working conditions. Employers may not attempt to comply by reducing the wages of any employee. Exceptions are allowed for wages that are based on a seniority system or a merit pay plan. The Equal Pay Act applies to federal, state, and local governments as well as to private commercial and industrial firms. Enforcement of the act became the responsibility of the Equal Employment Opportunity Commission in 1979, but the statute is less frequently used than Title VII since a violation of one is also a violation of the other and most attorneys prefer to bring suit under Title VII (McCulloch, 1981).

A question that frequently arises in litigation having to do with equal pay is how similar duties must be in order for two jobs to be considered as meriting equal pay. Courts have not always been consistent in defining the degree of required difference (Schlei & Grossman, 1976). It is common for female custodians to be assigned tasks that are less physically demanding than those assigned to males. For example, male custodians may be responsible for removing snow from school sidewalks and driveways, whereas female employees escape that duty. Males may be required to climb a ladder to change lightbulbs, install wiring, repair air conditioning equipment, and perform other tasks that female employees are not asked to perform.

Given these differences in assigned duties, is it justifiable to pay higher wages to the male employees? In the cases that have been tried under the Equal Pay Act, the answer to that question given by the courts has most often been *no.* The courts have held that the differences in the duties required of male and female custodians are not great enough to justify wage differences favoring males.

As a general rule, wage differences in favor of one sex are more likely to be sustained by the courts if the additional duties of the higher paid sex require a significant percentage of the employees' time or if they can be shown to require significant extra effort (Schlei & Grossman, 1976). For example, a school board could justify paying a male soccer boys' coach more than it pays a female girls' soccer coach if it could show that the boys' team played more games and spent more time practicing than the girls' team.

Rehabilitation Act of 1973 and Americans with Disabilities Act of 1990

The Vocational Rehabilitation Act (VRA) of 1973 and the Americans with Disabilities Act (ADA) of 1990 prohibit discrimination in employment decisions against qualified individuals with disabilities. The VRA applies to federal contractors and agencies that receive financial assistance from the federal government, whereas the ADA applies to most employers with 15 or more employees.

Both acts provide that an individual with a disability who is able to perform the "essential functions" of a position, with or without reasonable accommodation, is qualified for consideration for a position and may not be refused employment solely on the basis of the disability. *Essential functions* are defined as primary duties that are intrinsic to a specific job, not including those of a peripheral nature (Jacobs, 1993).

Three questions that are used to help identify essential functions of a job are (Fersh & Thomas, 1993):

1. Does the position exist to perform the function?
2. Are there only a limited number of employees available to perform the function?
3. Is the function so highly specialized that the person holding the position is hired for his or her ability to perform that particular function?

To help answer those questions, consider information obtained from written job descriptions, estimates of time devoted to various functions, suggested consequences of not performing a particular function, and the terms and conditions of collective bargaining agreements (Fersh & Thomas, 1993).

Some jobs have a limited number of essential functions. For a school nurse, essential functions include the ability to apply first aid and make decisions regarding follow-up actions when a child is ill or injured—for example, whether to contact parents to take the child home or call emergency services. Other jobs have multiple essential functions. School counselors discuss problems of personal adjustment with students and work with them to find solutions. But counselors also help students locate information about prospective careers, calm anxious or upset parents, prepare and mail transcripts, and administer and interpret standardized tests. All of these functions are essential, but the position of counselor does not exist solely to perform one of these functions to the exclusion of the others.

The EEOC defines *reasonable accommodation* as a modification or adjustment in the way a job is ordinarily performed that enables a qualified individual with a disability to perform the job without imposing an undue hardship on the employer (Schneid, 1992). Examples of accommodations are providing entrance ramps to allow access to persons in wheelchairs, granting time off for medical treatments or physical therapy, and purchasing special equipment or adapting existing equipment to enable people with disabilities to perform a job.

Other forms of accommodation include hiring an assistant to perform the tasks that the employee with disabilities is unable to perform and restructuring work assignments to limit those employees' responsibilities to tasks that are within their capabilities. An employer is not required to make accommodations that are unduly costly or disruptive to the operation of the business or agency (Schneid, 1992).

A person is considered to be disabled if he or she has a physical or mental impairment that substantially limits one or more major life activities or is regarded as having such an impairment. Individuals who have undergone drug rehabilitation are considered to be disabled, but those who are currently using drugs are not. Homosexuality is not considered a disabling condition, but AIDS is (Schneid, 1992).

The law does not require an employer to hire a person with disabilities who is less qualified than a person with no disabilities, but it forbids employers from refusing to employ individuals solely on the basis of their possessing a disability. Employers may legally refuse to hire an applicant with disabilities whose employment in a particular position would result in creation of a safety hazard for the employee or others when it is not possible through reasonable accommodation to eliminate the danger (Gordon, 1992). However, the employer should be prepared to produce evidence that the claimed hazard is real and not simply a pretext.

Deciding whether to employ individuals with disabilities as teachers requires administrators to consider the safety and well-being of students as well as the rights of the disabled. Districts that are able to show that they have carefully weighed a disabled applicant's qualifications to perform the job with reasonable accommodation against the potential risk to students created by hiring the person stand a good chance of prevailing in court.

On the other hand, districts that refuse to consider a disabled applicant's qualifications are almost certain to lose a legal challenge. A district that declined to allow a blind applicant to take a qualifying examination for a teaching position on grounds that her blindness made her incompetent to teach sighted students lost its suit and was required by the court to hire the teacher and provide back pay and retroactive seniority (*Gurmankin* v. *Costanzo*, 1977).

Interviewers should ask applicants with disabilities to indicate how they will perform essential functions of the position for which they are applying and what accommodations they will need in order to carry out their duties. Requests for accommodation should be treated on an individual basis and decisions should take in account both the expected cost and the potential for creating hardships for other employees (Sovereign, 1984).

One question that is still largely unanswered is to what extent the law protects employees who contract contagious diseases. The Eleventh Circuit Court held that the legislation did not exclude persons with such conditions as long as their presence did not pose a risk to other people. The case involved a teacher who had been dismissed from her job because she had tuberculosis (*Arline* v. *School Board of Nassau County*, 1985).

Constitutional Protections

All U.S. citizens have certain protections under the Constitution. Freedom of speech, association, and religion are guaranteed by the First Amendment, and the rights of due process and equal protection are secured by the Fifth and Fourteenth Amendments, respectively. Privacy rights also derive from the Constitution (Sorenson, 1987).

The Supreme Court has held that the free speech right of school employees must be balanced by consideration for the efficient operation of schools. In reviewing a case in which a teacher was dismissed for making public statements critical of the school board and the administration (*Connick* v. *Myers*, 1983), the Supreme Court held that discussion of issues related to public concerns was protected under the First Amendment but that comments about issues of a personal nature were not so protected. Unfortunately, the distinction is clearer in theory than in practice.

Criticism by teachers of student grouping practices and of the quality of the educational programs have been held to be matters of public concern and thus entitled to protection (*Cox* v. *Dardanelle Public School District*, 1986; *Jett* v. *Dallas Independent School District*, 1986). However, statements that were critical of school officials for changing registration procedures and for delays in purchasing teaching materials were judged to be matters of personal concern and thus not protected (*Ferrara* v. *Mills*, 1986; *Daniels* v. *Quinn*, 1986).

The Seventh Circuit Court held that a district action prohibiting teachers from holding prayer meetings at school before the school day started did not infringe on the teachers' right of free speech (*May* v. *Evansville-Vanderburgh School Corporation*, 1986). The right to privacy has been cited as protecting women who choose to bear a child out of wedlock from adverse employment decisions (*Eisenstadt* v. *Baird,* 1972). Policies that require pregnant teachers to begin mandatory maternity leave at a specific point in the pregnancy have been held to deny teachers' rights to equal protection under the Fourteenth Amendment (Director, 1973).

Types of Discrimination

Title VII of the Civil Rights Act of 1964 prohibits overt discrimination, also known as *disparate treatment.* This is the most flagrant and, fortunately, also the least common form of discrimination. It occurs when an individual who is a member of a protected group and who qualifies for or holds a job is discriminated against for legally indefensible reasons.

A more common form of discrimination is *adverse impact,* which occurs when employment practices that are neutral in intent have a discriminatory effect on a protected group. This is the most common form of discrimination (Miner & Miner, 1978). Among actions that can lead to charges of adverse impact are using screening tests on which members of one group score lower than other groups and establishing educational or experience requirements that adversely affect members of a protected group.

Once an adverse impact claim is established, the district must show that the practice is valid for the purpose intended. This is a "business necessity" defense. The Supreme Court accepted such a defense in allowing the use of the National Teachers Examination (NTE) for teacher certification and to determine employee salaries (*United States* v. *State of South Carolina,* 1978). However, in *Griggs* v. *Duke Power Company* (1971), the Supreme Court held that the use of a test of general intelligence for selection purposes was discriminatory because the test had an adverse impact on minority applicants and had not been validated for use in employee selection. The use of an arbitrary cutoff score as part of a selection process without prior investigation of the potentially harmful effects of such a decision is likely to be successfully challenged (Beckham, 1985).

Perpetuation of past discrimination refers to the lingering effects of discriminatory practices after the practices themselves have ended. Under segregation in the South, for example, Black staff members were assigned to schools that enrolled only Black students. These were often schools with outdated facilities and limited budgets. After integration took place, the effects of previous personnel assignment practices lingered until districts took action to reassign personnel in order to achieve balance in the racial distribution of staff members.

The fourth type of discrimination is *failure to make accommodation.* Section 504 of the Rehabilitation Act of 1973 and the Americans with Disabilities Act of 1990 require employers to make reasonable accommodations in order to enable employees who have disabilities to perform a job. Reasonable accommodations include improving accessibility; restructuring jobs; modifying work schedules; designing flexible leave policies; adjusting or modifying examinations and training materials; and providing qualified aides or assistants (Fersh & Thomas, 1993).

Sexual Harassment

Sexual harassment is a form of sex discrimination and is illegal under Title VII of the Civil Rights Act, although the term itself does not appear in the statute. Sexual harassment claims may be analyzed under either the disparate treatment or adverse impact theories, depending on the situation (Lindemann & Kadue, 1992).

Sexual harassment claims are usually one of three types—unwelcome sexual advances, gender-based animosity, or a sexually charged workplace. *Quid pro quo* discrimination occurs when an employee is the object of sexual advances that involve explicit or implicit promises of employment benefits in return for sexual favors. Hostile environment discrimination results from other employees or supervisors engaging in conduct that is offensive to an employee because of his or her gender, even if the conduct is not sexual in nature. For example, a woman who joins a previously all-male work group may be subjected to hostile comments and treatment by the male members of the group because of her gender (Lindemann & Kadue, 1992). Even if the actions of employees are not sexually suggestive, they constitute sexual harassment if the intent is to embarrass or humiliate another employee or to prevent that individual from doing his or her best work.

The Supreme Court, in *Meritor Savings Bank* v. *Vinson* (1986), held that sexual harassment violates Title VII's prohibition against sex discrimination even if the loss incurred by the offended employee is psychological and not financial. *Meritor* involved a sexual harassment claim against a supervisor by a female employee. The woman admitted that she had voluntarily had sexual relations with her boss on numerous occasions. The bank argued that the voluntary nature of the liaison freed the bank from liability, but the Supreme Court held that the test for sexual harassment was whether the woman had indicated that the sexual advances were unwelcome (Lindemann & Kadue, 1992).

Both genders are subject to sexual harassment in the workplace, but women experience it more often than men and are more likely than men to report it. That may be because men and women view certain types of behavior differently. Sexual advances that are viewed negatively by women are often thought of positively by men (Konrad & Gutek, 1986). The increased litigation involving charges of sexual harassment has led to greater awareness of this problem but has also created confusion about what types of behavior are appropriate in the workplace.

If one is not already in effect, a policy should be developed by school districts designating an individual who is responsible for investigating charges of sexual harassment. The individual assigned to investigate should be some-one who will treat the charges in a serious and professional manner, and the procedures followed should be thorough, prompt, and impartial.

The policy should also describe alternative procedures for investigating and acting on charges made by an employee against his or her immediate su-pervisor that do not require the employee to confront the supervisor. Care should be taken to avoid retaliating against employees who file charges of sexual harassment (Hubbartt, 1993).

Administrators must also be prepared to investigate charges of sexual ha-rassment made by students against teachers, counselors, or other school per-sonnel and, if a school employee is found guilty of harassment, to take prompt disciplinary action. Charges by students against school personnel are difficult to judge because of the strong emotions such charges arouse and be-cause of the difficulty of proving or disproving them. For students, sexual at-tention from a teacher or someone else in a position of trust frequently pro-duces confusion, guilt, and loss of trust. For employees, the charges can result in the loss of a job or even the end of a career. Even if the charges are found to be false, an adult who is charged with sexual harassment of a child is un-likely ever to fully recover the esteem and credibility that were lost.

When the person charging sexual harassment is a student, the investiga-tor must first establish that the student understands sexual harassment and is not simply misinterpreting harmless behavior. Most children today have a pretty clear idea about the types of behavior that are acceptable and unac-ceptable, but occasionally a child will misinterpret an innocent gesture by an adult. As a result, many teachers, counselors, and other personnel avoid touching students out of fear that they may be falsely charged with sexual harassment.

As unlikely as it seems, a student will occasionally charge a teacher or ad-ministrator with sexual advances in order get even with the adult for some-thing he or she has done to the student or a friend. Those who are responsi-ble for investigating students' claims should be aware of this possibility.

If the initial investigation establishes that the child understands sexual harassment and is not simply seeking revenge, the investigator's first con-cern must be to protect the child and any other children who might be at risk. If there is reason to believe that the child's charges have a basis in fact, police should be contacted. School personnel have a responsibility to pro-tect children in their care from exploitation. No other responsibility is more important.

Defending Personnel Practices

If a district is charged with discrimination in hiring practices, it may be able successfully to defend its actions by showing that the relevant characteristics of the applicant pool are comparable to the characteristics of the employees hired. Thus, for example, if 15 percent of applicants are members of a protected group and the district can show that an equal or greater percentage of persons hired were members of that group, that constitutes *prima facie* evidence of the absence of disparate treatment.

A more stringent test involves a comparison of the characteristics of those hired with the characteristics of members of the labor pool. This was the test used by the courts in the *Hazelwood* case. Hazelwood School District was charged by the Justice Department with violating Title VII of the Civil Rights Act by failing to recruit and employ Black teachers. The district's attorneys argued that, since the percentage of Black teachers employed by the district equaled or exceeded the percentage of Black students, the district was in compliance. The Supreme Court ultimately ruled that the relevant comparison was not the ratio of teachers to students but rather the ratio of minority teachers employed by the district to the number of qualified minority persons in the labor pool in the St. Louis metropolitan area. Hazelwood lost the suit and was required to hire and give back pay to minority applicants who had previously been rejected (*Hazelwood School District* v. *United States*, 1977).

Preventing discrimination before it happens is preferable to correcting it after it has occurred. School districts can prevent discrimination by developing and implementing personnel procedures designed to avoid it. Among the recommended practices are the use of structured interviews rather than open-ended questions for selection and establishing criterion validity for any tests that are used for personnel decisions. Districts are wise to avoid concentrating staff members of one race in a few schools and, where such concentrations exist, to reassign individuals in order to achieve a more equal racial balance (Beckham, 1985).

Establishing a Defense

Personnel practices that have disparate impact may nevertheless be allowed by the courts, provided that the district is able to show a bona fide occupational qualification (BFOQ) or business necessity. One school district was upheld by the courts after hiring a male applicant without a master's degree over a female with the degree by arguing the male could be hired at a lower salary and could also perform coaching duties. To successfully use business necessity as a defense, an employer must be able to show that the practice is necessary for the efficient operation of the district and that no acceptable alternatives with lesser racial impact are available (Valente, 1980).

Exclusion refers to the degree of pervasiveness of a particular practice. If personnel practices occasionally result in adverse impact to members of protected groups, there is a lower level of legal vulnerability than if the practices consistently result in adverse impact upon those groups. Employers are most likely to win a legal challenge when a practice involves a low degree of exclusion and a high degree of business necessity. Employers are most vulnerable when exclusion is high and business necessity is low (Schlei & Grossman, 1976).

Other factors that are sometimes considered in discrimination cases are the degree of potential risk to human health and safety or the potential for economic loss resulting from employee performance. An airline company may be able to justify exclusionary selection practices in hiring pilots by showing that the practices are necessary to reduce the chance of injury or death to passengers resulting from performance of inadequately trained employees. A hospital might support exclusionary hiring practices by showing that they are necessary to protect the health of patients. Exclusionary practices may also be defended by showing that they reduce the amount of potential economic loss to the employer resulting from employees who lack essential skills. Employers whose work involves lower levels of risk would be held to a comparably lower level of exclusionary practice in hiring.

Accurate and detailed records are a necessity to a successful defense if a district is charged with discrimination in employment practices. It is recommended that the district personnel office maintain charts showing the age, race, color, sex, and national origin of all applicants and similar information about those hired. Since collecting such information on the application form itself may itself constitute *prima facie* evidence of discriminatory intent, it is advisable to use a preemployment inquiry form to collect that data. This is a form that all applicants are asked to complete and return separately from the application form itself. The applicant has the option of filling out the preemployment inquiry anonymously in order to avoid the possibility of being identified.

The Uniform Guidelines on Employee Selection Procedures (1978) spell out procedural rules to help employers and licensing and certification boards to comply with the laws on discrimination. The guidelines cover such decisions as hiring, promotion, licensing, and certification, but they do not deal with recruitment (Caruth, Noe, & Mondy, 1988).

Affirmative Action and Reverse Discrimination

Employers with federal contracts as well as those who have been found guilty of discrimination or who have been ordered by a court to do so are required to adopt affirmative action plans. Other employers may decide voluntarily to implement such plans. The first steps in the process are to identify problems with existing personnel practices and develop a plan to correct them. The plan should specifically address recruitment, training, and promotion, and identify goals and time tables that will lead to eventual resolution of the problems (Jacobs, 1993).

The intent of affirmative action is to open job opportunities that have traditionally been closed to minorities and women. The purpose is not, as some have assumed, to achieve "proportional representation through preferential hiring" (Fullinwider, 1980, p. 159). There is little disagreement on the need for and importance of providing educational and employment opportunities to members of groups that have been subject to discrimination. However, preferential hiring, which is one element of affirmative action, arouses strong feelings from both proponents and opponents (Fullinwider, 1980).

Title VII of the Civil Rights Act of 1964 provides that employers are not required to grant preferential treatment to members of protected groups as a way of achieving balance in the racial or gender characteristics of a group of workers. This practice is known as *reverse discrimination,* since it sanctions discrimination against members of historically favored groups.

Reverse discrimination occurs when members of a protected group such as Blacks or females are given preference in employment decisions in order to correct the effects of previous discrimination. These actions have been approved by the courts when they have been designed specifically to correct past discrimination and do not do unnecessary harm to the rights of other employees.

However, the Supreme Court rejected an agreement between the Jackson (Michigan) Board of Education and the Jackson Education Association that was intended to protect the jobs of minority employees by requiring the district to maintain a constant proportion of minority workers. This meant that White employees with more seniority were laid off while minority employees with less seniority stayed on. The district argued that this protection for minority employees was necessary because of the severity and duration of societal discrimination.

The Supreme Court held that, in the context of affirmative action, racial classifications must be justified by a compelling state purpose and that societal discrimination alone was an insufficient basis for its use. An agreement such as that entered into by the board and the teachers' association could only be justified, the Court ruled, if there was evidence of prior discrimination by the employer. Since no such evidence was produced, the Court held that the clause was invalid (*Wygant v. Jackson Board of Education,* 1986).

Summary

Local school boards have the authority to employ, assign, transfer, suspend, and terminate teachers, and they are given wide latitude by the courts in the exercise of that power. States require teachers to have a valid teaching certificate. Boards may assign teachers to any school as long as there is no violation of the bargaining agreement or the teachers' contract. Reassignments are subject to legal challenge if they involve a demotion, but most courts have upheld the board in these cases.

Title VII of the Civil Rights Act affords protection against discriminatory employment decisions based on race, color, sex, religion, and national origin for all employees. The Pregnancy Discrimination Act extended the same protections to pregnant employees. The Age Discrimination in Employment Act protects employees above the age of 40 from age discrimination in personnel decisions, and the Equal Pay Act requires employers to pay women the same as men who perform similar jobs. The Rehabilitation Act and Americans with Disabilities Act make it illegal for employers to refuse to hire persons with disabilities because of their disabilities and require employers to make reasonable accommodations for such employees.

Discrimination is of four types—disparate treatment, perpetuation of past discrimination, disparate impact, and failure to make reasonable accommodation. Employers who hold federal contracts or who have entered into a consent decree with the Equal Employment Opportunity Commission may be required to implement an affirmative action plan. Preferential hiring under such plans is called reverse discrimination.

Suggested Activities

1. Examine the State Code of your state and identify the qualifications for teachers, counselors, and administrators. What qualifications are listed besides educational ones?
2. Does your state permit school boards to enact a residency requirement for its employees? What are the arguments for and against requiring teachers to live within the boundaries of the school district?
3. All states require teachers and other professional personnel to be licensed. They also provide for revocation of the license. What are the conditions for which a professional license may be revoked? Does the State Code spell out due process rights of employees whose licenses are revoked? If so, what are they?
4. Obtain a copy of a sexual harassment policy for a school district and answer these questions:
   a. What actions does the policy require a supervisor to take when he or she first learns about a charge of sexual harassment by a person whom he or she supervises?
   b. What procedures are recommended to ascertain the facts about a harassment charge?
   c. What corrective actions are suggested or required when a charge of sexual harassment is confirmed?
5. Suppose that you are the principal of a middle school. One of your teachers belongs to a religious group that requires its members to observe six holy days each year. Members are required to be absent from their work on those days. The bargaining agreement provides for three religious holidays and three days for conducting "necessary personal business." Personal business days are granted only if the employee can demonstrate need. The teacher in your school asks that he be allowed to use the per-

sonal business days for religious observance. This has not been done previously in the district. What will you tell the teacher? (The Supreme Court decided a similar case in *Ansonia Board of Education* v. *Philbrook*, 1986).

References

Ansonia Board of Education v. *Philbrook*, 478 U.S. 1034, 1047 (1986).

Arline v. *School Board of Nassau County*, 772 F.2d 759 (1985).

Beckham, J. (1985). *Legal aspects of employee assessment and selection in public schools*. Topeka, KS: National Organization on Legal Problems of Education.

Caruth, D., Noe, R., & Mondy, R. (1988). *Staffing the contemporary organization*. New York: Quorum.

Connick v. *Myers*, 461 U.S. 138 (1983).

Cox v. *Dardanelle Public School District*, 790 F.2d 668 (1986).

Daniels v. *Quinn*, 801 F.2d 687 (1986).

Director, J. (1973). Mandatory maternity leave, rules or policies for public school teachers as constituting violation of equal protection clause of Fourteenth amendment to Federal Constitution. *American Law Reports federal cases and annotations* (17 ALR 768). Rochester, NY: Lawyers Co-operative Publishing.

Education law (Vol. 2). (1989). New York: Matthew Bender.

Eisenstadt v. *Baird*, 405 U.S. 438 (1972).

Ferrara v. *Mills*, 781 F.2d 1508 (1986).

Fersh, D., & Thomas, P. (1993). *Complying with the Americans with Disabilities Act: A guidebook for management and people with disabilities*. Westport, CT: Quorum.

Fullinwider, R. (1980). *The reverse discrimination controversy: A moral and legal analysis*. Totowa, NJ: Rowman & Littlefield.

Gordon, P. (1992). The job application process after the Americans with Disabilities Act. *Employee Relations Law Journal*, *18*, 185–213.

Griggs v. *Duke Power Company*, 401 U.S. 424 (1971).

Gurmankin v. *Costanzo*, 556 F.2d 184 (1977).

Hazelwood School District v. *United States*, 433 U.S. 299 (1977).

Hubbartt, W. (1993). *Personnel policy handbook*. New York: McGraw Hill.

Hudgins, H., Jr., & Vacca, R. (1985). *Law and education: Contemporary issues and court decisions* (rev. ed.). Charlottesville, VA: Michie.

Jacobs, R. (1993). *Legal compliance guide to personnel management*. Englewood Cliffs, NJ: Prentice Hall.

Jett v. *Dallas Independent School District*, 798 F.2d 748 (1986).

Konrad, A., & Gutek, B. (1986). Impact of work experiences on attitudes toward sexual harassment. *Administrative Science Quarterly*, *31*, 422–438.

Lindemann, B., & Kadue, D. (1992). *Primer on sexual harassment*. Washington, DC: Bureau of National Affairs.

May v. *Evansville-Vanderburgh School Corporation*, 787 F.2d 1105 (1986).

McCarthy, M. (1983). Discrimination in employment. In J. Beckham & P. Zirkel (Eds.), *Legal issues in public school employment* (pp. 22–54). Bloomington, IN: Phi Delta Kappa.

McCarthy, M., & Cambron-McCabe, N. (1992). *Public school law: Teachers' and students' rights* (3rd ed.). Boston: Allyn and Bacon.

McCulloch, K. (1981). *Selecting employees safely under the law*. Englewood Cliffs, NJ: Prentice Hall.

Meritor Savings Bank v. *Vinson*, 106 S.Ct. 2399 (1986).

Miner, M., & Miner, J. (1978). *Employee selection within the law*. Washington, DC: Bureau of National Affairs.

Schlei, B., & Grossman, P. (1976). *Employment*

discrimination law. Washington, DC: Bureau of National Affairs.

Schneid, T. (1992). *The Americans with Disabilities Act: A practical guide for managers.* New York: Van Nostrand Reinhold.

Sorenson, G. (1987). Employees. In S. Thomas (Ed.), *The yearbook of school law* (pp. 1–44). Topeka, KS: National Organization on Legal Problems of Education.

Sovereign, K. (1984). *Personnel law.* Reston, VA: Reston Publishing.

Strahan, R., & Turner, L. C. (1987). *The courts and the schools.* New York: Longman.

Uniform guidelines on employee selection procedures. (1978). 29 *Code of Federal Regulations* 1607.

United States v. *State of South Carolina,* 434 U.S. 1026 (1978).

Valente, W. (1980). *Law in the schools.* Columbus, OH: Merrill.

van Geel, T. (1987). *The courts and American education law.* Buffalo, NY: Prometheus.

Wardwell v. *Board of Education of the City School District of Cincinnati,* 529 F.2d 625 (1976).

Wygant v. *Jackson Board of Education,* 476 U.S. 267 (1986).

13

COLLECTIVE BARGAINING
IN SCHOOLS

The work of most teachers in schools in the United States is governed by negotiated contracts between teachers' organizations and boards of education.
The process by which the parties reach agreement on a contract is known as
collective bargaining. Collective bargaining originated early in this century as
industrial unions fought successfully for better working conditions and the
right to participate in decisions about their work.

The National Education Association (NEA), the larger of two national organizations that represent teachers, is not affiliated with the labor movement, preferring the designation "professional organization." However, in its
actions, NEA resembles industrial unions; its tactics and objectives are quite
similar to those of the American Federation of Teachers (AFT), which is the
other, smaller organization for teachers. The AFT is affiliated with the national labor movement.

Board negotiators are sensitive to the dollar costs of union proposals but
pay less attention to their potential impact on instructional quality. The
unions seek provisions to protect job security, establish satisfactory conditions of work, and guarantee generous salaries and benefits. These and other
similar provisions may create barriers to improved instruction by limiting the
district's power to dismiss or transfer employees, change job descriptions, or
alter staffing patterns. Once incorporated into the contract, they are difficult
to change, and improving instruction becomes dependent on the willingness
of the union to accept modifications in the contract.

Plan of the Chapter

This book advocates an approach to collective bargaining that encourages
negotiators to consider the potential effects on instruction of contract
proposals, in addition to the usual attention given to issues of cost and

223

security. The following topics are covered in this chapter: (1) background on collective bargaining in schools, (2) scope of bargaining (3) new forms of collective bargaining, (4) negotiating processes, and (5) impact of collective bargaining on schools.

Background on Collective Bargaining in Schools

Collective bargaining has been called one of the three most significant developments in public education in the past quarter century (Mitchell, Kerchner, Erck, & Pryor, 1981). (The other two are desegregation and the introduction of categorical aid programs by the federal government.)

In 1959, Wisconsin became the first state to pass legislation governing collective bargaining between teacher unions and school boards (Cresswell & Murphy, 1980). Since that time, about 80 percent of the states have enacted enabling legislation. These laws vary in the degree of regulatory specificity and in the types of rights accorded unions. Some statutes provide an opportunity for teachers' unions to "meet and confer" with school boards, whereas others contain detailed and specific lists of what may and may not be negotiated.

The right to "meet and confer" gives employees' organizations an opportunity to meet with the board to argue for improvements in worker security, conditions of work, and benefits. The board is obligated to hear the teachers' presentation but is free to ignore their suggestions. "Meet and confer" is based on an assumption of commonality of interests of teachers and board members and it is the first stage in the evolution of a stable relationship between unions and boards.

The first stage breaks down when teachers realize that their goals are in conflict with those of the board, and teachers turn to militant tactics to win concessions, leading to acrimonious exchanges and occasional strikes (Jessup, 1981). Out of the conflict and strife emerges a second stage in the relationship, characterized by more equitable distribution of power (Mitchell et al., 1981).

This "second generation" of labor relations is characterized by acceptance by boards of teachers' right to bargain and by reduced conflict between the parties, leading to a period of relative stability (Mitchell et al., 1981). Teachers' organizations frequently wield considerable power during this stage, and quality standards are often allowed to slide in the interest of maintaining tranquil relations.

A more mature "third generation" of labor relations begins when parents begin to demand action to improve instruction and removal of incompetent teachers, or when the board decides on its own to initiate such actions. At this stage, boards are generally more sensitive to teachers' rights to due process and are aware of past neglect of those rights. When boards with a strong commitment to qualify education demonstrate a willingness to involve teachers in decisions on curriculum and instruction, significant progress can result (Mitchell et al., 1981).

Private Sector Bargaining

Collective bargaining in the private sector is regulated by the National Labor Relations Act, but there is no comparable federal statute governing bargaining involving public employees. Collective bargaining for public employees is governed by state statutes, case law, and administrative regulations (Cresswell & Murphy, 1980). Some state statutes are comprehensive, applying to all public employees, but others apply only to teachers.

There is general agreement on several points, however:

1. Strikes of public employees are unlawful or, if permitted, are closely regulated. Nevertheless, strikes among teachers are fairly common.
2. Bargaining units may not represent members of more than one employee group (Cresswell & Murphy, 1980). Both teachers and administrators may negotiate with the board, but they may not be represented by the same organization.
3. Parties are allowed to negotiate a procedure for resolving impasses and disagreements regarding interpretation of the contract. In some cases, the state requires binding arbitration if the parties are not able to arrive at a contract (Cresswell & Murphy, 1980).
4. When one organization represents all workers, it is called an *exclusive representative;* if each organization represents only its own members, it is called a *proportional representative.*

Scope of Bargaining

Topics of discussion between teacher organizations and boards of education are determined by the legal framework governing bargaining, the history of the relationship between the parties, and their willingness to negotiate an issue (Cresswell & Murphy, 1980). Legislation may specify mandatory topics (those about which the parties must negotiate) and exclude others from the bargaining table. Any topic that is not specifically mandated or forbidden is subject to negotiation if the parties agree. A list of items that are often included in teacher contracts appears in Exhibit 13.1.

Unions like to widen the scope of the negotiations to cover as many aspects of the work situation as possible, but management generally prefers to limit the scope of the talks in the belief that anything not covered in the contract remains a prerogative of management (Mitchell et al., 1981). In addition to negotiating salaries and conditions of work, teacher unions favor including in the contract policies relating to curriculum, student placement,

Membership
Negotiation procedures (dates, negotiation team authority,
      modification of the contract)
Grievance procedures (purpose, definition, rules)
Teacher organization rights and privileges
Employee rights
Leaves of absence (sick leave, temporary leaves, extended leaves)
Sabbatical leave
Vacations
School calendar
Work schedule (hours, duty-free time)
Teaching load (number of classes, number of students per class)
Extra duties (monitoring bus, cafeteria, playground, and hallways)
Personnel actions
Reduction in force
Evaluation of personnel
Curriculum and textbook committees
Professional development
Insurance
Protection of employees and property
Deductions from salary
Maintenance of standards
Management rights

EXHIBIT 13.1   Typical Provisions of Teacher Contracts

Sources: New Jersey Principals and Supervisors Association (1982) and National Association of Elementary School Principals (1982).

and teacher selection and assignment. Almost half (46 percent) of agreements in effect during the 1981–82 school year contained provisions on curriculum. About 64 percent had policies on student placement, and 96 percent provided for policies relating to teacher selection and assignment (Goldschmidt, Bowers, Riley, & Stuart, 1984).

Some contract provisions have more impact on instruction than others. Examples of proposals that could have an effect on instruction are shown in Figure 13.1. The figure shows the positions taken by the union and the board of education on each issue. In the middle, a marker indicates the position that would be most likely to promote instructional quality. The nearer the mark appears to the position taken by one of the parties, the greater the likelihood that that party's position is instructionally responsible. The issues are discussed in the paragraphs that follow.

Teacher Evaluation

Teachers' unions are seeking to define new roles and responsibilities for principals in the evaluation process. Through collective bargaining, teachers' unions push to include in the contract restrictions on evaluation practices that they believe are unfair or that might be used by administrators to punish teachers. The restrictions include limiting when and where teacher observations can be held and what data may be included in written evaluations. Unions also seek to write into the contract prohibitions against evaluating teachers on the use of one approved model of instruction, arguing that teachers may achieve equally good results using a variety of approaches (Black, 1993).

A review of current master contracts found that in some districts, principals were required to hold preconferences prior to scheduled classroom observations and to review with teachers during the preconference any instruments that were to be used for the observation. Some contracts required principals to write verbatim reports of what they saw and heard during the observation and to share those reports with teachers. Administrators were allowed to comment only on parts of the lesson that were included in the written report when they met with teachers for a follow-up conference (Black, 1993).

Some contracts stated that principals were not allowed to use data from a classroom observation to evaluate a teacher unless the principal was present in the classroom during the entire lesson. Principals were allowed to make unannounced visits to classrooms but could not refer to such observations for evaluation purposes (Black, 1993).

Transfer and Reassignment/Selection

Teacher transfer and reassignment policies have long been an area of contention between boards and unions (McDonnell & Pascal, 1979). Teacher unions prefer limiting involuntary transfers to situations involving declining enrollment or changes in programs and favor making seniority the sole criterion for deciding who is transferred (Cresswell & Murphy, 1980). Board negotiators favor allowing administrators to make these decisions under more general guidelines.

The importance for teacher morale of contractual safeguards against arbitrary decisions on transfer and reassignment should not be underestimated, but neither should the potential negative consequences for the quality of instruction be overlooked. A principal who is prevented from selecting the most qualified teacher is hampered in trying to improve the quality of learning in the school.

As school restructuring efforts proceed, organized teachers in some areas are pressing for authority to play a more active role in personnel decisions, arguing that this empowers teachers. They advocate a more direct voice for teachers in teacher selection and favor assigning teachers responsibility for assisting colleagues who are performing unsatisfactorily and for providing training for mentor teachers in induction programs. Boards generally agree

Issue	Teacher Position
Teacher evaluation	Limited number of classroom observations with advance notice
Transfer and reassignment	More senior teachers have choice of teaching assignments; no involuntary transfers
Selection	Teacher committee decides which applicants are hired
Class size	Specified upper limit; class divided or aide provided if limit exceeded
Preparations	Limit on number; additional planning time provided if exceeded
Extra duty	Duties required only if stated in agreement; pay for all extra duty
Planning time	Minimum number of minutes per week; no exceptions
Curriculum and textbook committees	Teachers volunteer and are paid extra
Reduction in force	Enrollment loss and program change only basis for reduction
	Reductions absorbed by attrition whenever possible; otherwise seniority governs
Maintenance of standards	Favor

FIGURE 13.1   Location of Most Instructionally Effective Position between Opposing Demands of Teacher Union and Board on Selected Issues

to teacher participation in these matters but view teacher control as intrusion and resist it.

Class Size/Preparations

Class size is another contentious issue between boards and teacher associations. The union argues that limiting class size facilitates teachers' work, and boards answer that reducing class size by even a small amount is expensive and produces no verifiable increase in student learning. Boards are especially opposed to provisions that require dividing a class or providing an aide if enrollment goes over a stated limit by only one or two students.

Limits on the number of different preparations a teacher may be assigned make sense from the point of view of instructional effectiveness. Again, however, such a policy is difficult to administer if expressed in absolute terms with no room allowed for administrative judgment.

Instructionally Effective Position						Board Position
—	—	—	—	X	—	No limit, no advance notice
—	—	—	—	X	—	Administrators decide, considering teachers' expressed preferences
—	—	X	—	—	—	Principal decides which applicants are hired
—	—	—	X	—	—	Principal decides optimum number based on teacher skills, budget, and student needs
—	—	X	—	—	—	Principal considers number of preparations but no absolute limit on number
—	—	—	X	—	—	Duties performed as needed upon assignment by principal; pay only if contract requires
—	X	—	—	—	—	Provided within limits of available resources
—	X	—	—	—	—	Teachers volunteer or are appointed; no extra pay
—	—	—	—	X	—	Enrollment loss, program change, budget cutbacks, and other factors allowed
—	—	—	—	X	—	Reductions absorbed by attrition if possible; otherwise seniority and other factors govern
—	—	—	—	—	X	Oppose

Extra Duty

Unions prefer that the contract specify the extra duties teachers are required to perform and include rules to ensure fairness in the assignment of those duties. They also favor provisions for additional pay for noninstructional tasks.

Duties that have traditionally been a part of teachers' responsibilities, such as sponsoring clubs and meeting with parents, have become optional under most negotiated agreements. In districts that do not pay extra for them, these jobs are often not done. Even teachers who are willing to donate their time are discouraged from doing so by union officers anxious to preserve the principle of extra pay for extra work (Mitchell et al., 1981).

Some extra duties are necessary for the efficient operation of the school, but an excessive number can interfere with good instruction. It is not always possible to anticipate what duties may be necessary, so some flexibility is needed. Everything considered, the best solution seems to be to include in the contract a statement acknowledging the administration's responsibility for fair and judicious use of extra duty and providing extra pay for the more time-consuming tasks. The statement should also acknowledge teachers' responsibility to perform the duties.

Planning Time

Teachers seek to include in the contract a statement that guarantees a minimum number of minutes of planning time each week. From an instructional point of view, these regulations are desirable, but overly prescriptive rules should be avoided.

Curriculum and Textbook Committees

The majority of contracts contain no provision dealing with curriculum revision and textbook selection committees (Cresswell & Murphy, 1980). These committees perform important functions, and teachers who serve on them should receive payment for their time.

Reduction in Force

Both sides have an interest in limiting the impact of reduction in force on employee morale. Usually both teacher and board negotiators are willing to discuss the order of release, but they sometimes disagree on the criteria to be used. Unions prefer that seniority be the only factor considered, whereas management argues for allowing considerations of performance and program needs in making reduction-in-force decisions (Cresswell & Murphy, 1980).

Reduction in force can impact instruction by depleting the faculty of a school of persons qualified to teacher certain subjects and by triggering bumping, which may lead to less qualified teachers taking over for those who are more qualified. Chapter 15 discusses this topic in more detail.

Maintenance of Standards

Teacher negotiators push to include maintenance of standards clauses in contracts, but board negotiators oppose them. This clause requires the administration to consult with the union before making any change in existing policy that has an impact on teachers' welfare or working conditions (Cresswell & Murphy, 1980). The purpose is to perpetuate existing conditions. The clauses are designed to be inflexible and have no redeeming feature.

In general, collective bargaining has positive effects on teacher morale, but if the process results in contracts that are excessively regulatory, it can have deleterious effects on learning. The position taken in this book is that contracts that provide for more flexibility of administrative decision making, combined with mechanisms that protect teachers' rights and professional autonomy, are most likely to create conditions that can lead to improved quality of instruction.

New Forms of Collective Bargaining

In recent years, a search has been undertaken to find new approaches to collective bargaining that will permit the parties to reach agreements more quickly and encourage boards and unions to cooperate in the interest of improving education. Several new models have been tried, with varying degrees of success. Among the new approaches are expedited bargaining, progressive bargaining, the win/win approach, principled negotiations, and strategic bargaining.

In *expedited bargaining,* the parties agree to limit the amount of time available to reach an agreement and the number of issues that will be discussed. The time limit is usually two to three weeks and the number of items to be discussed is usually no more than 10. Expedited bargaining avoids the protracted discussions that have in the past held up school operations and planning while negotiations were underway (National Education Association, 1991).

Progressive bargaining is the opposite of expedited bargaining. Progressive bargaining is intended to permit full discussion of any issue that either party wishes to raise. Because of the number of issues examined and the amount of time spent on each one, progressive bargaining sometimes continues for months. Issues are referred to subcommittees for study, and if a stalemate is reached, fact finding and mediation are used to resolve the impasses (National Education Association, 1991).

Win/win bargaining was developed by a sociology professor, Irving Goldaber, who specialized in conflict resolution and hostage intervention. This form of bargaining is highly structured, and includes detailed rules that govern negotiating sessions. At the outset, participants must agree that the needs of the institution take precedence over individual goals (Booth, 1993).

A neutral facilitator oversees the negotiations, and the facilitator and members of the negotiating teams take part in a communications laboratory before negotiations start. The parties meet over a three-week period to discuss issues and select those to be included in the contract. The issues are then assigned to subcommittees composed of equal numbers of union and management representatives. An intensive weekend negotiating session is scheduled to resolve issues on which the parties have not been able to reach agreement (National Education Association, 1991).

Principled negotiations was developed by the Harvard University Negotiation Project and is intended for use in any setting, including negotiations between employers and employees. The objective of this approach is to allow both parties to benefit without compromising their interests (Fisher & Ury, 1981, 1988).

The principled negotiations approach provides a set of guidelines for negotiators that help remove the most common stumbling blocks to agreement. Among these guidelines are the following (National Education Association, 1991):

1. *Separate the people from the problem.* Negotiators are encouraged to accept emotions expressed by the other side and to allow people to let off steam without reacting angrily. Negotiators are urged to listen actively and speak clearly.
2. *Focus on interests, not positions.* An individual's or group's position on an issue is a way of advancing an underlying interest. By trying to identify the interest, bargaining partners can identify other, more acceptable, positions that may be equally effective at advancing their interests.
3. *Invent options for mutual gain.* The idea here is to create new choices that satisfy both shared and separate interests. This guideline helps avoid situations in which both parties lock in to positions early and refuse to yield. It also helps the parties refrain from the assumption that a win for one side necessarily signifies a loss for the other.
4. *Evaluate options, not power.* The parties to the negotiations should establish a set of criteria by which proposals will be judged. The criteria might include fairness, cost, and practicality. In the absence of criteria, the final outcome is often determined by which party is more unyielding in its positions.

Strategic bargaining is the negotiating counterpart to strategic planning. In this approach, the parties are urged to develop a vision of the future for their organization and to identify potential hurdles that might be encountered in trying to actualize that vision. The power of strategic bargaining is its focus on the future and the underlying assumption that labor and management must contribute to building the future, that neither can do it alone (National Education Association, 1991).

Negotiating Processes

Both sides in collective bargaining know that they have the power to inflict damage on the other. The board can withhold the concessions teachers seek, and teachers can strike. (Even in localities in which strikes are unlawful, unions are sometimes willing to risk them in order to extract concessions). Most of the time, collective bargaining works because the two sides develop a level of trust that allows them to work cooperatively to reach a mutually acceptable agreement. This trust does not emerge immediately, however. As with most human exchanges, development of trust between negotiators takes time.

Successful negotiations occur in three stages, as depicted in Figure 13.2. In the first stage, demands are heard and agreement is reached on the issues to be negotiated (Lipsky & Conley, 1986). In Stage 2, the two parties acknowledge one another's legitimacy and begin to develop trust. In the third stage, serious bargaining takes place, with both parties making concessions on less vital issues in order to gain concessions on more important questions.

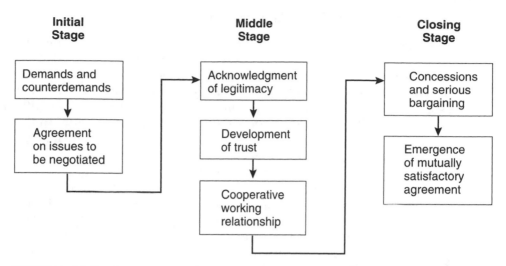

FIGURE 13.2   Stages in a Successful Collective Bargaining Relationship

Both sides learn what the other side hopes to gain from the negotiations early in the process, but it takes longer for them to begin to get a picture of what the other is willing to accept. Bargaining proceeds through a series of give-and-take exchanges with each party yielding on some demands in return for concessions from the other side (Mitchell et al., 1981). Teacher negotiators, for example, may demand a 10 percent salary increase, expecting to settle for 7 or 8 percent and prepared to strike if the board does not come through with at least 6.5 percent. The board, on the other hand, may approach the table prepared to offer 6 percent but preferring to settle for 5.5. Obviously one side must yield if a settlement is to be reached. However, neither side wants to make a concession too early in the process for fear of appearing weak.

As the distance between the parties narrows, bargaining becomes more difficult because the negotiators are nearing their final positions. Impasses are not uncommon at this point and are more likely to occur when one or both sides is poorly informed about the other's true position.

When the board signals that it is making its final salary offer, for example, union negotiators must decide whether the board is bluffing or will, under pressure, agree to a higher amount. Teachers' representatives may propose a figure they believe is slightly above the board's predetermined limit in hopes that board negotiators will yield in order to reach a settlement, but this strategy has some risks. If the teachers miscalculate, they may provoke a strike that neither side wants (Mitchell et al., 1981).

If the differences are resolved and an impasse avoided, an agreement is finally reached. The work is now finished unless the teachers or board members reject the settlement. If negotiators have stayed in close touch with their constituencies throughout the process, however, that should not happen.

Processes for New Forms of Bargaining

Negotiating models vary in the degree of importance attached to each of the stages in Figure 13.2. Several of the newer models of collective bargaining attempt to reduce the total amount of time devoted to bargaining. In win/win bargaining, identification of issues takes place prior to the initiation of bargaining. In the process of deciding which issues to negotiate, the bargaining teams begin to develop a cooperative working relationship, so that when negotiations start, the participants are ready to move immediately to the closing stage.

In progressive bargaining, the initial stage is prolonged as members of both teams discuss a variety of issues. These preliminary discussions allow the parties to become acquainted and to develop trust, so that by the time bargaining gets underway, an agreement can be reached quickly.

Expedited bargaining attempts to speed up negotiations by limiting the number of issues discussed and setting deadlines for reaching agreement. However, since this model does not provide for preliminary discussions, the parties are not always able to reach a satisfactory consensus on the issues they wish to resolve.

In its emphasis on principles and deemphasis on power, the principled negotiations model expands the middle stage of negotiations and devotes less time to the initial and closing stages. This approach is particularly effective at building trust and encouraging the emergence of cooperative working relationships.

Strategic bargaining shifts the focus of attention away from current issues toward consideration of the organization's future. It places considerably more emphasis than other models on the middle stage of bargaining. In arriving at an agreement about the future, the parties often are able to develop a trusting, cooperative relationship that permits them to move to the final stage of negotiations with confidence that they will be successful.

Resolving Impasses

The climate of negotiations is affected by several factors, including the personalities of the participants, the pressure each side feels from its constituencies, and the nature of the situation (Cresswell & Murphy, 1980). When trust breaks down and union and management representatives find themselves at an impasse, outside intervention may be needed. Mediation, fact finding, and arbitration are used to resolve differences in such a situation. Compulsory or binding arbitration involves a presentation by each side of its position on the issues they have been unable to resolve. After hearing both arguments, the arbitrator makes a decision that is binding on both sides. An alternative approach is final offer arbitration, which involves both sides making final offers to the arbitrator on the issues in conflict. The arbitrator then chooses one of the offers (O'Reilly, 1978).

In preparing for final offer arbitration, each side must consider how the other side is likely to respond. Teacher representatives making a final offer on salaries are aware that if they are unreasonably demanding the arbitrator will be likely to adopt the board's position. Similarly, board representatives must try to anticipate the position the teachers are likely to take in order to present an offer that has a reasonable chance of being accepted. Thus both parties are prevented by self-interest from making offers that are unreasonable or nonresponsive.

Impact of Collective Bargaining on Schools

There is agreement that collective bargaining has had a major impact on the operation of schools in the United States, but there is less consensus on whether schools and teachers are better off or worse off as a result of collective bargaining. Four questions that are frequently asked about collective bargaining are: (1) What effect does collective bargaining have on teachers' salaries? (2) In what ways does it affect the quality of instruction and how much students learn? (3) How does bargaining impact on principals' power? and (4) Is site-based management compatible with collective bargaining? In this section, we examine answers to these questions.

Teachers' Salaries

Collective bargaining in the private sector results in sizable gains in salary for workers who are represented by negotiators. Seven studies conducted during the 1970s found that the average increase in salaries of workers whose unions bargained collectively with employers ranged from 21 to 32 percent more than the gains received by workers in the same industry who did not bargain (Freeman & Medoff, 1984). Of course, employees of these firms might have received higher salaries anyway, even if they had not had collective bargaining, since other factors, including employee skill and aggressiveness and employer generosity, may have contributed to the outcome. But, even allowing for these factors, collective bargaining appears to lead to salary advantages for private sector employees.

However, findings from research on the effects of collective bargaining on teachers' wages are not so favorable. In one study it was found that the average difference in salaries of teachers in districts that bargain as compared to those without bargaining ranged from 0 to 12 percent (Johnson, 1988). The author of that study concluded:

> *Negotiation has increased teachers' salaries modestly, if at all. It seems unlikely that the precise effect will eventually be determined, because further research on this question is increasingly complicated by the expansion of*

bargaining and the virtual impossibility of identifying comparable bargain-
ing and nonbargaining districts and controlling for spillover effects. (p. 616)

Student Learning

Studies on the impact of collective bargaining on student learning suggest that bargaining is related to increased learning for average students but decreased learning for above and below average youngsters. One of the common concerns about unions is that they hold down productivity, but the reality seems to be somewhat more complicated. One study showed that unionized districts had higher student achievement gains than nonunion districts for average students. The difference in achievement test gains was about 7 percent, favoring unionized districts. However, for students who were above or below average in ability, nonunionized districts did a better job, by about the same margin (Eberts & Stone, 1987).

The authors of that study noted that the latter result was consistent with the view that unions tend to standardize work procedures. They also reported that instructional leadership by principals in union districts seemed to have had a positive effect on learning, but that a negative relationship was found between leadership and learning in nonunion schools. They attributed these results to the unions' role in keeping administrators informed about teachers' needs and concerns.

Potentially, the most damaging result of collective bargaining from the point of view of student learning occurs when negotiators reach an impasse and a work stoppage results. Strikes are traumatic events for school personnel. Everyone loses, and it may take years to repair the damage. Student learning is affected both by the length of a strike and by whether or not striking teachers are replaced by substitutes.

There has been relatively little research on the subject, but the available studies show, as one would expect, that shorter strikes are less harmful than longer ones. Mathematics achievement seems to be more sensitive to loss of instruction than reading. Mathematics is negatively affected both by the length of strike and by the presence of substitute teachers, whereas reading achievement appears to be affected more by the length of a strike than by the presence of substitute teachers (Crisci & Lulow, 1985). That may be because substitute teachers are less likely to be proficient in teaching mathematics.

For principals and personnel managers, the obvious lessons from this research are, first, to take actions that will prevent or limit the length of teacher strikes and, second, if strikes occur to seek to maintain normal instructional routines to the extent possible.

Work of Principals

Negotiated agreements limit the power of principals to make decisions related to administration and organization of the school by forcing the administrators to become interpreters of the contract (Ubben & Fulmer, 1985). District administrators pressure principals to adhere closely to the contract because of fear that leniency by one principal will lead to demands from teachers in other schools for similar treatment (Mitchell et al., 1981).

Principals sometimes express concern about the difficulty of dismissing incompetent teachers, whom they feel are protected by the unions. The teachers' organizations deny the charge and insist that they will support dismissal of teachers whose incompetence is adequately documented.

The truth is probably somewhere between these positions. Most administrators know of cases in which ineffective teachers have managed to keep their jobs with union support. However, it is also true that administrators have occasionally been careless in documenting poor performance or have simply lacked the courage to take action against an incompetent employee out of fear of the union's reaction.

Principals who are accustomed to a free-wheeling style of management may have difficulty adjusting to life under a negotiated agreement. Being successful in such a situation requires an individual with considerable flexibility—one who is careful to abide by the provisions of the master contract, yet able to inspire teachers to give more than the minimum effort in order to increase learning.

Most administrators will admit that collective bargaining has some positive features. Among these are the increased security that teachers feel and the increased clarity of teachers' work responsibilities. Principals who work in districts with contracts that detail duties teachers are expected to perform report that they have no problems in getting those duties carried out (Jessup, 1981).

All in all, administering a school that operates under a negotiated agreement probably require skills that are no different from those required in schools in which there is no agreement in effect. In both cases, the administrator must attend to details and provide leadership to move the faculty toward a goal of improved instruction.

Bargaining and Site-Based Management

Some authorities claim that collective bargaining is incompatible with site-based management (SBM) of schools or that, at the very least, there are likely to be problems encountered in the effort to implement SBM in districts with negotiated contracts. For example, these authorities express concern that teacher members of a school council might refuse to approve layoffs of fellow teachers even when such an action was needed. Some people believe that SBM is a tactic employed by teacher unions to seize control of schools (Walker & Roder, 1993).

However, there is not much evidence that teacher unions are promoting SBM, and some union officials have expressed strong concerns about it. One of the more optimistic union officials concluded that SBM will work if management agrees to share or relinquish some of its power and if the details of the plan have been fully discussed during negotiations (Poltrock & Goss, 1993).

In some districts with SBM, unions have agreed to a provision in the master contract to allow waiving parts of the contract that are in conflict with decisions of school councils. However, before embracing waiver provisions, unions usually insist that principals accept co-equal status with teachers in specified areas of decision making (Poltrock & Goss, 1993). Some union officials are adamant in their opposition to these concessions and warn that accepting waivers will lead to gradual erosion of employee rights (Clark, 1993).

Some school districts have implemented SBM successfully without prior bargaining about operational details. This appears to work in situations in which teachers and administrators are able to develop an informal approach that avoids confrontation over divisive issues. In another tactic that appears to have promise, unions have agreed to permit deviations from the master contract if the principal and a majority of teachers in a school agree on the need for the waiver (Clark, 1993).

Summary

Collective bargaining has been called one of the most significant developments in education in the past quarter century. The content of negotiated contracts is regulated by state statutes but generally covers compensation and working conditions. Some provisions of negotiated agreements may impinge on the quality of instruction in schools, and board negotiators should take those effects into account, along with attention to cost and administrative prerogatives, in reaching a settlement.

Negotiations proceed through three stages: (1) an initial stage in which the sides state their positions and agree on the issues to be negotiated, (2) a middle stage in which trust emerges and a cooperative working relationship is established, and (3) a closing stage in which both parties begin to bargain seriously, granting the concessions that are needed to reach a mutually acceptable agreement.

New approaches to collective bargaining are being tried in a number of school districts. Among the new approaches are expedited bargaining, progressive bargaining, the win/win approach, principled negotiations, and strategic bargaining. Several of these new forms of bargaining are designed to speed the negotiation process by setting deadlines for reaching an agreement and limiting the number of issues that can be discussed.

When the two sides are not able to reach agreement, outside assistance may be required. Mediation, fact finding, and arbitration are all used to help resolve impasses.

Four questions are frequently asked about collective bargaining. They are (1) What effect does collective bargaining have on salaries? (2) How does it affect the quality of instruction and student learning? (3) How does it affect principals' power? and (4) Is site-based management compatible with collective bargaining?

Suggested Activities

1. Following is a statement on class size proposed by the teachers' union. Take and defend a position for or against the proposal as written. (You are not allowed to rewrite it.)

    "We believe instruction is most effective when class sizes are kept small enough to permit teachers to diagnose students' needs and plan instruction to meet them. To permit the level of teacher attention needed for learning to occur, we ask the board to agree to place a limit of 20 students in classes in reading and English in grades 1–12 and to limit all other classes in grades 1–12 (except special education) to no more than 24 students. Each special education student assigned to a regular class will count as two students for purposes of calculating size limits."

2. Principals are sometimes excluded from joining the board's negotiating team because board members believe they might be inclined to side with teachers. Principals argue that they could help the board's representatives understand how proposed contract provisions might affect instruction, and thus avoid language likely to harm learning. Take and defend a position on this proposition:

    "Principals should be represented on the board's negotiating team."

3. Consider the statement on teacher evaluation that follows. If you were a member of the union bargaining team, what changes would you propose in the statement? If you were a member of the board team, what changes would you want made?

    "The union and the board recognize the importance of teacher evaluation for sound instruction. Teachers will be evaluated in the following way: The principal will observe each teacher at least twice during the school year, will evaluate the teacher after each observation, and will inform the teacher of the results. No later than April 15, the principal will prepare a written narrative describing the teacher's strengths and weaknesses and include the statement in the teacher's personnel file. If the teacher is completing the probationary period, the principal shall recommend that the teacher be tenured or terminated."

4. In schools with site-based management, school councils sometimes request waivers of certain provisions in the master contract. Should waivers be allowed? If so, what type mechanism should be used to review and approve such requests? Are there certain parts of the contract that should

be sacrosanct—that is, no waivers allowed under any circumstances? If so, which ones?

5. Review the principles for principled negotiations. Explain how each principle might help two parties to reach agreement on an issue on which they disagree. (*Example:* How does separating a problem from the person help advance negotiations?) What other principles can you suggest that might help two parties reach agreement on a divisive issue?

References

Black, S. (1993, October). How teachers are reshaping evaluation procedures. *Educational Leadership, 51,* 38–42.

Booth, R. (1993). *Collective bargaining and the school board member.* Springfield, IL: Illinois Association of School Boards.

Clark, R. T. (1993, Spring). School-based management—Problems and prospects. *Journal of Law and Education, 22,* 183–186.

Cresswell, A., & Murphy, M. (1980). *Teachers, unions, and collective bargaining in public education.* Berkeley, CA: McCutchan.

Crisci, P. E., & Lulow, R. J. (1985). The effect of school employee strikes on student achievement in nine Ohio school districts. *Journal of Collective Negotiations, 14,* 197–212.

Eberts, R. W., & Stone, J. A. (1987). Teacher unions and the productivity of public schools. *Industrial and Labor Relations Review, 40,* 354–363.

Fisher, R., & Ury, W. (1981). *Getting to yes: Negotiating agreement without giving in.* New York: Penguin.

Fisher, R., & Ury, W. (1988). *Getting together: Building relationships as we negotiate.* New York: Penguin.

Freeman, R. B., & Medoff, J. L. (1984). *What do unions do?* New York: Basic Books.

Goldschmidt, S., Bowers, B., Riley, M., & Stuart, L. (1984). *The extent and nature of educational policy bargaining.* Eugene, OR: University of Oregon, Center for Educational Policy and Management.

Jessup, D. (1981). *Teacher unionism and its impact: A study of change over time.* Washington, DC: National Institute of Education.

Johnson, S. M. (1988). Unionism and collective bargaining in the public schools. In N. J. Boyan (Ed.), *Handbook of research on educational administration* (pp. 603–622). New York: Longman.

Lipsky, D. V., & Conley, S. C. (1986, April). *Incentive pay and collective bargaining in public education.* Paper presented at the annual meeting of the American Educational Research Association, San Francisco. (ERIC Document Reproduction Service No. ED 277111).

McDonnell, L., & Pascal, A. (1979). *Organized teachers in American schools.* Santa Monica, CA: Rand.

Mitchell, D., Kerchner, C., Erck, W., & Pryor, G. (1981). The impact of collective bargaining on school management and policy. *American Journal of Education, 89,* 147–188.

National Association of Elementary School Principals. (1982, July). *School management handbook.* No. 6. Arlington, VA: Author.

National Education Association. (1991). *Collaborative bargaining: A critical appraisal.* Washington, DC: Author.

New Jersey Principals and Supervisors Association. (1982). *Negotiations primer.* Trenton: Author. (ERIC Reproduction Service No. ED 266530).

O'Reilly, R. C. (1978). *Understanding collective bargaining in education.* Metuchen, NJ: Scarecrow Press.

Poltrock, L., & Goss, S. (1993, Spring). A union lawyer's view of restructuring and reform. *Journal of Law and Education, 22,* 177–182.

Ubben, G. C., & Fulmer, B. (1985). The relationship of collective bargaining to the decision-making power of the public school principal. *Journal of Collective Negotiations, 14,* 141–150.

Walker, P., & Roder, L. (1993, Spring). Reflections on the practical and legal implications of school-based management and teacher empowerment. *Journal of Law and Education, 22,* 159–175.

14

MANAGING CONFLICT
IN SCHOOLS

Conflict occurs in all organizations, and although managers work to resolve or eliminate it, it is important to recognize that some conflict is inevitable and may even have beneficial effects (Pneuman & Bruehl, 1982). Conflict occurs when people disagree regarding values, information, and goals, or when individuals compete for scarce resources (Rahim, 1986). Organizational managers usually become involved when conflict occurs among members of the organization, and managers themselves are sometimes parties to conflict.

Conflict may occur between individuals, within or between groups, or between an individual and a group. Our concern in this chapter is with conflict involving school personnel and, in particular, that which involves two teachers or groups of teachers or a teacher and an administrator such as a principal. Conflict involving parties outside of the school is beyond the scope of this book. For example, issues of conflict between teachers and parents will not be addressed, even though many of the principles for handling various types of conflict are identical.

Plan of the Chapter

This chapter deals with the following topics: (1) nature of conflict in organizations, (2) resolving conflict in work settings, (3) managing conflict through the grievance process, (4) administering grievance procedures, (5) grievance arbitration in schools, (6) arbitration involving work rules, (7) other issues in arbitration, and (8) effects of arbitration on the district.

Example 1: A teacher in the mathematics department requests permission to attend a regional conference sponsored by the state mathematics teachers' association. The department head has also asked to attend, but there is not enough money in the budget to pay expenses for two teachers. The principal gives the department head approval to attend the meeting and denies the teacher's request. The teacher protests this action and accuses the principal of favoritism.

Example 2: An English teacher protests to the principal that he is being treated unfairly because he teaches 135 students each day, whereas an English teacher across the hall has only 119.

Example 3: The business education department requests money to buy two additional typewriters to replace two that are worn out. The request is denied, but the industrial arts department receives money to buy a new jigsaw for the woodworking shop. The business teacher complains that "the business department never gets any support from the principal."

Example 4: The principal of an elementary school admonishes a third-grade teacher for failing to notify the parents of a child whose grades have dropped so that they could intervene before report cards went home.

Example 5: A special education teacher requests personal leave in order to appear in court for the final hearing for the adoption of her son. The agreement states that personal leave may be used "only for unforeseen emergencies." The hearing is not an unforeseen emergency since the teacher has known about it for two months.

Example 6: The chairperson of the social studies department at a middle school tells the principal that other teachers in the department are complaining because one of the teachers in the department fails to show up for department meetings and has not participated in department committee assignments.

Example 7: A teacher complains that evaluation ratings given by the principal do not fairly represent the quality of her work.

EXHIBIT 14.1 Examples of Conflict Situations in Schools

Nature of Conflict in Organizations

In any human activity, some conflict is inevitable, and schools are no exception. Conflict in work settings, including schools, tends to center around one of four issues: (1) application and interpretation of rules and policies; (2) allocation of resources and privileges; (3) duties and responsibilities of employees; and (4) assessment of employee performance.

Exhibit 14.1 shows examples of these four types of on-the-job conflicts. Example 5 of Exhibit 14.1 deals with the interpretation and application of board policy. In Examples 1 and 3, the issue is the allocation of resources and privileges. Conflict about job duties and responsibilities is evident in Examples 2 and 6, and Examples 4 and 7 illustrate conflict related to assessment of individual performance.

Resolving Conflict in Work Settings

The principal or personnel administrator must act as conflict manager when disputes arise. There are certain actions the administrator may take that are more likely than others to lead to resolution of the conflict. If the dispute centers on something the administrator did, then he or she must be prepared to defend that action by citing the policy or rationale for it. If the decision was made in haste and not well thought out, it may be necessary for the administrator to change it. After hearing all sides, however, if the administrator continues to feel that the decision was correct, it should be left intact. Most employees will accept adverse decisions without bitterness if they have received a respectful hearing from a decision maker who has no "hidden agenda" (Yates, 1985).

When disputes center about group competition for resources, there is a temptation for conflict managers to attempt to resolve them by using the strategy of "something for everyone." However, in most school districts at the present time, resources are too scarce to be distributed "casually and generously" (Yates, 1985, p. 164) without regard to the implications for achieving the goals of the district. To preserve the manager's ability to use organizational resources to achieve identified goals, managers must be prepared to cite long- and short-term goals identified earlier through a strategic planning process (see Chapter 2).

Conflict Resolution Model

A recommended approach to resolving conflict in work settings is to encourage employees to take responsibility for their actions. One way to do that is to focus on the problem rather than the employee (Redeker, 1989). The following steps will help focus attention on the problem and lead to the resolution of much job-related conflict:

1. Clarify and discuss issues in the conflict.
2. Search for shared values.
3. Explore possible solutions.
4. Select a solution that satisfies those with a stake in the outcome.

Example 2 in Exhibit 14.1 illustrates a common complaint among workers—disparities in workload. At Step 1, the teacher and department head discuss the issues involved and attempt to understand how the problem arose. From the teacher's point of view, the issue is unequal teaching loads, but other issues are likely emerge as the two talk. The teacher with the lighter teaching load may have been given fewer students in return for agreeing to teach students with learning disabilities, or the differences in class sizes may have occurred because students' schedules changed or because some students transferred to other schools. Understanding how a problem arose often helps allay some of the feelings the problem arouses.

At Step 2, the parties search for shared values. The value advocated by the complaining teacher in the example is that teaching loads should be equalized. The department head is unlikely to disagree with that position but may argue that other values must also be considered. Adjusting class sizes to allow teachers to spend more time with difficult-to-teach students is one such principle.

If the disparities in workload resulted from schedule changes or transfers, then the question is whether students should have been reassigned in order to rebalance teachers' workloads. Most administrators are not willing to transfer students from one class to another after the first week or so of school solely for the purpose of balancing teaching loads, unless the disparities in class sizes are sizable. This is a case in which competing values must be weighed. Which is more important—equalized workloads or maintaining stability in students' class assignments? Some administrators are willing to tolerate some workload disparities in order to maintain stable student schedules. A point for discussion between the teacher and department head is: How large must the differences in workloads be before the decision is made to reassign students?

Examining Solutions

When common values have been identified, potential solutions are examined at Step 3. In the example, one possible solution is to formulate an explicit policy regarding adjustments in class size for teachers with difficult-to-teach students. If the difference in workloads resulted from student transfers, assigning new incoming students to the teacher with the lighter load will reduce the disparity somewhat. However, with a difference as great as the one in the example, this method is not likely to produce equal workloads in the near future.

At Step 4, the parties agree to a solution to the problem. In this case, the solution must be approved by other teachers, since they will be affected by it. If they reject it, they will be responsible for proposing an alternative that is acceptable to all.

The key to resolving conflicts that arise in work settings is finding a set of values about which the competing parties agree. Those involved in these disputes do not usually disagree with one another regarding basic principles, but difficulties are often encountered in reaching accord about which values should receive priority.

Principles for Resolving Conflict

Several principles of conflict resolution will help those who attempt to settle disagreements in the workplace. First, the chosen solution should be one that benefits the largest number of people and results in inconvenience or harm to the smallest number. In Example 2, this principle suggests that the parties should search for a solution that will help students without causing undue burdens for teachers. The second principle holds that the preferred solution is one that helps the organization achieve its mission. Since schools exist to impart knowledge, the solution settled upon should help teachers teach more effectively and enhance the prospects that students will learn.

A third principle that can be used to guide parties attempting to resolve conflict is to recognize that most individuals are motivated by self-interest but that they also value membership in the group and try to avoid violating group norms. It is human nature to seek a personal advantage, but the person who is attempting to resolve conflict can appeal to individuals' desire to be accepted by asking them to forego personal gain in order to help the group. This appeal carries more weight with most people than a request to sacrifice personal gain in order that another individual may benefit.

Managing Conflict through the Grievance Process

Much conflict that occurs in the workplace involves disagreements between employees and supervisors over disciplinary actions and conditions of work. Teachers and school principals agree about most aspects of school operations but disagree about a few. They generally agree that teachers should have a good deal of autonomy in deciding what to teach, in choosing instructional activities and materials, and in the relative emphasis given to instructional topics. They also agree that principals have the responsibility to supervise and evaluate teachers' work. Disagreements between teachers and administrators most often occur when the administration proposes to change teaching assignments or responsibilities, to prescribe certain instructional procedures, or to require teachers to perform nonteaching duties.

Negotiated contracts normally include a grievance procedure, which is an orderly process for resolving disputes over interpretation and administration of the contract (*Contract Administration*, 1983). In some cases, the denial of previously won employee rights occurs because of honest disagreements about the interpretation of particular provisions in the contract. Whatever the reason—lack of information, private interpretation, or honest differences of opinion—when disagreements arise, they must be resolved.

The grievance procedure is intended to prevent work stoppages by providing a means for employees to have their complaints heard without the time and expense that are required by courts of law. Grievance procedures usually work well in resolving disputes about work rules, leave time, and job duties, but they are less effective for resolving the types of conflict that are encountered in schools with site-based management.

The operational assumptions of SBM are different from the assumptions used in grievance processes. In schools with SBM, disputes are resolved through informal discussion, cooperation, and compromise. The search for solutions usually takes into account the interests of teachers, students, and parents. Grievance procedures, on the other hand, use an adversarial approach and ultimately rely on an objective outside party to hear the evidence and decide the issue. The procedures follow rigidly prescribed rules and focus on faithfully interpreting an agreement rather than seeking the best solution to a problem.

Resolving conflict in a school with SBM involves evaluation of options, with attention given to the school's mission and the well-being of the parties involved. Finding a solution often requires compromise. Grievance processes, on the other hand, seek to solve conflict by using historical data to decide which version of events is more accurate.

Some districts with SBM plans have developed, in collaboration with employee unions, a variation on existing grievance procedures that is intended to settle disputes on site rather than appeal them to arbitration. In Dade County (Florida) Schools, a grievance committee composed of administrators and union representatives hears grievances appealed from schools with SBM plans. If a dispute is not resolved by the grievance committee, it is appealed to a two-person panel composed of the district superintendent and a union vice president. Only if the panel fails to resolve the issue does it go to binding arbitration (Fossey, 1992).

Administering Grievance Procedures

Grievance procedures have a long history in industry. The first record of their use dates back to the early years of the twentieth century, but they did not come into widespread use in this country until World War II. A recommendation of the President's Labor-Management Conference that all labor contracts include a procedure for settlement of grievances gave impetus to their adoption. The U.S. Supreme Court gave additional support to their use when it held in a series of decisions that courts should not rule on the merits of disputes between labor and management but should limit themselves to enforcing arbitration awards and reviewing questions of arbitrability (Lovell, 1985).

At the present time, grievance procedures are pervasive in industries with negotiated labor agreements, and they are increasingly used to resolve employee/employer disputes in schools. In districts without negotiated agreements, written grievance policies govern the resolution of disputes. The grievance process is favored by most employers and many unions because it is a quicker and less costly way of settling disputes than strikes and lengthy litigation (Lovell, 1985).

Contents of Grievance Clause

A grievance clause in a master contract usually consists of a definition of *grievance,* tells who may initiate a grievance, and establishes deadlines for filing and processing employee complaints. The clause also details the procedural steps that are followed in processing the grievance, including the final step, which in many districts is binding arbitration.

Unions favor grievance plans that include binding arbitration as the final step because they feel that it guarantees employees a fair hearing for their complaints. However, most school boards prefer advisory arbitration, which leaves the final decision on a dispute in the hands of the board (Lovell, 1985). The grievance clause also specifies which parties may file grievances. In some districts, teacher associations and unions are allowed to file, whereas in others only individuals are permitted to grieve the employer's actions.

Steps in Resolving Grievances

Most grievance policies provide three or four steps through which a grievant may appeal a complaint. Step 1 commonly includes both an informal and a formal stage. The employee initiates action informally by bringing to the attention of the supervisor the decision or situation that originally aroused the employee's concern. If not satisfied with the response received, the employee may then proceed to Stage 2 of Step 1 by formally filing a written grievance with the same supervisor. In the case of teachers, Step 1 involves the principal of the school in which the grievant works.

In most districts, a form is provided on which the employee is asked to (1) describe the incident, decision, or practice that gave rise to the complaint; (2) cite the contract or policy provision that has been violated; and (3) explain what corrective action is being requested. Since there is usually a time limit for filing a grievance, the grievant must specify the date of occurrence of the precipitating event or the date on which the employee first learned about it.

Grievance Appeals Procedures

If the employee is unhappy with the decision at the first step, he or she proceeds to Step 2 by appealing to the next higher level, usually either the director of personnel or an assistant superintendent. Finally, Step 3 involves a hearing before the superintendent if the grievant has not received satisfaction. Step 4 in the grievance procedure is a hearing before the board of education or an arbitrator or arbitration panel. In districts with binding arbitration, the decision of the arbitrator is final, but in districts that use advisory arbitration, the recommendation of the arbitrator is reviewed by the school board, which has the final word about the employee's complaint.

Documentation of Decisions

Grievance hearings become more formal as the complaint advances from one administrative level to the next. The only written documentation required at the first step is the supervisor's written decision, but at the final step, a transcript of the hearing is prepared (Salmon, 1983). The transcript, along with the superintendent's written decision on the employee's complaint, is reviewed by the arbitrator or arbitration panel if the grievance is appealed to arbitration.

Both parties have an interest in settling grievances quickly and at as low a level as possible. For the district, each complaint that proceeds beyond Step 1 represents additional costs and increased risk of arousing antiadministration sentiment. Teachers incur both emotional and monetary costs in pursuing a grievance and so have an equally strong interest in reaching an early settlement. The teacher's monetary costs of pursuing a grievance are often paid by the union, especially if the case is one that involves an issue of interest to all teachers.

According to research, conditions in schools are conducive to the production of grievances. Schools have workers with generally homogeneous backgrounds who have similar working conditions and who have common free time during the workday. These conditions contribute to a relative increase in the number of grievances in an organization as compared to other organizations (Lutz & Caldwell, 1979). For this reason, principals must be alert to conditions that lower teacher morale or raise their feelings of frustration. When grievances increase in number, principals may be blamed for the increase even though they had nothing to do with creating conditions that led to it.

Of course, an increase in the number of grievances originating in a school may signal ineffective leadership by the principal, and district administrators should be sensitive to that possibility. A generally high frequency of grievances may also indicate a need to renegotiate portions of the bargaining agreement that are giving rise to the disputes. Statements that are ambiguous or that deal with emotion-laden issues can sometimes be clarified through negotiations, thereby reducing the number of grievances.

Benefits and Disadvantages

Several benefits accrue to employers from the use of a grievance procedure. An employer is less likely to experience work stoppages if employees have access to a mechanism for resolving disputes. And if a strike does occur, an employer who has agreed to resolve disputes through a grievance process with binding arbitration can obtain injunctive relief through the courts (*Boys Markets* v. *Retail Clerks*, 1970). A second benefit is that grievance procedures have the potential to improve employee morale and productivity by providing relatively quick and objective decisions about situations that involve possible violations of the contract. Finally, a grievance procedure lets management know what issues most bother employees (McPherson, 1983).

Grievance Arbitration in Schools

When an employee fails to achieve a satisfactory solution to a grievance after following all of the steps provided in the policy, the final step is arbitration. The rules on arbitration vary, depending on the state in which the individual works and on the provisions of the bargaining agreement. Some states require boards to include binding arbitration in contracts with employees, whereas others leave the decision to the negotiators. A few prohibit binding arbitration.

Certain powers of school boards are nondelegable and are considered nonarbitrable unless state law specifically permits review. Among these are the power to hire, promote, and discharge employees; establish the curriculum; and set standards of service (Lovell, 1985).

Courts generally prefer to allow arbitration procedures to operate without interference, but if nondelegable powers of school boards have clearly been abridged in the process of arbitration, courts are likely to intervene. In some states, the courts are less ready to grant arbitration the acceptance in the public sector that it has traditionally been accorded in the private sector (Lovell, 1985).

Selection of Arbitrators

A grievance may be heard by a single arbitrator or by a panel consisting of several arbitrators. The procedures followed in selection of arbitrators are those established by state legislation or by a professional organization such as the American Arbitration Association or an agency such as the Federal Mediation and Conciliation Service. The usual practice is for the designated agency to submit a list of five to seven names of qualified arbitrators, from which the representatives of the grievant and the board alternately delete names until only the required number remains (Ostrander, 1987).

The arbitrators' function is to determine whether the administrative decision or practice to which the employee objects is a violation of the bargaining agreement. Most disputes involve rights that union members claim to have received at the bargaining table and that management denies were granted. The arbitrator thus has the task of determining which interpretation is the one intended by the parties at the time the contract was signed (Ostrander, 1987).

Guidelines for Interpreting the Contract

In arriving at an interpretation of the contract, arbitrators are guided by several rules of contract interpretation. Among them are the following (Elkouri & Elkouri, 1973):

1. If the intent of the parties is clear, it should govern.
2. Words are given their ordinary and accepted meaning unless other meanings are specifically indicated.
3. The meaning given to a passage in the contract should be consistent insofar as possible with the intentions expressed in other parts of the contract.

4. When the agreement specifically includes something, it is assumed that that which is left unstated is excluded.

5. When there is a conflict between specific and general language, specific language should govern.

6. When there is no evidence to the contrary and the meaning of a term is unclear, the intentions of the parties should be viewed to be the same as those held during the negotiations that led to the agreement.

7. No consideration should be given to compromise offers or to concessions offered by one party and rejected by the other during the process that led to arbitration (Elkouri & Elkouri, 1973).

Exhibit 14.2 contains a summary description of a teacher's grievance. The arbitrator relied on several rules of contract interpretation in arriving at a decision. The arbitrator's decision and the reasoning that led to it are described below, but before you read abut them you may want to test your skill as an arbitrator by reviewing the case and making a decision on your own.

A teacher, Cynthia Ollendyke, received notice that she would be reassigned from high school science to a middle school science position. She received notice of the reassignment on May 27.

Section 6a of the current contract contained the following statement: "Teaching assignments for the oncoming school year will be provided in writing to employees no later than July 15th. If the employee must relocate his/her material prior to the first day of classes, said employee shall be provided with compensatory time. . . ."

Ms. Ollendyke wrote the principal on May 28: "How do I go about arranging for a paid moving day? I would like to do it Monday, June 8. Is that possible?" The principal informed the teacher that the contract provision dealing with compensatory time applied only if the notice of reassignment was received after July 15th.

The teacher grieved the principal's decision and the grievance ultimately went to arbitration. The board argued that a mutual drafting error led to omission of a phrase that altered the meaning of the provision.

The previous agreement had read: "Teachers shall be given notice of their assignment for the forthcoming year promptly after they are formulated, not after July 15th. When it is necessary for the District to change an employee's assignment, the employee shall be notified as far in advance as practicable of the change and the reasons therefor.

"If a teacher is notified of a change of assignment after August 1st that requires the teacher to pack and move his/her personal teaching material prior to the first day of classes, said employee shall be provided with compensatory time."

Both parties agreed that they had intended to change the deadline for notification of reassignment from August 1 to July 15 and had intended that only teachers notified after August 1 should receive compensatory time for moving.

EXHIBIT 14.2   Peters Township School District and Peters Township Federation of Teachers (90 LA 35)

Source: Reprinted with permission from *Labor Relations Reporter-Labor Arbitration Reports,* 90 LA 35-38. Copyright 1988 by the Bureau of National Affairs, Inc. (800–372–1033).

Arbitrator's Reasoning

As with most grievances that reach arbitration, contradictory elements were present in this one (Exhibit 14.2). The arbitrator found Section 6a of the contract to be "clear and unambiguous," but the decision hinged on the intentions of the negotiators, which were not as clear.

The arbitrator's review of the history of the negotiations led him to comment that while "the Federation did not *initiate* any request for broader compensatory time . . . , it is not at all clear from the evidence presented that such a concept was never even contemplated. . . ." He ultimately decided that "no clear conclusions [about the parties' intentions] can be drawn from the negotiations history" (*Peters Township School District*, 1988, p. 38).

The board contended that the change in deadline date was the only change the negotiators intended to make, but the arbitrator was not convinced, pointing out that if in fact no other change had been contemplated, all that would have been required was for the drafters of the contract to substitute the new date for the old. Instead, they rewrote the section, resulting in the omission of a key phrase.

The board presented as evidence of the teachers' intentions copies of a proposal that had been submitted by the Federation during negotiations. The proposal suggested changing the date of notification to May 15 but did not mention compensatory time. The board argued that this showed that there was no intention on the part of the union to request compensatory time for all teachers who were reassigned.

The board also cited past practice in support of its claim that the teacher's grievance was not justified. Although numerous teachers had been reassigned in the past, the board claimed that only one had asked for and received compensatory time and that that payment had been made in error. The arbitrator noted that past practice is only relevant when the contract language is ambiguous and that in this case the language was not ambiguous.

Arbitrator's Decision

The arbitrator sustained the grievance and directed the board to pay Ms. Ollendyke one day compensatory time. The factor that swayed the negotiator was the "clear, unambiguous" statement in the contract and the absence of compelling evidence that the parties had not contemplated offering compensatory time to all reassigned teachers.

Arbitration Involving Work Rules

Many grievances have to do with application of work rules. It has been noted that principals are expected to discuss disagreements concerning work rules with the involved parties and that doing so increases the chances that the principal will be successful in mediating future disputes (Lutz & Caldwell, 1979). Disagreements over work rules usually involve these three questions (Turner & Weed, 1983):

1. What action or activity is covered by the rule?
2. Under what conditions is the activity appropriate?
3. To whom does the rule apply?

Consider a policy that states, "Teachers will confer with parents upon request and at a mutually convenient time regarding students' academic performance." What actions are covered by the rule? If a teacher discusses a child's work with a parent by telephone, does that constitute conferring? What about an exchange of notes? If the request for a conference originates with the principal rather than a parent, does that constitute a "request" within the meaning of the policy?

Under what conditions is the activity appropriate? Suppose a teacher tells an inquiring parent that there is no need for a conference since the child in question is doing well. Has the teacher violated the rule? Suppose the teacher has a second job and cannot arrange a mutually satisfactory time for a conference. Is she exempt from the rule?

To whom does the rule apply? Are both part-time and full-time teachers obligated by the rule? Is a teacher who has a child for one period a day under a mainstreaming arrangement equally as bound by the rule as the child's base teacher? Is an itinerant teacher who spends only three or four hours per week in a school required to meet with parents who request it?

Deciding Which Rule Applies

In some disputes, a question arises regarding which of two or more rules governs. In one such case, the contract between teachers and the board of the Anoka-Hennepin District in Minnesota contained a provision stating that "teachers shall not be disciplined, reduced in rank or compensation without just cause." Teachers who missed school because of snow requested they be granted personal leave for the half-day they missed. The request was denied and the teachers lost one-half day's pay. They filed a grievance that ultimately went to arbitration. The teachers cited the "just cause" clause, but the district argued that its action was justified by a clause governing emergency leave. That provision held that absence from school because of the effects of weather on transportation would not be approved for emergency leave purposes. The arbitrator supported the district in this case (Coulson, 1986).

Interpreting Just Cause

Arbitrators are frequently confronted with the necessity of interpreting "just cause" clauses such as the one in the Anoka-Hennepin contract. The intent in using this phrase is to allow administrative discretion while protecting employee rights granted by the contract. Several criteria are used by arbitrators to determine whether administrative action meets the "just cause" standard. Among the questions an arbitrator is likely to ask are the following:

1. *Was the employee informed of management's rules and expectations?*
2. *Were management's rules and expectations reasonable?*
3. *Was adverse action necessary to maintain orderly, efficient procedures in the organization?*
4. *Was the employee given a chance to improve his or her conduct?*
5. *Was the imposed penalty reasonable? (Ostrander, 1981, p. 41)*

Teachers' Use of Force

Teachers are expected to take action to prevent students from fighting or to stop fights when they occur, yet the rules about the use of force in such situations are often unclear. In a junior high school in Michigan, a teacher who encountered two students fighting sent another child to the principal's office for help. The principal came and stopped the fight, but on the following day the principal placed a letter of reprimand in the teacher's file because he felt she should have been more aggressive and stopped the fight herself (Coulson, 1986).

A teacher in a school in Iowa got into trouble with the school principal for the opposite reason: He was too aggressive in separating two youngsters who were fighting. The teacher grabbed one of the students by the shoulder and pulled him away from the other boy, causing the student to fall and strike his head. He wrapped his arm around the other boy and pulled him into the office. The teacher was reprimanded for excessive use of force (Coulson, 1986).

Both teachers filed grievances seeking to have the reprimands removed from their personnel files. How would you rule if you were the arbitrator? It might help you to know that the first teacher had taught for a total of 30 years, 13 in the same system, and had never been previously reprimanded. The teacher in the Iowa school, however, had been warned by the principal about excessive use of force and had previously received a reprimand for the same offense.

The arbitrator in the first case decided, as you probably did, that the teacher should not have been reprimanded, but in the second case the arbitrator held that the reprimand was justified. In both cases, teachers were operating on the basis of expectations that were not very clear or explicit, but the second teacher, because of the principal's previous warning, was especially vulnerable to disciplinary action. Some use of force in these situations may be required, but a fine line exists between suitable or appropriate force and excessive force. In this case, the teacher crossed that line.

Grievances on Evaluation

A good many grievances filed by teachers concern evaluation procedures. In handling these disputes, administrators must be guided by the language of the contract. When contract language is specific with regard to evaluation procedures, any departure from the provisions will probably be rejected in arbitration. If the language is permissive, then an administrative decision is more likely to be upheld.

Some contracts specify who is responsible for making classroom observations but do not forbid others from observing in classes. It is common for contracts to state that the principal is responsible for making classroom observations as part of the evaluation process. In one case, a principal called in a central office supervisor to make an additional observation of a teacher, and the teacher filed a grievance, claiming that the use of the supervisor for a classroom observation violated the contract. The administration was upheld in that case on grounds that the contract did not specifically forbid the use of observers other than the principal (Ostrander, 1981).

Another complaint that teachers sometimes make is that principals use information for evaluation purposes that was not obtained by means of classroom observations. Arbitrators have held that such use of information from other sources is justified unless specifically prohibited by the contract.

Guidelines for Action

Being aware of the factors that arbitrators consider in deciding disputes over work rules can help administrators make better decisions and avoid some of the emotional cost of confrontations with employees. In disputes that involve employee absence or tardiness, arbitrators look for a pattern of employee behavior and are not inclined to support the board when an employee's infraction is limited to a single incident. Advance notification is also considered. A teacher who fails to notify the principal when she is absent from school is less likely to win an appeal of a reprimand than a teacher who has been more conscientious about notification (Ostrander, 1981).

Negative Norm Setters

Arbitrators also consider an individual employee's behavior in light of the behavior of other employees. A reprimand of a teacher who has accumulated "excessive" absences is unlikely to be sustained if other teachers in the district with equal or greater numbers of absences were not reprimanded. Employees whose behavior is poorest set the standard by which all employees are judged, so administrators must first take corrective action against these negative norm setters.

Noncompliance with work directives is a charge that most often arises in connection with noninstructional duties. Teachers are expected to monitor hallways, cafeterias, and restrooms in most schools. In some schools they also supervise the playground and bus-loading ramps. If the contract defines particular duties as voluntary, teachers may refuse to perform them without being subject to penalty. A question arises, however, when a teacher has agreed to perform a duty and later discontinues the activity before the task is complete. Consider a teacher who agrees to serve as sponsor of a cheerleading squad and resigns at midyear because of an increased workload related to a part-time job just taken on. Would a reprimand issued to a teacher in such a situation be sustained?

There is no way to predict what an arbitrator will decide in a given case, but if the contract is silent on the issue in question, then the arbitrator will use other information, including past practice, in making a decision. In this case, several factors must weigh on the decision. The arbitrator might consider whether the teacher understood that the assignment was for the full year, whether the teacher received supplemental pay for sponsoring the cheerleaders, and whether the teacher gave advance notice of her impending resignation and offered to help train a successor.

Other Issues in Arbitration

Arbitrability

One of the issues that frequently confronts arbitrators is the question of arbitrability. *Arbitrability* refers to whether a grievance is subject to arbitration. Grievances that deal with powers granted to the board by statute are not arbitrable, and those that are not timely are also likely to be judged nonarbitrable. Most grievance policies limit the number of days that may elapse after occurrence of an event before a grievance is filed. If the allowable number of days for filing a grievance is exceeded, it may be declared nonarbitrable unless the teacher failed to learn of the precipitating event until after it occurred.

Arbitrabilty also hinges on definitions of what is or is not arbitrable as stated in the negotiated contract or contained in state statutes. Certain disputes may be grievable but not arbitrable. (*Contract Administration,* 1983). In those situations, teachers have no appeal beyond the steps provided in the grievance procedure within the district.

Timeliness

Just as teachers must file a grievance within a specified number of days after the occurrence of the event they are grieving, administrators are required to respond to formal grievances within a few days of receiving them. Even though a grievance may arrive at a time when a principal is overwhelmed with other responsibilities, an answer must be given within the required time or the administration faces the possibility of losing in arbitration because of delay.

Questions of Law

Grievances frequently involve claims that state laws have been violated, but there is no unanimity of opinion regarding whether arbitrators should attempt to interpret the law in settling such disputes. Some people believe that arbitrators should not consider issues of law but should rather confine themselves to interpreting the collective bargaining agreement. Others argue that arbitrators are uniquely qualified to interpret the law as it applies to the parties to a collective bargaining agreement.

Past Practice

Past practice is frequently used by arbitrators as a guide in resolving disputes. If a particular practice has been consistently followed and there is nothing in the contract to indicate that the negotiators intended to change it, then any deviation from the practice by the administration is likely to be rejected. On the other hand, if the bargaining agreement specifies a procedure that is a clear departure from past practice, and the evidence suggests that both parties agreed to the change, then grievances appealing to past practices are unlikely to be upheld.

Problems most often arise when contract language appears to sanction a departure from previous practice but it is not clear that the negotiators meant to initiate the change. In one district, the contract specified that the "principal shall meet with the teacher following each classroom observation to discuss the results." When a new contract was negotiated, the language was changed slightly. In the new version, the provision read: "The principal shall meet with the teacher to discuss the results of classroom observations."

A teacher complained that the principal had not held a postobservation conference with her following a visit to the classroom and had informed her that a conference following every observation was no longer required. When the question reached arbitration, the arbitrator had to decide whether the negotiators had intended to drop the requirement. The board representative argued that such a change was intended, but the teacher representative denied it. In the absence of agreement that a change in practice was intended, the arbitrator held that principals should continue meeting with teachers after every observation.

In some cases, arbitrators have upheld departure from past practice when conditions warranted unusual actions. In one case, teachers participating in a mass "sick-out" to protest an action of the board were required by the administration to produce a physician's statement or have their pay docked for the time they were not at school. The penalized teachers grieved the decision, claiming that it violated past practice. The arbitrator upheld the administration on grounds that the teachers' actions justified the board's response (Ostrander, 1981).

Teacher Allegiance

Some issues are more important to teachers than others, and they will demonstrate flexibility on certain provisions of the contract while holding firm on others. Teachers are most likely to grieve what they believe to be violations of contract provisions affecting job security, transfers, class size, and assignment to noncontractual duties (Johnson, 1984).

However, most teachers feel allegiance to their school and to the principal and will try to work out disagreements before resorting to filing grievances. On occasion, teachers have even overridden the objections of union officials and performed duties that were not required by the contract in order to help facilitate a school's program (Johnson, 1984).

Effects of Arbitration on the District

Arbitrators' decisions can have considerable impact on district personnel policies. For that reason, most district administrators attempt to include in the contract language that narrowly defines which disputes may be taken to arbitration. Some administrators make it a practice never to go to arbitration unless they are certain of winning (Salmon, 1983). There is some wisdom in that position. Although the contract language may appear to be straightforward and clear to district administrators, there is no guarantee that the arbitrator will agree with their interpretation, and once an arbitrator's decision has been announced, it establishes a precedent that may be difficult to change (*Contract Administration*, 1983).

Maintenance Clauses

Unions often seek to include a maintenance of standards clause in the agreement. When such a clause is in effect, the administration may be unable to terminate programs that have outlived their usefulness or that the district can no longer afford. Consider a district that decides to remove physical education teachers from elementary schools to save money. The PE teachers all receive assignments elsewhere in the system, but teachers in the affected elementary schools will lose a planning period if the program change is made because the physical education teachers will no longer be available to take their students (*Contract Administration*, 1983).

If the district had intended for teachers to have a planning period and the bargaining agreement contains a maintenance of standards clause, the administration will almost certainly lose when the grievance reaches arbitration. Even if the planning time for teachers was an unplanned and coincidental part of the decision to implement the physical education program, the district may lose the grievance. For this reason, board negotiators generally oppose maintenance clauses, not because they are opposed to maintaining high-quality standards in the schools but because such clauses limit the flexibility of decision making that is needed to deal with changing conditions.

Threat of Grievance

The threat of a grievance may have as great an impact on personnel management practices as the actual grievance because administrators may avoid taking an action out of fear that to do so will lead to a grievance. That inhibiting effect sometimes accomplishes more for the union than it is able to gain through negotiations. A more healthy attitude is one that views the grievance process as a system of checks and balances that permits teachers who disagree with administrative decisions to seek redress (Johnson, 1984).

Some administrators are reluctant to take an unpopular position for fear of damaging teachers' morale. This is a consideration that all administrators must take into account, but it is not the only matter at stake in determining how disputes should be resolved. Often the issues in these disputes transcend a single school and have districtwide implications. If the principal of one school interprets the contract to favor teachers, personnel in other schools may demand the same concession. Such a decision can be costly for the district and limit the district's ability to win concessions from the other side in future negotiations.

A district-level administrator, usually the director of personnel, must monitor grievances if the district is to avoid unwanted and costly arbitration decisions (Hughes & Ubben, 1980). The grievance procedure provides the district with the opportunity to review decisions on employee grievances before they reach arbitration. The review process should include a careful analysis of the cost to the district of the precedent that may be established by an adverse decision.

Summary

Conflict in work settings usually involves one of four issues—interpretation and application of work rules, allocation of resources, duties and responsibilities, and assessment of performance. The effort to solve work-related conflict requires clarification and discussion of underlying issues, a search for shared values, exploration of possible solutions, and selection of one solution.

Increasingly, schools are relying on grievance procedures developed through the process of collective bargaining to resolve disputes. Arbitration is a component of the grievance procedure in many districts with bargaining agreements. A grievance process permits employees to have their complaints heard by managers or administrators in the organization and, ultimately in most cases, by an impartial arbitrator. Grievance procedures reduce the cost of settling disputes for both employees and employers by taking issues out of the courts and reducing the time required for resolution.

Arbitrators who review disputes between management and labor must decide whose interpretation of the contract is correct. Guidelines that are used by arbitrators to help them arrive at an accurate interpretation of contract language include the rule of consistency and the rule of intent. Arbitrators must frequently deal with complaints that involve interpretation and application of rules. Questions they must answer include to whom rules apply and what actions are either required or forbidden by a rule. "Just cause" complaints refer to contract clauses in which the administration is prohibited from withholding an employee benefit without good reason. These grievances are usually decided on the basis of reasonableness in behavior.

One of the principles used by arbitrators in resolving grievances is past practice. Unless it is clear that the board and the teachers' union intended to institute a new practice, the arbitrator usually holds that previous practice will remain in effect.

Suggested Activities

1. Read Exhibit 14.3 and prepare to present either the grievant's or the board's case before an arbitration panel. Stage a simulated hearing before three classmates representing the panel. After both sides have presented arguments, the panel will make its decision. You may want to locate the case in *Labor Arbitration Reports* to find how it turned out.

2. The principal of an elementary school informs teachers that he is concerned about student behavior in the cafeteria and proposes that they sit with their students while they eat rather than sitting together at one end of the room. There are strong objections from some teachers. There is no policy or contractual agreement that prevents the principal from directing teachers to sit with their students, but he prefers to avoid conflict if possible. How would you advise the principal to resolve this conflict?

3. Interview a principal or director of personnel to learn more about the types of conflict situations that arise with regard to interpretation and application of work rules and how they are usually resolved.

4. Look at Examples 1 through 5 in Exhibit 14.1. Take the position of one person in one of those disputes and explain the values held by that individual. Contrast those values with the values held by the other party to the conflict. What are some possible solutions to the individual's problem? Which of solutions are congruent with the values held by both parties?

The grievant, a Chapter 1 aide in a junior high school, was dismissed from her position after her husband was arrested for growing marijuana. The husband told police officers that he smoked marijuana for relief from migraine headaches and reported that his wife knew about the plants.

At the arbitration hearing, three employees testified that the aide had told them she did not know about her husband's marijuana. However, the Superintendent, who had obtained a copy of the official police report, pointed out that police said both the woman and her husband admitted that she knew about the marijuana. At that point the aide broke down and conceded that she did have knowledge of her husband's illegal activities. The Superintendent suspended the aide pending an investigation and, ultimately, she was dismissed from her job.

Testimony at the arbitration hearing showed that the district had a record of inconsistency in dealing with employees who were subject to discipline.

Three district employees had received DUI citations, but only one was terminated, and that person was later rehired. In the other cases, no disciplinary action was taken. An employee who had been arrested for growing marijuana was terminated, and another employee was dismissed for, among other reasons, lying to a supervisor.

The district argued that it was important for children to have positive role models and said that teachers and aides were expected to respect and obey the law and exemplify personal integrity and honesty. They said it was especially important for children in Chapter 1 programs to have upstanding role models.

The district stated that the instructional aide was discharged equally for reasons of untruthfulness and failing to control the use of her property.

The association argued that the employee did what she could reasonably have done to disassociate herself from her husband's activities. (She had left her husband on two occasions but had returned both times because the separation was hard on her daughters.)

The association also suggested that since the district had no rule regarding the consequences for employees of illegal activities by relatives, the aide had no way of knowing that her husband's activities could result in the loss of her job. The association said that employees should not be responsible for actions of people not under their control. Finally, the association pointed out that employees who had been charged or convicted of alcohol abuse had all received a second chance.

The district suggested that the grievant knew the probable consequences of acquiescing in her husband's drug activities and argued that expectations held for the employee were reasonable since her outside activities had the potential to reduce her effectiveness on the job.

The contract specified that an employee who was not performing his or her job satisfactorily could be terminated and that employees who were dismissed for theft, deception, willful disobedience, intoxication or being under the influence of drugs did not have the right to an explanation of the action, nor did they get a chance to improve their performance.

EXHIBIT 14.3   Grievance Pertaining to Dismissal of an Instructional Aide

Source: Reprinted with permission from *Labor Relations Reporter-Labor Arbitration Reports,* 100 LA 496. Copyright 1993 by the Bureau of National Affairs, Inc. (800–372–1033).

References

Boys Markets Inc. v. *Retail Clerks, Local 770,* 398 U.S. 235 (1970).

Contract administration: Understanding limitations on management rights. (1983). Eugene, OR: University of Oregon, Center for Educational Policy and Management. (ERIC Document Reproduction Service No. ED 271842).

Coulson, R. (1986). *Arbitration in the schools: An analysis of fifty-nine grievance arbitration cases.* New York: American Arbitration Association.

Elkouri, F., & Elkouri, E. (1973). *How arbitration works.* Washington, DC: Bureau of National Affairs.

Fossey, R. (1992). *Site-based management in a collective bargaining environment: Can we mix oil and water?* (ERIC Document Reproduction Service No. ED 355644).

Hughes, L., & Ubben, G. (1980). *The secondary principal's handbook: A guide to executive action.* Boston: Allyn and Bacon.

Johnson, S. (1984). *Teacher unions in schools.* Philadelphia: Temple University Press.

Lovell, N. (1985). *Grievance arbitration in education.* Bloomington, IN: Phi Delta Kappa.

Lutz, F., & Caldwell, W. (1979). Collective bargaining and the principal. In D. Erickson & T. Reller (Eds.), *The principal in metropolitan schools* (pp. 256–271). Berkeley, CA: McCutchan.

McPherson, D. (1983). *Resolving grievances: A practical approach.* Reston, VA: Reston Publishing.

Ostrander, K. (1981). *A grievance arbitration guide for educators.* Boston: Allyn and Bacon.

Ostrander, K. (1987). *The legal structure of collective bargaining in education.* New York: Greenwood Press.

Peters Township School District, 90 LA 35 (1988).

Pneuman, R. W., & Bruehl, M. E. (1982). *Managing conflict.* Englewood Cliffs, NJ: Prentice Hall.

Rahim, M. (1986). *Managing conflict in organizations.* New York: Praeger.

Redeker, J. (1989). *Employee discipline: Policies and practices.* Washington, DC: Bureau of National Affairs.

Salmon, H. (1983, April). *A superintendent's perspective of the grievance process.* Paper presented at the annual meeting of the National School Boards Association, San Francisco. (ERIC Document Reproduction Service No. ED 251927).

Turner, S., & Weed, F. (1983). *Conflict in organizations.* Englewood Cliffs, NJ: Prentice Hall.

Yates, D., Jr. (1985). *The politics of management.* San Francisco: Jossey-Bass.

15

TERMINATION AND
REDUCTION IN FORCE

The emphasis in this book has been on how to improve teacher quality and performance through the application of sound principles of personnel management. This positive approach, when carried out consistently over time, will produce significant gains in student learning.

However, there are times when less pleasant actions must be taken. When enrollments decline or funds are lost, reductions in force may be necessary, and when a teacher who appeared promising proves to be unable to manage a classroom successfully, termination must be considered. These actions are the subject of this chapter.

Plan of the Chapter

This chapter deals with the following topics: (1) carrying out a reduction in force, (2) reduction in force and employees' rights, (3) discipline of school personnel, (4) incompetence in the classroom, (5) legal requirements for dismissing teachers, (6) documenting unsatisfactory performance, and (7) rights of dismissed teachers.

Carrying Out a Reduction in Force

The purpose of a reduction-in-force (RIF) policy is to permit the district to achieve necessary cutbacks in the number of employees on the payroll without disrupting services. That outcome is most likely to be achieved if a policy providing fair, efficient, and consistent procedures for carrying out cutbacks has been developed in advance of the need (DeKalb County School System, 1979).

The need for reductions in the number of employees can arise in several ways. Developments that most often result in layoffs are declining enrollments, funding shortfalls, discontinuation of programs, and reorganization or consolidation of school districts. About four-fifths of the states have legislation that legitimizes reductions in force for one or more of those reasons (Zirkel & Bargerstock, 1981). In addition to those reasons, some states permit layoffs for "good or just cause."

If a state statute does not expressly identify a particular factor as a legitimate basis for laying off an employee, then the school district may be on shaky ground if it implements reductions for that reason. A Pennsylvania court reinstated a teacher who had been laid off by a district that had experienced a budget shortfall because financial exigency was not identified in the state statute as an acceptable reason for laying off employees (Zirkel & Bargerstock, 1981). However, some state courts have held that declining enrollments in one program may justify staff reductions, even though total enrollments are not declining (Caplan, 1984). The seven steps involved in carrying out a reduction in force and the individual or department responsible for each are shown in Exhibit 15.1.

Determining That a Surplus Exists

The first step in carrying out a reduction in force is determining that layoffs are needed. If enrollment drops or funding is cut, the district may not need as many personnel. When the number of excess personnel is small, normal attrition may achieve the needed reductions, but if it doesn't, other possibilities, including reduction in force, must be considered. The decision to lay off personnel is made by the district superintendent after consultations with

Step	Responsible Individual or Department
1. Determination that surplus exists	Superintendent (in consultation with principals and other administrators)
2. Identification of position classifications and certification fields affected	Personnel department (or official designated by superintendent)
3. Review of alternative actions	Superintendent, personnel department, finance department, and principals
4. Identification of a potential reduction-in-force pool	Personnel department, director of instruction, and union officials
5. Rank individuals in the pool using criteria established by law and policy	Personnel department with assistance from principals and others
6. Review of ranked list to remove protected individuals and groups	Personnel department with assistance from superintendent, principals, and other administrators
7. Implementation of reduction in force	Superintendent, personnel department, and principals

EXHIBIT 15.1   Steps Involved in Implementing Reduction in Force

other administrators. Among the factors to be considered before a final decision is made are enrollments, state statutes, accreditation standards, financial condition, court rulings, and program priorities (DeKalb County School System, 1979).

Identifying Classifications Affected

Once the superintendent has declared a personnel surplus, the personnel department is faced with the task of determining surplus personnel by position classification and certification field. If enrollments have dropped in business education courses, for example, the personnel department may declare a surplus of business education teachers. The number of surplus teachers will depend on the size of the enrollment decline, the number of teachers with business education certification employed by the district, and the number of teachers required to maintain the program.

Reviewing Alternatives

Layoffs are a traumatic experience for individuals involved. When layoffs occur, even employees who are not directly affected may experience feelings of depression and anxiety out of empathy for colleagues who are being laid off and feelings of concern for their own future security. It is sometimes possible to avoid the stress of layoffs by taking action to postpone or avoid the need to carry out a reduction in force. Among the actions to be considered are early retirement, unpaid leaves of absence, half-time employment, assistance in finding alternative employment, and retraining.

Early Retirement

Early retirement is one of the most widely used methods for avoiding reductions in force because it solves the problem of surplus personnel without the trauma of layoffs. On the other hand, early retirement is expensive and is not always a satisfactory solution. It works best when enrollments are declining at an equal rate in all grade levels and programs and when the district has a relatively large number of personnel nearing retirement age. If personnel surpluses are concentrated in a few programs or grade levels or if few individuals are close to retiring, early retirement is less likely to be a viable solution.

Leaves of Absence

Unpaid leaves of absence have the advantage of allowing employees to continue in-force insurance policies that are provided by the district. An employee is thus able to secure health insurance for self and family at rates below those that are available to individuals. Normally, the individual must pay the premium for the policy, but in some instances that cost is borne by the district. Employees on unpaid leave will be reinstated if a position is available at the expiration of the leave. Unpaid leaves offer psychological support at a crucial time by letting employees know that the district still values their contributions and wishes to continue the employer/employee relationship.

Part-Time Employment

Half-time or substitute positions are sometimes offered to employees who otherwise would be laid off, in the belief that most people would rather work part time than not work at all. If one position is assigned to two half-time employees, both have some income, whereas an employee who is laid off receives no income. As a temporary measure to give employees time to find alternative employment, half-time work helps.

Job-Hunting Assistance

Providing assistance to help individuals who are laid off to find new jobs is a psychologically sound strategy, since it motivates these employees to take action and move forward. Employees who receive layoff notices are sometimes immobilized by the hope that they will quickly be recalled. Rather than try to find another job, they sometimes waste months waiting for a recall notice. Beginning a systematic and wide-ranging job search can help them cope more realistically with their situation by assessing their strengths and examining their options.

Retraining Teachers

Retraining teachers who are about to be laid off is a viable strategy if enrollments in the subjects in which they are retrained are expected to remain stable. Teachers who are near to being certified in critical subjects are sometimes allowed to begin teaching classes in those subjects on temporary teaching certificates while they continue to take courses to qualify for full certification. However, teachers who lack the necessary subject matter competence should not be permitted to teach until they acquire it.

Identifying the Potential Pool

If alternative actions are not feasible, or if after such actions are taken an oversupply of teachers remains, the district then begins the crucial step of preparing a list of employees who are subject to being laid off. The list is prepared by reviewing personnel files of all individuals in the affected positions, using criteria established by the reduction-in-force policy. In the example used earlier, the pool might include all business education teachers or, in a large district, business education teachers with fewer than a specified number of years seniority.

It is wise to involve the director of instruction early in the process. Some programs require teachers who are certified in certain subspecialties in order to operate effectively, and the director of instruction can provide that information. A good example is a music program that involves offerings in chorus, band, and orchestra. A school with several tenured band teachers and no tenured chorus or orchestra teachers may end up with an oversupply of band teachers if seniority is the sole criterion for making reduction-in-force decisions. The director of instruction can identify needed adjustments in the pool in order to maintain well-balanced instructional programs.

Rank Ordering the Pool

Personnel files of employees who are included in the pool are reviewed and any who are considered essential for the continued operation of school programs are protected by being moved out of the pool. A teacher who is endorsed in a subject in which shortages exist or one whose teaching duties cannot be assumed by others in the department may be removed from the pool. This is a good time to review the bargaining agreement and state statutes to ensure that those documents are not violated in the process of carrying out the reduction in force. If there is a question about the interpretation of contract or statutory provisions, union officials and the board attorney should be consulted.

Factors Considered

Factors that may be taken into account in determining which employees are assigned to the pool, in addition to seniority and tenure status, are performance ratings, extra duty assignments, and additional certification areas. Teachers who perform extra duties, such as department head or cheerleader sponsor, may be protected from layoff over teachers with more seniority who do not perform extra duties.

Reviewing of Ranked List

At this point, a final review of the ranked list is carried out, with involvement of principals and various district staff members. The purpose of the review is to make deletions and additions that may be needed in order to avoid violating provisions of state law, negotiated agreements, and district policy, and to provide safeguards against disruptions of programs and unnecessary harm to program quality. When the review is complete and the superintendent has signed off, individuals on the list are notified that they are subject to layoff. In districts in which seniority is the only criterion used to determine the order of layoffs, a seniority list is published to inform employees of their status.

Implementing Reduction in Force

The final step in the process is to notify the individual employees who are to be laid off from their jobs. This is usually done by letter from the superintendent or the director of personnel. The letter identifies the date that the reduction in force becomes effective and outlines the employee's rights under the law and the bargaining agreement.

Reduction in Force and Employees' Rights

Collective bargaining agreements and state statutes grant certain rights to employees who are subject to being laid off. These rights include privileges earned through seniority, the opportunity to continue health insurance in effect at the employee's expense, and future reinstatement when funding permits.

In general, more senior workers are protected against layoffs when other employees with less seniority hold the same job. However, administrators sometimes decide to lay off a teacher with more seniority while retaining one with less seniority. When that happens, the district may expect to face a court challenge.

An example involved a Pennsylvania school district. The superintendent retained a teacher with less seniority as coordinator of a program for gifted students and laid off teachers who had more seniority. The administrator's rationale was that the teacher who was retained was more qualified for the position because she had been involved with the program since its inception, had more experience with arts and humanities, and was better at interacting with students and members of the community. Those arguments might have prevailed in some states, but the Pennsylvania Supreme Court held that the law of that state required the district to lay off employees with the least seniority (*Dallap* v. *Sharon City School District,* 1990).

Under collective bargaining agreements in force in many school districts, employees who are threatened with layoffs may replace or "bump" an employee with less seniority. However, this right has limitations. The bumping teacher must possess a valid certificate to teach the subject taught by the teacher being bumped and must have more seniority than the bumped teacher. It is common to require teachers who bump other teachers to have had recent and successful experience teaching the subject to which they are requesting to transfer. In some districts, the bargaining agreement gives the principal of the school receiving a replacement teacher the prerogative of reviewing the transferring teacher's credentials to determine whether that individual's qualifications are sufficient to maintain program quality (Johnson, 1982). In districts with such a policy, a teacher who received certification to teach a subject many years earlier but has never taught in that field and has taken no recent coursework would not be permitted to replace a teacher with more up-to-date credentials and experience.

Protections for Minorities

Minority employees who have been hired under affirmative action programs often have the least seniority in their districts and therefore are most vulnerable to reductions in force. Bargaining agreements sometimes provide protection from layoffs for these individuals. In one case involving such a plan, the Supreme Court held that the board failed to show a "compelling purpose" in arguing that past societal discrimination justified the plan and so rejected it. The Court stated:

> *Societal discrimination alone is [not] sufficient to justify a racial classification. Rather, the Court has insisted upon some showing of prior discrimination by the governmental unit involved before allowing limited use of racial classifications in order to remedy such discrimination. (Wygant v. Jackson (MI) Board of Education, 1986)*

However, in a case tried under Title VII of the Civil Rights Act, the Supreme Court upheld a plan that benefitted individuals who had not been identified as actual victims of discrimination (Geier v. Alexander, 1986).

Layoffs in Site-Based Schools

Most reduction-in-force policies were developed for districts in which uniform personnel allocation formulas are in effect in all schools, but under site-based management, staffing patterns may vary from school to school. Schools are allowed to decide whether to use established staffing ratios to decide how many teachers and other staff members to hire or to adopt alternative formulas and, for example, hire fewer teachers and more technicians and aides (Odden & Picus, 1992).

Alternative staffing practices raise complex questions when a layoff is necessary. Suppose a school has given up one teaching position in exchange for three instructional aides. If the school is scheduled to lose a teaching position in a reduction in force, should it have the option of releasing either one teacher or the three aides?

A similar question might arise in a school that uses multimedia instructional methods and hires a computer technician in place of a teacher to assist in producing instructional materials. Suppose that a RIF takes place and the faculty decide that they cannot operate the program without the technician's assistance. Should the technician be retained and a teacher laid off? When a reduction in force occurs, the district specifies the departments and subjects that will lose staff. Since the technician assists teachers in all subject areas but is not assigned to any one department, is he or she immune from being laid off?

In some localities, school councils are given the option of transferring funds across budget categories and may reallocate money from one account to another (Clune & White, 1988). Suppose that teachers in a school agree to teach larger classes and apply the salary savings to the purchase of books and materials. Since the school has in effect already reduced its staff size, should it be immune from further personnel cuts during a reduction in force?

In all of these situations, the answer to the question depend on board policy, past practice, and the collective bargaining agreement. When districts adopt school-based management, employee unions are often asked to agree to permit waivers of certain provisions of the master contract (Poltrock & Goss, 1993). Some have agreed to do that, but other unions have refused to permit any deviation from contract language related to reduction in force (Clark, 1993). Districts need to develop clear and specific guidelines governing layoffs, so that when questions such as these arise they can be answered.

Staffing Adjustments Required

When a reduction in force takes place, principals are required to make adjustments in staffing by redistributing instructional and noninstructional assignments among the remaining staff members. In the case of elementary schools, this may involve nothing more than reducing the number of classes in the affected grade levels and reassigning students, but it often involves much more. In middle and high schools, principals are faced with making adjustments in the master schedule to reflect shifting enrollment patterns brought about by the elimination of some course offerings. For example, if fewer classes are offered in the business education department because of staff reductions, existing classes in that department as well as in other departments may increase in size, as a result of the reduced number of elective options available to students.

These changes in enrollment patterns also have implications for the purchase of equipment, materials, and supplies. If available business education classes increase in size, it may be necessary to purchase additional typewriters or computers to accommodate the increased enrollment.

If teachers who were laid off were sponsors of student clubs or activities, it will be necessary for the principal to arrange to recruit other teachers to take over those duties rather than let the programs languish. If the layoffs involved nonteaching personnel, such as guidance counselors, the principal must see to it that the workload is redistributed equitably among remaining staff members.

The decision to carry out a reduction in force is not an easy one, but it is simple compared to the difficulty and distress that faces an administrator who attempts to terminate a teacher. The next section addresses the topic of teacher discipline and termination.

Discipline of School Personnel

On occasion, disciplinary action must be taken against a school employee who has been guilty of breaking the law or violating board policy. In a progressive disciplinary system, the action taken depends on the seriousness of the incident and whether it is a first-time offense. For a minor offense, the usual disciplinary action is an oral reprimand. For example, an oral reprimand would be an appropriate response for a teacher who oversleeps and arrives late for school but fails to call ahead to notify the office.

A more serious disciplinary response is a written reprimand, which is issued after an employee has broken a rule several times, or, in the case of a more serious infraction, after the first offense. A written reprimand would be appropriate when a school bus is involved in a traffic accident as a result of carelessness on the part of the driver of the bus. The next disciplinary steps, in order of progressive severity, are suspension with or without pay and non-renewal or termination. In addition to these actions, in some states salary adjustment is used for disciplinary purposes.

The contents of an oral or written reprimand are similar. In both cases, the administrator issuing the reprimand identifies the action that is the basis for the reprimand and cites the policy that has been violated. The employee is reminded to refrain from the action in the future and warned of the consequences of failing to do so.

Exhibit 15.2 shows an example of a written reprimand issued by a principal to a tenured teacher who engaged in an altercation with a student. The administrator describes the actions for which the reprimand is issued, cites the policy that was violated, and admonishes the teacher to refrain from fu-

---

Ms. Wanda Olson
Price Elementary School
Clearfield, OH 43236

Dear Ms. Olson:

On Thursday, October 11, you engaged in an argument with a student, Mary Anne Carter, during which you admit calling her a "lame brain" and making derogatory remarks about her appearance. When Mary Anne's mother called you to complain, you admit that you refused to discuss the incident with her and suggested that she call me.

Let me remind you that board policy states that teachers in Clearfield Schools will avoid harsh, abusive, and profane language in front of students. The policy also states that teachers will, when asked, arrange to meet with parents to discuss questions and concerns. In the incident described above, you were in violation of this policy.

I realize that the student's behavior was provocative, and I have taken appropriate disciplinary measures with the student. However, the child's behavior, while not acceptable, does not excuse your actions. Therefore, I am issuing this reprimand and directing you to avoid further violations of this policy. If you ignore this directive, more serious measures will be taken. I hope and trust that you will exhibit professional behavior in all future dealings with students and parents. A copy of this letter will be placed in your personnel file, but if you finish the school year without further violations of board policies, the letter will be removed.

Sincerely,

Mark W. Williams
Principal

EXHIBIT 15.2   Letter of Reprimand to a Teacher

ture violations. One copy of the written reprimand goes to the employee, and a second copy is placed in his or her personnel file. The file copy may be removed after a time if the employee has no further infractions.

Suspension is used as a disciplinary technique when an employee is suspected of a serious violation of a regulation, policy, or law. A teacher who is arrested on drug or morals charges would probably be placed on suspension by the district pending a court decision on the individual's guilt or innocence. If the charge is less serious, an individual might be suspended for a limited period of time. For example, a coach who strikes a referee during an argument following a disputed call might be suspended without pay.

The purpose of employee discipline is not to punish people but to make employees aware of rules, policies, and laws and to impress upon them the importance of compliance. It is most effective when it is viewed as an educational tool, is applied consistently and fairly, and is used sparingly.

Incompetence in the Classroom

Some observers believe that the greatest impediment to the improvement of instruction in schools is the quality of teachers. It has been argued that teacher competence is the most severe problem facing the schools and that school administrators have been lax in failing to take firm and prompt action to dismiss teachers who are not performing satisfactorily (Johnson, 1984).

Bridges (1985) has argued the point forcefully:

> *Most teachers in our nation's schools are competent, conscientious, hardworking individuals. All too often their efforts are overshadowed by the poor performance of a relatively small number of incompetent classroom teachers. These incompetents must be identified and assisted, and if they fail to improve, they must be dismissed. (p. 19)*

Scriven (1980) took an even more critical position:

> *The current state of teacher personnel policies is that they are reasonably fair to teachers—a great improvement over the pre-union situation—and extremely unfair to students, parents and taxpayers. They protect all, but they excessively protect the congenital incompetent, the once-but-no-longer-competent and the competent non-performer. . . . We have teacher policies that ruthlessly sacrifice productivity for equity. Productivity without equity is morally intolerable; equity without productivity is socially irresponsible. (p. 2)*

How accurate are these charges? Is quality of teachers a critical problem in the schools? Are administrators remiss in failing to act to remove incompetent performers? Are we overly concerned with protecting the rights of poor performers at the expense of students? These are important questions that will be examined in this chapter.

Views of Teacher Quality Problem

Most observers agree that teacher quality is a problem. The degree of seriousness attached to the problem depends on who is asked. About 7 percent of public school parents responding to the 1993 Gallup Poll on attitudes toward the public schools cited "difficulty getting good teachers" as a problem for the schools, down from 11 percent five years earlier (Gallup & Elam, 1988; Elam, Rose, & Gallup, 1993). Among problems cited in the 1993 poll as more serious than teacher quality were lack of financial support, drug abuse, lack of discipline, fighting and violence, and quality of education.

In the 1988 survey, 89 percent of public school parents agreed that public schools needed to attract more capable students into teaching. Large majorities also favored requiring experienced teachers to take and pass a competency test in their subject area and creation of national standards for certification (Gallup & Elam, 1988).

Not surprisingly, teachers are less likely than parents and administrators to agree that teacher quality is a major concern. However, even teachers agree that a problem exists, and those who teach with incompetent teachers often report that they feel demoralized. Some are discouraged because they feel they try hard to do a good job while some of their colleagues do nothing more than the minimum (Johnson, 1984).

Administrative Responsibility

Few teachers are willing to take a personal position on incompetence in the profession or to pressure union officers to do so. However, many of them believe that administrators should set high standards for teacher performance and take action against teachers who do not meet those standards (Johnson, 1984).

Many administrators and some teachers believe that unions protect both incompetent teachers and those who have lost interest in teaching but remain in the classroom. However, others, including many administrators, believe that poor teachers can be removed from classrooms if the procedures that are available are put into use by principals (Johnson, 1984).

One of the concerns expressed by administrators and union leaders alike is that in the current concern for school productivity teachers' rights are likely to be overlooked. Gross (1988) pointed out the danger and suggested a possible solution:

> *Requiring fact rather than assumption as a basis for disciplinary action may appear on the surface to make it more difficult to dismiss immoral or incompetent teachers. On the contrary, identifying and eliminating unfairness*

in the current disciplinary system for tenured teachers will require school districts to develop hiring, evaluation, promotion, and disciplinary policies and practices that can be validated with competent evidence. (p. 2)

If selection and evaluation procedures are in place and working well, there should rarely be a need to dismiss teachers. Yet, even when care and thought are exercised in selecting and placing teachers, and when opportunities for professional growth are provided, there will still be a few who do not perform the job satisfactorily or who lapse into substandard performance after a time. Districts should monitor the performance of all teachers and be prepared to take action against those few who fail to meet their standards of performance.

Legal Requirements for Dismissing Teachers

State statutes identify specific causes for which teachers may be dismissed. The most common grounds for dismissal are incompetence or neglect of duty, immorality or unprofessional conduct, and insubordination. Some states allow dismissal for "good or just cause" and "inefficiency" (Neill & Custis, 1978).

Dismissed teachers have been charged, among other things, with failing to maintain classroom control, abuse of students, excessive tardiness, failure to maintain self-control, and refusing to accept supervision. Dismissals have also been based on failure to use up-to-date teaching methods, failure to use tact in dealing with students and co-workers, and low student achievement. In most cases of incompetence, teachers fall short of an acceptable standard of performance in several areas.

Incompetence or Neglect of Duty

Incompetence covers a broad range of conditions and behaviors. Physical or mental incapacity and lack of knowledge of subject are examples of behaviors that have been successfully cited as evidence of incompetent teaching. Other examples include failure to maintain appropriate discipline, mistreatment of students, failure to adopt new teaching methods, lack of cooperation, and personal misconduct in or out of school (Valente, 1980).

Courts generally interpret statutes on teacher dismissal to favor teachers, which places on the district the burden of assembling substantial documentation to show that the teacher was guilty of persistent dereliction of duty or lack of cooperation. Testimony of department heads, supervisors, other teachers, parents, and even students may be introduced to establish incompetence and to show a connection between the teacher's conduct and his or her performance as a teacher. If the board is not successful in convincing the court of the teacher's incompetence, it may be ordered to reinstate the teacher and pay lost wages and damages (*Education Law,* 1989).

Physical disability may not be used as the basis for dismissal of an employee except when the individual has a contagious disease or is so severely impaired that even with reasonable accommodation he or she is unable to perform effectively in a job. *Reasonable accommodation* is defined by the Equal Employment Opportunities Commission (EEOC) as modifications to the manner in which a job is customarily performed that enable a qualified individual with a disability to perform the essential functions of that position (Schneid, 1992).

When a district contemplates terminating a tenured teacher for incompetence, it must explain to the teacher in what areas his or her performance is deficient. Time must then be given to the teacher to correct his or her problems. As a rule, a single incident of poor judgment or incompetent behavior is not sufficient to justify termination of a tenured teacher. Courts look for patterns of behavior, and if none is found, they are likely to support reinstatement.

An example of one such case involved a teacher from Maine who worked outside of school as a gunsmith. The teacher inadvertently brought a revolver and some ammunition to school in a jacket pocket. The jacket, with the weapon inside, was stolen and the teacher was later dismissed by the school committee, which argued that bringing the revolver and ammunition to school were evidence of grave lack of judgment that justified dismissal. The court reversed the committee's action, noting that dismissal was not justified when the individual's ability to teach effectively was not in question (*Wright v. Superintending School Committee,* 1976).

Immoral or Unprofessional Behavior

Dismissing a teacher on grounds of immoral or unprofessional conduct places on the board the burden of showing that the teacher's behavior had an adverse impact on students or teachers. There is no absolute standard against which such behavior is judged. Rather, the courts take into account such factors as age and maturity of the students, degree of adverse impact, motive for the behavior, and the likelihood that it will be repeated (Alexander & Alexander, 1985).

Teachers have been discharged on grounds of immoral behavior for engaging in sexual misconduct with students. Some courts have held that when sexual involvement occurs between teacher and student, a presumption of adverse impact is justified without additional proof (McCarthy & Cambron-McCabe, 1987). Other examples of immoral behavior for which teachers have been discharged are physical abuse of students, use of profanity, misconduct involving drugs or alcohol, and misappropriation of funds.

Homosexual behavior has been allowed as grounds for dismissal in some courts, but not in others (Landauer, Spangler, & Van Horn, 1983). As a general rule, private sexual behavior, whether homosexual or heterosexual, is regarded by the courts as grounds for dismissal only to the extent that it affects the individual's effectiveness as a teacher. But it should also be noted that teachers are regarded as exemplars and that their actions "are subject to much greater scrutiny than that given to the activities of the average person" (*Chicago Board of Education* v. *Payne*, 1982).

A teacher who is convicted of a crime of moral turpitude may be dismissed. However, an arrest alone is not usually sufficient grounds for dismissal, although it may be justifiable grounds for suspension. Sexual crimes are considered irremediable and are sufficient to justify dismissal. Use of drugs can justify immediate suspension pending dismissal (*Education Law*, 1989).

Insubordination

Insubordination is a lawful cause for dismissal of teachers in many states. Actions that may be construed as insubordinate include failing to follow rules and regulations pertaining to use of corporal punishment, absenteeism, tardiness, and failing to complete required reports.

Insubordination also includes a teacher's refusal to perform properly assigned duties. Administrators may assign duties that are not specified in a bargaining agreement as long as they are reasonably related to the instructional program and are not unduly time consuming or burdensome. However, a teacher may not lawfully be dismissed for refusing to perform duties for which he or she lacks competence or that are unrelated to the school program (*Education Law*, 1989).

Some courts have held that a single incident of insubordination is sufficient to justify dismissal. A teacher in Kansas was dismissed after he had his wife call the school to report that he was ill while he was actually in Texas interviewing for another job. The teacher had earlier requested and been denied leave. The principal of the school at which the teacher taught learned of the deception when the principal of the Texas school in which he interviewed called for a recommendation. The Kansas Court of Appeals upheld the decision to terminate the teacher's contract, noting that a single incident of insubordination could be sufficient to justify termination (*Gaylord* v. *Board of Education*, 1990). A similar conclusion was reached by the Colorado Supreme Court, which held that a district was justified in dismissing a teacher who had used profanity in front of several students after having been ordered by the superintendent to refrain from doing so (*Ware* v. *Morgan County School District*, 1988).

A board is most likely to win a legal test of a decision to dismiss a teacher for insubordination if it can show that the teacher knew about but repeatedly violated a rule, regulation, or directive, thereby causing harm to the school. The board's case will be further buttressed if the teacher's behavior is considered irremediable (Landauer et al., 1983).

Documenting Unsatisfactory Performance

Most teachers occasionally violate school rules and policies, but most of those violations are minor and many of them are ignored by principals. When serious or repeated violations occur, the principal is obligated to take action. This involves preparing written documentation of the teacher's actions and the actions taken by the principal or others to remediate the problem, sending a copy to the teacher, and placing a copy of it in the individual's personnel file. Performance evaluation reports and descriptions of classroom observations are also included in the personnel file.

Five types of records prepared by principals are involved in documenting unsatisfactory performance: specific incident memoranda, private notes, descriptions of classroom observations, evaluation reports, and summary memoranda. If a teacher takes an action (or fails to take action) that constitutes violation of policy, the principal should immediately hold a conference with the teacher to discuss the infraction and to remind the teacher of the policy that has been violated. If the teacher's behavior is serious enough, this conference may be followed by a specific incident memorandum in which the principal summarizes the actions taken by the teacher that violated policy and describes any corrective action the principal has taken, including issuance of a reprimand (Frels & Cooper, 1982).

Specific Incident Memoranda

The specific incident memorandum should contain an objective description of the teacher's act or failure to act, a comment on the detrimental effect of the action on students, a description of suggestions or directives given the teacher by the principal or supervisor, and a statement indicating whether the teacher complied with the directives or followed through on suggestions (Neill & Custis, 1978).

It is advisable to ask the teacher to acknowledge receiving the memorandum by signing a copy to be placed in the individual's personnel file. The teacher should also be given the opportunity to prepare a written response explaining circumstances surrounding the incident and presenting the teacher's version of the facts. This response is also placed in the personnel file (Frels & Cooper, 1982).

Private Notes

Brief private notes about teachers may be kept by a principal as reminders for followup action but should be destroyed as soon as possible. For example, a principal may make a note to remind a teacher that students must be given at least one day's notice before being assigned to after-school detention in order to allow them to arrange transportation home. If the teacher continues to violate the rule after meeting with the principal, the administrator may reprimand the teacher or may place a note in a private file that serves as a reminder to comment on the teacher's actions in the performance evaluation report (Frels & Cooper, 1982).

Observation Reports

In most school districts, principals are required to observe teachers' classroom performance and to note the results of these observations in a memorandum or on a form provided by the district. These records are retained in teachers' personnel records and, if a teacher is dismissed, are used as part of the documentation. Notes prepared by the principal should be as detailed as possible, since relying on memory to recall events from an observation that occurred several months or years earlier is extremely risky.

Evaluation Reports

Evaluations of teachers' performance become part of a permanent documentary record. Evaluations are usually based on classroom performance but may include ratings on other aspects of the teacher's work. Some teachers may perform satisfactorily in the core tasks of teaching, such as planning and presenting instruction, but have problems working with administrators, teachers, and parents. These problems should be noted in the evaluation summary since they may be central to a subsequent action to dismiss.

Most teachers receive satisfactory performance ratings, even though their performance does not always justify them. It is extremely difficult to convince a court that a teacher's performance falls below the minimally acceptable standard when over a period of years the teacher has consistently received satisfactory performance ratings from principals. This problem is not exclusive to schools; it happens in most organizations (Bridges, 1984). However, organizations that do not grant tenure to their employees have more discretion in discharging unsatisfactory performers. When the decision is made to terminate a tenured teacher, the district should be able to produce evidence over a period of at least three years showing a pattern of unsatisfactory performance. Moreover, the board should be prepared to show a connection between identified deficiencies and loss of learning (Barton, 1984).

Summary Memoranda

A summary memorandum outlines the results of several incidents or classroom observations. It is used when the principal wishes to call to the teacher's attention several related instances of rule or policy violations or to summarize several classroom observations. The summary memorandum is used when the individual actions are not serious enough to warrant writing a specific incident memorandum but which, taken together, constitute a pattern of behavior that requires attention.

Global	Specific
Had poor classroom management procedures	3 students were out of their seats and 4 others were talking, ignoring the teacher
Violated the school policy on collection of payments and fees	Failed to issue receipts to 3 students who paid $5 locker fee
Inadequately prepared for teaching	Had not prepared a lesson plan for the class; used part of class time to show a movie that was only tangentially related to the topic being studied
Classroom appearance poor	Bulletin board displays unchanged for 6 months; books and papers piled atop bookcases and teacher's desk

EXHIBIT 15.3   Global Versus Specific Documentation

The documentary record should be a complete, accurate, and specific compilation of facts about an individual's performance. Complete and accurate records benefit both the district and the individual, since courts will uphold a termination action when documentation exists to show that a teacher's performance fails to meet the standards required by the district. Courts will dismiss the action when documentation is not available to substantiate the charge.

Principals who are documenting unsatisfactory performance by a teacher should be prepared to write objective, factual descriptions about what is observed in classrooms or in other areas of the school. Global descriptions are likely to be challenged in court and should be avoided. In their place, principals should use specific descriptions of classroom events or teacher actions. Sample descriptions of both types are provided in Exhibit 15.3.

Rights of Dismissed Teachers

A district may refuse to renew the contract of a nontenured teacher without stating reasons for the decision, except in states with statutes that require notification. Tenured teachers, however, are entitled to certain protections prior to dismissal. Successful dismissal of a tenured teacher requires that the district strictly observe these procedural requirements.

The following list enumerates the due process protections that are provided tenured teachers by various state statutes (Cambron-McCabe, 1983):

1. A statement of charges
2. Access to evidence and names of witnesses
3. A choice of an open or closed hearing
4. Opportunity to be represented by counsel

5. Opportunity to introduce evidence, call, and cross-examine witnesses
6. A transcript of the hearing upon request
7. A written decision
8. Right of appeal

A teacher may be suspended without a hearing if his or her presence in the school represents a potential threat to students or other persons, or if the individual is charged with a crime involving moral turpitude.

Constitutional Protections

The Constitution grants certain rights to all American citizens, and employees are protected from employers' actions that infringe those rights. The Fourteenth Amendment provides that government shall not "deprive any person of life, liberty, or property without due process of law." Tenured teachers and nontenured teachers under contract have potential property and liberty interests that are jeopardized by termination. They are entitled to procedural due process before being terminated. Due process involves, at a minimum, notice of charges and an opportunity for a pretermination hearing at which evidence must be presented to show that the charges are true and support the proposed action (Hill & Wright, 1993).

The First Amendment guarantees freedom of speech, but the Supreme Court has held that that right must be balanced with employers' interest in maintaining an efficient operation. In *Pickering* v. *Board of Education* (1968), the Court held that speech that interfered with employee performance, created disharmony, or undercut supervisory authority was not extended the same protections as other forms of expression.

In *Connick* v. *Myers* (1983), the Court held that to be protected, an employee's statement must deal with public—and not merely private—concerns. Determining which issues are private or public involves considering whether the expression advances a purely personal or community interest and whether or not there is general public interest in the issue (Frels & Schneider-Vogel, 1986).

A legal challenge under the First Amendment is likely to occur when an employee is terminated after openly criticizing district policy. The district may argue that the decision to dismiss was based on performance deficiencies and not on the employee's statements, but if the two events are proximate in time, questions are certain to be raised about the district's true motives (Frels & Schneider-Vogel, 1986).

In 1990, 40 states required prospective teachers to pass a test in order to be certified (National Center for Education Statistics, 1993), and a few states have enacted legislation that requires testing of practicing teachers. Both types of laws have been challenged in court.

In Texas, state law requires public school teachers and administrators to pass the Texas Examination for Current Administrators and Teachers

(TECAT), which tests basic reading and writing skills. An organization representing teachers and administrators challenged the law, claiming that it was an unconstitutional impairment of teachers' and administrators' contracts. The Texas Supreme Court rejected the claim and upheld the test (*State* v. *Project Principle,* 1987).

In Alabama, the required test was the National Teachers' Examination (NTE). The Supreme Court of that state held that the board had properly refused to renew contracts of 106 teachers who had failed to attain the required score on the examination (*York* v. *Board of School Commissioners,* 1984).

Teachers who are threatened with dismissal are often given the option of resigning in order to avoid embarrassing and damaging publicity. Administrators should use care in attempting to persuade a teacher to resign, because courts may view the resignation as coerced and order the teacher reinstated. For the same reason, administrators should avoid trying to obtain a resignation by increasing a teacher's workload or transferring the individual to an inconvenient or undesirable location.

Remediation

A question that is often raised in dismissal cases is remediability. If the behavior for which a tenured teacher is dismissed is considered remediable, then the board has an obligation to permit the teacher the opportunity to correct the behavior before it takes action to dismiss. The board's decision on the question of remediability is subject to judicial review. If there is a question about remediability, administrators are wise to assume that the behavior in question is remediable and to permit the teacher the opportunity to correct it. There is no absolute standard for judging how much time should be allowed for remediation. Although five weeks was found to be insufficient in one case, eight weeks was considered adequate by another court (Landauer et al., 1983)

Eight types of remediation are provided for teachers whose performance is judged to be unsatisfactory. They are listed in Exhibit 15.4 along with examples of actions appropriate for each.

The district is not expected to provide all of these various types of assistance to one individual, but the more different kinds of help it gives, the better the chance the teacher will achieve significant improvement in performance. If no improvement results, the courts are then more likely to validate the board's decision to dismiss the teacher.

The first six remediation actions in Exhibit 15.4 should be carried out together. Although districts sometimes take one of these actions alone (for example, goal setting or instructional input), the chances of success are much greater if all six are used.

Goal setting was discussed in Chapter 6 as a motivational technique. In working with a teacher who has significant deficiencies in instructional performance, it is advisable to help the individual establish learning and

Goal setting:	Help the teacher establish instructional and behavioral goals for students.
Instructional input:	Arrange for the teacher to take a class or attend a workshop to learn new skills.
Modeling:	Provide released time for the teacher to observe a colleague who has the skills the teacher is learning.
Practice:	Arrange time for the teacher to practice new skills in a nonthreatening environment.
Feedback:	Provide feedback to the teacher who is attempting to master new skills.
Reinforcement:	Provide rewards, including praise, for correct use of newly learned skills.
Therapy or counseling:	Arrange for intensive emotional support for the teacher who has severe emotional problems.
Environmental change:	Arrange for the teacher to transfer to a different assignment.

EXHIBIT 15.4   Actions and Examples for Teacher Remediation

Source: *Managing the Incompetent Teacher* by E. M. Bridges, 1984, Eugene: University of Oregon ERIC Clearinghouse on Educational Management.

behavior goals to achieve better classroom control and increased student achievement.

Instructional input equips the teacher with the knowledge and skill needed to achieve the goals. Modeling, practice, feedback, and reinforcement help the teacher to refine the skills and acquire facility and confidence in their use. Teachers who are having difficulty implementing instruction effectively may need to be reminded about the conditions under which learning occurs. Teachers help students to learn by establishing clear learning objectives, choosing appropriate learning tasks, expressing confidence in students' ability, providing rewards to practice new skills, and creating conditions under which transfer of learning can occur (Tyler, 1985).

Therapy/counseling and environmental change are less often used. They may be applied together, in conjunction with other techniques, or alone, depending on the nature of the teacher's problem. Teachers whose problems are related to their life situation may profit from therapy or counseling, and those whose difficulties emanate from their work assignment often perform better in a different setting. Sometimes it is necessary to provide psychological support along with environmental change.

Summary

Reductions in force and termination of employees are occasionally necessary personnel actions. Policies governing both contingencies should spell out the actions to be taken and define the rights of employees involved.

The purpose of a reduction-in-force policy is to permit the district to achieve necessary cutbacks in the number of employees on the payroll without disrupting services. Reduction-in-force policies should describe a procedure for declaring that a surplus of employees exists and for identifying the employee classifications and positions affected. It should also specify alternatives that may be taken to avoid layoffs. Preparation of a layoff pool should be done in consultation with the director of instruction in order to avoid harm to instructional programs.

Teachers may be dismissed for reasons related to incompetence, immoral or unprofessional behavior, and insubordination. Tenured teachers who are dismissed must be accorded due process rights, and all teachers are protected against loss of constitutional rights.

Principals anticipating the need to dismiss a teacher should prepare a detailed documentary record of the individual's performance deficiencies. Specific incident memoranda, private notes, observation and evaluation reports, and summary memoranda are all used to establish a record of evidence. An effort must be made to provide remedial assistance to tenured teachers if the deficiency is considered remediable.

Suggested Activities

1. What action would you, the principal, take in the following situations? Give reasons for your decision.

   a. A teacher tells you that she observed a male eighth-grade teacher from your school attending a movie with one of his female students the previous evening.

   b. At a basketball game, you observe the coach walking unsteadily as enters the gym with his players. As you approach him, you can smell alcohol on his breath.

   c. A teacher from your school gives a speech to a local environmental organization criticizing the superintendent and school board for deciding not to introduce an environmental education program into the curriculum.

2. Discuss reasons why seniority should or should not be used as the sole factor to be considered in deciding which employees will be laid off when a reduction in force is necessary.

3. Review the actions used for teacher remediation (Exhibit 15.4). Explain under what circumstances goal setting would be the best approach for helping a marginal teacher improve his or her performance. When would instructional input and environmental change be most appropriate?

4. Read Case Study III (at the end of the book) and answer the questions that follow.

References

Alexander, K., & Alexander, M. (1985). *American public school law* (2nd ed.). St. Paul, MN: West.

Barton, M. (1984, April). *What you ought to know about termination and due process.* Paper presented at the annual meeting of the National School Boards Association, Houston. (ERIC Document Reproduction Service No. ED 247641).

Bridges, E. (1984). *Managing the incompetent teacher.* Eugene: University of Oregon, ERIC Clearinghouse on Educational Management.

Bridges, E. (1985, January). It's time to get tough with the turkeys. *Principal, 64,* 19–21.

Cambron-McCabe, N. (1983). Procedural due process. In J. Beckham & P. Zirkel (Eds.), *Legal issues in public school employment* (pp. 78–97). Bloomington, IN: Phi Delta Kappa.

Caplan, G. (1984). Current issues in reduction-in-force. In T. Jones & D. Semler (Eds.), *School law update . . . preventive school law* (pp. 15–22). Topeka, KS: National Organization on Legal Problems of Education. (ERIC Document Reproduction Service No. ED 244321).

Chicago Board of Education v. *Payne,* 430 N.E.2d 310, 315 (Ill. App. 1982).

Clark, R. T. (1993, Spring). School-based management—Problems and prospects. *Journal of Law and Education, 22,* 183–186.

Clune, W., & White, P. (1988). *School-based management.* New Brunswick, NJ: Rutgers University, Center for Policy Research in Education.

Connick v. *Myers,* 461 U.S. 138 (1983).

Dallap v. *Sharon City School District,* 571 A.2d 368 (Pa. 1990).

DeKalb County School System. (1979). *A policy and administrative procedure for reduction in force.* Decatur, GA: Author. (ERIC Document Reproduction Service No. ED 228690).

Education law (Vol. 2). (1989). New York: Matthew Bender.

Elam, S., Rose, L., & Gallup, A. (1993, October). The 25th annual Phi Delta Kappa/Gallup Poll of the public's attitudes toward the public schools. *Phi Delta Kappan, 75,* 137–152.

Frels, K., & Cooper, T. (1982). *A documentation system for teacher improvement or termination.* Topeka, KS: National Organization on Legal Problems of Education.

Frels, K. & Schneider-Vogel, M. (1986). *The First Amendment and school employees: A practical management guide.* Topeka, KS: National Organization on Legal Problems of Education.

Gallup, A., & Elam, S. (1988). The 20th annual Gallup Poll on the public's attitudes toward the public schools. *Phi Delta Kappan, 70,* 33–46.

Gaylord v. *Board of Education, School District 218,* 794 P.2d 307 (Kan. App. 1990).

Geier v. *Alexander,* 801 F.2d 799 (1986).

Gross, J. (1988). *Teachers on trial: Values, standards, and equity in judging conduct and competence.* Ithaca, NY: ILR Press.

Hill, M., & Wright, J. (1993). *Employee lifestyle and off-duty conduct regulation.* Washington, DC: Bureau of National Affairs.

Johnson, S. (1982, March). *Seniority and schools.* Paper presented at the annual meeting of the American Educational Research Association, New York. (ERIC Document Reproduction Service No. ED 221931).

Johnson, S. (1984). *Teacher unions in schools.* Philadelphia: Temple University Press.

Landauer, W., Spangler, J., & Van Horn, B., Jr. (1983). Good cause basis for dismissal of education employees. In J. Beckham & P. Zirkel (Eds.), *Legal issues in public school employment* (pp. 154–170). Bloomington, IN: Phi Delta Kappa.

McCarthy, M., & Cambron-McCabe, N. (1987). *Public school law: Teachers' and students' rights.* (2nd ed.). Boston: Allyn and Bacon.

National Center for Education Statistics. (1993). *Digest of education statistics.* Washington, DC: U.S. Department of Education.

Neill, S., & Custis, J. (1978). *Staff dismissal: Problems and solutions.* Arlington, VA: American Association of School Administrators.

Odden, A., & Picus, L. (1992). *School finance: A policy perspective.* New York: McGraw-Hill.

Pickering v. *Board of Education,* 391 U.S. 563 (1968).

Poltrock, L., & Goss, S. (1993). A union lawyer's view of restructuring and reform. *Journal of Law and Education, 22,* 177–182.

Schneid, T. (1992). *The Americans with Disabilities Act: A practical guide for managers.* New York: Van Nostrand Reinhold.

Scriven, M. (1980, October). *Teacher personnel policies: Equity, validity, and productivity.* Paper presented at the Midwest Policy Seminar, St. Louis. (ERIC Document Reproduction Service No. ED 206741).

State v. *Project Principle,* 724 S.W.2d 387 (Tex. 1987).

Tyler, R. (1985). Conditions for effective learning. In M. Fantini & R. Sinclair (Eds.), *Education in school and nonschool settings* (pp. 203–229). Chicago: University of Chicago Press.

Valente, W. (1980). *Law in the schools.* Columbus, OH: Merrill.

Ware v. *Morgan County School District,* 748 P.2d 1295 (Colo. 1988).

Wright v. *Superintending School Committee,* 331 A.2d 640 (Me. 1976).

Wygant v. *Jackson Board of Education,* 476 U.S. 267 (1986).

York v. *Board of School Commissioners of Mobile County,* 460 So.2d 857 (Ala. 1984).

Zirkel, P., & Bargerstock, C. (1981, January). Reduction-in-force. *A Legal Memorandum,* pp. 1–8.

16

TECHNOLOGY IN PERSONNEL MANAGEMENT

Effective management of personnel requires collecting, storing, and analyzing large amounts of information. The information is the basis for decisions about programs and staffing, and the speed with which it can be retrieved influences its potential value to users. Information that is available immediately is valuable, whereas that which requires extensive effort to retrieve or which is available only after a protracted delay is likely to be worthless.

Because of their speed, computers enhance the value of information by making it possible to retrieve data quickly and by permitting users to transform data into formats that accommodate the needs of decision makers. This chapter examines the use of electronic technology for collecting and managing personnel information in school systems.

Plan of the Chapter

The chapter focuses on the processes by which information about personnel is collected, stored, and retrieved and shows how personnel management practices are being reshaped by current technology. Computers are an integral part of personnel information management in school districts, and administrators need to be well informed about how their use can improve personnel practice and result in more effective school programs. Topics covered in the chapter are: (1) value of information, (2) uses for personnel information, (3) information management, (4) computer applications in personnel management, and (5) legal issues in managing personnel information.

Value of Information

Not all information is of equal value in an organizational setting. Value is determined by the quality, utility, and impact of the information the organization collects (Orna, 1990). Factors to consider in judging quality are accuracy, comprehensiveness, credibility, relevance, and validity. Utility is measured by degree of accessibility, ease of use, and flexibility. Information has the potential to have an impact on organizational productivity, effectiveness, and finances.

Two common methods used by schools to collect information are application forms and registration or student locator forms. The *locator form* contains parents' names and addresses, telephone numbers, parents' employers, the name and address of a close relative, and information about any medical conditions the child may have. One use for this information is to enable the school to contact parents in case of an emergency, so it is important that the information be complete and accurate.

Application forms vary from one district to another, but they are usually more comprehensive than locator forms. A comprehensive form includes questions about all of the factors that might be considered in deciding whom to hire. If a form omits questions about educational attainment or previous work experience, it is not as valuable as a more comprehensive form would be.

Information obtained from locator and application forms is about equally accurate. However, since applicants might stand to gain by furnishing incomplete or inaccurate information, the information they provide is not as credible as that furnished by parents on locator forms. An individual who stands to gain by providing misleading information has less credibility than a person with no such expectation.

Relevance is determined by whether information serves the purpose for which it was collected. Information about previous teaching experience is relevant for deciding whether to hire an applicant to fill a teaching position, but an applicant's religious affiliation and marital status are not. Validity has to do with the degree to which a piece of information is an accurate indicator of the trait or quality it is intended to measure.

Utility of Information

Utility refers to accessibility, ease of use, and flexibility. Accessibility and ease of use are related. Information may be accessible without being easy to use, but it cannot be easy to use if it is difficult to access. Information is flexible if it can be transformed from one format to another without excessive expense or loss of accuracy.

An example of flexibility of information that is important in screening applicants for a teaching position is whether applicant files can be sorted to select those with specified characteristics. If a school needs a biology teacher and a soccer coach, the selection process is facilitated if decision makers are able to sort data on those characteristics to a produce a single list of applicants qualified in both areas. The ability to sort applicants on two or more critical characteristics reduces the amount of time required for reviewing applicants' files.

Uses for Personnel Information

In schools, personnel data are used for a variety of management functions. The three principal managerial uses for personnel information are (1) to inform decisions about individuals, (2) to prepare periodic reports informing those holding key positions in the district about indicators of system performance, and (3) to monitor the internal environment of the organization in order to anticipate the need for action.

Examples of decisions about individuals include whom to hire, whether to place a teacher on tenure, which of three candidates to promote to a principalship, and whether to terminate an employee. Examples of reports that might be prepared by a personnel department for key decision makers are number of teachers who have received Master's degrees during the previous year, mean National Teachers Exam (NTE) score of teachers hired during the year, and mean number of days absent from work for various classifications of employees.

Information that is used to monitor the internal environment of an organization includes reports on the number of employee grievances filed over a given period of time, the number of teachers who receive ratings of "exceptional" or "needs improvement" on annual or semi-annual performance reviews, the number of principals nearing retirement age, and the number of teachers assigned to teach classes outside of their field of preparation.

Information Management

Information is an important resource that, when properly managed, yields significant results in the form of improved decision making. Whenever a problem is encountered, it is more likely that a satisfactory solution to it will be found if employees and managers have rapid access to accurate information than if information is unavailable or if what is available is incomplete or scattered across several units. In many school districts, information resources are fragmented and poorly managed.

Personnel information is often stored piecemeal in several departments, with the result that access to data is difficult and time consuming. Until recently, a large hotel chain represented an extreme example of information fragmentation. When an employee of the company received a salary increase, four departments were involved in recording and storing the information. The payroll department was responsible for changing the amount of the employee's paycheck, but changes in salary-based benefits were made by the benefits department. The human resources department updated the individual's personnel file, and the compensation department updated the file used for salary surveys. Since each of these transactions required separate data entries, the chances of an error were high (Santora, 1992).

In 1989, the company decided to move away from several separate personnel data systems and to integrate all information into a unified database. The changeover was not easy. Four different methods of coding and entering data had to be combined into a single standardized set of procedures, and employees had to be trained to use the new methods. However, the savings of time and money and increased accuracy of personnel records justified the cost (Santora, 1992).

Under the new system, data are entered one time only, and all of the company's records are automatically updated. For example, when an employee's salary changes, salary-based benefits are automatically updated to reflect the change. Information is shared across departments so that all users have access to current information (Santora, 1992).

The new information system installed by the hotel chain saved money for the company, but employees also reaped benefits. A flexible benefits plan, which would have been too cumbersome under the previous system, was introduced, and employees were allowed for the first time to choose their fringe benefits (Santora, 1992).

Information Management Policy

Integration of personnel data files allows a district to take advantage of the full power of the computer in processing information and frees decision makers from dependence on an antiquated management system. The first step in the process of merging separate databases is to develop a comprehensive management policy. Such a policy deals with what information is to be acquired, recorded, and stored and how those actions are to be carried out. It details how information will flow through the system, for what purposes it will be used, and how information-related activities will contribute to achieving an organization's mission (Orna, 1990).

The need for an information management policy becomes more important as the ability to process information increases. Computers have greatly increased the power to process, store, and transmit large amounts of data, but without a well-thought-out policy on the management of information, decision makers can be overwhelmed by the quantity of data with which they must deal.

Information management policy harnesses information power to organizational purposes. The policy should clarify what information is to be collected and identify which units are responsible for collecting it. It should also commit the organization to incorporating validity checks into the process of collecting and storing information, in order to ensure accuracy.

The introduction of technologically advanced communication and data-processing capabilities has greatly expanded the power of organizations to gather and process information about all aspects of their operations. Personal computers have placed sophisticated information-processing technologies in the hands of individuals at school sites and have made it possible to transmit large amounts of data rapidly and cheaply.

It is now possible, for example, for the principal of a school to have access online to all of the personnel data that the director of personnel can access, and it is possible to provide to the district superintendent detailed information about the academic performance of each child in the school system. But principals rarely need information about personnel in schools other than their own, and superintendents ordinarily do not have time to review the records of all students in the schools.

One of the purposes of information management policy is to specify how much and what kind of information is to be made available to decision makers at each level of the organizational hierarchy. Because information represents power, it is not unusual for individuals to attempt to control access to it. Limiting access results in poor quality decisions.

The same result occurs when more information is available to decision makers than they are able to use. When the capability exists to transmit large amounts of data, there is a temptation to do it, and when that happens, decision makers are likely to be overwhelmed by the quantity of information they must process. There is rarely a need for upper-level decision makers to have access to information at the level of detail that is required by those at lower levels (Welsh, 1993).

Information management policy must reflect the organization's best judgment about the amount of aggregation required at each level of the organization. Classroom teachers need information about the performance of individual students, but principals are more interested in the performance of groups of students by classroom or grade level, and the director of instruction wants to know how well schools are performing. The level of aggregation should reflect the responsibilities assigned to each organizational level.

Computer Applications in Personnel Management

Computers have been used for many years to maintain employee records and process payrolls, but with recent technological developments, many more applications are now possible. Among these applications are applicant tracking, testing, employee training, benefits administration, job evaluation, Equal Employment Opportunity (EEO) compliance, communication, management reporting, electronic meeting systems, and adaptive technology (Forrer & Leibowitz, 1991; Filipczak, 1993). Some of these applications are described here.

Important among the technological developments that make it possible to carry out these applications are relational database management systems and graphical user interfaces. Relational databases enable computers to exchange and cross-reference information from several sources.

The payroll department prepares employee paychecks. In order to correctly calculate the amount of an employee's check, the department needs information about the rate of pay, number of hours worked, number of dependents, and amount of deductions. If that information is stored in separate databases, the computer must be able to access it. Relational databases make it possible for the payroll department to retrieve information from several databases and use it to perform the calculations involved in preparing a check (Ogden, 1993).

Graphical user interfaces (GUIs) are the menus, icons, and help screens that facilitate the work of individuals who lack an extensive background of preparation in computer programming languages. A secretary who wishes to double space a document produced by a word-processing program can, with the stroke of a key or push of a button, bring a menu up on the screen that displays several options for formatting a document.

The secretary selects double-spacing from the menu, and the GUI activates a stored sequence of commands that accomplish the desired result. The only skills the secretary needs for this operation are the ability to read and knowing which key or button to push to bring up the appropriate menu. If he or she is not sure how to access the menu, most word-processing programs even provide a help screen to explain how to do that. Without the GUI, the secretary would have to be an accomplished programmer in order to change the formatting of a document (Ogden, 1993).

Management Reporting

One of the advantages of a computer-based personnel record system is the ability to use data from employee records to produce reports and graphics to facilitate planning and administrative decision making. An example is a monthly report showing which employees are due to renew their professional certificates. That information might be used by staff developers to plan workshops and course offerings. Reports can also be prepared to notify principals about which employees are due for performance appraisal, to produce a count of the number of employees eligible for retirement by job type, to monitor trends on employee absences, or to monitor expenditures from various budget accounts.

Programs are also capable of producing reports that show what subjects teachers are qualified to teach, in addition to those they are currently teaching. They can identify teachers who have indicated an interest in various types of extracurricular assignments. For example, if a tennis coach or yearbook sponsor is needed in a school, a list of teachers in the district with previous experience or interest in those activities can be prepared.

Figure 16.1 shows hypothetical examples of graphic displays of data on employee absences, ages, and attrition. Spreadsheet programs use data downloaded from a database to produce graphs such as these.

Graph A charts the percentage of employee time lost to absences for each month of the year. Graph B indicates the number of days absent from the job over a period of one year by employees of a district. The age distribution for administrators in a school district is shown in Graph C. In this particular district, the profile shows a large number of administrators who are middle aged (40–54). Since individuals in that age group will begin to retire in a few years, the district may need to begin planning for preparing replacements. Graph D shows attrition from a cohort of teachers over the first 10 years of employment. As the trendline indicates, attrition is high in the first few years of employment and then levels off.

Recruitment

In large school districts, keeping track of personnel vacancies is a challenge. Every week experienced employees resign and new people are hired. Effective recruitment requires accurate information on vacancies, but without a computerized record system, keeping an up-to-the-minute list of vacancies is difficult and time consuming. A database that is kept updated can be used to produce a daily or weekly list of openings, including job duties, location, and required qualifications (Carolin & Evans, 1988).

Personnel Testing

Computers are an essential part of testing programs in industry, and their use in school systems is growing, albeit somewhat slowly. Computerized tests are used as an aid to the selection process. For example, applicants for a secretarial position might be asked to complete a typing exercise on a computer that automatically calculates typing speed and error rate. Likewise, a person seeking a job that involves spotting imperfections in machine parts might be tested on discriminatory ability by being asked to identify which one of three drawings is different from the other two.

Computerized tests have several advantages over paper-and-pencil exams. The computer can be programmed to select items at random from an item pool, so that every examinee receives a unique set of questions, thus reducing the incidence of cheating. The computer can also be instructed to prepare individualized exams based on pretest scores, resulting in tests at a suitable level of difficulty and eliminating the feelings of frustration aroused by having to take a test that is either too easy or too difficult.

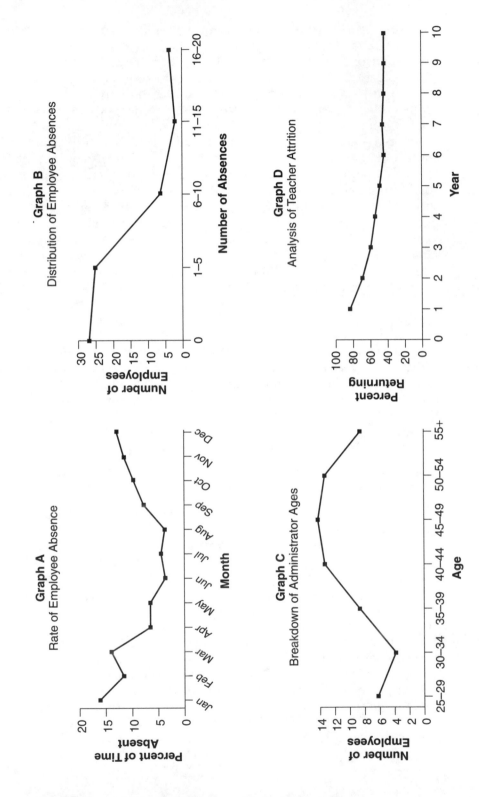

FIGURE 16.1 Computer-Generated Graphs: Using Data on Employee Absences, Age, and Length of Service

Applicant Tracking

Most school districts receive many more applications for employment than there are vacancies to be filled. Simply keeping track of applicants and informing them when an action is taken is a major task. In recent years, this process has been automated, a development that has simplified the job considerably.

When a personnel search is underway, information about applicants is entered into a computer file as soon as it is received. It is possible to read the information from the application form directly into the computer using a scanner. In addition to information from the application form, the applicant's computer file may include comments from references, copies of transcripts, and test scores. Interviewers' comments and ratings may also be included.

Most districts keep this type of information on file at the district office, but a computer network can make it accessible from any school in the district. Thus, teachers and administrators are able to review information on applicants without leaving their buildings, and may select for interviews those whose credentials appear to best meet the needs of the school. When an employee is hired, the computer can be programmed to prepare a letter to the new employee and to generate forms used by the personnel department to establish a personnel file (Forrer & Leibowitz, 1991).

Equal Employment Opportunity Compliance

Applicant tracking can be used to produce evidence of an employer's compliance with legislation on equal employment opportunity (EEO). Information about characteristics of the applicant pool that are relevant to affirmative action—including age, gender, race, ethnicity, and religion—can be used to produce comparative analyses of the number of people who applied and were hired from each demographic group. The critical measure in determining whether discrimination has occurred is the ratio of hires to qualified applicants in the appropriate labor market. Using a ratio of hires to applicants cannot prove that discrimination did not take place, but it may indicate that discrimination did occur.

Staff Development

Several technological developments have promise for making an impact on staff development practices. One such breakthrough is videodisc technology. A *videodisc* is a data storage device that reproduces high-quality sound or video. Videodiscs are valuable for training purposes because of their ability to store large amounts of data that can be used to produce text, voice, and visual images. A 12-inch disc holds a half million pages of text or 100,000 images (Sampson, 1992). Videodisc technology has been slow to catch on because of the expense, but as the technology becomes more refined, the cost is expected to drop.

Videodiscs have many of the same capabilities as videotape, but they also have important advantages over tape. Consider a videodisc designed to train employees of the transportation department to service a school bus. Using a training program on videodisc, an employee could choose any of several topics for study, depending on the individual's job assignment, previous training, and experience. He or she might review relining brakes, tuning an engine, or replacing the refrigerant in the air conditioning unit.

Videodiscs produce high-quality audio as well as still and motion images and are especially useful for explaining the operation of a process and simultaneously demonstrating it. A program might include a pretest to assess a worker's readiness for instruction on a topic and, using the employee's responses, assign the learner to an appropriate entry point in the instructional sequence.

Some programs are designed with a branching format, or an employee can create his or her own branches by selecting for review topics that provide the necessary background for understanding new material. For example, a worker might temporarily exit a lesson on tuning an engine in order to brush up on the function and operation of the catalytic converter and then return to the study of the engine. Branching on videotape must be done manually and is an awkward operation.

An individual who learns best by repetition can go over material on the videodisc repeatedly until he or she has mastered it. Rewinding and replaying videotape or moving from place to place in a program is an awkward and clumsy operation, but a videodisc machine can shift from one spot on the disc to any other designated spot easily and quickly. The combination of voice with both motion and still visual images holds learners' interest and helps reinforce the lesson content.

Assessment Centers

Computer programs are being developed to automate certain features of assessment center testing. An assessment center (Chapter 5) consists of a series of activities, ranging from paper-and-pencil in-basket exercises to leaderless group projects, that are used to assess leadership ability. The measures have been shown to be valid indicators of leadership potential, but the process has the drawback of being highly labor intensive and therefore expensive. A computer program now being developed promises to reduce the amount of time required for assessment for both participants and assessors.

Career Development

School systems routinely provide vocational guidance for students but seldom offer such services to employees. However, it is now possible to offer individualized vocational planning at modest cost to employees who are about to be laid off from their jobs or who are considering an early retirement offer and want to investigate other fields.

Interactive computer programs now on the market provide information on a number of occupations, including job prospects, advancement opportunities, and salary. Some programs are interactive, using input from an individual to identify occupations that fit the individual's interests, work preferences, and income needs ("Computers for Career Planning," 1993).

Record Maintenance

Computers can be used to store information on almost any phase of school operations. One useful application of this ability is maintaining records on employee training. These records maintain a log of employees' training activities over time and are useful for identifying individuals who might be interested in advanced training on a topic. They also make it possible to create an inventory of skills that can be searched when a vacancy occurs and the district needs to find individuals qualified in certain areas. The information can also be accessed to determine future training needs (*Personnel Records and Statistics,* 1985).

Compensation and Benefits

Spreadsheet programs have simplified administration of compensation and benefits programs by making possible rapid calculation of the cost of proposed changes in salaries and benefits. For example, budget planners wish to know the total cost, with benefits, of raising teachers' salaries 4.3, 4.5, or 4.7 percent. Those figures can be obtained in seconds using a spreadsheet program in combination with a database containing information on the number of teachers at various levels of education and experience and their preferences of fringe benefit packages.

The trend toward a "cafeteria" approach that allows employees to choose the benefits they prefer from a menu of options has increased the need for accounting systems that permit fast calculation of the cost of a variety of insurance and leave options. Increased government regulation of benefit plans has also contributed to the need for fast and accurate systems for maintaining records on employee benefits.

Interactive computer programs are being used by some companies to help employees make better-quality decisions about their fringe benefits. Many employers now offer Keogh plans, which are employee-managed retirement accounts. Earnings from these accounts are untaxed during the employee's working years in order to allow individuals to accumulate a larger nest egg for their retirement years. However, some employees tend to invest Keogh funds in conservative investments that are unlikely to produce sufficient earnings to sustain an individual throughout his or her retirement years.

To make employees aware of the need to choose investments with greater potential for growth, some employers now use interactive computer programs that allow individuals to enter information about their age, income, family responsibilities, and objectives, which the computer uses to produce individualized investment recommendations ("The Many Faces of Benefits Communication," 1992).

Personnel professionals are now contemplating taking the ultimate step of making personnel data available to individual employees. A teacher who wants to know how much money she has accumulated in her retirement account, or a secretary who wishes to know how much sick leave he has available could access that information directly from a personnel database containing that information ("The Many Faces of Benefits Communication," 1992).

Collective Bargaining

Computers are used by both union and management during collective bargaining. A common use of computers during negotiations is to calculate the cost of proposals presented by the other side. If teachers ask for a 10 percent salary hike for individuals with 12 years' experience or less and 8 percent for those with more than 12 years' experience, board negotiators need to be able to calculate the cost of the teachers' proposal. That can be done easily using a spreadsheet program and a database containing information on the number of teachers at each level of education and experience.

Analyzing costs is only one of several uses for computerized databases during collective bargaining sessions. Programs are available that will compare contracts across units. For example, if teachers in School District A wish to determine whether their board's offer compares favorably to features of a contract recently negotiated in District B, a computer program is available that will make such a comparison possible (Extejt & Lynn, 1994).

Electronic Meeting Systems

Meetings consume a great deal of school administrators' time, but electronic meeting systems can reduce that loss by eliminating travel. Electronic meetings involve individuals or small groups linked together by computers or on a telecommunications hookup that transmits both audio and visual information. With the telecommunications link, participants are able to see and hear one another and to transmit visual images. By adding a FAX machine, they are also able to transmit documents. One of the uses for such a system is to conduct interviews with applicants.

A computer network allows individuals to talk to one another and to send and receive written messages but lacks the visual component. If all participants have a computer, they may offer comments anonymously, which has a facilitating effect on people who are disinclined to speak out in groups. Software is available that can be used by the group to prepare an agenda; record comments, ideas, and votes; and keep detailed records of the meeting (Davis & Hamilton, 1993).

Adaptive Technology

The Americans with Disabilities Act has changed the landscape with regard to recruitment and selection of personnel. It is no longer legally permissible to refuse to employ an applicant who is able, with or without accommodation, to perform the essential functions of a position, on the basis of a disability. To ensure compliance, personnel department staff members need to be able to identify the essential functions of all positions and to be well informed about types of accommodation that will enable individuals with disabilities to perform the work successfully.

Adaptive technology is the generic name for equipment, tools, devices, and procedures that help individuals who are disabled to perform a job. Few educators can be experts in this field, but specialists are available to help identify adaptations that will work in a given situation. National organizations such as the Easter Seal Society and the United Cerebral Palsy Association, state agencies such as vocational rehabilitation departments, and universities are valuable sources of information about adaptations that can assist individuals with disabilities to perform effectively on the job. The cost to the district of adaptive devices varies. Some are prohibitively expensive, but under certain conditions, state rehabilitation agencies will share or even pay the entire cost of such equipment (Filipczak, 1993).

Computers make it possible for some individuals with disabilities to perform jobs they would not otherwise be qualified for. Some of these devices are designed to assist individuals who are unable to read because of visual impairments or dyslexia. For example, a computer can be programmed to enlarge the size of type on a screen or to "read" a document in a synthesized voice. By combining a scanner and voice synthesizer with a computer, a machine can be produced that will scan a printed page and read it aloud (Filipczak, 1993).

Individuals with limited use of their arms and hands can operate a computer with their eyes, using an electronic device that bounces an infrared beam off the cornea. By moving his or her eyes, a worker can change the position of the beam on the computer screen and relay commands to the computer's central processing unit (Filipczak, 1993).

Other devices help individuals to compensate for physical limitations. An adjustment to a keyboard, for example, allows a secretary to type capital letters using one hand. The secretary touches the shift key and then the letter to produce a capital. People with limited use of their arms and hands are sometimes slow to remove a finger from a key, and the lingering pressure produces an unneeded string of letters. However, by deactivating the repeat function, the problem is easily solved and the worker's productivity increases (Filipczak, 1993).

As the use of computers for processing personnel information increases, the possibility of data being used in unauthorized or illegal ways also grows. School administrators need to be on guard against misuse of information from district personnel files. They need also to become informed about legal requirements for collecting and reporting personnel data.

Legal Issues in Managing Personnel Information

Personnel files include a great deal of information of a sensitive nature. Employee files usually contain the application form or resumé with educational and work experience, a letter of appointment, professional licenses or certificates, test scores, record of immunizations and verification of health or disability status, income tax withholding form, benefit enrollment forms, personnel evaluations, and an information log. The information log contains an ongoing record of personnel transactions, including leaves, changes in pay or benefits, changes in job classification, disciplinary actions, and training or course work completed (Levesque, 1993).

In addition, federal legislation requires employers to collect and keep on file certain information about characteristics protected under equal employment opportunity legislation. The Immigration Reform and Control Act of 1986 requires employers to obtain a completed and verified I-9 form from each individual hired, showing that the person is eligible to work in the United States (Levesque, 1993). Employers with more than 100 employees are required to submit an annual report to the Equal Employment Opportunity Commission showing the number of employees in each of a number of categories.

Privacy Rights

Because they contain a wealth of sensitive information, personnel files can easily be misused unless action is taken to establish safeguards to protect individual privacy. Individual employee files are private records, and legislation has been enacted in a number of states to grant employees the right to review their personnel files and to prevent unauthorized disclosure of information from the files. Four principles embodied in the Privacy Protection Act of 1974 can be used as guides to ensure protection of employees' privacy rights. These principles are (Walker, 1993):

1. Collect and store only data that are relevant to district operations.
2. Allow employees to review their records and correct inaccuracies in them.
3. Allow disclosure of information from personnel files only to those with the right and need to receive the information.
4. Do not allow data collected for one purpose to be used for other purposes.

Employees' rights are least likely to be violated by the release of private information if employers develop and enforce information management policies that spell out in detail procedures to be used for storing and handling the information. Procedures should also specify who should and should not have access to the information. One other important action that employers can take to safeguard employees' privacy rights is to ensure that any information recorded in employees' files is accurate.

Summary

Information is an important resource that, when properly managed, yields significant results in the form of improved decision making. Personnel management involves collecting, storing, and analyzing large amounts of data about employees. Most personnel offices now use computers to store and process personnel information. The value of information is determined by its quality, utility, and impact. An information management policy identifies what information is to be acquired, recorded, and stored. It also specifies how information is to be used and how information-related activities will contribute to achieving the organization's mission.

Administrators who manage employee information systems should be aware of legal requirements that apply to collecting and reporting such information. It is important that they take action to prevent misuse of personnel information. Four principles that should be followed in this regard are to collect only information that is relevant to district operations, to provide opportunities for employees to review their records and correct mistakes, to disclose information from personnel files only to people with the right to receive the information and who need it, and to be certain that data collected for one purpose are not used for other purposes.

Suggested Activities

1. Investigate the policy on employee access to personnel records in a school district. Do employees have the right under the policy to review their own files? Under what conditions is such access granted? Are employees allowed to copy material from the file or to add material to it? Is there a procedure in place by which an employee can contest and request removal of incomplete or false information from the file?

2. Computers are used to prepare enrollment projections and estimate the number of teachers needed to staff the schools. List the items of information that would be needed to develop enrollment projections and estimate personnel needs for a small school district and identify the source of each element of information. (Refer to Chapter 2 for a discussion of enrollment projections.)

3. This chapter discussed the increased efficiency achieved by an integrated personnel information management system, but no mention was made of possible disadvantages of such a system. What are the disadvantages of placing all information about employees in a single computer file?
4. Interview a person who is familiar with adaptive technology to find out more about new technological devices that are used to help individuals with disabilities perform work. Describe your findings to the class.
5. Some corporations offer extensive educational programs to help their employees manage their finances, plan for retirement, learn about nutrition, or acquire new skills. Interview the personnel or training director of a corporation to find out what programs are offered by his or her company. Compare them to the programs offered to employees of a school district in your area.

References

Carolin, B., & Evans, A. (1988, July). Computers as a strategic personnel tool. *Personnel Management, 20*, 40–43.

Computers for career planning. (1993, October). *Training, 30*, 17, 89–90.

Davis, G., & Hamilton, S. (1993). *Managing information: How information systems impact organizational strategy.* Homewood, IL: Irwin.

Extejt, M., & Lynn, M. (1994). Applications of decision support systems by teacher union negotiators. *Journal of Collective Negotiations in the Public Sector, 23*, 59–72.

Filipczak, B. (1993, March). Adaptive technology for the disabled. *Training, 30*, 23–29.

Forrer, S., & Leibowitz, Z. (1991). *Using computers in human resources.* San Francisco: Jossey-Bass.

Levesque, J. (1993). *Manual of personnel policies, procedures, and operations* (2nd ed.). Englewood Cliffs, NJ: Prentice Hall.

Many faces of benefits communication, The. (1992, February). *Personnel Journal, 71*, 58.

Ogden, D. (1993, February). Reaping the benefits of new technologies. *HR Focus, 70*, 18.

Orna, E. (1990). *Practical information policies: How to manage information flow in organizations.* Brookfield, VT: Gower.

Personnel records and statistics. (1985). Chicago: Commerce Clearing House.

Sampson, K. (1992). *Value-added records management.* New York: Quorum.

Santora, J. (1992, January). Data base integrates HR functions. *Personnel Journal, 71*, 92–100.

Walker, A. (1993). *Handbook of human resource information systems: Reshaping the human resource function with technology.* New York: McGraw-Hill.

Welsh, T. (1993). The politics of valuing in information system construction. In D. Chapman & L. Mahlck (Eds.), *From data to action: Information systems in educational planning* (pp. 92–114). Oxford, England: Pergamon Press.

CASE STUDIES

Case I

The three teachers serving on the committee to select a teacher to fill a vacancy in the mathematics department at Camden Park High School were interviewing an applicant, Margaret Dannen. She was the last of three candidates to be interviewed. Mrs. Dannen had recently moved back to the area after having lived and worked in several other states.

The interviewers were Ralph Nunez, a biology teacher; Sandra Torrey, an English teacher; and Nancy Glass, head of the mathematics department. Camden Park was a site-managed school, and all applicants for teaching positions were interviewed by teacher committees. The committee had the responsibility to recommend an applicant for the vacancy. Mrs. Dannen had taught 12 years. She was 41 years old, had two daughters, ages 13 and 15, and was a widow.

Sandra Torrey opened the interview. "We appreciate your coming for an interview. I understand you grew up in this area."

"Yes," Mrs. Dannen said. "I graduated from Dickinson High."

Torrey asked, "Did you know Bob Allbright and Marilyn Price at Dickinson?"

"I knew who Bob was, but he was a year or two ahead of me," Mrs. Dannen replied. "I didn't know Marilyn."

"They graduated the same year. I think it was 1970 or 1971."

"I graduated in 1972."

Mr. Nunez broke in with a question. "I know you have been living out of state for a number of years. How did you happen to move back to this area?"

"Actually, we lived in Iowa a couple of years and in Ohio before that. My husband died last November, and I wanted to move back here because this is where most of my family live. Iowa really didn't seem like home to me."

"I'm sorry," Mr. Nunez said.

"It has been a difficult year, but if we can get resettled I think we will be fine," Mrs. Dannen replied. "This job is really important to me because I don't have any other source of income."

Nancy Glass spoke. "The job involves teaching mostly ninth- and tenth-graders. You'll have two classes of algebra and one of geometry, also two classes of prealgebra. Have you had experience teaching those subjects?"

"I haven't taught prealgebra since I was a student teacher, but I have taught algebra and geometry regularly."

"Would it bother you to teach prealgebra?" Ms. Glass asked.

"Oh, no. That's no problem. I don't think I would want to teach it exclusively, but I wouldn't mind teaching one or two classes. These students will be preparing to take algebra in tenth grade, right?"

"Yes," Ms. Glass replied. "About two-thirds of our students take algebra."

Mr. Nunez broke in. "How many of your students in Iowa took algebra?" he asked.

"About 90 percent of the students in the school where I taught took algebra. They were required to take three years of math."

"Did you teach mostly college-bound students?" Mr. Nunez asked.

"Yes, the majority were expecting to go to college, but we had some who didn't attend."

Ms. Torrey asked, "How do you feel about requiring all students to take algebra?"

Mrs. Dannen replied, "Actually, I think it's a good idea. If they have the background for it and it's taught the right way, I think most students can learn algebra. Our students did pretty well because the teachers were patient and worked with them one on one. For the slowest ones, algebra was a two-year course."

"How do you feel about teaching in a school like Camden Park?" Ms. Torrey asked.

"I think I would enjoy teaching here," Mrs. Dannen said, "and it would help stabilize my family situation. This has been a difficult year for my daughters."

Ms. Torrey continued, "I ask you that because Camden Park is probably different from schools where you have taught. About 60 percent of the students at Camden Park are minorities. I don't know how much experience you've had with minority students."

"The school where I taught in Iowa had a few African American and Vietnamese students," Mrs. Dannen said, "but I don't expect to have any problem working with minority students."

Ms. Glass spoke. "Changing the subject: Do you know yet where your daughters will be going to school?"

"I haven't decided definitely," Mrs. Dannen said. "Angela will be a sophomore, and if she goes to public school she'll be at Benson High. But I may send her to private school. I understand the classes at Benson are pretty large and the students don't always get much personal attention. Angela does not do well in large classes. Denise will be in the eighth grade. She'll probably go to Falk Middle School."

Mr. Nunez asked, "Shouldn't a teacher in the public schools send her children to the public schools?"

Mrs. Dannen reflected a moment. "I believe in public schools," she said, "and I work hard to provide the best education I can for the students I teach. But I also feel I have an obligation to give my daughters the benefit of the best schooling I can."

Ms. Torrey gave Mr. Nunez a look of disapproval. "I agree with you," she said to Mrs. Dannen. "It's no one's business where your daughters go to school."

"We're about out of time," Ms. Glass said. "Is there anything you would like to ask us?"

"Yes," Mrs. Dannen said. "I'm curious about site-based management. How long has it been in operation here, and how well does it work?"

Ms. Glass said, "This is the third year Camden Park has been in the program, and I'd say it works pretty well."

Mrs. Dannen asked, "Do you really have a say in decisions?"

Ms. Torrey responded, "Yes, I have more input here than I've ever had before in 20-plus years of teaching."

"It takes time, though," Mr. Nunez added. "I spend an extra four or five hours a week working on committees, and I don't get paid any extra for it. But I do it because I think it's important."

"Are you still expected to teach five classes?" Mrs. Dannen asked.

"Yes."

"Ralph's right," Ms. Torrey commented. "It does take time and you don't get time off for the extra work you do. We've probably put in a total of 20 or 30 hours on this committee—reviewing applicants, telephoning references, and interviewing. After this we have to meet to decide who we want to recommend, but the nice thing is that our recommendation will be taken seriously."

"It sounds like a major responsibility," Mrs. Dannen said. "I'm not sure I would want to spend that much time on administrative matters."

Mr. Nunez started to ask a question, but Ms. Glass cut him off. "I'm afraid we have to stop," she said. She rose and extended her hand to Mrs. Dannen. "I've enjoyed meeting and talking with you. We expect to make a decision within a week, and we'll let you know as soon as we can. Thanks for coming by."

Questions for Case I

1. The interviewers asked several questions about matters that were not related to job duties or applicant qualifications. In what situation is it ap-

propriate to ask questions about applicants' personal lives? When are such questions not appropriate?

2. Mrs. Dannen made an emotional appeal to the members of the committee about needing the job. If you were a member of the selection committee, would you be more likely to recommend Mrs. Dannen for the position because of her situation? Should the fact that an applicant needs the job influence the selection decision?

3. Would you be influenced in your recommendation by the fact that Mrs. Dannen is considering sending her daughter to a private school? Should that be a factor in deciding whether to hire her? Why or why not?

4. Mrs. Dannen expressed reservations about committee work. Since Camden Park is a site-managed school, committee service is important. Should her reluctance be a factor in deciding whether to recommend that she be hired? Why or why not? Ms. Glass ended the interview without allowing a clarifying question about that issue. What question might have been asked to obtain more information?

5. Identify the selection criteria for the mathematics position at Camden Park High School as you understand them, assuming committee members' questions reflect the criteria. Rate Mrs. Dannen on those criteria. Based on your analysis, do you recommend hiring or rejecting the applicant? What other information about this applicant would you like to know before deciding?

6. What suggestions would you give the interviewers that might help them to do a better job the next time they interview an applicant?

Case II

Barbara Cullen was proud to be a teacher. She had taken her first teaching job and had been assigned to teach third grade at Windsor Elementary School. She visited the school frequently in the weeks before classes started to arrange her room and post bulletin boards. She was anxious for school to start and looked forward to meeting her students for the first time.

Third grade was not Ms. Cullen's first choice. She had asked for first grade, but the woman in the Human Resources Department explained that the district did not assign beginning teachers to first grade. "We like for you to have some experience before you teach first-graders," she said.

Ms. Cullen had met Margaret Homer, the principal at Windsor School, on her first trip to the school. One of the things Mrs. Homer had told her in that first meeting was that she would assign a mentor teacher to help her "learn the ropes."

Ms. Cullen wasn't sure what the function of a mentor was, so she asked Mrs. Homer. "A mentor is your friend," Mrs. Homer explained. "She will answer your questions or find someone who can."

A week before classes started, teachers reported for staff development activities, assembling in the cafeteria, where doughnuts and coffee awaited them. Returning teachers greeted one another warmly and exchanged stories about their summer activities. Mrs. Homer circulated through the room, welcoming the teachers back.

Ms. Cullen was one of three new teachers. She and one other were starting their first teaching assignment. The third newcomer was a woman who had taught seven years in another district.

Mrs. Homer greeted Ms. Cullen. "Welcome to Windsor Elementary," she said. "Are you ready for a big year?" "Oh, yes, I'm excited about getting started," Ms. Cullen replied.

"Good. I want to introduce you to someone." Mrs. Homer took Ms. Cullen by the arm and guided her across the room, where she introduced her to a slender young woman with dark hair and friendly eyes. "This is Nancy Field," she said. "Nancy is going to be your mentor. She will answer any questions you have and introduce you to all the teachers." Ms. Field shook Ms. Cullen's hand. "It's good to meet you," she said. "I've been looking forward to this."

Ms. Cullen responded, "Me, too. I'm really happy to meet you and to know that we'll be working together."

"You're third grade, right?" Ms. Field asked.

"Yes. You too?"

"No, I teach fourth grade." Ms. Field's expression grew serious. "I have to warn you," she said, "you're the first teacher I've mentored. I told Ms. Homer that I didn't know much about what a mentor does, but she insisted that I do it. So I'm willing to try."

"We'll learn together," Ms. Cullen said.

After the two teachers had chatted for a few minutes, Ms. Field walked with Ms. Cullen across the room and introduced her to half a dozen other teachers. By that time, the program was beginning and the teachers began to settle into their seats.

The first week of classes flew by. Ms. Cullen found herself much busier than she had imagined she would be. There was little time for anything other than preparing her lesson plans, teaching, and sleeping. After school she hurriedly cooked and ate her dinner, then devoted the rest of the evening to planning instruction for the following day. She saw Ms. Field only twice during the week, once on the parking lot after school and a second time in the hallway.

As the weeks passed, she was accumulating questions that she hoped to find answers to, but she never seemed to be able to catch Ms. Field. Twice she went by her classroom after school, but Ms. Field was gone. Toward the end of the first month, Ms. Cullen decided to arrive at school early in hopes of catching Ms. Field before classes got underway. Monday morning she pulled into the school parking lot 20 minutes earlier than usual and made her way to Ms. Field's classroom.

Ms. Field was recording grades. "I'm sorry to interrupt you," Ms. Cullen said. "But I've been wanting to see you, and it seems this is the only time we're both free."

Ms. Field's smile was warm and friendly. "How's it going?" she asked.

"I think things are going pretty well," Ms. Cullen said, "but I have a problem I'd like to talk with you about, if you have time."

"I'm really trying to get these grades recorded before the children arrive," Ms. Field said, glancing at her watch. "I meant to do it last night, but Jim's mother came by and didn't leave until nearly 11:00."

"That's OK," Ms. Cullen said. "I'll catch you another time."

"How about right after school?" Ms. Field asked. "I'll come to your room."

"That sounds good. See you then."

After school, Ms. Cullen waited 20 minutes before Ms. Field finally arrived. "I'm sorry," she apologized. "Brenda Widby's mother came by and I had to talk to her."

Ms. Cullen pulled two chairs together and gestured to Ms. Field to have a seat. "It's no problem," she said. "I understand."

The two teachers talked only about 10 minutes before Ms. Field had to leave. Ms. Cullen talked about a child in her class who was proving to be a problem. "It's nothing really bad," she said. "He just seems to ignore what I say. He gets out of his seat without permission, and when I tell him to sit down, he just looks at me and keeps going."

Ms. Field made two suggestions. One was to move the boy to the front of the room so that Ms. Cullen could corral him before he could get out of his seat. She also suggested that Ms. Cullen warn the boy that if he didn't stay in his seat she would send him to the principal.

"That seems to be a pretty harsh punishment for something no more serious than that," Ms. Cullen protested.

"That's what I would do," Ms. Field replied. "Sometimes you have to do it—or at least threaten to do it or students take advantage of you."

The next day, she tried Ms. Field's suggestions. She moved the boy near her desk and told him that she expected him to remain in his seat unless he had permission from her to get up. When he left his seat and started toward the back of the room, she stopped him. "Charles," she said. "I didn't give you permission to be out of your seat." The boy stopped and looked at her, then he turned and walked toward the rear of the classroom.

"What did I tell you, Charles?" she asked. The boy didn't answer.

She felt a rush of anger. "Charles, take your seat or you will have to go to the principal's office." Charles pulled a book off a shelf and leafed through it, ignoring the teacher.

Ms. Cullen walked to the back of the room and took the boy's arm. She guided him toward his seat, and when he sat down, she took the book from his hand and laid it on her desk.

She was pleased at having prevailed in this encounter, and she wanted to share her triumph with Ms. Field, but when she stopped by the teacher's room after school, Ms. Field was talking with another teacher. Ms. Cullen waved to her from the door and left.

A couple of days later, Ms. Field stuck her head in the door of Ms. Cullen's classroom before school. "How's it going?" she asked.

Ms. Cullen was busy assembling a bulletin board, but she put the stapler aside and walked over to the door. "I'm doing fine," she said.

"Oh, I almost forgot. I have something for you," Ms. Field said. She handed Ms. Cullen a calendar with a bright drawing of children jumping. "I thought you might like this."

"Oh, it's nice," Ms. Cullen said. "Thanks. I'll put it up by the door. The children will enjoy it."

"Sorry I have to run. Your room looks pretty."

Ms. Cullen's success with Charles was short-lived. After a day or two, he again began leaving his seat and wandering around the room. The first time it happened, Ms. Cullen had directed him to return to his seat and then had approached him and tried physically to steer him in the direction of his seat, but he had resisted. He ducked under her arm and ran to the back of the room. He stayed there, sitting in a corner looking through a book, for almost an hour, when he decided voluntarily to return to his seat.

She was perplexed, but she hated to talk to Ms. Field again. She felt somehow that she had failed, and she dreaded admitting that to her mentor.

Another third-grade teacher whose room was nearby took her class to the cafeteria at the same time as Ms. Cullen. The two chatted over their lunches, and occasionally the other teacher stopped by Ms. Cullen's room to comment on the bulletin boards or offer to share materials. Her name was Donna Holland, and she had been teaching at Windsor for 12 years. Ms. Cullen decided she would ask Ms. Holland to suggest ways of dealing with Charles.

She brought up the subject at lunch the next day. "What do you do when a child won't stay in his seat?" she asked. Ms. Holland thought a moment. "I don't have that problem very often," she said. "I try to give students enough interesting things to do at their seats that they don't have any reason to wander around. But I know it's a problem with some children. Who is the child?"

"Charles Stamper."

"You might talk to Mrs. Bowden. I think she had him last year, and she might be able to suggest something."

"Thanks," Ms. Cullen said.

Ms. Cullen talked with Mrs. Bowden the next day, but she didn't get any help. Mrs. Bowden said that Charles was frequently "off in the clouds" but that she didn't remember his ever leaving his seat without permission.

Ms. Cullen was aware that she spent more time with Charles than with other children, and it bothered her. When she assigned seatwork, she found herself hovering near Charles's desk, ready to offer assistance if he needed it, hoping that if he was able to do the assignment he would be more inclined to stay in his seat. It seemed to be effective; Charles had only been out of his seat without permission once all week.

On Friday, though, Charles resumed his wandering. Shortly after math class started, Charles wandered to the back of the room and leaned against a bookcase, looking out the window.

Ms. Cullen paused. After a few moments, she said his name. There was no reaction. She repeated his name with more emphasis. "Charles. Return to your seat."

Again, the boy gave no indication of having heard. Without warning, Bennie left his seat and made his way across the room to where Charles stood. He looked out the window and then at Charles.

Other students were stretching to see what the boys were watching outside. Ms. Cullen felt an urgent need to get the situation under control. "Bennie!" she said. The boy turned to look at her. "Take your seat."

"I'm just trying to see what Charles is looking at," Bennie said. "There's nothing out there."

"Of course, there's nothing out there," Ms. Cullen said. "Sit down."

Bennie returned to his seat, but Charles continued to stare out the window. Ms. Cullen debated with herself whether to proceed with the lesson and ignore Charles or to demand that he sit down. She chose the latter course.

"Sit down, Charles," she said in the firmest voice she could muster. Charles did not move. His head rested in his hands, and he stared out the window as if absorbed in some spectacle on the playground.

"Charles, if you don't sit down immediately I will have to send you to the principal."

She waited. Charles did not respond.

"Charles, you give me no choice. You will report to the principal's office now."

Charles finally turned and looked at the teacher. His face was impassive and he said nothing. He walked to his seat and sat down.

Ms. Cullen felt both relief and confusion. She didn't know whether to insist that the boy leave the room and report to the principal or let the incident drop. She chose the latter course.

After school, she went to Ms. Field's room. The teacher was talking with two students, but Ms. Cullen stepped into the room and said to Ms. Field, "Excuse the interruption, but I need to talk to you. Can you come by before you leave?"

"Come on in," Ms. Field said. "I'll be finished with these girls in a couple of minutes."

Ms. Cullen took at seat at a reading table until Ms. Field finished talking to the girls and they left. She described to Ms. Field what had happened. "I'm so confused I don't know what to do," she said. "I'm afraid that others are going to start acting like Charles."

"It's not a good idea to tell a child to go to the principal and then let him get away with not doing it," Ms. Field said. "After a while they get the idea you don't mean what you say."

"I know that, but at the time it seemed best to get on with the lesson."

"I think if I were you, I would talk first with the boy to see if you can find out what's going on. Then I'd talk to his parents with the boy present. That usually works well with my students. But I haven't taught third grade, and I don't know what works best with that age. Maybe you should talk to a teacher in your grade level. Ms. Bennett or Ms. Holland might be able to help."

"That helps," Ms. Cullen said. "I think I will try talking to Charles."

Two days later, she met with Charles after school. "Tell me why you get out of your seat when you're supposed to be listening or working," Ms. Cullen said. Charles shrugged.

"Is there a reason?"

"I guess so," said Charles.

"What is the reason?"

"I don't know," Charles mumbled.

"In the future, I want you to stay in your seat, unless you have permission to get up," Ms. Cullen said. "If you leave your seat without asking, I'll have to send you to the principal." Charles shrugged again but said nothing.

"Do you understand?" the teacher asked.

"I guess so," the boy said.

"I need to talk to your mother and father about your behavior," Ms. Cullen said. "When is a good time to call them?"

For the first time, Ms. Cullen observed a reaction from the boy. He sat up in his seat, and a look of concern crossed his face.

"I'll stay in my seat," he said.

Ms. Cullen was surprised. She felt she had discovered a secret weapon. The threat to call his parents seemed to get Charles' attention better than anything she had tried.

She decided not to call the boy's parents but to wait and see if his behavior improved. For the rest of that week and the following week, there was no problem. Charles seemed to be more attentive than he had ever been.

Then the wandering resumed. The first time it happened, Ms. Cullen simply called his name. After hesitating, Charles stopped and looked at her, then returned to his seat. But the next time, he ignored her.

"Charles," she said. "Sit down or I will have to send you to the principal's office."

There was no response. She repeated her warning, and again the boy did nothing.

"Charles, go to the principal's office," she said.

The boy left the room without looking at her and headed down the hall.

Ms. Cullen went back to the lesson, feeling disappointed that Charles had chosen to face the principal rather than accept her direction. After she had given her students a seatwork assignment, she asked the teacher next door to watch her students while she went to the office.

There was no sign of Charles in the waiting room, and when she asked the secretary about him, she was told that he had not been there. Mrs. Homer was in her office. Ms. Cullen explained what had happened. "I sent him down here 20 minutes ago," she said. "I can't imagine what happened."

"You look around the building. I'll check the playground," Mrs. Homer said.

There was no sign of Charles in either place. Mrs. Homer said, "He probably went home. I'll call and see if he's there. You'd better get back to your class. I'll let you know what I find."

She did not hear from the principal the rest of the day. After the students left, she stopped by the office. When she entered, the secretary whispered, "Charles went home. His mother found him. She's with Mrs. Homer now. You are to go on in."

Mrs. Cullen tapped lightly at the door and then entered. Mrs. Homer greeted her and introduced her to the parent. "Charles decided to go home when you sent him to the office," Mrs. Homer said. "When I called, Mrs. Stamper went out looking for him and found him on the street. He didn't understand that he was supposed to report to the office."

"I think it was very clear that he was supposed to see the principal," Ms. Cullen said.

"What did you send him to me for?" Mrs. Homer asked.

"He's been getting out of his seat. I had warned him many times but it didn't seem to do any good. I finally told him that if it happened again I would send him to see you."

"When you send a child to the office, you need either to come with him or send a note explaining the problem. You should also call the secretary to tell her the child is on the way."

"I'll do that next time," Ms. Cullen said.

Mrs. Homer turned to Mrs. Stamper. "I'm very sorry this happened," she said, "and I can assure you it won't happen again. The safety and welfare of our children is our number one priority. We will take every precaution in the future to prevent a recurrence. Now I suggest that we talk about Charles's problems in class and see if we can find out what is going on."

Ms. Cullen related the story of Charles's frequent excursions out of his seat and of the efforts she had made to solve the problem. "Nothing I tried seemed to work," she said.

"Did you talk to your mentor teacher?" Mrs. Homer asked.

"Yes, several times."

"Was that no help?" Mrs. Homer asked.

"When I was able to talk to her, she gave me some suggestions, and I tried them, but they didn't seem to make much difference. Charles continued to wander around the room."

"Mentor teachers are there to help you with problems like these," Mrs. Homer said. "But you have to let them know what is going on. Ms. Field can't help if you don't ask."

"But I did ask," Ms. Cullen protested. She hesitated, sensing that Mrs. Homer did not believe her. "I really tried to get help," she explained, "but nothing seemed to work."

"Then you should have come to me," Mrs. Homer said. "Don't let problems fester. Take action to solve them."

Questions for Case II

1. Do you agree or disagree with Mrs. Homer's description of the role of a mentor? Did Ms. Field fulfill that role? Explain.
2. What does the case study suggest about ways that a principal might help mentors to better understand their roles and be more effective in carrying them out?
3. What criteria do you recommend using when choosing a mentor for a beginning teacher? What criteria did Mrs. Homer appear to have used in assigning Ms. Field to work with Ms. Cullen?
4. Is it likely that Ms. Cullen might have had an easier time if she had had a different mentor? Explain the type of mentor you believe might have been most helpful. Would Ms. Holland have been a better choice as mentor to Mrs. Cullen? Why or why not?
5. In this school district, no induction program was offered for new teachers. Mentor teachers were apparently expected to carry out induction functions. Is that a legitimate expectation for mentors? Why or why not?

Case III

Donald Becker, principal of Lawson High School, wrote a sentence on the sheet of paper in front of him and reread it silently. He thought about the words briefly and then scratched them out. After a moment, he discarded the paper and pulled a fresh sheet from his drawer.

"Dear Ms. Diamond," he wrote. He paused, reflecting on the events of the previous two days.

In his mind he went back to the telephone call he had received the previous Sunday from Pat Simmons, orchestra teacher at the school. Ms. Simmons had told him that Abby Diamond had called her Friday night and asked her to take her place at the regional band competition on Saturday. Ms. Simmons said that she had reluctantly agreed to do so because students would have been terribly disappointed if the trip had been cancelled.

Abby Diamond was the band teacher at Lawson High. It was her first year at the school. She had transferred to Lawson from a middle school in the district where she had taught for three years, and she had caused problems for Mr. Becker almost from the day she arrived.

On Monday, Mr. Becker had stopped Ms. Diamond in the hall before classes to ask her why she had not made the trip with the band. She had told him that she was ill and hadn't felt like accompanying the band to the competition. "You had a responsibility to call and let me know if you weren't going," he had said. "In the future, let me know if you are unable to meet your responsibilities."

"Pat Simmons agreed to go in my place," Ms. Diamond had replied. "I knew she would do a good job with the band."

"The band isn't Pat's responsibility," Mr. Becker told her. "You are the band teacher. What would have happened if Pat couldn't have gone?" Ms. Diamond had shrugged and walked away.

The trip was the latest in a series of actions by Ms. Diamond that Mr. Becker felt showed indifference toward her responsibilities. He had decided to write a letter for her personnel file to impress on the teacher the importance of being more conscientious about her work and to warn her to avoid a repetition of Saturday's incident.

He felt that it was important to reiterate to Ms. Diamond that, as band teacher, she was expected to accompany the band on all trips and that if she was unable to go, she was to notify him. He sat for a minute deep in thought, recalling months of frustrating experiences with Ms. Diamond.

Earlier in the year, Mr. Becker had learned from several students that Ms. Diamond had on several occasions left a student in charge of the class and left the room. They had told him that the first time or two it happened she had returned near the end of the period but that on one occasion she didn't return to the class at all. One parent had even called him to complain about Ms. Diamond leaving the band class unsupervised.

Mr. Becker had explained to Ms. Diamond that board policy required teachers to remain in the classroom at all times when students were present or to arrange for a teacher or aide to supervise the class if they had to leave. She had assured him that she would observe the policy in the future. But a week later, when he had gone into the teachers' lounge in the middle of a period, she had been sitting there with a soft drink in her hand, leafing through a magazine. "Who's taking care of your class?" he had asked.

"I left Yolanda in charge for just a minute," Ms. Diamond had replied. "I have a migraine headache, and I needed to get away for a few minutes. I'm going right back."

Mr. Becker warned Ms. Diamond that she was not to leave her classroom unattended and that if she did so again she would be reprimanded. Ms. Diamond had assured him that it would not happen again.

Unsupervised classes and missed trips weren't the only problems Mr. Becker had had with the teacher. One parent had complained that she was treated rudely when she called to ask Ms. Diamond to help her daughter locate some sheet music that the girl said she had returned to the teacher. Ms. Diamond insisted that the music had not been returned and told her that she would have to pay for it. When the parent asked her to see if she could locate the sheet music, the teacher had replied, "That's not my responsibility. These kids have to learn to take better care of their things."

Other parents had complained about Ms. Diamond's choosing the same small group of students to perform for school programs and PTA meetings. Mr. Becker assured the parents she was choosing the better musicians for special events, but some of the parents disputed that. "She only selects her favorites," one parent charged. "There are some excellent musicians in the band who are never picked to perform on programs."

Mr. Becker was puzzled. Ms. Diamond was a likable person, but he had never known a teacher who took responsibilities so lightly or who could find so many ways to evade her obligations. He wondered if she had behaved that way when she was teaching at the middle school before coming to Lawson and, if so, how she could have received tenure. Ms. Diamond had arrived at Lawson High with a favorable recommendation from the principal of the middle school, and Mr. Becker wondered if the principal had simply given a good reference in order to get rid of a problem teacher.

With a sigh, he picked up his pen and prepared to finish the letter.

Questions for Case III

1. Is a letter of reprimand an appropriate response for Abby Diamond's failure to make the trip to the regional band competition? What other disciplinary options might Donald Becker have considered? What action would you recommend? Should the principal have taken disciplinary action sooner? Explain.
2. What should Mr. Becker say in the letter of reprimand? Besides the band trip, should he also mention parents' complaints about the teacher? Why or why not?
3. Draft a letter of reprimand to Abby Diamond for Donald Becker's signature.
4. What should a principal do when asked to furnish a recommendation for a teacher whose performance is unsatisfactory? Is it ethically acceptable to give a favorable recommendation in order to encourage such a teacher to transfer to another school?

INDEX